Shorelines

Space and Rights in South India

Ajantha Subramanian

Stanford University Press
Stanford, California

Stanford University Press
Stanford, California

Printed in the United States of America on acid-free, archival-quality paper

Library of Congress Cataloging-in-Publication Data

Subramanian, Ajantha, 1969–
Shorelines : space and rights in South India / Ajantha Subramanian.
    p. cm.
    Includes bibliographical references and index.
    ISBN 978-0-8047-6146-8 (cloth : alk. paper)
        1. Mukkuvars—Civil rights—India—Kanniyakumari (District)   2. Fishers—Civil
rights—India—Kanniyakumari (District)   3. Catholic Church—India—Kanniyakumari
(District)—Clergy—Political activity.   4. Village communities—India—Kanniyakumari
(District)   5. Space—Political aspects—India—Kanniyakumari (District)   6. Catholic
Church—India—Kanniyakumari (District)—History.   I. Title.

    DS432.M77S83   2009
    305.9'6392095482—dc22

                        2008046634

Typeset by Thompson Type in 10/14 Minion Pro

Contents

Illustrations

Map

Figures

Tables

Acknowledgments

AS WITH MANY ACADEMIC BOOKS, this one too has been a long time in coming and has accrued many debts along the way. I researched and wrote this book with support from the SSRC-Macarthur Program in International Peace and Security, the Mellon Foundation, the Harry Frank Guggenheim Foundation, and the Rockefeller Foundation. I am grateful for permission to use the resources of numerous libraries and archives: India Office Library, London; London Missionary Society archive, SOAS, London; Tamilnadu Archives, Chennai; Tamilnadu Department of Fisheries, Chennai; International Collective in Support of Fishworkers, Chennai; Kanyakumari District Department of Fisheries, Nagercoil; Kottar Bishop's House, Nagercoil; Kanyakumari District Collectorate, Nagercoil; Revenue Divisional Office, Thuckulay; Center for Development Studies, Trivandrum; Programme for Community Organization, Trivandrum; South Indian Federation of Fishermen Societies, Trivandrum; Kerala State Archive, Trivandrum; National Fishworkers Forum, Trivandrum.

This book benefited from the support and guidance of Richard G. Fox, Orin Starn, David Gilmartin, Katherine Ewing, and Irene Silverblatt. Orin and David have continued to be invaluable readers and mentors. Over the years, I have also added other mentors to the list, most importantly K. Sivaramakrishnan and Mahesh Rangarajan, whose enthusiastic support and suggestions have strengthened the manuscript considerably.

South Indian fisheries are a particularly fertile political arena, in part because of the tireless activism of people such as Nalini Nayak, John Kurien, Fathers Thomas Kocherry, Arulanandam, Pierre Gillet, James Tombeur, and

Edwin, Sisters Patricia, Philomene Mary, Mercy, Alphonsa, and Fatima, V. Vivekanandan, A. J. Vijayan, and Sebastian Mathew, all of whom have helped me give shape to my ideas and arguments. I am especially grateful to Professor John Kurien, who generously agreed to regular meetings at the Center for Development Studies, Trivandrum, to discuss the history of mechanization and sectoral conflict in South Indian fisheries. In Kanyakumari, I thank Mary Therese, Johnsy, and Baby Celine for their friendship and guidance. I first met them in 1994 during a brief stint with the Tamilnadu Fishworkers Union, and they remained close friends during my years of fieldwork. In Thirumalai Ashram, where I lived for much of my time in the district, I was humbled by the lifelong service of Babuji and Lieve Akka. In Trivandrum, Vanita, Chandan, and Avanti Mukherjee welcomed me into their home with incredible warmth and generosity. The glorious food, music, and conversation to be had there were a wonderful escape from the doldrums and solitude of academic research. On the Kanyakumari coast, I was invited into the homes of so many fishermen and women who patiently listened to my many questions, shared their meals with me, and engaged me in passionate argument over a wide range of issues. I thank each one of them for making my time in the district so intellectually meaningful and personally transformative.

My time in North Carolina was also one of building lasting friendships, without which the experience would have been much diminished. For making Durham a real home, I thank Julie Byrne, Mandakini Dubey, Katy Fenn, Paul Husbands, Vasu Kilaru, Scott Kugle, Sangeeta Luthra, Surajit Nundy, Gillian Silverman, Amardeep Singh, Subir Sinha, and Rashmi Varma. In Massachusetts, Geeta Patel, Kath Weston, Ami Zota, and Harpreet (Nishu) Singh have been sisters to me and aunties to my kids. During the many moments of frustration and doubt over the manuscript, and academic life more generally, Geeta and Kath offered wise counsel and intellectual sustenance that magically put everything in perspective. Smita Lahiri and John Gibson were ideal everyday friends who shared impromptu meals over meandering conversation. Others have been constants from before and beyond academia: Raoul Daruwala, Kalyani Gandhi, Kalpana Karunakaran, Rebecca Ladbury, Rosanne Lurie, Meaghan McCauley, Arunah Pandiarajan, Babar Sobhan, Zafar Sobhan, and Phoebe Walker are the kind of lifelong friends some only dream of.

At Harvard, Smita Lahiri, Engseng Ho, Lucien Taylor, and Asad Ahmed were comrades in arms who eased the trials of junior faculty life. With his insatiable curiosity about the world and remarkable lack of intellectual condescension, Stanley Tambiah was a true inspiration to me. Michael Herzfeld enthusiastically read my material and offered valuable guidance on all manner of things, from publishing books to eating out. With his characteristic economy of words, James (Woody) Watson made me feel at home in William James Hall. Mary Steedly graciously guided me through my first promotion, and Steve Caton injected a healthy dose of irreverence and humor into departmental life. Within the Anthropology Department, the Political Ecology Working Group has been a wonderful space for intellectual exchange, good humor, and a free meal. A number of graduate students within and outside the group—Will Day, Ujala Dhaka, Paula Goldman, Rusaslina Idrus, Rheanna Parrenas, Miriam Shakow, and Anthony Shenoda—have made my time at Harvard especially inspiring. Outside the department, Lori Allen, Mandakini Dubey, and Maria Grahn-Farley read my work when it most needed a fresh pair of eyes and helped me see its political import when I lost sight of the larger purpose of the project. I've been fortunate to be part of a wonderful writing group of women anthropologists in the greater Boston area who offer that rare mix of warm friendship and intellectual critique. Jennifer Cole, Elizabeth Ferry, Smita Lahiri, Ann Marie Leshkowich, Janet McIntosh, Karen Strassler, and Christine Walley watched this manuscript become what it is, thanks in part to their input.

I benefited greatly from the feedback I received at the many workshops and conferences at which I have presented my work, including the workshop on Violence and the Environment at Berkeley, the panel and workshop on Indian Regional Modernities at Madison and Yale, and the workshop on Displacement and Environment at Cornell. Before joining the Harvard faculty, I was fortunate to spend a year at Yale's Agrarian Studies Program, where I enjoyed and learned from conversations with Jim Scott, Harry West, Donna Perry, Teferi Abate, Alexander Nikulin, and Guadalupe Rodriguez Gomez. My year as a visiting assistant professor at Cornell also generated its share of friends and interlocutors, in particular, Amita Baviskar, Cindy Caron, Dia da Costa, Shelley Feldman, Gaston Gordillo, Sondra Hausner, Ron Herring, Farhana Ibrahim, Gayatri Menon, Viranjini Munasinghe, Cabeiri Robinson, and Andrew Willford.

Working with Stanford University Press has been a pleasure. I thank senior editor Kate Wahl, anthropology acquisitions editor Jennifer Helé, and assistant editor Joa Suorez for the insight, enthusiasm, and speed with which they got my book through the various stages of the publication process. I am also grateful to the two anonymous readers for the press who responded so positively to the manuscript and offered such productive advice.

It is difficult to account for the ways family members shape one's pursuits. My parents, K. S. Subramanian and V. Vasanthi Devi, have always wholeheartedly supported my political, intellectual, and personal commitments, offering advice only when asked, engaging my endeavors enthusiastically, and providing comfortable homes in which to work and relax. My brother and sister-in-law, Narendra Subramanian and Minakshi Menon, have, over long conversations, indulged my reflections on work and life with warmth and good humor. My parents-in-law, Manuelita and Willie Brown, have been wonderful additions to the family who, in their understated and charming way, have given me a home in the United States. My precious daughters, Zareen and Anisa, have been the best distraction from the self-containment of academic life. They charm, delight, and exasperate me every day and are living reminders that intellectual pursuits are only a small part of what makes life meaningful. Over the last fourteen years, Vincent Brown has been my best friend, critic, and companion. He has helped me sharpen my ideas, strengthen my commitments, and take pleasure in dreaming possible futures. This book is first and foremost a tribute to the countless conversations we've shared.

Note on Terminology

I have used the term *fishers* as the best gender-neutral plural for people work-ing in the fishing industry and, more broadly, members of the Mukkuvar fishing caste. Although older anthropological works have used *fishermen* or *fisherfolk* to refer to these populations, I have adopted *fishers* to avoid the in-appropriate gender generalization and primitivism now associated with these previous uses.

Shorelines

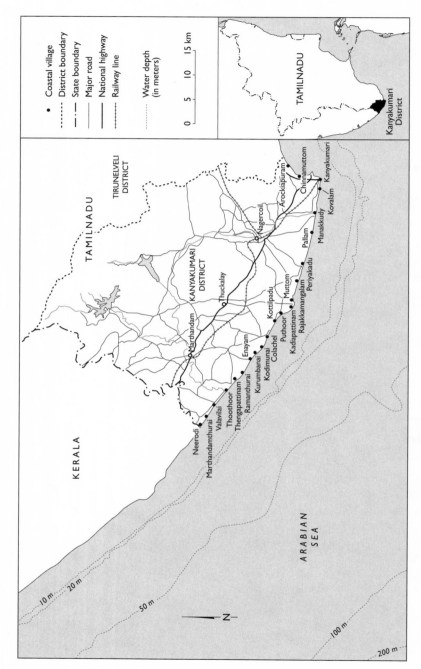

Map 1 Main coastal villages, Kanyakumari District. Courtesy of GIGA Information System, Trivandrum, Kerala.

Introduction

IN JUNE 1997 CATHOLIC FISHERMEN AND FISHERWOMEN from a coastal village in India's southwestern Kanyakumari District took their bishop to court. The fishers' unprecedented decision to wield state law against their religious leadership came in response to a clerical sanction that prevented village inhabitants from fishing for a week. They had provoked the anger of the clergy by initiating an attack on the mechanized trawling boats of a neighboring village. The attack ruptured a church-brokered peace on the coast and was one in a series of confrontations between groups using artisanal craft and gear, such as catamarans, canoes, and fishing hooks and lines, and groups using mechanized trawlers. It signaled the buildup of artisanal opposition to the trawling of southwestern waters and the depletion of marine resources. But unlike other occasions when religious sanctions against violence among coastal Catholics held sway, this time fisher artisans accused the church of overstepping its authority. Instead of submitting to the clerical order, they sought justice in the courts against unconstitutional barriers to their livelihood.

In their court petition the fishers called on the state as benefactor of the poor and patron of the artisan to recognize and protect their rights as custodians of the local sea and to regulate trawling. Significantly, the village councillors who drafted the petition on behalf of fifteen artisanal fishing villages made a point of distinguishing between the district officials, whom they encountered in their negotiations with trawler owners, and the state as a moral umbrella that, unlike the church, transcended the vicissitudes of local politics. One of them, a fisherman in his 60s who had served as a village councillor for ten years, stated this distinction most clearly and vehemently to me:

"Shame on the Bishop and Fisheries Director! Instead of protecting us, they have established a rule of corruption that favors the rich. The state is our protector, our benefactor. These people are betraying the state with their immoral neglect of the poor."[1]

The extraordinary nature of the fishers' decision has to be understood against the historical backdrop of the Catholic Church's role in the region. Located at the southwestern tip of the Indian subcontinent, the Kanyakumari coast is inhabited by about 150,000 Catholics from the Mukkuvar fishing caste. With Portuguese expansion in the sixteenth century, Catholicism spread along the west coast of India, when a sizable section of the western coastal population from Bombay in the north to Kanyakumari in the south was converted through a series of pacts between the Portuguese crown and different native kingdoms. Since that time, the church on the southwestern coast has been landlord, tax collector, and religious authority—an imposing trinity that has served as the primary intermediary between the fishing population and successive rulers. The religiosity of the landscape is unmistakable. Kanyakumari's forty-four fishing villages are each distinguished by a towering church steeple and many smaller chapels. The insinuation of the church into the everyday life of the fishing village has lent coastal space a seamless quality; church parish and fishing village appear as one and the same. Visually, the parish church marks the territoriality of the village. Village festivals—saints' feast days, Easter, Christmas, Tamil New Year—are oriented around the churchyard, a bustling space where villagers and visitors exchange stories, buy trinkets from vendors, and show off their new garments. The parish council remains the dominant institution of village governance, overseeing the administration of local justice. Councillors manage a system of marine resource access and use, and the parish priest's moral authority underwrites penalties for transgressions of norms governing the coastal commons.

Why, then, did fisher artisans turn to the courts to make their claims on the sea? Why did they align themselves with the state and against the church? And why did they cast the state in the guise of a patron?

Taking the church to court marked a new phase in a coastal politics of rights and mirrored strategies at the heart of a globally proliferating environmental rights politics. However, seeing the fishers' actions as a by-product of global environmentalism would be to misrecognize long-standing forms of political maneuver that have structured relations between the coastal fishing population and various sovereign authorities. Indeed, the fishers' alignment with the state even contradicts standard environmentalist accounts that picture communities dependent on natural resources shrugging off the oppressive weight of the modern state in order to claim local autonomy. The fishers' actions are also poorly explained by conventional understandings of Indian democracy. Claims to rights by communitarian minorities—particularly against the dictates of religious authority—are supposed to be an anomaly. Fisher use of patronage as an idiom of rights further confounds expectations of how modern subjects appropriately express political self-determination. That Kanyakumari's fishers combined the desire for state recognition with the will to navigate formal institutional mechanisms and the dissonantly archaic idiom of patronage invites a rethinking of postcolonial democracy and of environmental politics and rights politics more generally.

In this book I chronicle lineages of rights in India's southwestern region that inform contemporary dynamics of postcolonial democracy. By showing rights to be historically constituted forms of long standing, I argue for an understanding of democracy as a politically and culturally embedded process. In this sense, I seek to go beyond the current impasse in South Asian studies between those invested in the nonmodernity of South Asia and others concerned with the expansion of political democracy. By illuminating democratic rights politics as the product of particular histories of caste, religion, and development, I "provincialize" (Chakrabarty 2000) democracy as a specific cultural formation that departs from universalist expectations of secular modernity and liberal subjectivity.

Let me be clear. This is not a book about how universal concepts such as rights circulate and accrue particular meanings in different contexts. Such a formulation keeps in place an origin story of rights that, by virtue of its modularity, renders later adoptions derivative. What I mean to do is upset this spatiotemporal hierarchy of origin and destination by showing how rights politics in any place, be it revolutionary France or contemporary India, is in continuity with previous histories of claim making. To understand rights politics, then, we need to attend to both regional histories of claim making and transnational histories of circulation.

One practice in particular is pivotal to my analysis of histories of rights in southwestern India. In the region a spatial mode of organizing power has geographically separated the socially high from the low, the developed from the primitive, and citizen from subject, tying social and political status to physical location.[2] However, space has not been simply an instrument of rule; claim making in the region has also drawn on geographical imaginaries and practices to contest injustice. Although other social groups have also suffered and challenged spatial marginalization, political, economic, and cultural transformations since the mid-nineteenth century have contributed in particular to the increasing separation of the "democratic inland" from the "primitive coast," where fishers are now thought to exist as free savages or cowed subordinates of religious authority. In this book I track the spatial dynamics of marginalization and fisher contestation. I show that fisher claim making was not simply a form of negotiation *within* spaces of unequal power. The political projects that fishers embarked on—regionalism, marine common property, alternative technology, and fisher citizenship—generated politicized geographies that ranged beyond the coast, challenging its representation as a self-enclosed domain of religious patronage and caste primitivism. Each geography of rights is a testament to how longer histories of claim making have intersected with new political currents: Regionalism crosscut fisher battles for enhanced caste status within the Catholic Church with political Dravidianism; marine common property crosscut village sovereignty with state law; alternative technology crosscut moral economies of artisanship with liberation theology; and fisher citizenship crosscut local community with civic belonging. It is by illuminating such political conjunctures as constitutive of rights that my work demonstrates the emergent character of Indian democracy.

Weaving together histories of space and rights allows me to make the book's central argument: Kanyakumari's fishers are best understood as subjects inhabiting a shared political universe. Departing from the current preference within South Asian studies, history, and anthropology for framing Indian subalterns either as ineradicably different or as products of governmentalized procedures, my work joins others (Chari 2004; S. Guha 1999; Ludden 2001; Sinha 2003; Sinha et al. 1997; Sivaramakrishnan 1995, 1999; Sivaramakrishnan and Agrawal 2003; N. Sundar 1997) in recovering a dialectical understanding of Indian subalternity. The thorough imbrication of state and community institutions and practices makes it clear that South Asian sovereigns and subjects are cut from the same historical cloth. Rather than see such groups as India's southwestern fishers as nonmoderns inhabiting a bounded cultural world or as moderns wholly captured by a statist logic, in this book I illuminate how they constitute themselves as subjects of rights in relation to existing histories and hegemonies.

Historical Sediments

The southwestern "fishery coast" has been given its contours by the economic, cultural, and political crosscurrents of the Indian Ocean. Its inhabitants are a testament to this past. Their faith, the crafts with which they ply the rough waters of the Indian Ocean, their very names—the Portuguese Febola, Mary Therese, and Constantine—suggest such long-standing interactions.

Yet the fishing village is routinely characterized as a place without history and its inhabitants as quintessential locals mired in static time and space, modern primitives whose culture is a mere extension of sand and sea. Although scholarship on India's west coast acknowledges its well-established identity as a space of transoceanic trade routed through flourishing coastal urban centers (e.g., Boxer 1969; Chaudhuri 1985; Das Gupta 2001; Das Gupta and Pearson 1999; Ho 2006; Subrahmanyam 1993), the people who actually live and work on the seashore are given scant mention. Their absence as historical subjects in scholarship on the coast is reflected in popular discourses about coastal fishers. Speaking with inland communities and state officials about fishing populations, one commonly hears such remarks as "They are as volatile as the ocean they sail"; "Mukkuvars have no sense of the world. What they know is prayer and fish"; "The coast is a theocracy and the priest is the Mukkuvars' god. He can tell them to do anything and they'll do it!" Such remarks derive the very character of Mukkuvars from their environs. Bound to the shore at land's end, they appear to be easy prey for an authoritarian clergy seeking a pliant body of followers. Their trade—working artisanal craft in waters dominated by the industrial trawlers of transnational fishing—seems to further consign them to a perennial social marginality on the fringes of the Indian nation-state.

Surprisingly, comments about fisher backwardness typically come from agrarian low caste groups who, a mere century ago, were themselves subject to disparagement by landed high castes, state developmentalists, and Protestant missionaries. Indeed, agrarian castes such as the Nadars not only shared the Mukkuvars' low status but were also subjected far more to daily rituals of subjugation than their fisher counterparts. That Nadars now place themselves higher on a developmental ladder suggests significant shifts in the organization of social power and caste status in the region.

Understanding how historical processes of caste formation, Christianization, state making, and capitalist transformation have produced coast and inland as particular kinds of spaces and the fisher artisan as a particular kind of subject is part of my task in this book. It is only by recognizing the postcolonial present as made up of such historical sediments, I argue, that we can properly understand contemporary political practices and idioms.

The significance of space is a case in point. Explaining its power in structuring both rule and rights in postcolonial Kanyakumari requires turning back to earlier articulations of sovereignty and claim making.[3] As I show in the first part of this book, the consolidation of native sovereignty in the princely state of Travancore, the rise of agrarian low caste movements, fisher challenges to caste privilege within the church, and late colonial developmentalism were all key factors that shaped the spatial contours of political imagination and practice in southwest India. On the coast, fishers battled caste stigma within the Catholic Church and clerical dominance over coastal villages. Navigating a complex world of institutional authorities, from the local diocese of Kottar to Rome's Propaganda Fide, the English East India Company, and the Protestant London Missionary Society, fishers crafted claims to higher caste status, clerical representation, and village sovereignty.

Simultaneously, different processes unfolded in the inland world of agrarian Travancore. Hindu and Protestant low caste struggles to open up proscribed high caste geographies concentrated first on physical territories, such as roads and temples, and then on representational spaces, such as the state bureaucracy. In the process, low caste Hindus and Protestants refigured inland high caste spaces, first as battlegrounds of civic rights and later as democratized geographies where social equality triumphed over caste hierarchy (S. Bayly 1989, 1999; Chiriyankandath 1993; Daniel 1985; Jeffrey 1976; Kawashima 1998; Kooiman 1989; Saradamoni 1999). This did not mean, however, that caste ceased to matter. Indeed, in southern Travancore, social equality accrued a distinct caste flavor, promoted as it was by specific agrarian low castes and their Protestant missionary patrons. The experience of these groups came to assume paradigmatic status in regional narratives of modernity, the yardstick against which other castes, such as the Mukkuvars, would mark their own progress. Ironically, then, the emergence of an inland discourse of civil rights contributed to the circumscription of the coast as an atavistic space of caste backwardness and feudal Catholicism, obscuring a history of fisher claim making.

This trend of primitivizing the coast was further entrenched by the spatial practices of late colonial fisheries development. In colonial documents from the end of the nineteenth and early twentieth centuries, one sees the circulation of ideas about the caste nature of fishers, which is increasingly perceived as arising from their labor and the very landscape they inhabit. Unlike the industrious farmer in his tight-knit village, fishers are deemed as rough and volatile as the waters they ply; the mobility of fishing is thought to make them incapable of social organization, and the unpredictability of the fish harvest mistakenly imbues them with flightiness and resistance to thrift. At the same time, colonial fisheries development advocated a gradual pace of change for a fishery deemed ill-equipped for modernization.

The historical production of a line separating inland from coast and low caste moderns from low caste primitives informed postcolonial dynamics. With independence, another shoreline internal to the coast emerged, this time produced by postcolonial fisheries development. Capitalism has long been a space-making project (Goswami 2004; Harvey 1996, 2001, 2006; D. Mitchell 1996, 2003; Smith 1984). Colonial capital built the metropolitan core by extracting from colonized peripheries, which were reduced to sources of raw material (S. Amin 1976; Frank 1975). This political economic drama of capital—that is, its accumulation on a global scale through the development of underdevelopment—generated spatial distinctions within empires. In the British colonies, the experience of the unevenness of the imperial economy fueled anticolonial sentiment. By the last decades of the nineteenth century, the end of colonial underdevelopment and the birth of national development had become a rallying cry of Indian anticolonial nationalism. Independent India promised a new beginning: economic growth through self-rule. Postcolonial statesmen took up with gusto the mantle of development, which had been cleansed of the taint of the civilizing mission by its rebirth as modernization (Bose 1997; Cooper 1997; Wallerstein 1992). Unlike the colonial "drain of wealth," postcolonial development aimed to generate prosperity for a newly enfranchised national citizenry.

As is evident from the opening anecdote, however, national development was anything but a rising tide that lifted all boats. Across rural localities, state developmentalism divided Indian haves from have-nots, generating new forms of inequality and disenfranchisement.[4] In some instances, the Indian state even exceeded its colonial predecessor in its zealous commitment to accumulation at the expense of equity. This was certainly the case with marine harvest. Unlike the cautious colonial approach to the capitalization of subcontinental fishing, the postcolonial state urged the modernization of the fishery. Although the Indian state initially pursued social development policies of cooperative technology ownership and fish marketing to enhance domestic food consumption, these policies were rapidly superseded in the 1960s by a new emphasis on private ownership of trawlers for export-oriented growth. Particularly in southern India, regional governments subsidized the purchase of mechanized trawlers, underwriting their enhanced levels of resource extraction.

Across fishing societies, the terms of marine resource access and use have long been a source of fierce contestation. These dynamics reflect the character of a resource very different from land. Fish are fugitive. Unlike land, fish cannot be subject to political borders or rigid forms of territorial exclusivity. Whereas the impact of the nonhuman world on the human one is arguably in evidence across a variety of economic systems, the agency of nature (Callon 1986; Latour 1988, 2005) in shaping the contours of social custom and capital accumulation is particularly visible in fisheries. There is no guarantee that fish species will abide by expected migratory patterns. Two fishermen working a narrow stretch of sea with the same craft and gear can have radically different harvests. Nevertheless, territoriality is a key principle in marine fisheries regulation. Unlike forms of land enclosure, however, marine territoriality specifies a regime of use rights without any possibility of permanent resource alienation (McCay and Acheson 1987).[5] Unlike other natural resource economies, then, marine fishing precludes the private ownership of the raw material of production. To the extent that there is private ownership, it is in the technological means of production. For this reason, technology is a key determinant of equity. When some fishermen are equipped to harvest marine resources at far higher levels, the uneven spread of capital-intensive technology undercuts an important principle of reciprocity in common property. When unequal forms of technology use are underwritten by powerful institutions, such as the state, the regulatory power of common property systems is called further into question.

In India, trawling technology, an icon of advancing capitalism, transformed a marine common property system into an open-access regime. State-led mechanization permitted the entry of new players into the fishery: entrepreneurs interested purely in the promise of profit. The 1970s witnessed an explosion in the international market for fishery products, particularly the sharp escalation in value of one commodity: prawn. With the discovery of extensive prawn grounds in India's southwestern waters, investment capital flooded the fishery. The "pink gold rush" transformed a technologically varied economy suited to the species diversity of the tropical ecosystem into a monoculture industry privileging the extractive power of a single technology. Trawling boats vied with artisanal craft and gear for resource control in a mad scramble for prawn. And artisanal fisheries, previously subject to the regulative mechanisms of village councils, encountered a new stakeholder in the developmental state, one whose executive and legal power far exceeded theirs (Achari 1986; J. Kurien 1978, 1985; J. Kurien and Achari 1990; J. Kurien and Mathew 1982).

Trawlerization in Kanyakumari differed in some measure from other coastal locales. In contrast to many other parts of the Indian coastal belt, where outside entrepreneurs invested economically in the fishery, Kanyakumari's trawler class arose from within the Mukkuvar Catholic fishing caste. One village—the natural harbor of Colachel—was chosen as the test case of fishery mechanization and the regional state's key beneficiary; this choice generated tensions between the emergent trawler class and the coast's artisans. State support for the unrestricted mobility and unlimited productivity of trawlers contradicted the intervillage regulatory regime, exempting Colachel from coastal norms. In the ensuing battle, trawler owners and artisanal fishers alike invested the coastal environment and Mukkuvar identity with different meanings using a sedimented repertoire of cultural terms: caste and Catholicism, coast and inland, territory and sovereignty, development and moral economy, primitivism and modernity.

Since India achieved independence from colonial rule in 1947, earlier struggles over caste, religious authority, and territory have taken on new significance as they inform a politics of citizenship. It is to this more recent politics, complete with its own spatial and social contours and hierarchies, that I now turn.

Citizenship in a Postcolony

That the coast has long been a crossroads of religious, political, and economic currents of transformation is evident from the histories that fishers narrate—histories that feature a motley crew of characters from Portuguese priests to high caste soldiers and community reformers. The postcolonial state also plays a central role in coastal stories, particularly around the fraught issue of trawlerization.

I first arrived in Kanyakumari in 1994 to work as an activist for the district's artisanal fisher union. I had been encouraged by friends active in struggles for artisanal fisher rights to lend my support to their campaign against the federal government's 1991 decision to license foreign industrial vessels to fish in Indian territorial waters. At the time, I knew that the domestic battles between artisanal craft and trawlers were a serious problem, but the focus of our efforts was on a more distant threat. According to my activist friends, artisanal and trawler organizations had come to an uneasy truce for the purpose of combating what they characterized as the new colonialism: the claim to national marine resources by foreign capitalists aided and abetted by the Indian government. Novice that I was in such matters, I was grateful for the crash course I received from fishermen and fisherwomen and their activist supporters on the twists and turns of national fisheries policy. Sometimes, these lessons came in expected ways, at rallies and union meetings. At other times, I learned things unexpectedly. Talking to a young fisherman, I was told that the worst thing for the coast was "dungle." Puzzled, I asked what this dungle was, and, after a prolonged discussion, I learned of the Dunkel draft, the document named after Arthur Dunkel, director general of the General Agreement on Trade and Tariffs from 1980 to 1993. The Dunkel draft embodied the results of the Uruguay round of multilateral trade negotiations (December 20, 1991) that culminated in the formation of the World Trade Organization. That "dungle" had become a household word was indicative of the success, at least on a discursive level, of the mobilization work of such groups as the National Fishworkers Forum, an umbrella body of artisanal fisher unions that spearheaded the campaign against the licensing of foreign vessels.

When I returned for my doctoral research in 1996, both struggles were continuing in tandem, but the most heated conversations with people from the coast revolved around the problem of domestic intersectoral conflict. Although the intrusion of foreign vessels was still a concern, I realized that most fishers viewed local class conflict as the more intractable problem. Some bemoaned the breakdown of community solidarity and harkened back to a time when the social glues of faith and caste secured a coastal moral order; others saw antitrawler violence as the positive sign of a strengthened artisanal class fighting the excesses of capitalist development. The extent to which "community" had survived the assault of capitalist transformation was in dispute. However, fishers were unanimous in identifying the state as the precipitator of the crisis, first with its initial investment in the uneven spread of mechanized trawling craft and then with its subsidies for capital-intensive fishing. No one I spoke to on the coast, whether fishers or priests, wrote the state out of the equation.

This consensus on the imbrication of the state in contemporary coastal dynamics stood in sharp contrast to the comments of state officials and inland inhabitants on the causes and solutions of coastal strife. In conversations with state officials, I noticed a persistent tendency to diagnose problems of coastal poverty and conflict as self-generated, a natural outgrowth of coastal culture rather than an outcome of political processes. Indeed, those I met from inland caste groups often expressed surprise that I was interested in coastal *political* life and not in religiosity or economic underdevelopment, the two organizing ideas in most discussions about the coast. To the extent that fishers had a political life at all, it was assumed to be an expression of church dictates. Such assumptions about the coastal world as an antidemocratic space of religious orthodoxy and caste backwardness were not merely rhetorical; they resulted in the actual political isolation of the coast.

This was particularly so when it came to antitrawler activism. Despite the state's role in disseminating and subsidizing trawling technologies since the 1960s, fishery officials consistently isolated associated tensions as an internal matter. By mid-1996, when antitrawler activism was at its peak, the three bureaucrats overseeing coastal economic and political life had handed over coastal conflict management entirely to the Catholic bishop of the coastal diocese of Kottar who had religious jurisdiction over Kanyakumari's fishing villages. The district collector, fisheries director, and revenue divisional officer all opted for a "community" resolution to class conflict, an approach seen to be in keeping with the coast's culture of church patronage. Unlike other parts of the Indian coastline where state fishery officials would typically negotiate matters of resource use and access with fisher *panchayats* (village councils), the institutions that formed the bottom rung of the state administrative machinery, here they turned to the Catholic Church as the chosen intermediary. Despite the presence of institutions such as fish marketing associations, trade unions, and credit societies, which fell outside the purview of the church and which more directly represented fishers as economic and political actors, state officials opted for church mediation, signaling its recognition of only one authoritative institution on the coast. State practices thus reinforced the predominance of the church at a time when, as evidenced in the opening anecdote, lay institutions and rights claims directed to secular authorities were becoming ever stronger.

This presumed weakness or absence of the state and other lay institutions on the coast and the associated privileging of church authority constituted fishers first as wards of the church and only second as citizens. Significantly, trawler owners who shared caste and faith with their artisanal adversaries were exempt from such "sensitivity" and were treated by state officials less as wards of their church than as citizen interest groups. This difference largely had to do with the expectation by both bureaucrats and mechanized fishers themselves of shared social affinities between trawler owners and inlanders that culturally delinked the fisher middle class from the coast and linked it instead to the "democratic" interior.

Assumptions about coastal isolation shaped attitudes toward fishers among fishery bureaucrats and equally within district law enforcement. Police officials routinely bemoaned the wall of silence that confronted them when they investigated coastal crimes. The district commissioner of police complained to me that perpetrator and victim would join hands when faced with an outsider, preferring an internal solution to one mediated by the state. He gave me the impression that the coast was a space antithetical to law and order, where the arbitrary rule of clerical power allowed for anarchic social relations. The commissioner's contradictory picture of coastal folk as at once an uncontrollable mob and a consolidated force that would stand together against an outsider was one widely shared across different inland social groups. An oft-repeated image that surfaced in conversations with fishery and police officials and inland castes was that of the tolling church bell that called fishers to arms. The higher levels of police brutality when dealing with fishers suggest that law enforcement officials anticipate violence and act preemptively to curb it.

A particularly graphic instance of such preemptive action by the police when dealing with the coastal population dates back to 1982. Late 1981 and early 1982 witnessed the peak of Hindu nationalist mobilization in the southwestern region; Hindu low caste agriculturalists in particular were recruited to join the paramilitary group, the Rashtriya Swayamsevak Sangh (RSS, or National Volunteers' Organization), and fight district Christians. Although Hindu nationalists targeted all Christians rhetorically, physical violence was reserved largely for the fishing population, which was seen as conveniently isolated both geographically and socially. Despite evidence of propaganda disseminated by Hindu organizations, such as the RSS, the Vishwa Hindu Parishad (VHP, or World Hindu Council), and the Hindu Munnani (Organization for Hindu Uplift), that scapegoated fisher Catholics and requests from coastal parish priests for police protection, no help was provided.[6] In the violence that erupted in early 1982, fishing villages became the target of both

Hindu activist and police violence. Although Hindus carried out the bulk of attacks—burning churches and leaving Hindu symbols standing in their place, leveling homes, destroying fishing craft and gear, and literally driving Catholics into the sea—the only victims of police firing were fisher Catholics.

The report of a state-appointed commission that was formed to look into the causes of violence speaks volumes about official attitudes toward fishers. One paragraph in particular is indicative of administrative attitudes toward the coast, here tied to fears of religious minority ascent.

> The 1980 Census showed that Christians have become the majority community in Kanyakumari district and that is when trouble for the district started. When a minority community becomes the majority community in any particular area, it tends to function as a militant, defiant and aggressive group in that pocket. Kanyakumari district is no exception to this general rule. The fishermen in the coastal areas, devoid of education and immersed in abject poverty have become the "fighting wing" of the Church. (Report of Justice P. Venugopal Commission 1986: 3)

The report goes so far as to characterize the Catholic population as an organism, with the church as its brain and the fishing community as its brawn, acting at the behest of its religious leadership. Significantly, this characterization of Catholics as a consolidated force waging religious war finds no parallel in the report's assessment of inland Hindus, despite the prominent presence in the district of Hindu paramilitary organizations working to unify Hindus politically by vilifying southwestern Christians. What we get instead is the expression of an administrative rationality that reproduces sedimented meanings about the coast—its culture of violence, the rough nature of the fisher, and the arrogance of the parish priest who holds sway over a gullible population—which are taken together to exemplify the difference between the feudal coast and democratic inland. Here, fisher Catholics appear as a politically unconscious, easily manipulated population whose actions are attributable to outside orchestration or to irrational spontaneity, not to political maneuver.

The circumscription of the Kanyakumari coast as a space of religious orthodoxy, caste backwardness, and political immaturity reinforces the assumption that political life in postcolonial India is defined by the simultaneous proliferation and partiality of democratic processes. Universal adult franchise dramatically expanded the electorate; development projects insinuated the state into the everyday life of the producer; rights discourses injected new life into ongoing challenges to hierarchy and authority; and diverse forms of associational activity burgeoned throughout Indian society. However, the rapid spread of political institutions and processes only seems to have confirmed the suspicion that independent India retained pockets of feudalism—such as the southwestern shore—where democratic consciousness had yet to take root. These spaces of unfreedom marked the unevenness of citizenship and its staggered progression across the Indian political landscape. In them, representation was assumed to follow older colonial patterns; so-called traditional elites whose authority rested on cultural kinship would act as intermediaries of the state. Here, custom and community retained their preindependence stature, and identity, not interest, was the name of the political game. In a form reminiscent of colonial indirect rule, the postcolonial state enthroned "natural leaders," such as the Catholic clergy, to oversee such communities of custom.

The opposition between the freedom of modern society and the shackles of premodern community is a familiar trope in scholarship on the postcolonial world. Derived from nineteenth- and early-twentieth-century social science formulations that contrast *Gemeinschaft* (community) and *Gesellschaft* (society), organic and mechanical solidarity, and traditional and rational-legal authority, postcolonial modernization theory continues the legacies of these older traditions of thought. Despite a stated commitment to overcoming colonial legacies, postcolonial statecraft also sustains the distinction between the rational, willed actions of modern social agents inhabiting civil society and the irrational, compelled motivations of nonmodern communitarian subjects that underpin a colonial sociology of knowledge.

As I have already indicated, since the mid-nineteenth century, southwestern fishers have been increasingly consigned to the category of nonmodern community. The church is thought to operate with impunity as a feudal patron and overlord, subjecting a docile low caste population to its whims. A widely held belief that priests dictate electoral choices from the pulpit only underscores the sense of the coast as a space of, first, religious orthodoxy and, only secondarily, part of a plural democracy. Even when fishers take to the streets to protest state neglect or when they enter the space of the court to demand the rights of equal citizenship, as they did in 1997, their use of political idioms, such as patronage, is taken as indicative of their political immaturity.

In the agrarian inland, the spheres of religion, economy, and polity are deemed distinct, but the interpenetration of these spheres on the coast is widely regarded as an impediment to the expression of political sovereignty. When fishers refer to favorable interventions by political party leaders in terms that suggest divine intercession or when they use a spiritual vocabulary to talk about the morality of particular economic or political configurations, their sense of their social landscape is deemed politically immature. Separate spheres as indicative of a modern polity is a noted trope of the European Enlightenment. Talal Asad demonstrated how the compartmentalization of religion as a form of interiorized belief set apart from public spheres of economy and polity was a founding tenet of European liberal secularism (Asad 1993, 2003). Through the instrumentalities of colonial rule, this idiom of interiority extended to public arenas in the non-West, relegating a colonized public to the domain of culture outside politics proper. Evolutionary paradigms determined that this native cultural world is prepolitical, not quite as mature as the bourgeois public spheres of the industrialized West. Scholars of South Asia (Chatterjee 1993; Freitag 1989; Gilmartin 1988; Pandey 1990) have narrated the colonial life of this parochialized public, illustrating the political implications of its ideological coding as the space of community separate from both state and civil society. The British colonial state used the existence of supposedly primordial, insular, and mutually exclusive communities to deny the possibility of Indian political self-determination, arguing that Indians could not possibly transcend the limits of their particularistic communities of identity to form the universal collectivities of interest that made up the modern public.[7]

Even with the establishment of representative institutions in British India, the mechanisms of representation distinguished these from their European counterparts. Farzana Shaikh observes that British colonial authorities based the principles of native political representation on the sociological map of India, implying that "Indian 'political society' was essentially an extension of its 'civil society.'" Because the primary categories in use were almost always sociological, officials were led increasingly to rely upon a notion of representation that stressed social correspondence, rather than any aspect pertaining to political activity as such" (Shaikh 1989: 69). For Indians, being representative translated as "being typical of the represented, rather than of acting politically for or on their behalf" (Shaikh 1989: 69). Representation was intended more as a tool of governmentality than as a tool of political enfranchisement. As far as the British government was concerned, the goal of Indian representatives was the descriptive goal of yielding information about the communities they represented, not the substantive goal of engaging in political action on their behalf.

Anticolonial nationalists challenged these limits on self-determination by claiming the nation as the universal form of political community transcending their particularistic designations. However, in India as elsewhere (e.g., Ferguson 2006; Mamdani 1996; Mbembe 2001), the divide between civil citizens and communitarian subjects persisted after the postcolonial transition, only now it marked differences internal to a national citizenry. The divide between citizens and subjects was instantiated differently in different places, depending on the regional or local histories that gave it meaning. In the southwest the distinction was social and spatial. The line drawn in the sand distinguished fisher Catholics ill-equipped for political sovereignty from mature inlanders able to identify and mobilize their interests. Caste, faith, and labor all combined to consign Mukkuvars to a space of nonfreedom. Indeed, even when fishers try to forge relations with state institutions unmediated by the church, the representative logic of state power dictates their return to the clerical fold.

Citizenship and Subalternity

Recently, a number of scholars studying the non-Western world have repudiated accounts of historical process that impose a singular teleology on all societies and the associated universalization of modernist categories of experience. In scholarship on South Asia, writers of the Subaltern Studies school of Indian historiography have been particularly vocal in claiming for South Asia different spatiotemporal coordinates and in claiming for South Asian subalterns a different epistemological orientation.[8] The intellectual commitments of Subaltern Studies have shifted from the earlier concern of seeking a more culturally grounded social history of peasant and working class struggle to a concern with colonial knowledge and the constitution of the colonized subject. In the process, subalternity has shifted away from Antonio Gramsci's original formulation (1972) in which the subaltern is a class subject formed within a relationship of cultural hegemony. The Indian subaltern has become a non-Western subject situated within an autonomous cultural space untainted by secular modernity. In the process, Gramsci's hegemony has been transformed into domination, and elites and subalterns have been separated into opposing, discrete epistemological camps, with the elites representing Western modernity and the subalterns representing non-Western tradition. The assumption that the Indian subaltern's worldview is wholly distinct from Western modernity has generated a wealth of research on forms of subaltern political collectivity and cultural affinity that runs counter to a modernist imaginary. In such works (e.g., Chakrabarty 2000, 2002; Chatterjee 1993, 1997a, 1997b; Ranajit Guha 1983), we see efforts to provincialize the modern as a particular cultural formation and to bring into view other forms of sociality and subjectivity.

Dipesh Chakrabarty's "The Subject of Law and the Subject of Narrative" (in Chakrabarty 2002) exemplifies this effort to bracket the modern in order to illuminate other cultural and political experiences and expressions. In this essay, Chakrabarty makes a case for considering forms of political intervention in situations of injustice that do not involve the "citizenly" invocation of the law and the state. Specifically, Chakrabarty considers narrative—testimonies in diaries, novels, and so on—as a form of intervention that honors the intimate particulars of the act of injustice and the irreducible singularity of the subject in a way that the abstractions of law and rights do not. Chakrabarty argues that, based, as law is, on "the idea of the abstract, homogenized citizen and his rights and duties" (2002: 113), there is no space in the sphere of rights for a form of justice that does not commit the violence of generalization and the erasure of the "radical alterity of the other" (2002: 112). Chakrabarty concludes with a rhetorical question: "Can we imaginatively bring into being modern civil-political spheres founded on the techniques of the dialogic narrative even as we live and work through those built on the universalist abstractions of political philosophy?" (2002: 114).

Chakrabarty's opposition of law and narrative, rights and justice, and citizen and cultural self rests on certain assumptions: that "law" in South Asia is a modular formation that faithfully reproduces an Enlightenment ideal and that, by extension, rights and citizenship as legal forms are incapable of encoding cultural particularity. If we follow his rationale, then to engage in citizenly action in India is to subscribe to a uniform conception of the modern rights-bearing subject. It is to be trapped within the ideological parameters of "universalist political philosophy."

In anthropology two key strands of work on rights replicate different parts of Chakrabarty's argument. The first, seen, for instance, in Sally Merry's work, adopts a model of culture contact to narrate the meeting of rights and culture and the forms of legal and cultural hybridity that emerge from the process. Merry, it must be said, has a far more dynamic conception of the law than Chakrabarty. Addressing the flow of human rights discourse to non-Western locales, she writes, "Rather than viewing the emerging regime of global human rights as the imposition of Western cultural forms and legalities, we need to see it as open text, susceptible to appropriation and redefinition by groups who are also players in the global legal arena" (Merry 1996: 68). Merry is also careful to critique static notions of culture that underpin more radical frameworks of cultural relativism; indeed, her work is exemplary in showing the flexibility of cultural forms and their capacity to accommodate legal knowledge and practice in unpredictable ways. Finally, Merry is careful to note that human rights is also a culture all its own and not the universalistic framework that it claims to be (2005, 2006). Although this last observation in some ways echoes Chakrabarty's, Merry takes the Western culture of human rights as simply a starting point that does not preclude its adoption for a variety of projects that move well beyond the sway of a liberal ethos.

Ultimately, however, Merry, like Chakrabarty, assumes that non-Western culture and rights begin as distinct phenomena, with rights flowing from the West outward to become "vernacularized." As she puts it, "The process of vernacularization is one in which the global becomes localized, no longer simply a global imposition but something which is infused with the meanings, signs, and practices of local places (Merry 1996: 80). Her language here clearly suggests that rights come from without into non-Western locales, where they are given new interpretations and put to new uses. For Merry, as for others addressing the relationship of culture to rights (e.g., Cowan et al. 2001), it appears that a focus on the *semantics* of rights predetermines the history of rights as the discursive flow of particular concepts from West to non-West. This kind of analysis relies on following the semantic trail rather than on considering the structures of feeling—embeddedness within a world of institutional authority, relationships of mutual obligation that bind institutional authorities and subjects, and a sense of their due on the part of subjects—that constitute a political culture of rights.

A second anthropological approach to rights identifies them as a form of governmentality through which subjects are incorporated into a normative legal framework. Elizabeth Povinelli's work exemplifies this second strand in its emphasis on the incorporative force of the law as a site of both regulation and production. In *The Cunning of Recognition: Indigenous Alterities and the Making of Australian Multiculturalism* (2002), Povinelli elaborates the work of "feeling" in shaping the contours of Australian multiculturalism. She argues that, despite its intentions of recognizing the past sins of the settler state and embracing the Aboriginal right to culture, multiculturalism in Australia hangs on the repugnance toward cultural differences that do not fall within majoritarian norms of acceptability. To secure their rights to land, Australian Aborigines have to perform an acceptable form of cultural authenticity that is neither too recognizably similar nor too repugnantly different, a form of culture that is in effect produced in the very encounter with the state. For Povinelli, then, rights are a governmental technology that produces new legal subjects *and* new notions of cultural difference. As she puts it, "Law is one of the primary sites through which liberal forms of recognition develop their disciplinary sides as they work with the hopes, pride, optimisms and shame of indigenous and other minority subjects" (Povinelli 2002: 184). Like Chakrabarty, Povinelli essentializes the law as a fixed juridical structure to which subalterns seeking recognition are forced to conform, in the process becoming so many disciplined subjects who are absorbed into Australian liberal nationhood only by leaving the less palatable markers of their alterity behind. Also like Chakrabarty, Povinelli seeks forms of political engagement outside the law that do not erase the "radical alterity of the other."

These approaches to the study of rights have much to commend them, but they all suffer from two problems. First, they replicate an understanding of rights as emanating from modern liberalism. This diffusionist framework of rights keeps in place a European origin story that renders later adoptions derivative. Second, these approaches to rights all begin with Chakrabarty's distinction between the (Western) civil-political sphere and the (non-Western) narrative-cultural sphere. This binary of law and narrative, with one falling within the sphere of the modern and the other outside it, disregards how the law actually works and how people are constituted as subject of rights. By contrast, fisher politics illuminates a far less static, more dialogical relationship between claims and rights in which the practice of claim making is generative of new understandings and subjects of rights. This means not just the reconstitution of law through the infusion of new cultural meanings or the production of culture through the generative power of law but also a shift in emphasis away from the encounter between law and culture toward the historicity of rights. It means treating rights as a *structure of feeling*—a dynamic cultural formation that encodes understandings of justice and accountability—that is not simply of Western origin.

What does thinking of rights in more historical, processual terms do to our understanding of postcolonial democracy? Another member of the Subaltern Studies collective, Partha Chatterjee, has recently addressed the relationship between democracy and subaltern politics in his book *The Politics of the Governed: Reflections on Popular Politics in Most of the World* (2004). Chatterjee argues that, in the postcolonial world, civil society is not the sphere of democratic possibility that it is touted to be but the domain of the elite, a world of norms where order trumps justice. Rather than arising from this heavily policed elite arena, democracy actually emerges, Chatterjee maintains, from those spaces outside—what he calls "political society." For Chatterjee, political society is the domain not of subaltern autonomy or alterity but of governmentality, inhabited by so many distinct "populations" rendered legible by a state policy apparatus. It is here that a transformative democratic politics is forged. By appropriating governmental categories and transforming them into forms of moral community, "the governed" become a political counterweight to civic norms and force transformations in the workings of democracy.

By locating subaltern political agency squarely within the sphere of governmentality, Chatterjee challenges the binaries of state and community assumed in much subalternist and postcolonial scholarship. At the same time, however, he retains a republican understanding of civil society and the rights-bearing subject. For Chatterjee, the classical ingredients of modern citizenship—sovereignty, equality, and rights—all fall squarely within the space of modern civil society. As he puts it, "A modern civil society, consistent with the ideas of freedom and equality, is a project that is located in the historical desires of certain elite sections of Indians" (Chatterjee 2004: 46). In contrast to civil society's rights-bearing subjects, the subalterns of political society merely deal in pragmatic maneuvers to change *how* they are governed. Chatterjee's bifurcated scheme does not allow for the possibility that subalterns could be both objects of governmental power and subjects of rights. Instead, he equates the subject of rights with the "proper" citizen, who, in the case of India, is the elite inhabitant of civil society. I suspect this is because, even as Chatterjee recuperates democracy as something other than a Western derivation, he is unwilling to accommodate histories of rights that depart from the modular forms of Western modernity. Ultimately, Chatterjee also trades in the binaries of elite and subaltern, Western and non-Western, that cut against a more integrated political history (Dubois 2006).

By contrast, my work argues for the inadequacy of treating rights as simply a by-product of Western modernity or colonial governmentality. Instead, I show how rights claims are embedded in dense histories of struggle and, in this sense, are not distinct from other cultural expressions of relationality and obligation. Finally, in my account, postcolonial politics is necessarily the outcome of interaction between social actors and spaces that would be kept apart in more culturalist accounts. In making these arguments, I build on the insights of Tania Li, Donald Moore, and Frederick Cooper, all of whom illuminate the historical sediments that comprise postcolonial political subjectivity and practice.

Cooper's argument against the analytic purchase of the term *modernity* has been particularly illuminating for me in prying apart rights and liberalism (Cooper 2005). Cooper questions the notion of an epistemic break into the modern period that is par for the course in much social scientific theorizing: What is obscured analytically by treating modernity as a coherent project, a causal agent, or a temporally delimited condition? How useful is it to work with a notion of the modern that is a distinct epoch that is discontinuous with the past, stretches seamlessly for 200 years, and is constituted by a packaged set of traits? Cooper exhaustively interrogates this package of traits, questioning their appearance in the aggregate, and shows each trait to be anything but uniformly present across "modern" society as well as present in prior historical moments (Cooper 2005). For me, Cooper's challenge underscores the problem of treating rights consciousness and practice as a by-product of a modern political rationality and a "trait" disseminated from Europe.

Like Cooper's work, Donald Moore's research illuminates the continuities of practice and meaning that cut across regimes of power, leaving sediments that work against the consolidation of a singular, cohesive project of rule. Writing about the Zimbabwean locale where he conducted his research, Moore notes, "Kaerezi's landscape of rule was not the result of a serial succession of new rationalities and administrative designations occluding previous power relations. Rather, previous sedimentations remained consequential even as they became reworked" (Moore 2005: 3). Moore locates these sediments spatially and shows how the past constitutes the very landscapes people inhabit, thus "entangl[ing] subjects and territory" (2005: 12). I take from Moore his attention to the historicity of space, what he calls an "enlivened geography" that encodes long histories of power and politics.

Tania Li's work meticulously documents what she calls "the practice of politics" (Li 2007), a term that she uses to illuminate governmentality "as a project, not a secure accomplishment" (2007: 10). Writing against scholars who frame governmental rule as a form of power that successfully depoliticizes projects and subjects of development, Li contends that the effort to "render technical" political economic realities is quite often reversed by these subjects themselves. As she puts it, "I am interested in the 'switch' in the opposite direction: in the conditions under which expert discourse is punctured by a challenge it cannot contain; moments when the targets of expert schemes reveal, in word or deed, their own critical analysis of the problems that confront them" (Li 2007: 11). Citing Foucault's notion of "permanent provocation," Li suggests that we remain attentive to the openings and closures generated at the interface between the will to govern and a strategy of struggle. I take from Li this attentiveness to politics as a state of permanent provocation, where government is a project but not necessarily an accomplishment of rule. I also take from her the recognition that government and politics are dialectically constituted rather than government being an orchestrating force that simply imposes its will on the population.

Building on these insights into temporality, space, and political agency, in my work I illuminate the political dynamics of rights as a sphere of negotiation informed by past histories of claim making and spatialization, histories that have brought Catholic fishers into creative engagement with Portuguese and British missionaries, native kings, and Hindu inlanders. To use Chakrabarty's term, I illustrate the provincial character of democracy as a set of idioms and practices that emerge from histories of political maneuver. But *unlike* Chakrabarty and others who identify Europe lurking behind universalist categories and, on that basis, reject their application to the postcolonial world, I propose that we provincialize democracy not as *European* but as always the product of particular cultural histories.

What I show instead is that subaltern politics *can* be informed by notions of sovereignty, equality, and rights, even as it uses idioms and forms of negotiation that appear antithetical to a politics of self-determination. A case in point is the claim to marine common property that I discuss in Chapter 4. Fishers opposing trawler activity claimed the 3 miles of inshore sea adjacent to the shore as the sovereign domain of the fisher artisan. This understanding of sovereignty did not privilege the bourgeois, law-abiding individual citizen. Claims to the inshore sea were articulated through street protests, invocations of fisher caste primordiality, and the moral economy of the artisan, constituting a form of sovereignty based on cultural history, political collectivity, and subalternity. These elements of political subjectivity are much more akin to Chatterjee's political society; however, they were mobilized to claim territorial sovereignty and to insert the fisher artisan into the state's juridical framework as a new legal subject. In transforming claims into rights through political maneuver, fisher politics actually forced a reconstitution of both governmental categories and legal frameworks and, by extension, the meaning of citizenship.

What are the implications of opening up rights-based citizenship as an arena of cultural contestation rather than a predetermined structure of power? First, we are able to recognize the dynamism of subaltern politics. Fishers did not simply reject or insert themselves into statist rights discourse. In the interplay of fisher claims and state responses, we see give on both sides. Mukkuvars' use of idioms of relationality have pulled state actors into new obligations. At the same time, as self-proclaimed clients of the state, they think of themselves as subjects whose political affiliations extend beyond the coast. This is by no means a closed universe; rather, new political currents render fluid the terms of negotiation and the idioms of rights. Second, thinking of citizenship in processual terms challenges the conceptual underpinnings of modern political theory, with its discrete spaces of community, civil society, and state. Fisher politics generated new political geographies that transgressed such neat spatial distinctions. Attending to actually existing subaltern rights politics thus releases citizenship from its normative equation with a predefined civic sphere and brings it to cultural life.

The equation of the subject of rights with the modern secular subject reinforces the binary between community and civic spaces. In the process, the normative parameters of citizenship are left unchanged and subalterns are relegated to a separate nonmodern sphere that appears spatially and temporally out of step. This persistent need to draw cultural boundaries around groups that are outside certain spheres of influence reinforces their outsider status and undercuts the project of narrating a more integrated political history (Dubois 2006).

Instead of definitively separating modern and nonmodern political epistemologies and their correlated civic and communitarian spaces, in this book I join others (Brown 2008; Cooper 2002; Ferguson 2006; Haugerud 1995; Matory 2005; Moore 2005; Palmié 2002; Sivaramakrishnan 1999; Tsing 2006; Walley 2004; West 2005) in narrating the circulation of ideas, practices, and strategies within shared arenas of power. Mukkuvar Catholics are neither strangers to regimes of rule nor simply individuals incorporated into subservience within structurally unequal political orders. Rather, they creatively negotiate norms of sociality and justice in ways that transform the very terms of participation.

Modernity and Difference

The question of who occupies the subaltern slot and what this means epistemologically and politically is a key concern of this book. As I show, groups in southwestern Indian society did not occupy fixed positions in a status hierarchy. From the mid-nineteenth century to the late twentieth century, the political fortunes and social standing of groups in the region kept shifting. From untouchable agrarian laborers, members of the inland Nadar caste became economic and political entrepreneurs who defined the terms of regional political modernity. At the same time and like other groups in Tamil society who experienced upward social mobility (Chari 2004), Nadars narrated their present with constant reference to their subaltern past, even making their change of status itself a by-product of their subalternity. From low castes sharing a comparable status to Nadars, Mukkuvar fishers became coastal primitives situated outside the boundaries of civil society. With the Blue Revolution in fishing technology, fisher beneficiaries of the developmental state parted ways with their caste brethren to claim a status as Mukkuvar moderns whose loyalties lay with inland and nation. These shifts call for a thoroughly historicized understanding of subaltern identity and politics rather than one derived from a cultural substratum. Indeed, subalterns in this account not only speak (Spivak 1988), often quite volubly, but also adopt changing strategies of self-representation in response to wider political currents.

Mukkuvar approaches to religious authority are indicative of the dynamism of subalternity. Within the Subaltern Studies project, the Indian subaltern's exteriority to modernity is represented first and foremost through the structural logic of religion. The subaltern's universe is depicted as a religious one animated by spiritual concerns that fall outside the purview of secular society. Indeed, even when subalterns engage in exercises that could be perceived as civic in nature, such as struggling for political independence or demanding the restoration of common property rights, subalternists have been careful to unearth a wholly "other" rationale for their actions.

What comes across most clearly within this framework is the need to delineate the world of subaltern enchantment from the mundane sphere of secular matters. We see here the scholarly fetishizing of religiosity and its treatment as a foundational worldview that anchors a supposedly autonomous domain of subaltern life. However, when we look at the organizational and political life of such groups as the Mukkuvars, who would be ideal candidates for representing subaltern religiosity, it becomes extremely difficult to maintain stark distinctions between the religious and the secular, or the spiritual and the material. Rather than the religious encompassing all of Mukkuvar life, one sees the traffic between religious and civic interpretations of authority, community, and rights that resists its characterization as either a wholly religious universe or one that is being inevitably secularized.

The dynamic relationship between fishers and priests at the village level captures some of the nuance of coastal rights politics and the irreducibility of fisher actions to either the civic or the religious domain. We might surmise from the opening anecdote of this introduction that the coast in the postcolonial period witnessed a process of secularization, the supplanting of religious authority and outlook with a civic sensibility. However, coastal dynamics belie such a teleological interpretation. The same fishers who registered a court case against their bishop continued to treat parish priests as the primary representatives at the village level. Indeed, when I first went to the village of Kovalam, the village that most of the case petitioners hailed from, I was predictably asked to let the parish priest know of my visit. Similarly, in the village of Muttom, which housed one of the most successful artisanal fisher unions, the priest had been the chosen representative at negotiations with the regional director of marine fisheries over the duration of a monsoon ban on trawling. The village of Mannakudy, which sought the construction of a bridge over a picturesque lake to invite tourism, also elected their priest to argue their case to the Public Works Department. Significantly, this was an instance in which the priest reluctantly performed his appointed task, because, as he confided to me later, he was opposed to using tourism to enhance village revenue. What was more, the villagers coerced him into wearing his cassock to the meeting, a garment that he typically donned only when he led Mass, so that he could present a more authoritative figure to the Public Works Department director.

There are also other instances of villagers rejecting the priest as the conduit of state law. In Ramanthurai, villagers militated against the required postmortem on an unmarried girl who had committed suicide as a violation of her bodily integrity and as causing additional violence to a hapless victim. When the priest insisted that the police required a postmortem to avoid criminal investigation, the villagers questioned his loyalty to the village and to Catholic principles and called him a stooge of the government. Such examples suggest a far more fluid relationship with secular and sacred authorities and affiliations than would be suggested by a totalizing depiction of subalterns as fundamentally religious in nature.

Granted, as in the case of Manakkudy, often fishers themselves would elect parish priests to represent them at negotiating sessions with state officials and trawler adversaries or to provide them with information on how to navigate the state bureaucracy. What was obscured for state officials, however, was that the representative role of the parish priest was often a conscious choice on the part of fishers rather than an automatic by-product of unquestioned clerical authority. Coastal life neither delineated religious and civic spheres nor wholly encompassed the civic within the religious. Rather, fishers appealed to civic *and* religious authorities and expressed a variety of spiritual *and* material aspirations through these appeals.

Fisher negotiations of religious and civic authority blur the rigid distinction between tradition and modernity that underpins arguments about subaltern difference. Indeed, southwestern regional histories of caste suggest the status of modernity not as a form of historical ontology associated with objective shifts in an evolutionary timeline or as a rupture into a new form of political rationality, but as a folk category of description and self-representation (Cooper 2005; Ferguson 1999; Sivaramakrishnan and Agrawal 2003; Walley 2004). Modernity, in this sense, references a set of meanings interacting with older social forms and processes rather than a rupture into a new historical condition.

A number of postcolonial theorists have pointed out that the Westerner has long been privileged as the Subject of History (Bhabha 1994; Chakrabarty 1992, 2000, 2002; Chatterjee 1993; Dirks 1992; Prakash 1995). This charge against a modular history was echoed in the discipline of anthropology; since the 1980s the role of anthropologists in spatially and temporally delimiting the non-Western localities we study, and the political implications of doing so, has been widely debated (Fabian 1983; Fox 1991). Eric Wolf was among the first to charge that European colonialism, with anthropology as its handmaiden, reduced non-Westerners to "people without history," in part by assuming the spatial containment of their worlds (Wolf 1982).

Although it is undeniably the case that a particular cultural narrative has underwritten projects of Western supremacy, modernist and postcolonial perspectives share the assumption that its discursive sweep has been so total that modernity everywhere references a Western subject. In doing so, these perspectives obscure other understandings of modernity that are neither derivative nor mimetic of a Western original. Part of my task in this book is to narrate a cultural politics of modernity that involves the elevation to paradigmatic status of the non-Western subject, one intimately linked to region and caste. Here, the subject of history is the agrarian inlander whose claim to modernity rests on notions of caste status and political sovereignty.

Both the politics of modernity and the negotiation of religious authority on the coast suggest the need to rethink a dyadic notion of difference that freezes the subaltern in an ahistorical mold (Sivaramakrishnan 1995). My work seeks instead to historicize subalternity as a moving target that is relationally constituted and politically mobilized for particular ends.

Chapters and Method

The structure of this book tracks the ongoing production of the coast and of fisher rights politics. Part 1 chronicles the forms of spatialization and claim making through the first half of the twentieth century that continue to shape postcolonial political dynamics. Chapter 1 offers snapshots of the coast over a 500-year period and highlights the political dynamism of coastal Catholicism, a world both local and translocal in makeup. I argue that perspectives of the coast as a space of premodern religious patronage mask the dynamism of the coastal world, in particular, the ongoing negotiation over the caste status of Mukkuvars and the sovereignty of coastal space. The history I narrate in this chapter is culled primarily from Catholic church histories (Narchison et al. 1983; Schurhammer 1977; Villavarayan 1956), histories of caste and Catholicism in India (Ballhatchet 1998; S. Bayly 1989), histories of Travancore state formation (S. Bayly 1984, 1999; De Lannoy 1997), and my own research conducted in the archives of Kanyakumari's Kottar diocese and in the archives of the London Missionary Society housed in the School of Oriental and African Studies, London. I have also supplemented these written records with oral histories of the Mukkuvar caste narrated by older fishermen and fisherwomen I befriended. Together, these sources provide a number of historically dispersed instances of Mukkuvar political maneuver that illustrate the use of patronage as an idiom not of subservience but of justice used to secure caste and territorial rights.

In the other two chapters of Part 1, I narrate the spatialization of the coast as local and of Mukkuvar Catholics as primitives located in a premodern universe. In Chapter 2 I move from the coast to the agrarian interior to understand coastal marginality from the inland out. I situate the shifting meanings of inland political space within a dynamic of state sovereignty and social contestation in the southwestern princely state of Travancore. With the advent of British indirect rule, the leadership of agrarian low castes and their Protestant missionary patrons in mobilizing discourses of popular sovereignty lent a particular caste flavor to an emergent sphere of democratic politics. Elevated to paradigmatic status in regional narratives of democracy, the experience of these castes constituted the sphere of inland modernity as distinct from coastal primitivism. Alongside these social struggles, rhetorical battles between Hindu sovereign and Protestant missions over the future of the princely state further relegated fisher Catholicism to a premodern past. In the chapter I finally turn to the creation of postindependence Kanyakumari as a separate district, which resulted in a radical transformation of the demographic balance between castes and religious communities. The new territorial boundary gave agrarian low castes political dominion, reinforcing the paradigmatic status of "their" modernity. As in Chapter 1, I blend ethnographic material on inland and coastal understandings of caste difference with missionary histories (Forrester 1980; Jacob 1990; Mateer 1871, 1883), histories of Travancore (Chiriyankandath 1992, 1993; Daniel 1985, 1992; Jeffrey 1976, 1978; Kawashima 1998; Kooiman 1989, 1995; Ouwerkerk 1994), and my own primary research of Travancore State administrative documents pertaining to the coast in the Kerala State Archives.

In Chapter 3 I consider another space-making project—twentieth-century developmentalism—which ran alongside the making of inland modernity and had a significant impact on the spatialization of fisher artisanship. I offer a historical account of administrative rationality, in particular, how spatial imaginaries informed developmental strategies. Using administrative reports and research papers of the Madras Presidency's Fisheries Bureau, I juxtapose the perspectives of three colonial fishery administrators—Nicholson, Hornell, and Sundara Raj—on the fraught question of trawling to parse overlaps and divergences among fishery bureaucrats in an era of imperial development. Three spatial imaginaries of the coast emerge from their writings: a bounded locality inhabited by subsistence fishers existing on the margins of an agrarian heartland; one node of an oceanic world of trade, technological diffusion, and cultural exchange; and a subset of an emerging nation. I show how these images informed specific developmental interventions on the southern coast over the first three decades of the twentieth century. I then shift to postcolo-

nial developmentalism, when the future of fishing was reset to the prerogatives of an economy imagined on a national scale. I use the administrative
reports and research papers of the Tamilnadu State Department of Fisheries
to show how, while in some ways similar to the colonial imagining of coastal
artisanship, the postcolonial fisher artisan was set apart not just from the inlander but also from the modern fisher.

Part 2 contains the last three chapters. It addresses the articulation of postcolonial fisher rights politics through space making and makes up the book's
ethnographic core. Together, the three chapters form a chronological narrative spanning the first forty postindependence years. In Chapter 4 I consider
the state's gradual shift from wealth redistribution to capital accumulation
as the basis of postcolonial developmentalism and its impact on coastal understandings of community and moral economy. Methodologically, the chapter provides the ethnographic counterpart to the latter half of Chapter 3 by
turning to fisher memories of the first two postindependence decades and the
experience of state-led development. The 1950s and 1960s witnessed the overlap between the production of a new shoreline separating trawler owner from
artisan and the transformation of both into national citizens. This chapter
asks how the pairing of development and democracy played out on the coast.
How did Catholic fishers, who were rendered increasingly marginal to the
consolidation of inland caste power, experience postindependence development? What did the transition to postcolonial rule mean socially and spatially
on the Kanyakumari coast? I show that mediating structures of sovereignty
and sociality persisted within the postcolonial developmental grid and generated forms of uneven citizenship, even as the postcolonial state proclaimed
its commitment to undifferentiated national belonging. At the same time,
fishers in these first two postindependence decades were beginning to articulate preexisting understandings of coastal moral economy with new state-
disseminated notions of rural community, thus setting the stage for later
political projects through which the artisan emerged as a distinct political
subject.

Chapter 5 follows chronologically from Chapter 4, taking us into the 1970s
and 1980s, when cracks in nationalist hegemony gave way to new political
experiments. Three shifts—the embrace of regionalism, the agitation for an
inshore artisanal zone, and the use of motorized technology—generated an
intermediate space of politics. All three—political, territorial, and technological—challenged the enforced marginality of artisans and respatialized them

as supralocal actors with claims to a wider polity. Combining an analysis of government documents, nongovernmental organization literature, and clerical autobiographies with the accounts of fishers engaged in the various projects, I argue that these projects of intermediacy capture the real limitations and possibilities of the nation-state in a way that localism and cosmopolitanism do not. While engaging in party politics, technological development, and state legislation, coastal actors consciously scaled their politics to be betwixt and between locality and nation, and nation and world, and in the process expanded the parameters of political rights.

In Chapter 6 I narrate shifts in the idioms and practices of fisher politics in the 1990s decade of neoliberal reforms. In the fisheries arena, this decade witnessed the juxtaposition of state-led neoliberal deterritorialization and oppositional call for a robust national territorial sovereignty that suggests a shift in both economic policy and political organizing. Judging from the literature produced by social movements in the fisheries sector, activist clergy, and their political party supporters, the space of intermediacy carved out by earlier negotiations was eclipsed by a new emphasis on anti-imperialist nationalism. Yet I show that when we turn back to Kanyakumari, we see more than the battle of sovereign nation against transnational capital. Ethnographic inquiry into fisher responses in the district shows that rather than a rupture with fishery politics of the previous decades, discourses of ecological sovereignty offered new tools of space making for domestic adversaries in the 1990s trawler wars that strengthened class opposition. They also offered the state occasion for reinforcing church authority over coastal space, now as the instrument of community resource management, a shift I document through interviews with state and church officials. By narrating the two trajectories of nationalization and localization and describing who engaged in each space-making project and what tools they used, I argue for an understanding of 1990s neoliberalism as part of a longer history of uneven development and contested citizenship, not as a rupture into a wholly different political paradigm.

I end this book by addressing the implications for postcolonial democracy of articulating space and rights diachronically. The Conclusion begins with a brief account of the devastating impact of the 2004 Asian tsunami on the Kanyakumari coast and the ensuing continuities and shifts in relations between state, church, and fishers. I then suggest that a Gramscian understanding of subalternity that highlights its dialectical nature is critical for scholarly work on conservation and for a truly participatory approach to rights. Within such a framework, state and community would be mutually implicated in long histories of rule, resistance, and collaboration. Postcolonial citizenship would be not a derivative juridical construct that is a less authentic expression of cultural subjectivity but a dynamic, locally constituted process through which people envision their relationship to nature, community, nation, and state. Approaching state and community as necessarily intertwined then allows for an approach to conservation as neither state science nor community practice. Rather, the thorough imbrication of states and communities suggests that any effort to redress the ills of overdevelopment has to be a joint one. In Kanyakumari the efforts of both artisanal and trawler fishers to draw state actors and institutions into their resource conflicts suggests a willingness on the part of local producers to recognize a role for the state in allocating resource rights. It is amply clear that they see the state as internal to locality and a key player in community conflicts. The question remains, however, whether the state is willing to challenge its cherished binaries of science and folk knowledge and of modernity and primitivism that distinguish state from community space and underwrite its monopoly on national development.

Genealogies of Inequality and Rights

Figure 1. Fishing village church, Kanyakumari District. Courtesy of International Collective in Support of Fishworkers, Chennai, India.

1 The Coastal World

Spatial Jurisdictions and Meanings

IT IS SOMETHING OF A TRUISM to say that the lives of Mukkuvars are oriented around the sea. Kanyakumari's shoreline is crowded with fisher huts and cement homes that open out to the Indian Ocean. India's southwestern fishermen spend their days casting craft into the roughest waters of the subcontinent's coastal belt. After spending their day at sea using an array of nets, hooks, and lines suited to specific species of fish, fishermen return to shore to sell the day's catch to waiting small fish vendors and bigger traders. Many of the smaller vendors are fisherwomen who load the fish into containers, which they then carry on their heads to nearby markets. These fish provide cheap protein to inland consumers and income for the fisherwomen's own household staples. Much has changed in the last fifty years with the introduction of mechanized trawlers, the entry of numerous long-distance fish merchants into the trade, and the expansion of a coastal proletariat who work as labor on artisanal and mechanized craft, but fishing is still the primary occupation on the coast. Even though some Mukkuvars have branched out into other occupations—the clergy, teaching, civil service, secretarial work, and social work—most coastal dwellers continue in the trade of their ancestors.

Fishers' lives, then, have long been oriented around the sea both socially and economically. When one considers this orientation in the context of the territorialized dynamics of the modern nation-state, this seemingly facile statement acquires deeper meaning. In the southwestern region, two histories unfolded in tandem, one oriented outward around the Indian Ocean and the other oriented inward around land, agriculture, and state. The southwestern coast was fully integrated into transoceanic circuits of trade and religion even as it became increasingly marginal to the state-making politics of the agrarian inland. While Mukkuvar fishers were looking out to sea, the agrarian world was closing ranks around new understandings of status and belonging. In Chapter 4, we will see the meeting of these two worlds through the initiative of the postindependence developmental state. State interventions in fishing in the mid-twentieth century subjected southwestern fishers to the turbulence of capitalist restructuring that had transformed agrarian lives a century earlier. With the introduction of new technologies came new institutions and political currents that knitted coastal and inland lives together in unprecedented ways.

In this chapter I explore the world of the coast inhabited by Catholic fishers before the onset of postcolonial state developmentalism. I highlight the political dynamism of coastal Catholicism, a world both local and translocal in makeup. Beginning in the mid-sixteenth century, the southwestern coast of India became part of a network of Catholic places, people, and politics that spanned the globe. Although southwestern fishers were not maritime traders and transoceanic travelers like the seafarers of Calicut or the merchants of Gujarat, faith and trade linked them to places beyond their immediate social world. At the time, Catholicism was a world unto itself, one both hierarchical and heterogeneous, uniting its members in faith and dividing them across lines of social difference. These fishers were also part of a wider world of fishing whose interconnections reached further into the past. Their craft and gear suggest transoceanic borrowings: The *kattumaram* is thought to be of Polynesian origin, and the *vallam* bears the impression of Arab influence. Similarly, Mukkuvar fishing techniques encode histories of conquest and trade: The boat seine, or *thattumadi*, is of Spanish origin, and the Portuguese brought the shore seine, or *karamadi*, to the southwestern coastal belt (J. Kurien and Mathew 1982).

Today's landlocked centers of state power and capital accumulation make it difficult to comprehend the vibrant dynamics of the Indian Ocean world and the place of fishers within it. The enduring historiographic focus on the inland public arenas of nineteenth- and twentieth-century Travancore, the princely state that included the southwestern region, only compounds the problem. Taking their cues from the states of the subcontinent, historians have focused their research on the agrarian worlds prized by modern states for their sedentarism and revenue (Arunima 2003; Daniel 1985, 1992; Jeffrey 1976, 1978; Kawashima 1998; Kooiman 1989, 1995; Menon 2004; Ouwerkerk 1994;

Saradamoni 1999; Yesudas 1975). In the historical literature, the agrarian inland is the space of prosperity, penury, and politics, and land, lord, peasant,
and state are the key ingredients of historical formation and transformation.
By contrast, fishing and fishers are conspicuously absent, marking with their
absence their insignificance to the coffers of the powerful. Even in the literature on the Indian Ocean trade, spice merchants, military entrepreneurs, and
imperial powers take precedence as historical actors over fishers.[1]

That these fishers are Catholic only compounds the problem of historical invisibility.[2] With a few exceptions (Ballhatchet 1998; S. Bayly 1989, 1981;
Boxer 1978; Houtart and Lemercinier 1981; Houtart and Nayak 1988; Nayak
et al. 2002; Ram 1991; Stirrat 1981, 1982), discussion of the Roman Catholic
coast as a dynamic space in its own right is almost exclusively limited to ha-
giographic church histories with their own obvious blinders. This historical
black-boxing of the church and its congregants has obscured from view the
social and political turbulence within the church over caste rights, the organization of fishing, and territorial jurisdiction. When we pull away the curtains,
we are witness to a remarkable set of dynamics bringing fishers of the western
coast into contact with a variety of institutional authorities from the parish
priest to the regional bishop, the Portuguese archdiocese of Goa, Rome's Propaganda Fide, and the English East India Company.

The forms of negotiation that fishers engaged in reflect a keen sense of
the overlapping circles of power and authority in which they were embedded;
this was a population that had a decidedly nonlocal political imagination.
When fishers appealed to the East India Company for a change of jurisdiction from Rome's Propaganda Fide to Portugal's Padroado, when they wrote
to the Vatican urging an end to caste prejudices within seminaries, or when
they demanded from their diocesan bishop a new parish priest who would not
extract so much from their daily catch for the church fund, fishers expressed
an understanding of hierarchies and scales of authority and demonstrated the
wherewithal to maneuver within and across them.

Although these other political arenas of the parish, the diocese, and the
imperial church fall outside the conventional parameters of Travancore historiography, they are no by means subject to a completely different set of dynamics. Indeed, the sources and patterns of conflict have striking overlaps—
opposition to taxation, demands for low caste representation within the
clergy, lay threats of conversion, and resistance to institutional norms of social
morality—that mark both inland and coastal politics. In both spaces, low castes

were issuing challenges to structural inequalities of caste, class, and religion and in the process transforming the institutions that governed their lives.

Perspectives of the coast as a space of premodern patronage mask the dynamism of the coastal world, in particular, the ongoing negotiation over the sovereignty of coastal space and the caste status of its fisher inhabitants. The church has been an awesome force in fishers' lives since the early days of its establishment on the coast in the sixteenth century. It was patron and intimate, an everyday influential presence. It is equally clear, however, that church authority was not accepted without question. In small and bigger acts of political maneuver, fishers negotiated the terms of coastal sovereignty. At times, they wove village and parish seamlessly together; at other times, fishers' claims to coastal space privileged village over parish; at still other times, fishers would proclaim their sovereignty over the village church, refusing the overarching authority of higher echelons of the Catholic hierarchy. In their negotiations of material and spiritual circumstances, we witness both allegiance to institutional patrons and claims to self-determination that belie a sharp distinction between patronage and rights. To put it differently, the intimacy of fisher relations to their church requires an understanding of institutional authority not as an exteriority to community but as woven into its very definition. When fishers defined themselves as a community, they often included the church as a collective symbol.

Modernist histories of social transformation that assume a linear progression from patronage to rights—as many of the inland-based histories do—fail to recognize the nuances of patronage that allowed southwestern fishers to, for instance, both invoke the church as lord and master and evict parish priests who did not subscribe to village standards of justice. The rigid distinction between patronage and rights, arguably the basis of much modern theorizing on democracy, does not hold up when one considers coastal dynamics. Mukkuvar claim making since the eighteenth century reflects an understanding of collective justice and patronage, of community and authority, as inextricably linked. As I show in this chapter, Mukkuvar claim making typically opposed the injustice of one authority by turning to another for protection, exhibiting a politics of affiliation and allegiance that sits uneasily with modernist notions of rights as individual self-determination.

The dominance of either an inland, agrarian orientation or an oceanic orientation around long-distance trade and militarism has meant a dearth of historical information on the Catholic fishers of the southwestern coast. In my quest for Mukkuvar cultural histories, I found glimpses of coastal dynamics in Catholic Church histories, European travelogues, Travancore state manuals, diocesan records, and a smattering of secondary historical literature. More recently, debate between development economists and fishery activists on the ecological and social fallout of the postcolonial state's fisheries development effort has generated a considerable amount of writing. Although this literature illuminates the particularities of coastal life since the 1950s, especially the socioeconomic context for the introduction of new capital-intensive technologies, it offers little on the preindependence period. What follows in this chapter, then, are several snapshots of the coast over a 500-year stretch culled from a variety of sources. I show the entrenchment of the coastal church as landlord, tax collector, and religious authority and illuminate how patronage as a mode of power and sociality became the basis not simply for the exercise of power but also for challenging it.

The Coastal Church

What emerges most clearly from the available patchwork of historical information is the social subordination of Mukkuvars first to royal and then to clerical patrons. Writings by early travelers to the Fishery Coast speak of the "lowly fishers" who formed the lowest rung of the region's social hierarchy. The Ming dynasty traveler and chronicler Mahuan, who visited the west coast trading center of Cochin in A.D. 1409, wrote, "There are five classes of men. The Nayars rank with the king. In the first class are those who shave their beards and have a thread or string over their shoulders. These are looked upon as belonging to the noblest families. In the second are Mahomedans, the third the Chetties who are the capitalists; in the fourth Kolings who act as commission agents, the fifth the Mukuvas, the lowest and poorest of all" (Nagam Aiya 1906: 65). In the early nineteenth century, English botanist and statistician Francis Buchanan referred to the Mukkuvars as a "tribe," a pejorative term indicating a place outside the caste order: "The Mucua or in plural Mucuar, are a tribe who lived near the sea-coast of Malayala, to the inland parts of which they seldom go, and beyond its limits, anyway, they rarely venture" (Buchanan 1807: 527). In the *Travancore State Manual* of 1906, Nagam Aiya reproduced a common, although unverified, story about women of rebel high caste families being sold as slaves to the Mukkuvars by Travancore ruler Marthanda Varma (Nagam Aiya 1906: 338). Whether or not this tale has any basis in fact, the ignominy of slavery is clearly enhanced in the account by bondage to a caste as lowly as the Mukkuvars.

However, there is no neat continuity between Mukkuvar *social* subordination of the past and their *geographical* marginality today. In the pre-nineteenth-century world, Mukkuvars were not spatially segregated outside a societal mainstream. Unlike today, when they are typecast as primitives inhabiting a wilderness outside the agrarian heartland, fishers were very much part of a society whose accumulation of wealth and state making were oriented around coastal trade. A long history of material, political, and cultural exchange linked the western coast of India to the continents of Africa and Europe (cf. Boxer 1969; Das Gupta and Pearson 1999; Subrahmanyam 1993). Trade routes were also pathways for the transmission of new faith traditions to the subcontinent, and conversions marked new military alliances as much as they did change of religious affiliation. Scholars date the Christian presence in India back to the visit in the first century of Thomas the Apostle, who established the Syrian Orthodox Church on the western coast. The establishment of the Roman Catholic Church followed in the sixteenth century, when the seafaring Portuguese traveled east in search of fabled lands of prosperity and lost Christians.

The Portuguese quickly insinuated themselves into regional dynamics, becoming one among many warring kingdoms and social groups seeking to further trade, military, and state-making agendas. To them, religion and trade were intertwined activities, and the Jesuits who traveled with the Portuguese navy were military contractors as much as missionaries. Patrick Roche puts it succinctly: "Portuguese officialdom was characterized not only by captains and factors but also by the padres. Both captains and clerics acted as partners in Christianization and colonization as servants of the king. Indigenous groups found that the clerics were powerful negotiators in winning the protection and support of the Portuguese officials" (Roche 1984: 41–42).

Among those who sought Portuguese naval support were the Paravar fishers of the southeastern coast. Paravars were a caste that enjoyed a virtual monopoly over the Coromandel Coast's pearl fishing industry. Unlike the Mukkuvars, this fishing caste enjoyed a renown chronicled in a rich body of historical evidence. Social histories of this population make clear the initiative of the Paravar caste elite in sending deputations to the Portuguese seeking protection from Muslim pirates and neighboring kings and offering conversion in exchange. The Paravar *jaati thalaivar* (caste headman) is said to have himself converted and commanded his subordinates to convert with him. By 1537, some 20,000 Paravars had been baptized and brought under the Portuguese military wing.

The second mass conversion of coastal fishers to Catholicism followed in 1544 with the entry of the Mukkuvars of the southwestern kingdom of Venad into the church. In the scholarship on Christian conversion in South Asia, conversion has increasingly been interpreted through the agency of the convert (cf. Kent 2004; Kooiman 1989; Oddie 1997, 1998; Viswanathan 1996, 1998). Placing converts at the center of conversion provides a crucial corrective to earlier interpretations of conversion as the manifest will of the missionary, with the converts moving from ignorance to enlightenment largely in spite of themselves. Anthropologist Kalpana Ram, who has written one of the few ethnographies of Kanyakumari's Mukkuvar Catholics, offers a speculative interpretation of their conversion that dovetails with this "second wave" of literature on conversion.

> To be untouchable, to be able to worship Hindu gods only from the outer wall and to be confined to the sea shore to protect caste Hindus from one's polluting qualities would seem reason enough to seek to escape Hinduism. In addition, we have seen that fisherpeople are quasi-independent of upper caste power and patronage, with all relations with the wider society mediated by trade. When an opportunity presented itself for the Mukkuvars to resolve the anomalies of their position in caste society, they took it. . . . Among the Mukkuvars, conversion was the result of a (probably explosive) combination of factors: the humiliations of untouchability being sharpened by the aspiration to autonomy and economic independence. This interpretation finds support in the literature on mass conversions to Christianity in the nineteenth century. (Ram 1991: 31–32)

Although convert intentionality and agency are certainly welcome frames through which to understand the mass conversions of South Asia, we must be cautious not to apply them across the board. A case in point is the Mukkuvar fisher conversion of the mid-sixteenth century. There is little evidence that this second exchange of guns for souls was, as Ram suggests, at the behest of the Mukkuvars themselves. Rather, it appears to have been part of a military agreement struck between the king of Venad and the Portuguese. Church histories of the period record that, in the interest of trade, the Portuguese sent Francis Xavier as a secret emissary to the king of Venad, one of four rulers of the west coast who controlled the best harbors and the richest spice zones. Xavier offered Portuguese naval support against the neighboring king, Vettum Perumal. In exchange for this support, the king of Venad affirmed his willingness to allow the socially powerless but strategically situated coastal Mukkuvars to be baptized by the Jesuit priest. With this decision, the Mukkuvars were transferred from royal to church patronage.

To read Mukkuvar conversion as an expression of the desire for autonomy and self-determination seems an untenable interpretation of existing historical evidence. Although Mukkuvars would certainly have had their own interpretation of conversion that possibly cut against those of king and church, it seems highly unlikely that they set the process in motion or had ultimate control over its outcomes. Indeed, it appears that Ram's reading of Mukkuvar conversion has more to do with her own preference for a model of subaltern consciousness and practice that privileges autonomy over a more dialectical understanding of the relationship of subalterns to elite patrons.

It is this interpretive angle that then allows Ram to charge the church with undercutting Mukkuvar aspirations: "Whatever the Mukkuvars hoped to gain from conversion, the Catholic Church has not made it its business to alter their place within the overall social structure" (Ram 1991: 32). Throughout her rich and compelling ethnography, Ram offers us a portrait of the church as external to community, or, as she puts it, the "petty Raja of the Mukkuvars" (Ram 1991: 29). We get little sense of the intimacy between the church and its coastal congregants, or even that the coastal clergy were increasingly drawn from the Mukkuvar caste. Instead, Ram's is a two-tier world in which a subaltern cultural stratum endures beneath the overlay of church authority and institutional Catholicism.

I highlight my argument with Ram's interpretation of Mukkuvar history only to make a larger point about hegemony. Many subalternist scholars invoke the Gramscian notion of hegemony, a term that figures prominently in Ram's (1991) subtitle, in order to underscore the autonomy of subaltern consciousness and practice. However, this predilection for treating the subaltern as an autonomous social actor marshalling an independent worldview into purposeful action runs counter to the dialectical valence of the term in Gramsci's work. Gramsci maintains that the "history of subaltern social groups is necessarily fragmented and episodic" and that they "are always subject to the activity of ruling groups, even when they rebel and rise up" (Gramsci 1972: 55). Rather than autonomy, then, what characterizes subaltern politics for Gramsci are complex affiliations with dominant strata and multiple forms of popular alliance.

Gramsci's notion of hegemony as a field of power within which subalterns maneuver for position and stake claims, often using the same discursive terms deployed by the powerful, seems to best characterize the relationship of Mukkuvars to their church. Church patronage exerted a tremendous amount of power over coastal congregants. Yet patronage did not imply absolute domination; this was not a feudal stranglehold. The glimpses we get into Catholic fisher practice reveal many instances of maneuver *within* the framework of patronage. Although fishers rarely staked out positions completely outside the parameters of Catholic community or even religious authority, they nevertheless articulated demands for justice and equality. Throughout this book, I argue that these examples of collective politics should force us to rethink the liberatory subject of rights. Instead of looking for insurrectionary subalterns inhabiting spaces outside power and expressing a politics of radical autonomy, we should be more attentive to the actual substance of subaltern agency, be it the quest for alternative patrons or appeals to higher echelons of religious authority. Only then will we be able to shed the social blinders imposed by our own liberation orthodoxies and see rights politics at work in all its myriad forms (see, e.g., Anderson and Guha 2000).

Church patronage over the southwestern coast was hugely consequential. Its reign extended new laws, institutions, and technologies of coercion and allegiance. First, it transformed the organization of the coastal village. Church histories date Francis Xavier's west coast baptisms to November 1544, when, starting in the village of Poovar, he initiated the mass conversion of 10,000 Mukkuvars. Mansilhas, another Jesuit accompanying Xavier, completed the Mukkuvar baptisms and originated the parochial setup of a *kanakapillai* (catechist), *modom* (overseer of ecclesiastical duties), *ubadesiar* (sacristan), *vaadiyar* (teacher in the religious school), and *melinchi* (jail attendant). Although we have no sense of what predated these village functionaries or how Mukkuvar villagers adapted this new parochial structure to their own understandings, it appears that by the end of Mansilhas's tenure, the foundation had been laid for a self-supporting church. Church histories also claim that by 1568 the local population financially supported the priests of the southwestern coastal parishes (Narchison et al. 1983; Schurhammer 1977; Villavarayan 1956).

The parish church's ability to sustain itself rested in part on its right of taxation, perhaps the most far-reaching of its powers. The king of Venad had levied a fish tax before the Mukkuvar conversions of 1544. Stone inscriptions dating back to 1494 at Kumari Muttom, one of the easternmost villages of the Fishery Coast, contain an edict of the king authorizing the levy of a light duty on the fishermen and on the transport boats that carried paddy and other cargo along the coast (Narchison et al. 1983; Schurhammer 1977). After the 1544 conversions, this tax passed from the hands of the king to the Catholic Church as part of the king's contract with the Portuguese Crown. The church was also granted ownership of coastal land and a landlord's claim to all its products, including coconut and coir.

Francis Xavier's self-sustaining village church so glorified in church hagiographies rested, then, not on consensus but on the coercive extraction of a tax-in-kind from coastal inhabitants. Until 1954, when the Catholic diocese of Kottar abolished the tax, the church would extract a percentage of the daily catch—anywhere from 25 percent to 35 percent of the meager surplus from fishing nets—as the *kuthagai*, a term that originally referred to the tax levied by the Venad ruler. That the church sustained itself on the backs of its coastal parishioners is made clear by additional documents detailing the method of tax collection. To facilitate the process, and perhaps to obscure its own problematic role as tax collector, the church would auction the right to collect this tax to merchants with the means to secure their bid. Whoever won the auction—the man designated fish contractor—also claimed the right to appropriate a portion of the tax as his commission. Interestingly, this role appears to have been largely reserved for inlanders because of the coastal population's general state of impoverishment. Hindu and Muslim merchants from the inland, and the occasional wealthy Mukkuvar, would participate in the church auction and, having secured the bid, enter into a three-way contract with church and fishers.

Apart from sustaining the church fund, the *kuthagai* system further entrenched mercantile power on the coast. Fishers are one of the most indebted of rural populations for several reasons. The volatility of marine fishing, subject to the wind, the swell of the ocean, and the unpredictability of a fugitive resource, makes for an unreliable harvest. Navigating a treacherous sea subjects craft and gear to sudden damage or loss, making fishers even more vulnerable to the burden of debt than inland farmers. Typically, fishermen will secure loans for repair or for purchase of craft and gear from merchants through whom they are then obligated to sell their fish. This means that fishermen not only lose a substantial portion of their daily catch to the church-appointed contractor but also get a meager sum for the remainder of their harvest. Historically, the church has been only too willing to underwrite mercantile power; when villagers refused to hand over the designated portion of catch to the anointed fish contractor or sought alternative channels for selling their fish, the church would in turn refuse them the sacraments or excommunicate them.

In addition to the church being the key intermediary between coast and king and between fishers and inland merchants, its parochial structure played a pivotal role in defining the boundaries of village community and the operations of the economy. Parish priests oversaw the complex system of cooperation that knitted villages together. Villagers had collective rights to the fishing grounds extending out from their village shore, and these grounds were understood to fall under the jurisdiction of the parish. The rules of access and use of village fishing grounds were enforced by a village council, but it was the parish priest who imposed sanctions against those who violated the codes governing use and access of the marine commons. The parish priest also collected a small fee from outsiders who launched their craft from the village shore; this fee contributed to the upkeep of the village church. The system of intervillage cooperation was maintained by the moral and religious power exerted by the church to ensure the payment of fees (Narchison et al. 1983; Ram 1991; Thomson 1989; Villavarayan 1956).

Finally, the church was a key broker in the flourishing military labor market of the eighteenth century. Travancore's imposition of *chumkam*, the tax on the import and export of pepper, was the most important source of income for the king. The English and French acceded to the tax and paid an additional tribute to the Travancore palace in exchange for control over parts of the coast; the Dutch, however, resorted to more overt military tactics to try to wrest the coastal trade from Travancore. Mukkuvars, through their church, were recruited into the eighteenth-century battles between the Dutch and Travancore over control of the lucrative west coast trade in pepper. Nagam Aiya, author of the multivolume *Travancore State Manual*, goes so far as to say that the Mukkuvars formed a dependable corps of soldiers for Marthanda Varma in his battle against the Dutch (Nagam Aiya 1906: 350).

Whether Nagam Aiya exaggerated the military role of Mukkuvars or not, they certainly do seem to have been drawn into the battles of the era's trading powers. One oft-repeated instance of Mukkuvar military participation is the Colachel War of 1740–1741. Some accounts—by historians and fishers alike—chronicle the triumphant role of the inhabitants of Colachel fishing village in staving off Dutch attack. The story goes that these fishermen lined the beach, their oars at their shoulders, forming the first line of defense that at a distance appeared armed and dangerous. By tricking the Dutch into seeing tools of harvest as weapons of war, Colachel's fishers managed to repel the Dutch advance, at least temporarily. The Dutch eventually succeeded in taking over Colachel, prompting the fishing population to flee inland en masse. Identifying the Mukkuvars as a potentially useful labor force, the Dutch approached the resident Jesuit priests to deliver fisher coolies for building a fort. Clearly, the Dutch recognized the church as the ultimate coastal authority wielding unquestioned power over its fisher congregants. However, this story also attests to fishers' own ability to negotiate terms, not only with their church but also with warring military powers. Colachel's villagers apparently did not accede to Dutch demands conveyed to them by their clergy. Furthermore, they sought to curry favor with the Travancore king by delivering to his soldiers a Dutch corporal and interpreter who had requested boat transport to the Dutch-controlled coastal town of Kanyakumari (De Lannoy 1997).

The Dutch were among many who assumed that the secular and ritual power of the coastal church meant its absolute authority over fishers. The church on the coast is undoubtedly a curious beast, at once internal and external to community. To this day, the insinuation of the church into the everyday life of the village lends coastal space a seamless quality in which parish and village appear as one and the same. Since the eighteenth century, the church has emerged as a key vehicle of social mobility for young Mukkuvar men, making it central to the creation of a coastal white-collar minority. Church leaders were certainly invested in equating coastal village with Catholic parish. As late as 1946, Kottar's Bishop Agniswami wrote to the parish priest of Mel Manakkudy village, "It is regrettable to note that some of the members of one or two families who have joined the Lutheran Mission some years ago still persist in their blindness. The parish priest should make every endeavor by prayer and persuasion to see that this blot on the parish is removed."[3]

All these dimensions of church patronage suggest the church's exclusive reign as the singular coastal authority. Other accounts, however, reveal that the relationship of Mukkuvars to the church has been far from smooth; the church's tenure on the coast has been met with frequent opposition by fishers trying to elbow more room for themselves within a clerical structure mired in caste hierarchy or challenging the church's stranglehold over coastal property and produce. Two key forms of claim making emerge from the historical record of the Fishery Coast: claims by an emerging coastal elite for caste representation within the Catholic clergy and claims by poorer fishers for village sovereignty and economic justice. Both types of claim elaborated a link between community, authority, and space. Mukkuvar clerical aspirants argued for the right to enter seminaries and to oversee particular church territories. Poor fishers also spoke the language of justice, although from a somewhat different vantage point. They sought to wrest control of village economy (most notably the allocation of fishing surplus) and village morality (e.g., the policing of sexuality) from a clerical and mercantile elite. Beginning in the early twentieth century, the question of the church's status vis-à-vis the village was frequently raised. With the entrenchment of a Mukkuvar clerical elite in the 1930s, fisher claims were increasingly in tension with caste brethren staking representative authority over the coast.

The claims that Mukkuvars made, whether for clerical representation or for economic justice, were typically crafted in the language of faith and patronage. They insisted that their demands were in accordance with the tenets of the faith, and they sought patrons who could help secure their claims. Even when they issued threats of conversion, which they did frequently, they did so as subordinates and in the language of filial piety, addressing clerical authorities as "Our Holy Father," "Your Excellency," and "Our Benefactor." One example of this, which I elaborate on later, concerns a village scandal surrounding the parish priest of Pallam village. Writing to the archbishop of Verapoly, Pallam's villagers demanded the priest's transfer, threatening conversion if their demands were not met: "Prostrating before Your Lordship, we humbly beg before Your Excellency to issue order to His Excellency the Bishop of Kottar to give sudden transfer to Rev. Fr. Borjia, the Parish Priest of Pallam, so that our religion may not be spoiled and also our faith may not be changed."[4]

Territorializing Caste Within the Church

The caste character of the Roman Catholic Church in India underwent a dramatic change between the eighteenth and twentieth centuries, largely because of the escalation of low caste protest against caste-based segregation of churches and demands for clerical ordination. By 1956, when Kanyakumari District was carved out from the erstwhile princely state of Travancore and merged with the state of Tamilnadu, the Catholic clergy of Kottar diocese had a low caste majority. Kottar diocese was not the only diocese that had become a low caste stronghold; in Catholic pockets across India, churches that had previously enforced low caste subordination to high caste congregants and clergy now had to contend with increasing numbers of low caste clergy. The changing composition of clerical power had far-reaching effects on the institutional culture of churches, sometimes carving out caste-specific churches and at other times making rights conflicts an intrinsic part of church dynamics.

Claims to fisher caste rights within the church were typically made by those Mukkuvars aspiring to join the clergy. Historian Kenneth Ballhatchet points out that, in this effort, the aspirants were aided by the jurisdictional conflicts between Portugal and Rome that beset Catholic India beginning in the seventeenth century. At the end of the fifteenth century, Pope Alexander VI divided up the newly colonized parts of the world, entrusting the western region to Spain and the eastern region to Portugal for missionizing. Through the Padroado, or Privilege of Patronage, the pope extended control over dioceses in India to the king of Portugal. This arrangement was repeatedly recognized by declarations of Rome from 1534 to 1606. But with the flagging of Portuguese missionary energies and rampant questioning of papal authority within Portuguese circles in the seventeenth century, the Vatican began to feel the need for a complementary authority. In response to rising tensions with the Padroado, the Vatican established the Propaganda Fide, or Congregation for the Propagation of the Faith, in 1622 and sent out its own missionaries to areas beyond Portuguese reach. To conciliate the Portuguese and underscore the lack of overlap between territorial jurisdictions, the pope assigned Propaganda Fide's vicars apostolic to territories under Muslim or other forms of "infidel" rule, such as Travancore, where Catholic dioceses were yet to be formed. However, Portuguese authorities were never reconciled to the Propaganda Fide, which they saw as an evasion of the letter and spirit of the Padroado. Policies inaugurated by the Portuguese government in the latter half of the eighteenth century that privileged administrative expansion over an expansion of the faith further exacerbated tensions between Rome and Lisbon. Toward the end of the eighteenth century, the Catholic map of India had sharp divisions reflecting the ongoing battle between the Padroado and the Propaganda Fide.

Caste struggles intersected with these battles over jurisdiction. Different caste groups within the Catholic Church used the conflict over jurisdiction to lay their own claims to caste status and representation. Although there is little information on how these jurisdictional battles played out in Travancore, Ballhatchet offers a portrait of Mukkuvar claim making in those territories directly ruled by the English East India Company. He notes that Mukkuvars appear in the company's records because of the frequency of complaints they registered against their religious leadership. Even though they rarely sought an escape from Catholicism, Mukkuvars liberally used the conflict of jurisdiction between the Portuguese Padroado and Rome's Propaganda Fide to challenge Vatican accommodation of caste hierarchy. Typically, this involved a request for transfer to Portuguese patronage because the Cochin Seminary under the Padroado made a point of ordaining Mukkuvar priests between 1838 and 1886. Before 1886, when a successful concordat was signed between Rome and Lisbon, Mukkuvar Catholics frequently sought the intervention of the East India Company, which was responsible for authorizing transfers of jurisdiction, on grounds of caste prejudice. Not only did fishers succeed in carving out a space for themselves within the Padroado, but their actions also had a trickle-up effect that reached all the way to the pope. The danger that these applications posed for the Vatican increased the frequency of papal intervention in the practices of its Indian churches. Time and again, papal decrees were issued outlawing the operations of caste in the church, but, just as often, they were ignored by the clergy in India (Ballhatchet 1998).

Controversies around caste have plagued the Roman Catholic Church in India since as early as the 1600s. The most famous proponent of accommodating caste was Robert de Nobili of the Madurai Jesuit mission in British-ruled Madras Presidency. De Nobili lived like a Brahmin, observed caste practices strictly, and managed to convert some Brahmins to Catholicism. Although his actions aroused controversy, de Nobili's contention that the observance of caste had no religious implications was eventually accepted, and his methods were ratified by Pope Gregory XV in 1623. Toward the end of the century, de Nobili's methods came under review once more, and in 1739 Pope Clement XII ruled that missionaries in both India and China must take an oath not to compromise the faith through accommodation of indigenous social hierarchies. In 1744 Pope Benedict XIV followed with a ruling that all Catholics, whatever their birth, should hear mass and receive communion in the same church at the same time. However, de Nobili's legacy remained strong within the Indian church, and in 1778 the Propaganda Fide allowed separate places and entrances in churches and separate cemeteries for high and low castes for the purpose of furthering evangelization. The question was raised again in 1783 regarding a church that had built a wall separating high from low castes within the church; in response, the Propaganda Fide condemned the erection of walls but conceded that, for the time being, such practices could be accommodated for the greater goal of growing the church.

The mixed signals sent by papal policy only exacerbated low caste protest within the church and increased demands for equality in worship and the ordination of low caste priests. The recruitment of native priests was a policy that the Propaganda Fide had entrusted to its Indian vicariates since 1630. Although there were differences among the various Catholic orders, when it came to the ordination of native priests, there was greater uniformity of practice. Regardless of the order, indigenous clergy who were ordained under the Propaganda Fide through the eighteenth century were overwhelmingly from higher castes.

This was certainly the case in Travancore, where the Carmelite Order was given charge of fostering an indigenous clergy. Despite repeated demands for seminary training and ordination of Mukkuvar boys since the end of the eighteenth century, little changed in southern churches until the late nineteenth century (Ballhatchet 1998: 8–9). It was the 1886 concordat between Portugal and Rome that precipitated changes in the Vatican's attitude to caste. By the time of the concordat, many more Mukkuvar priests had been ordained under the Padroado. The first Indian archbishop installed after the concordat was the Portuguese João Gomes Ferreira, whose previous experience in Macao had inspired him to come to India to inaugurate a more liberal era of church policy. Seeing the progress that fisher priests in northern territories had made during the years under Portuguese ecclesiastical authority, Ferreira instituted a territorial adjustment. He created a new Mukkuvar diocese of eleven churches with 10 fisher priests and 26,000 parishioners. These parishioners came to call themselves the 500 families, and they established their own rules in reaction to high caste restrictions on Mukkuvar clergy entering their churches. They declared that no high caste priest could enter Mukkuvar churches if their priests could not enter high caste churches (Ballhatchet 1998).

This first claim to territorial sovereignty on the part of Mukkuvar priests sent shock waves through the church hierarchy. In addition, Ferreira's activities confirmed high caste fears that a Portuguese bishop would favor the fishers, who had openly showed their preference for the Padroado in the years before the concordat. Ferreira's open opposition to caste prejudice made them even more wary. Those clergy who were against fisher caste assertion argued even more forcefully for caste-segregated seminaries. Bishops and archbishops from Goa, Madras, Cochin, and Travancore advised Ferreira not to encourage fisher ambitions, for fear of destabilizing the church. Some reflected that, although the caste system encouraged immobility, it also contributed to tranquility. Without it, how could a small number of Englishmen have ruled so many millions of Indians?

Despite clerical conservatism on the question of caste, the ordination of Mukkuvars continued apace throughout the nineteenth century. In the final decades of the century, the church emerged as a key means of social mobility for Mukkuvar Catholics, and many boys went into the seminaries as a means to higher education and a ticket out of the coast. In 1907, this trend precipitated the opening of the St. Francis Institute at Nagercoil, the urban heart of southern Travancore, to train Mukkuvar youth as teachers and catechists (Narchison et al. 1983; Villavarayan 1956). To ease clerical duties, Bishop Benziger of Quilon proposed in 1929 to Rome that the Quilon diocese be divided into three—Quilon, Trivandrum, and Kottar—and that Kottar be "confided to the native clergy." On May 26, 1930, an apostolic letter sent from Rome authorized the creation of three distinct dioceses. As requested, the diocese of Kottar was entrusted to the care of Indian clergy. Kottar was the third native diocese in India, and its first bishop, Lawrence Pereira, was the third Indian to become a bishop within the Roman Catholic Church hierarchy. In their address on October 5, 1930, to Bishop Benziger, Kottar's clergy made specific mention of this fact: "Our last and best thanks are reserved for the last and best gift you have bestowed on us—the gift of Indianization for which you have been most responsible" (quoted by Narchison et al. 1983: 43).

Of course, the exact meaning of Indianization, with its ethic of native sovereignty, is open to debate. It could simply mean the establishment of an Indian clergy or, more specifically, a clergy drawn from the locality or even from a particular caste. My oral histories with Kottar's parish priests attest to the palpable tensions and open conflicts among clergy from different castes around sovereignty of the diocese. It was unclear which native castes—high or low, local or translocal—would assume diocesan power. If it was to be shared, how would jurisdictional authority be apportioned? Spatially? In terms of caste constituencies? After much wrangling, an emergent Mukkuvar clergy drawn from a coastal elite took the opportunity provided by the delineation of Kottar as a separate diocese in 1925 to stake unprecedented claims to representation. However, the reigning high caste Syrian Christians and Vellalas were loath to give up their control. In the end, sheer numbers and sustained effort appear to have favored the Mukkuvar clergy within the diocese, at least in claiming Mukkuvar villages as their own. By the time Kanyakumari

District merged in 1956 with Tamilnadu State, Mukkuvars made up a majority of diocesan clergy, and most of them served in coastal parishes.

To recap, then, struggles over caste rocked the Catholic Church on India's western coastal belt. In the north, Portuguese patronage allowed Mukkuvars to assert themselves as an emergent clerical and lay force within the church, but it was not until the turn of the twentieth century that southern Mukkuvars successfully staked their claim to clerical ordination and then to diocesan territorial sovereignty. By the 1950s, the Kanyakumari coast looked overwhelmingly like a domain of caste sovereignty, with Mukkuvar priests overseeing Mukkuvar parishes.

It was into this setting that the postcolonial developmental state entered in 1956. As I show in the second part of this book, postcolonial rule rekindled tensions over coastal sovereignty. The consolidation of an indigenous clergy claiming caste solidarity with their congregants allowed the postcolonial state to treat coastal Catholics as an undifferentiated community subject to its natural leaders. Ironically, as we will see in Chapter 4, this statist sense of social cohesion and consensus crystallized at precisely the moment when state developmental intervention in fishing produced a lasting cleavage on the coast between a new class of trawler owners and the larger population of fishers, who came to be constituted as "artisans."

The nineteenth-century claim to clerical caste representation was largely a middle-class politics. Spearheaded by the 500 families and then taken up farther south by fisher clergy, the call for an end to caste favoritism in the church did not affect the everyday lives of poorer fishers. These Mukkuvars found their own ways of negotiating social hierarchies. The church was no less relevant in their lives. To them, it was intimate and patron, an institution whose relevance in their lives was as unquestionable as ties of blood. The rituals of the life cycle—birth, marriage, and death—were inextricably tied to the workings of spiritual authority, making fisher dependence on clerical intercession absolute. Nevertheless, fisher responses to excesses of clerical power reflect a sense of village sovereignty as irreducible to church jurisdiction and an understanding of spiritual power as distinct from the precise authority of the Catholic clergy.

Wielding Protestant Conversion

Whereas tensions between the Padroado and the Propaganda Fide equipped elite Mukkuvars with the means to secure a place for themselves among the clergy, the entry of Protestant missionary societies into Travancore enabled poorer fishers to perform other types of maneuver. In 1806, the Nonconformist London Missionary Society (LMS) began its operations in southern Travancore. The archives of the LMS attest to the society's preference for particular native converts over others. In diaries, travelogues, meeting minutes, and letters to their London headquarters, LMS missionaries speak of their work among Travancore's agrarian Hindu low castes and their goals of freeing them from the bonds of agricultural slavery, the despotism of Hindu rule, and heathenism. Mukkuvar Catholics appear in these documents only as evidence of the failure of the Catholic Church to elevate their converts out of heathenism (as elaborated in Chapter 2) or as a fringe population in thrall to their church. More practically, the LMS perceived its twin goals of conversion and destabilizing native rule as better achieved in the inland. For them, the position of Catholic fishers outside the agrarian social relations of increasing significance to the maintenance of princely rule made them less desirable converts to have in the LMS's arsenal. For their part, Mukkuvars also made little effort to approach the Protestant missions. When they did, as in the case of the LMS's Parassala Mission, it was as much to threaten the Catholic Church with conversion in order to extract certain concessions as to actually embrace a new faith.

James Emlyn, who served as the LMS missionary in the Parassala Mission in southern Travancore from 1886 to 1892, recorded his temporary success with the Mukkuvar Catholics. At the beginning of his work on the coast, Emlyn reported, "Our success has been considerable—not only do a large number remain steadfast—thus far; and give promise of continuing as, by means of our success the work is spreading and all the fishermen from Cape Comorin to Quilon have obtained a measure of freedom never before known" (London Missionary Society 1888: 80). In the first five years, about 500 Catholic fishers from five coastal villages joined the LMS mission. Within a few years, however, most had returned to their old faith, and Emlyn concluded that the work among the Catholic fishers had proved "a complete failure" (London Missionary Society 1897: 67).

Despite Emlyn's short-lived success, his writings provide important insights into the relationship between the Catholic Church and its fishers and into how fishers negotiated the wider arena of religious patrons. As with most low caste converts to Protestantism (S. Bayly 1989; Forrester 1980; Oddie 1997) and unlike their own earlier conversion to Catholicism, it was Mukkuvars themselves who approached Emlyn's mission. Emlyn attests that fishers from four villages led by "one Joseph Alcander of Vallavilai" initially approached him for conversion. They told him that they had "already been for some three or four years without a priest and needed someone immediately to conduct marriages, and prevent disorders" (London Missionary Society 1887: 13). The priest had left, they explained, because of a conflict over the Vallavilai church, which they claimed was the property of the village and not of the Roman Catholic hierarchy. Upon their takeover of the church, the Roman Catholic bishop of Quilon filed a lawsuit against them, demanding a restitution of church property (London Missionary Society 1887: 11–13). Not wanting to relinquish the village's right to the church, they requested that the LMS mission send them catechists. Their need was evidently grave, Emlyn concludes, because despite the poor fishing season, the villagers of Vallavilai were willing to gather money collectively to meet the expenses of the LMS missionaries during their stay on the coast.

Emlyn remarks that this instance of tension between the Catholic Church and coastal villagers appears to have been part of a long-standing pattern. From time to time, especially during poor fishing seasons, fishers would refuse to pay the tax levied by the church, claim church property as the communal property of the village, or, in the most extreme cases, physically evict the parish priest from the village territory. In most cases the disputes would be resolved by the bishop in favor of the church and against lay fishers. In the case of the Vallavilai fishers, however, the persistence of villagers in their claim to the church led the bishop to turn to the "secular courts" for resolving the dispute. The presence of the LMS mission as a new intermediary further complicated matters. Emlyn decided to intervene in the case filed by the Quilon bishop in the district court against Vallavilai's villagers by appealing to the High Court, where he was able to obtain a verdict in favor of the villagers. Following the successful appeal, the Quilon bishop sent a complaint to the directors of the LMS mission against Emlyn's unorthodox intrusion into the affairs of the Catholic Church and "demanded his transfer to some other station." Despite the LMS leadership's voluble criticism of the Catholic Church's theocratic hold over the coast, it followed the bishop's request and transferred Emlyn. Before Emlyn left Parassala, he witnessed the kinds of ostracism to which those who left the Catholic fold were subject. A fish famine hit the coast alongside a cholera epidemic and, while others went inland to stay with relatives and friends, the LMS fishers were "received nowhere; for having become 'reprobates' the priests had forbidden Roman Catholics receiving them or giving them any help" (London Missionary Society 1889: 27). In addition, crucial services, such as those of a barber, "a necessary functionary at every wedding and burial," were denied them. The one barber who sided with the rebels was threatened with his life, a horrified Emlyn reported.

Even leaving room for Emlyn's denominational bias, one can draw from his account the force of church authority and its territorial hold over the coast. The church could dictate the terms of sociality and exclusion by wielding the weapon of sacramental censure. What Emlyn does not emphasize, however, and what is particularly compelling in his narrative, is the way fishers contested clerical authority over the village church through the intercession of other authorities. For Vallavilai's fishers, the church was *theirs*, and they were determined to secure their claim to it even if it took turning to other religious authorities to sustain its spiritual life. Their ultimate turn to the LMS suggests the necessity of patronage in securing a village claim. This was a landscape of power where patronage—religious, royal, or mercantile—was ubiquitous and did not permit any simple recourse to autonomy.

Lay fisher strategies of seeking protection through affiliation and allegiance must be thought of not as capitulation to the powerful but as forms of maneuver in a social world of entrenched hierarchies. As the case of Vallavilai's villagers shows, seeking a new patron was not opposed to a rights claim but a mechanism for securing such a claim. Such a politics of patronage, in which fishers sought out new patrons to hold at bay or to coerce a particular response from old ones, has been a repeated pattern on the coast, with the pitting of the Padroado against the Propaganda Fide, the Catholic Church against the Protestant mission, and as we shall see in later chapters, the state against the church.

Parish Conflicts in a "Native Diocese"

The growing presence of a clergy dominated by Mukkuvar priests born within the diocese must have enhanced the intimacy between church and fishers. Coastal boys increasingly sought priestly ordination as a ticket to education in distant seminaries, access to a white-collar profession, and social respectability. Many were appointed to serve in their home diocese. Although they were restricted from serving in their native villages, they could serve in any one of the other forty-three villages of Kottar's coastal belt. The Mukkuvar clergy's religious authority, backed by the institutional power of the church, certainly gave them an awesome local presence. They were quintessential native authorities, born of the locality, bred in distant seminaries, and returned to rule. At the same time, ties of kinship and childhood memories mediated their reception as religious leaders.

From existing records, it is difficult to say how exactly the establishment of Kottar as a native diocese and the increasing number of Mukkuvar clergy shaped lay fisher politics. What is clear from the volume of correspondence between coastal parishioners and the Kottar bishop is the willingness, even eagerness, of fishers to express grievances. As representatives of the church in the village, and increasingly as locals themselves, parish priests commanded great respect *and* bore the brunt of fisher resentment. Mukkuvar priests in particular were in the tenuous position of being both caste brethren and church authorities, a mix of affiliations that rendered them all too human and subject to criticism. In letters and petitions, parishioners were quick to hold a mirror up to their parish priests in challenging excesses of clerical power, asserting a separation between the church and the village, or even claiming for themselves a greater commitment to the faith. From the correspondence of three villages—Pallam, Mel Manakkudy, and Keezh Manakkudy—with the Kottar Bishop's House, we get a sense of the range of issues that cropped up repeatedly as points of tension between diocesan clergy and coastal parishioners.

Most of the early-twentieth-century conflicts focused on the church's right of taxation and the tension over the exact terms of the church's hold over coastal land and marine harvest.[5] A letter from the parish priest of Pallam village, for instance, complains of villagers' tendency "to lease church property without permission and keep the money to themselves."[6] Yet another missive from the priest of Mel Manakkudy insists that the bishop make fishers obey the terms of the fish contract and hand over 25 percent of their daily catch to the Hindu merchant who had won the church auction. A number of letters passing between parish priests and the bishop go to lengths to spell out the exact terms of the fish contract and of frequent fisher violations, either through refusal of payment or by setting up independent contracts with other merchants unauthorized by the church. Each violation emptied parish coffers and called into question the ability of village parishes to support their priests and maintain the upkeep of their churches. The parish priest of Mel Manakkudy expressed this concern about his parishioners' neglect of their church: "They all do not commit themselves to the common income of the church. May I, therefore, humbly request Your Excellency to consider the above situation of the villagers and make a settlement towards the income of the church and thus free the church from further debts."[7] The frequency with which this intervention by the Bishop's House was required suggests a breakdown of fisher compliance with religious authority, even at the cost of excommunication or denial of sacraments. It further suggests that for many fishers the "common income of the church" appeared more a matter of the village subsidizing the church than of a common pool of funds being redistributed to villagers according to their needs.

One particularly drawn-out negotiation became controversial enough to warrant the constitution of a clerical commission to investigate charges of violating church law. Arulappan Fernandez of Keezh Manakkudy had assumed the role of fish contractor in direct opposition to the church-appointed contractor, an inland Hindu named Thangappan Nadar. It appears that Fernandez had drawn up a separate four-year contract with fifteen village elites who owned *karamadis*, large shore seines that each employed up to 100 fishermen. This agreement contravened the church's contract with Thangappan Nadar that bound villagers to make their fish contributions to him over a two-year period.

Hearing of the countercontract, the Bishop's House intervened by issuing an official warning and then setting up a clerical commission to investigate the matter. The commission determined that the unsanctioned contract was "highly unlawful" on two grounds: first, that Fernandez's payments to the church could not be used to conduct church functions because all contracts with ecclesiastical purpose had to be sanctioned by the bishop; and second, that Fernandez's contract was in direct opposition to the sanctioned contract in operation. Having thus deprived the church of its rightful income, Fernandez was required to pay 1,300 rupees to cover the payments due to Thangappan Nadar and the parish church. In addition, the fifteen fishers who had signed on to the unsanctioned contract were to pay fines to the church and henceforth transact only with the official contractor. Although Fernandez and the fifteen fishers submitted "humble apologies" for their infringement of the official contract, neither party paid their dues to the contractor or church and they were excommunicated from the church until they made good their payment.

The church's decision to excommunicate Fernandez solicited the intervention of Pedru Vasthian, a schoolteacher and prominent member of the diocese based temporarily in Colombo. Vasthian wrote to the Kottar bishop expressing concern over the excommunication of the parishioners of Keezh

Manakkudy, even chastising him for allowing events to spiral out of control. "It is a pity," he wrote, "that Your Lordship, even though you are from the very high Society of Jesus, have not imbued into the hearts of the priests, especially the very young priest at Keezh Manakkudy, that they cannot now expect in this modern world (with all its atrocities) to keep our Lord's flock together if they act in the Mohammedan way of the 'Quran and the sword.'" With this crafty rhetorical comparison of the clergy's out-of-date Catholicism with Islam, Vasthian goes on to laud Fernandez for assuming the proper role of the parish priest and to deny any wrongdoing on the part of either Fernandez or the fifteen fishers so grievous as to require excommunication: "There was no necessity in the poor people being excommunicated from the church as long as they had not done anything wrong against the Law of the Church. What, after all, is the Law of the Church? Had it not been for the steadfast faith in Mr. Fernandez, I am sure that a very good part of the people of Keezh Manakkudy will now be following the Lutheran faith, and the one man to answer to our Lord for the conduct of the poor illiterate people would have been the parish priest."[8] With a remarkable sleight of hand, Vasthian attributes to Fernandez a truer commitment to the faith and a greater ability to keep congregants faithful than the parish priest. He also contradicts the church commission's determination that Fernandez's actions ran counter to church law by emphasizing his role as a keeper of not only his but also the people's faith. Surely, Vasthian implies, the absolute authority of the church over its parishioners is a bygone practice, one that, like Islam, is keeping the church out of step both with the modern world and with parishioners' sentiment. At the same time, the exercise of church power through excommunication is met with the threat not of rejecting religious authority but of seeking the protection of a competing faith tradition. Ultimately, then, even someone like Vasthian with his rhetoric of modernization speaks from within the parameters of patronage.

Other letters address the church's tense mediation of coastal villagers' relations with the "secular inland." Even though the church invited inlanders to facilitate certain aspects of coastal life, such as the fish contract, it secured its sovereign authority over the coast by keeping its congregants from independently engaging with inland institutions or by mediating such transactions. The coast was to be kept Catholic and the village indistinguishable from the parish. Letters from the Bishop's House to coastal parishioners reference the "threat" of the "secular inland," with its courts, its banks, and its state officials. The perceived gulf separating the Catholic coast from the secular inland may have served to secure the church's institutional hegemony over the coast, but it could also work against the church. A case involving the Palai Central Bank, the Kottar bishop, and the congregants of Mel Manakkudy is one instance of this double-edged sword.

The parish priest typically stood as guarantor of loans received by his congregants; if they defaulted, inland banks would proceed up the church hierarchy, approaching first the parish priest and then the bishop. In this sense, coastal villagers were treated very much as wards of their church by inland institutions that would only offer loans to fishers that were underwritten by the bishop himself. However, its status as patron also came at a cost to the church. Coastal villagers would routinely default on loans, citing a lean fishing season, debts incurred by sudden accidents at sea, or the payment of dowry, passing on the burden of payment to the church.

In one 1941 case, several fishers from Mel Manakkudy defaulted on a loan borrowed from the Palai Central Bank Ltd. of Nagercoil in the name of the bishop. Significantly, the bank manager's first step was to approach the parish priest, demanding that he force payment from his parishioners. When payment was still not forthcoming, the manager wrote to the diocesan vicar-general, who then wrote to the parish priest asking him to "order your parishioners in our name to execute a fresh promissory note and thus save themselves from being dragged to the secular Courts which, no doubt, will entail heavy expenses and untold miseries."[9] This threat of being left unprotected in secular society was common, but in this case it apparently did not have the desired effect. The villagers were fully aware of the advantages of their treatment by the secular courts as wards of their church—that in the event of a court case, it would be the bishop who would be "dragged" into the domain of secular law. Months passed with no action on the part of Mel Manakkudy's villagers, at which point they were excommunicated. What followed was a drawn-out series of negotiations between bishop, parish priest, village elites, and parishioners over the terms of the penalty incurred that did not involve the bank manager or anyone else from Palai Central Bank; the negotiations finally concluded with the villagers paying a nominal fee to the parish church fund. This, then, was yet another instance of maneuver within the parameters of religious community that belies the notion of the Catholic coast as a space of incarceration. Although the church's practice of excommunication was certainly a fearsome weapon, it did not actually place the excommunicated outside the domain of community. Indeed, excommunication was often an invitation to a negotiation that made other forms of power and affiliation visible. In this case, other moral economies came into play that challenged the bishop's abdication of responsibility for poor parishioners. Mel Manakkudy's parish council called on "Your Excellency, Our Father" to resume his power of patronage and restore the excommunicated "to their rightful place within the parish."

The Catholic Church has achieved a special notoriety for its role in the policing of sexuality. In Kottar diocese the church not only micromanaged sexual relations but also enhanced its revenue by issuing financial penalties for marital infidelity or for "spoiling" unmarried girls or by forcing youngsters who had engaged in premarital sex to marry under threat of excommunication and extracting fees for betrothal and marriage. A letter from the bishop to the parish priest of Mel Manakkudy is typical of church intervention in sexual matters and its tendency to resolve social tensions through enforced monetary transactions.

> A complaint has been made here that one Michael Venthupillay of Manakkudy has spoiled Innacial Annammal of Alikal, Pillaitope. The delinquent appears to have admitted his guilt and even promised to marry the girl in question. It is reported that with this object in view, the relatives of the girl put together some money for jewels and handed it over to the parish priest. The boy now, it is said, refuses to marry the girl and proposes to marry another girl from Manakkudy. You will do your best to persuade the boy to marry the girl whom he has spoiled which he is in justice bound to do. If however he refuses to do so, you will demand that the boy pays Rupees 100 as compensation to the girl before you proceed with the marriage.[10]

Notwithstanding the easy resolution of the issue through the penalty of 100 rupees, it is clear that the church regulated village sexual dynamics with a heavy hand.

At the same time, the bishop, as an overarching paternal authority, also provided recourse for those whose marriages were forbidden by family. Parishioners, even young ones such as Adimakanoo Tobias of Keezh Manakkudy, would beseech the bishop to intervene on their behalf so they could marry their chosen partners. "I am a parishioner of Keezh Manakkudy and I am now 22 years old," wrote Tobias. "I wish to marry Miss Netnammal aged 18, daughter of Silva Cruz and Mrs. Susai Ammal of Kadiapattanam. My parents are not willing for the marriage and so they want to throw all sorts of obstacles to our getting married in the Holy Church at Kadiapattanam. The parish priest is not willing to give permission. Hence, I most humbly pray Your Excellency to issue an order to the parish priest." In response, the bishop wrote to Tobias's parish priest ordering him to proceed with the marriage on condition that the boy "pay a fine of Rupees five for not attending Catechism, and the additional fees for Betrothal and Marriage."[11]

Moral censure could also work against parish priests, who became easy targets of sexual scandal. A case involving the priest of Pallam shows the vulnerability of priests at the village level when their actions invited the hostility of village elites. The village teacher and catechist of Pallam, superseding the authority of the Kottar bishop, wrote to the archbishop of Verapoly beseeching his intervention in the "scandalous conduct of Father Borjia Peters." The letter begins: "Fr. Borjia owing to deep love with a girl named Lawranjial Victorial educated her in the Training School at Mulagamudu last year. She is now put up in the Primary School at Pallam as a 3rd class teacher. Whenever one wants to see him he can be seen talking with Victorial. Moreover he visits her home during the night and day. He freely mingles with her and by and by she comes to know that she is pregnant. Medicines are given to prevent her conception. Thrice he has done this." As if sexual misconduct were not enough, the parishioners then proceed to state that Father Borjia further displayed his affections when, during the "Kottar feast he has bought a dozen of bangles, sweets for Rupees 5, a powder tin, a scent bottle, and has given them to Victorial." The charges of sexual misconduct and favoritism then escalate to blasphemy: "He says in his sermons that he is Altar Christ and also he is the Second King for Catholics. He also says that Jesus is in the power of his hands, whenever he wishes he can call Jesus to come and ask Him to go." Having submitted their long, varied list of complaints, the parishioners end with a threat of conversion delivered in the most subservient tones: "Prostrating before Your Lordship, we humbly beg before Your Excellency to issue order to His Excellency the Bishop of Kottar to give sudden transfer to Rev. Fr. Borjia, the Parish Priest of Pallam, so that our religion may not be spoiled and also our faith may not be changed."[12]

That even a letter as fantastical as this had traction is evidenced by Father Borjia's lengthy response in which he painstakingly elaborates his intentions and trials as a parish priest. He begins his letter with a general comment about his commitment to social uplift through education and the difficulty of achieving this goal in light of the entrenched hierarchies of Pallam.

As I am one from their community I could not bear the sight that they were so backward both spiritually and socially. The only reason I found for their backwardness in these times is that they are uneducated. So I wanted to force their education, which alone could make men morally good and spiritually pious. From my first day in this parish, daily I went around the village, speaking with the people, advising them to send their children to school which alone will bring salvation from their poverty and backwardness. This sincere act of mine made some of the leaders get angry with me. For, as these people are illiterate and poor, they are slaves to the leaders who can do with this poor people anything they like; they could use them for their views and fancies. Many priests have tried and failed to change things on account of the objection of these proud Pharisees.[13]

This is a common narrative of Mukkuvar "enlightenment" through clerical training. It is a story of low castes assuming a modern subjectivity through the seminary and then returning to their home territories as crusaders against lay village authority. It is equally a commentary on caste modernity and the centrality of education to the elevation of low castes out of "backwardness." It is this same paternalistic tone that suffuses Father Borjia's own description of his relationship with Victorial, in defense of which he writes:

Victorial is a girl from a poor family who passed her VSLC [teachers'] training. As there was a vacancy in the parish school last year, I recommended her for the spot. But the leaders didn't want the girl's status raised and so they objected and did not appoint her. This year, there was another vacancy and this time, I appointed her to the position without consulting the village leaders. They objected as she is the only woman on the school staff, but the parishioners were very happy with her as she does more work than all the men.[14]

Father Borjia then proceeds to list several other instances where his intervention toward "reform" worked against the interests of village elites: his dismissal of a favored teacher from the school, his nosing out of a bribe for the fish contract, his refusal to grant a land title (*patta*) to certain elites who wanted to make a profit by leasing church land to paddy farmers. With this tally of his good deeds, Father Borjia ends with his own accusation that reproduces the trope of benighted Islam: "So they are defaming me using a girl who was pregnant illegally, possibly due to visiting Mohammedans who stayed in Pallam for fish trade."

The clergy's assumption of a vanguardist role in ushering the coast into the modern world is one that was, by no means, received with equanimity.

Indeed, any priest who stepped on the toes of the locally powerful typically found his days in the parish numbered. Parish priests fashioned themselves as local patrons and were no doubt treated as such, but they were also the bottom rung of a vertically integrated institutional hierarchy that could just as easily work against them. This was especially so when local elites were better versed in working the levels of the institutional order to their advantage, of appealing to overarching forms of patronage to root out the middleman. This was certainly the case with Father Borjia. His speedy transfer out of Pallam to another parish attests to how circumscribed clerical authority could be and how ambiguous the terms of coastal sovereignty really were. Far from an uncontested "petty Raja," then, the Mukkuvar priest was part of a dynamic world of maneuver in which the outcome of negotiations involving fishers and clergy was certainly weighted but by no means determined. Although the "secular inland" inhabited a position of exteriority to the coast and although the church did occupy pride of place as the key patron of the fisher, there was nevertheless room for maneuver within the parameters of coastal space. From the vantage point of the inland, however, coastal patronage was the antithesis of a culture of negotiation and rights. As we will see in Chapter 2, the consolidation of an inland political culture of caste modernity increasingly framed the coast as a domain of spatial and temporal discontinuity, consigning Catholic fishers to a savage slot of primitivism.

Patronage and Rights

Mukkuvar political maneuver before the end of colonial rule illuminates the use of patronage for claim making. I have argued that the rigid distinction between patronage and rights that forms the basis of much modern theorizing on democracy does not hold up when one considers coastal dynamics. Mukkuvar claim making since the eighteenth century reflects an understanding of collective justice and patronage, of community and authority, as inextricably linked. Mukkuvars articulated claims to caste representation and village sovereignty by opposing the injustice of one authority and turning to another for protection, exhibiting a politics of affiliation and allegiance that sits uneasily with modernist equations of rights with autonomy and individual self-determination.

In Part 2 we will see how these early forms of political negotiation informed later contestations over rights, illuminating the emergent character of Indian democracy. Mukkuvar contestation of caste status, religious authority, and territorial sovereignty in postcolonial South India shows clear continuities with these earlier instances of claim making. Understanding contemporary rights politics, then, requires attending to both regional histories of political maneuver and transnational circuits of discourse and practice. As stated in the Introduction, it is my hope that attending to such regional histories of claim making will upset the European origin story of rights by showing how rights politics in any place—contemporary India in this book—is in continuity with earlier strategies and understandings of justice and entitlement.

Figure 2. *Kattumaram*s on shore. Courtesy of International Collective in Support of Fishworkers, Chennai, India.

2 From the Inland Out

Caste Purity to Caste Modernity

WHEN I WAS DOING MY FIELDWORK, I was continually struck by the pride with which fishers would assert their difference from the castes of the agrarian inland. During one conversation with John Rose, a *kattumaram* owner with a remarkable eye for social drama, I asked whether coastal and agrarian low castes ever made common cause politically. He reacted sharply to my question: "Nadars, Dalits, these are people who have been slaves to others. Not us. We people of the shore [*kadalkarai makkal*] have never had to bow and scrape before superiors." This claim derives from a pride in artisanship as a trade of independents in sharp contrast to the wage or bonded labor to which agricultural laborers have been historically subject. It further underscores a sense of the sea as unclaimed and uncontrollable space, beyond the strictures of property.

In her 1991 ethnography of gender and capitalist transformation on the Kanyakumari coast, Kalpana Ram addresses this tension between Mukkuvar fisher marginality and sovereignty: "Their geographical location is a metaphor not only for the social and economic marginality of the Mukkuvars but for the possibilities of an independent cultural identity which this marginality provides" (Ram 1991: xiii). This is in some sense true, but the shaping of an inland mainstream at the expense of the Mukkuvar margin continues to this day to profoundly constrain fisher efforts to secure economic justice and political recognition. The castes that John Rose disparages for their historical "servility" currently enjoy a degree of sociopolitical power that eludes most Mukkuvars. And indeed, during other conversations, Rose expressed an acute awareness of fishers' contemporary status as caste inferiors whose inability to claim a narrative of emancipation from servitude was part and parcel of their subordination.

The sense of the difference between coast and inland is shared by inland castes, although they invert the values ascribed to each space. In 1998, I began a conversation with a Tamilnadu state archivist from Nagercoil, the district capital of Kanyakumari. He reminisced about his school days in the south, remembering that although there had been a few Mukkuvar boys in his class, he had not gotten to know any of them. "They tend to stick together," he explained, "and it's very difficult to get close to them or to trust them. It was strange—I could never tell if they were being serious or pulling my leg. I never felt like it would be possible to truly know them."

The archivist's comments echo similar impressions of the coast's inhabitants that I heard expressed time and again by inlanders. A well-respected writer who has penned some of the most popular novels on the district's caste and religious dynamics regretfully told me that his writing did not address the coast and its people; somehow, it had never struck him to include them in his chronicles of the region. A policeman assigned to the coast grumbled about how impossible it was to get anyone from the fishing community to testify to coastal crimes. "They band together like a tribe," he commented. "They'd rather ask their parish priest to adjudicate than provide evidence to the police." Asking a locally prominent low caste Protestant politician about voting patterns, I was told, "Only the coast stands apart. They hardly seem to be part of our district."

This sense of Catholic fishers as a population existing at a remove from inland sensibilities and practices was shared by people I met from all walks of life and from all social groups, be they Protestant Nadar educationists (like the archivist), Hindu Nadar coconut farmers, Brahmin novelists, Vellala politicians, or Dalit activists. More striking even than impressionistic accounts of the coast as a place mired in religiosity and clerical orthodoxy, as an unsanitary environment, or as a domain of drunkards was the pervasive sense of its opacity. To most of those I spoke with in the district capital of Nagercoil and surrounding rural areas of Kanyakumari, the coast was a space *outside*, unfamiliar and inaccessible and distinguished from the shared social world of "the inland" (*ul naadu*).

Over my two years in the district, I was struck time and again by the repeated description of the inland as a space of democratic politics and the equally insistent placing of the coast outside this umbrella. Two questions emerged for me out of these conversations: How did inland Kanyakumari come to be defined as a haven of democracy? And why were the coast and its inhabitants seen as outsiders to this world? It seemed that investigating the historical production of southwestern India's inland as a particular kind of political space would best address these questions.

This chapter has three parts. In the first part I situate the shifting meanings of inland political space within a dynamic of state sovereignty and social contestation. Over a century and a half, notions of caste equality and political self-determination emerged to challenge older understandings of status and sovereignty. The leadership of particular agrarian low castes and their missionary patrons in mobilizing discourses of popular sovereignty lent this emergent sphere of democratic politics a particular caste flavor.[1] In south Travancore, the Nadars were particularly important in marshalling new ideas of self-worth and self-determination to their cause. The experience of this caste came to assume paradigmatic status in regional narratives of democracy, the yardstick against which other castes would mark their own progress. Most important, inland low castes lay claim to modernity and subalternity *at the same time*. It was precisely their historical journey from slavery to freedom that marked them as quintessential moderns. Moreover, this was a history that played a recursive role in their claims to political sovereignty. Unlike other upwardly mobile castes, they did not retroactively cleanse their past of the taint of oppression; rather, they returned to it as a legitimating narrative in their claims to political and social power. To put it differently, their subalternity in relation to high castes remained a crucial defining feature of their collective identity even as they placed themselves above other low castes, such as the Mukkuvars, who were now constituted as primitives.

The opposition between caste moderns and primitives that crystallized through the political battles of the nineteenth and twentieth centuries mapped onto the opposition between democracy and patronage. Those castes who fought against monarchical power for "responsible government" claimed for themselves a modern caste status that distinguished them from the defenders of patronage, whether princely or religious. As I show in later chapters, this opposition between democracy and patronage had an afterlife in postcolonial rule. It lived on in the relationship between the coast and the inland, with Catholic fishers constituted as primitive subjects of religious patronage and inland inhabitants viewed as modern citizens of a democratic republic.

In the second part of the chapter I shift from the role of political action in generating caste modernity to the parallel discursive construction of caste primitivism. I look at how low caste Catholics came to be constituted as caste primitives through the rhetorical battles between the Travancore palace and the London Missionary Society (LMS). By the beginning of the twentieth century, the palace promoted an incipient regional variant of Hindu nationalism, and South Indian Protestants wielded an incipient form of civic religiosity. Even as they pushed against each other to carve out new domains of authority, Hindus and Protestants used Catholic low castes as a *rhetorical presence* underpinning competing claims to modernity and progress. Through these debates, religious adversaries together constituted a space of political modernity juxtaposed against fisher Catholicism.

In the final part of the chapter I narrate the confluence of both political and discursive currents in the making of Kanyakumari. The district actualized caste modernity in territorial sovereignty. The carving out of the district from the rest of Travancore radically transformed the demographic balance of castes and religious communities, giving inland low castes, particularly Hindu and Protestant Nadars, political dominion. Through this reterritorializing of caste, the historical experiences of Nadars assumed hegemonic force in the makeup of the state and the meaning of the public. These subaltern sovereigns monopolized the space of both disenfranchisement and rule.

As a whole, in this chapter I illustrate the relationality of subaltern identity by showing how yesterday's subalterns can become today's sovereigns and can even use a past of subalternity as a legitimating ground for making sovereign claims. Rather than a fixed status, then, subalternity is a processual category that occupies shifting historical ground and resists permanent location as a position outside power. I also argue strongly for a situated understanding of democracy. In south Travancore, democracy took on meanings that could not be simply derived from some European original. Rather, histories of caste struggle shaped notions of popular sovereignty and rights, giving them a collective, culturally embedded character distinct from the modular form of the individual rights-bearing subject.

The political space of inland Travancore—the territorial location of particular social groups and their access to key thoroughfares and institutions, the forms of collective participation in representative politics, and the symbolic expression of state sovereignty—was remade not through an autonomous state spatial imaginary but as a result of the negotiations between the state and social movements. The battle over space that swept Travancore in the late nineteenth and early twentieth centuries had both ritual and representational dimensions. Initially, low caste struggles to expand public space concentrated on opening up proscribed territories, such as roads and temples, to castes that were deemed ritually impure. Gradually, this focus on physical-territorial space was enhanced by struggles to open up representational space in state institutions and newly created forums of political representation. Agrarian change attended these changes in political space. The capitalist transformation of agriculture and the end of state monopolies over trade threw into sharp relief the contradiction between changing economic relations and state-mandated social orthodoxy. By the 1930s, challenges to the autocratic power of the *raja* (king) and *dewan* (councillor) gained force as more and more of Travancore's subjects began to agitate for "responsible government." As they formed corporate institutions—caste and religious associations and political parties—they lent a new civic charge to caste and religious identities that altered their earlier ritual meanings without displacing them completely.

Even the transition to representative government and integration into independent India in 1947 did not lull political ferment. In the following decade, Travancore's southern Tamil-speaking castes began to press for their own vision of linguistic sovereignty through merger with the neighboring Madras Presidency and its majority Tamil population. With the 1956 Linguistic Reorganization of States, their demands bore fruit with the carving out of Kanyakumari District and its merger with the newly created state of Tamilnadu (Land of the Tamils). The merger actualized a spatial imaginary territorializing Tamils within their "own" sovereign domain. Significantly, the creation of Kanyakumari District was the condition of possibility for the *political* ascendance of agrarian low castes, who, through a century and a half of rights struggles, had come to think of themselves as caste moderns.

To write about the transformation of political space in Travancore, then, is to write about space-making acts of protest. Each period of state formation and reformation involved the circulation of competing spatial imaginaries that territorialized the region's social groups differently. Although conflict over different visions of space, caste, and rights intensified over the nineteenth and twentieth centuries, their interplay itself became a key ingredient of regional politics. As in the eighteenth century, power was distributed unevenly across a spatially differentiated social world; in the nineteenth and twentieth centuries, however, power was increasingly tied to location within a newly defined democratic arena. In the process, social groups at the margins of this political world were increasingly typecast as outsiders to a future-in-the-making, in a space outside a politics of rights.

As I argue in this chapter and throughout the book, this political space of rights was by no means a derivative modernity approximating a distant democratic ideal. Rather, the modernity of caste—understood primarily as the will to political sovereignty—became the final determinant of inclusion in the inland political arenas of the southwestern region. The shift in the terms of political integration over a century was from caste purity to caste modernity, both elaborated through spatialized social difference.

Forming and Transforming Hindu Kingship

Travancorean Hindu kingship was an eighteenth-century invention. As with other regional powers that arose in the aftermath of the Vijayanagara empire, warrior-king Martanda Varma (r. 1729–1758) extended the reach of his principality, Venad, through conquest of neighboring territories. He secured his sovereign authority over the newly expanded and named state of Travancore through rituals of legitimation involving a claim to divine kingship and the establishment of a rigid caste order. Hindu kingship was not religiously exclusive. It accommodated particular non-Hindu social groups, such as the mercantilist Syrian Christians, who were accorded an upper caste status. Social difference was organized along lines of caste *and* religion, but ritual or caste purity was the final determinant of access to social power.

Although Christianity has had a longer presence on the western coast of the Indian subcontinent than in most other parts of the world, the classification of Christians as a religious community distinct from Hindus is of more recent vintage. In an effort to consolidate his newly expanded, increasingly centralized state, Martanda Varma crafted new rituals of sovereignty and incorporation, such as dedicating his kingdom to Sri Padmanabha, the tutelary deity of his family, importing Brahmins from the north and east as *dewans*, and enforcing the strict separation of ritually pure and impure castes to maintain the sanctity of his kingdom. At first glance, these foundational principles of his state would certainly suggest that Travancore was Hindu. However, ritual purity and incorporation into palace culture were not contingent on being Hindu. Rather, Travancore's rulers perfected the "flexible techniques of state-building by incorporation" (S. Bayly 1984: 180). The prohibitions that applied to low caste Hindus and Christians, for instance, did not apply to the elite Syrian Christians, classed as *savarna*, or people of clean caste and ritual standing in the Hindu moral order and allowed right of access to Hindu temples and sacred precincts. The relationship between Travancore's Hindu rulers and Syrian Christians was one of mutuality: Travancore's kings gave the Syrian

Christians privileges and honors that distinguished them as a mercantile high caste, and Syrians came to rely on kingly mediation in deciding disputes over ecclesiastical authority within their church (S. Bayly 1984, 1989). This particular logic of integration also extended to other martial and commercial castes whose cooperation underpinned the stability and power of the state. That groups we would now imagine to be outside the norms of Hindu orthodoxy enjoyed such privilege suggests that state patronage was organized along principles more complicated than mere religious adherence. Indeed, Susan Bayly has argued that "the style of patronage followed by these rajas displayed almost no concern with formal religious or sectarian boundaries" (S. Bayly 1984: 191).

Caste and occupation overlapped neatly to form a highly stratified agrarian social structure: High caste Brahmins dominated the priestly and administrative services; high caste Nairs and Vellalas monopolized agricultural land; low caste Ezhavas and Nadars served as labor on high caste land; and the slave castes of Paraiyas and Pulayas took on the most polluting tasks of waste disposal, tanning, and meat production. Those castes outside agrarian society, such as the Mukkuvar Catholic fishers, were accorded a low caste status but were not subject to the daily ritual subjugations that shaped the lives of agrarian low and slave castes.

Ritual status in precolonial Travancore marked rigid social *and* spatial distinctions. A number of scholars have commented on the particularly dehumanizing form of ritual pollution that was attached to low castes in the state; not only were they not to touch high caste individuals, but they were also forbidden from even approaching for fear of pollution through proximity. Throughout the region, strict rules of exclusion banned the low ranking from Hindu temple precincts and from the streets and ceremonial procession routes adjoining temples, palaces, and other places associated with both royal and divine power (S. Bayly 1989; Jeffrey 1976, 1978; Kawashima 1998). This had a significant impact on the social makeup of public spaces. Because most thoroughfares were built to accommodate some kind of sacred or ceremonial function, this meant that low castes were barred from just about every town and village street that was not designated specifically for them. The intimate link between ritual and state space further meant that ritual prohibitions against entering certain physical territories literally kept whole social groups out of institutions at the heart of state power. Susan Bayly puts it most succinctly: "As in so many other aspects of south Indian life, there was no clear distinction between 'secular' administrative tasks and the organization of corporate rituals. Both served to order and integrate the state's political networks, and both fell within the domain of Hindu office-holders" (S. Bayly 1989: 289).

It was only in the nineteenth century that this nexus between territorialized ritual status and state power was loosened. With the expansion of British dominion over the subcontinent, Travancore, along with many other Indian states, entered into a military alliance with the English East India Company. Under the treaties of 1795 and 1805, the Travancore maharaja was forced to recognize British paramountcy and pay an annual subsidy in exchange for continued military protection as a subsidiary ally. He was allowed to retain his own administration, pass his own laws, and levy taxes on the condition that he agreed to rule in accordance with the advice given by a British resident, the company's representative in the princely state (Fisher 1991; Jeffrey 1978; Ramusack 2004). In addition to this limit on his sovereign authority, the maharaja had to give up control over his state's external and military affairs. This was an awkward negotiation of sovereignties that required a new vocabulary and new rituals of signification. As Michael Fisher puts it, "'Paramountcy' was one of the terms coined in the nineteenth century to refer to the concept of limited sovereignty. . . . European politicians and bureaucrats tried to reconcile their desire to perpetuate the sovereignty of the indirectly ruled state with their need for the right to intervene whenever their policy demanded. Theoreticians created concepts such as 'paramountcy' and 'suzerainty' to explain the relationship between the imperial European sovereign and a sovereign (but subordinate) indigenous Ruler, stripped of many of the key attributes of sovereignty" (Fisher 1991: 13). Dick Kooiman further notes that "the Indian States Committee overseeing the relationship of the Company to the Native States was of the opinion that the concept did not allow for a precise definition and simply concluded that paramountcy had to define itself according to the shifting necessities of time and circumstance. . . . Under this interpretation the states had to remain both subordinated and isolated, as no state, big or small, could justifiably claim to negotiate with the paramount power on a footing of equality" (Kooiman 2002: 17).

The relationship of British residents to the Travancore palace in the first half of the nineteenth century was fraught, with the native state permanently on the knife-edge of annexation. Throughout the nineteenth and early twentieth centuries, British authorities were caught between promoting their civilizing mission and maintaining a policy of religious neutrality. Although the perceived barbarism of native custom certainly made them sympathetic to missionary critiques, if not their strategies, they were equally wary of social disturbances that might produce resistance to British rule. Colonel C. Macauley was appointed the first resident of Travancore, followed in 1810 by Colonel John Munro. Macauley's and Munro's attitudes to the Travancore palace—their hostility toward the very notion of Hindu sovereignty—was best exemplified in the active support they provided for the work of the Christian Missionary Society (CMS) and the LMS in northern and southern Travancore, respectively.[2] Despite fierce opposition from Travancore's upper castes and the East India Company's official neutrality on religious matters, both British residents encouraged the work of the missions among the untouchable castes and native Catholics. During Macauley's tenure, East India Company troops protected the fledgling missions in Travancore against upper caste attacks. For Macauley, the missions served the function of destabilizing native authority, and he encouraged mission activity not so much because of his Christian faith but because his faith in liberal empire conflicted with his assumptions about Hindu despotism. Munro, who was a fervent evangelist committed to fighting "heathenism," "native superstition," and "popery," went further in obtaining land and providing financial support for the LMS and the CMS (Kooiman 1989: 54). As Munro wrote to the Madras government, "The support of a respectable body of Christian subjects would contribute to strengthen the British power."[3] His commitment to the spread of Protestantism in Travancore extended even to the unprecedented appointment of an LMS missionary as a civil judge. During his period as resident, a missionary army flooded the region and turned the southwest into the most active mission field in India (S. Bayly 1989; Kooiman 1989).[4]

The first half of the nineteenth century saw the LMS missionizing against different aspects of native rule, often with the tacit support of the resident. Ironically, the "plight" of the Syrian Christians was key "evidence" of Travancore's autocratic rule. Protestant missionaries came armed not just with the gospel but with a sense of the primacy of religious identity (S. Bayly 1989; Forrester 1980; Kooiman 1989). For them, Hindu and Christian were irreconcilable essences, each with its own sovereign cosmology. It followed that, for them, the complex ritual and material coexistence of the Travancore palace and Syrian Christians was merely a smoke screen for what was in actuality religious oppression at the hands of a fanatical and bigoted Hindu overlord. To them, the place of Syrian Christians in the Travancore palace—their tribute payments to the maharaja and his role in adjudicating clerical succession—could only mean coercion. Indeed, they took Hindu monarchical power all too literally as a form of religious domination that necessarily suppressed all other religious affiliations.

Until the 1850s, the LMS agitated against elements of the caste order—untouchability, slavery, *uliyam* (forced labor), and taboos maintaining a rigid physical and symbolic separation between upper and low castes—and demanded that their converts be released from these "disabilities." Missionary willingness to do battle for them brought low castes—in particular, the Nadar caste of toddy tappers[5]—to the LMS in large numbers demanding conversion *as castes*. LMS missionaries responded ambivalently to these demands, which smacked, they thought, of materialistic opportunism. How, they questioned, could the individual psychological transformation that propelled "true" conversion be reconciled with these collective requests for a change of religious affiliation? Surely they were driven more by the perceived material opportunities afforded by a link to the missions and did not represent an actual relinquishing of ties to heathenism. The timing of mass conversions—during the 1810–1812 famine, after the appointment of the missionary Mead as a civil judge in 1818, after the visit of the *raja* and his *dewan* to the mission in 1835, when they gifted a number of teak trees in appreciation of its educational efforts—struck the LMS as particularly suspicious.

However, even the LMS missionaries could not resist the draw of such an army of souls for their political goal of destabilizing native rule and laying the groundwork for the unfettered spread of Christianity. In any case, they had set in motion processes that were no longer under their control. Beginning in 1822, LMS converts had begun to push against the territorial proscriptions of caste. With missionary backing and the occasional endorsement of the Madras Presidency, the headquarters of the Travancore resident, they agitated for access to high caste spaces—schools, courts, temples and surrounding roads and tanks, wells, and so on—that were out of bounds for low castes. This nineteenth-century battle against ritually mandated spatial exclusions often exploded into violence as low and high castes clashed in street battles across Travancore. Missionaries encouraged low caste converts to press for access to privileged temple streets and procession routes and to engage in acts of intentional pollution directed against upper caste Hindus and their shrines. In response to low caste assertions of right to spaces deemed ritually pure, high caste state and private armies attacked convert groups, often using public shame as a threat against future transgression (S. Bayly 1989: 293).

A typical example of low caste challenges to ritual prohibition were the so-called breastcloth agitations of the 1820s. One marker of caste status that distinguished the ritually pure from the impure in Travancore was the cloth covering a woman's breasts that was permitted only to high caste women. During the breastcloth agitations, Nadar convert women violated expected custom, donned breastcloths, and appeared in public. On the first occasion of this public breach of ritual boundaries in 1822, the women were stripped by high caste Nair men and forced to flee. During several repeat performances later in 1828, Nair gangs ratcheted up the violence, burning Christian houses and churches. Finally, the *raja* issued a proclamation in 1829 permitting low caste convert women the right to wear loose jackets, although not in the style of high castes. The agitations continued against the maintenance of caste-specific codes of dress until, in 1858–1859, Nair and state attacks on Christians provoked the intervention of Charles Trevelyan, then governor of Madras. With this explicit intervention by British India, then maharaja Utram Tirunal Marthanda Varma (r. 1847–1860) issued a second proclamation removing all caste-based dress restrictions (Jeffrey 1976; Kooiman 1989).

Unlike Munro and Macauley, not all residents were sympathetic to missionary activism. This was especially the case after the Great Rebellion of 1857 against East India Company rule; the rebellion shook the northern states, and its epicenter was those states most recently annexed by the British. The replacement of the East India Company with direct Crown rule that followed the rebellion ushered in a new relationship between Britain and the native states. In response to widespread feeling that missionary disturbance of the caste order had precipitated the uprising, the Crown proclaimed its neutrality on religious and social matters, officially disowning missionary campaigns against caste and native rule in the princely states. The new policy toward the native states upheld princely sovereignty as a necessary buffer against the rising tide of rebellion against empire. It underwrote the territorial sovereignty of the princes in exchange for their loyalty to the Crown.

The proclamation seemed to consolidate the space of the princely state as an unquestioned domain of the native sovereign, but in fact the period after the rebellion witnessed the most far-reaching changes to the relationship between sovereigns and subjects. By the early decades of the twentieth century, new economic arrangements, political affiliations, and representative institutions had transformed the meanings and practices that constituted the space of the state and the public.

In part, this transformation was due to a discrepancy between the official policy of nonintervention and the subsequent development of institutions and practices that pushed against the divide between British and native India. Just after the colonial state took over from the East India Company, new pressures forced the redefinition of sovereignty, both in England and in the colonies. The British trading lobby and missionaries, incensed by the colonial state's decision to preserve India's princes, questioned their ability to represent their people and ensure good governance. This challenge to the Indian aristocracy paralleled similar challenges faced by Britain's own aristocrats, whose sovereignty was increasingly challenged by an emerging financial and industrial middle class and by an urban and rural underclass demanding rights. In this late-nineteenth-century context, the idea of "representativeness" became a new measure for gauging the legitimacy of rulers, a necessary accommodation to the age of nationalism and rights politics. As Mridu Rai shows in her work on Kashmir, "the principle of descent and tradition providing legitimacy would have to be complemented by the ideal of service and accountability to populations deemed to possess political rights" (Rai 2004: 132). Having pronounced India's princes as legitimate sovereigns by lineage in midcentury, the colonial state just a decade later compelled them to assume more responsibility to their subjects and demonstrate their achievements in "good governance."

This compulsion to good governance generated its share of economic, political, and cultural changes. Greater pressure by European capitalist interests forced an end to Travancore state monopolies on trade. In 1860, the monopoly on pepper was abolished, followed in 1863 by tobacco. In 1865, Travancore joined the British Indian system of free trade, adopting British Indian tariffs and removing most of the duties on trade between Travancore and British India. Indeed, when it came to trade, native sovereignty rapidly became meaningless. As Manu Goswami notes, "The external physical-territorial boundaries of colonial India constituted the principle of division between internal-domestic and external-foreign transactions. In fact, princely states or so-called native territories were subsumed within the overarching classificatory scheme of internal, domestic trade" (Goswami 2004: 82). Through the large-scale investment of private foreign capital in coffee, tea, and rubber plantations and in coir and coconut oil agroprocessing industries, Travancore was gradually integrated into an international commodity market dominated by European capital. European firms predominated, exerting near total control over commercial and financial activity. By the late nineteenth century, the

Travancore economy was "an essentially export-oriented agro-based industrial complex characterized by the overall predominance of foreign capital" (Mahadevan 1991: 167).

Land reform accompanied the revamping of trade, again as a result of colonial state pressure to break up matrilineal landholdings and institute individual property rights.[6] In 1865, the Travancore *dewan*, Sir T. Madhava Rao, granted full ownership rights to peasant cultivators of *sirkar*, or government, lands. He also allowed the unrestricted transfer of landed property, soon followed by reforms ensuring tenants of private landlords legal protection and permanent occupancy rights (Kooiman 2002: 56). The commodification of land broke up Nair landholdings, permitting low caste Ezhava and Nadar peasant cultivators new property rights and attendant economic mobility. Government land grants to the missions also exposed them to commercial agriculture. In addition to working on mission lands, an increasing number of Nadar converts also began to travel to Ceylon for work on coffee plantations, where their mission connections availed them of both labor and lower level management jobs. Low caste mobility was not limited to Protestant converts. Hindu agrarian low castes similarly benefited from changed circumstances. In northern Travancore, Hindu Ezhavas took advantage of the liberalization of trade by supplying coir to British India and became middle-class entrepreneurs in their own right. Across Travancore, this combination of employment and trade opportunities and new access to education propelled the economic and social mobility of agrarian low castes. Indeed, their success was so apparent that Maharaja Sri Mulam Tirunal Rama Varma (r. 1885–1924) made a point of referring to low caste entrepreneurialism at the Lahore Industrial Congress of 1909.

Although Travancore's agrarian world experienced the drama of late colonial political economic change most dramatically, the coast was not entirely insulated from these processes. The liberalization of trade most directly affected the export of salt fish to British India and the Arabian Gulf, where the British army became one of its main consumers. As further elaborated in Chapter 3, the volume of fish exports expanded nearly tenfold between 1870 and 1917. This lucrative trade consolidated the profits and power of Mukkuvar merchants and moneylenders, especially in northern Travancore from where the trade was organized, but it left most fishers in the same social and economic position. The absence of anything on the coast akin to the land reforms of agrarian society meant that class relations on the coast remained relatively unchanged, except for greater concentration of power in the hands of a tiny elite.

Alongside these new processes, other processes, such as low caste conversion to Protestantism, continued unabated from the early to the late nineteenth century. Although the Crown's proclamation was a serious setback to missionary progress, the economic and social mobility of previous converts brought increasing numbers of low castes flocking to the missions demanding mass conversion. Steady pressure applied by the LMS and the CMS on the Travancore government, both directly and through the resident, contributed to the abolition of slavery in 1853, adding to the attraction of ex-slave castes to the missions. The numbers of converts increased rapidly throughout the nineteenth century; from modest beginnings in 1806, the LMS enlarged its flock to 17,000 in 1850, to 40,000 in 1875, and to 63,000 in 1900, the overwhelming majority from the low and ex-slave castes (Kooiman 1989: 71).

Contemporary Kerala, the postindependence state comprising most of erstwhile Travancore, is well known as a "development miracle," largely because of its high literacy rate. Far from a postindependence accomplishment, the commitment to education began at the turn of the twentieth century and was largely due to a transformed relationship between the palace and missions in the post-1858 period. Even before 1900, the government had started to distribute educational grants-in-aid to Protestant missions to meet the swelling demand for schools from low castes. Missionary schools proliferated and soon came to dominate the Travancore educational system, providing low castes with the education they were forbidden by the ritual prohibitions on their entering government schools.[7] State support for private education advanced the missions' attraction for low castes, but it also gave the Travancore palace a "progressive" aura and elevated it in the eyes of British modernizers.

By the time Maharaja Rama Varma ascended to the throne in 1885, Travancore had acquired the reputation of being a model native state. Among princely states, it was the first to introduce a census along the lines of the British Indian census, to secularize education, to liberalize trade, and to commercialize agriculture. All these changes—political, economic, and social—had a significant effect on popular perceptions of and engagements with caste and sovereignty. It also set the stage for the fierce debates between the Travancore palace and the Protestant missions over state sovereignty, Hindu culture, and native Christianity, to which I now turn.

Progress and Primitivism, Caste and Christianity

The struggles over political space waged by low castes and Protestant missionaries against the Travancore palace and high castes strengthened the link between the inland polity and caste modernity. While battling over the future social and political makeup of the region, adversaries and allies generated a shared discursive arena in which they debated questions of how the state should relate to its subjects, what defined Hinduism, and whether Christians were natives.

Unlike my earlier discussion in this chapter, which highlighted low caste Catholic invisibility in the public arena, here we find Catholics to be more of a presence not as persons but as symbols. Protestant missionaries contrasted the enlightened, entrepreneurial convert to Protestantism with the ignorant, submissive, and heathen native Catholic; in the process, they put in circulation notions of Christian progressivism and primitivism that privileged their own converts over those of the Catholic Church. Even as the Travancore palace pushed against missionary and Protestant convert demands for ending caste prohibitions, state elites crafted a defense of Hindu sovereignty that reproduced Protestant missionary classifications of low caste Catholics. They also identified differences among Christians; however, in state ideological frameworks, Catholics appropriately inhabited caste as cultural feeling, whereas Protestants inappropriately wielded it as a basis for political rights. Although the state appeared to reward Catholics by placing them and not Protestants firmly within the fold of native culture, this distinction actually constituted Catholics as unthreatening inferiors easily assimilated to a lower rung of Travancorean social hierarchy.

The period after 1858 was especially critical in reshaping the relationship of the Travancore state to Protestant missions and of each of these to agrarian low castes. Before the 1857 rebellion, Travancore witnessed open hostility between rulers and missions, with the missions bent on delegitimizing native rule and making a case for the state's annexation by British India. Even after the rebellion, the standoff between missionaries and the state persisted in some form, with the Madras Presidency intermittently weighing in on the side of the LMS and the CMS. By the 1880s, however, the tide had begun to turn. Increasingly, Protestant missionary demands for low caste rights and protections for their converts fell on deaf ears as British imperial policy shifted in a conservative direction. The missions suddenly found themselves without an imperial ally, as the Madras Presidency and British Indian viceroys increasingly favored princely sovereignty over intervention on behalf of native Christians. Protestant mission societies had to seek princely state patronage for their activities.

The rhetorical role of Catholic low castes in these negotiations suggests that they became pawns in battles over sovereignty and rights and indicates the changing terrain of caste. Before 1857, the LMS and the CMS articulated a staunch anti-Catholicism carried over from Europe and reshaped by conditions in Travancore. Through their attacks on Catholic low castes, the two missionary societies took aim at their main targets: heathenism and Hindu state tyranny. By the beginning of the twentieth century, however, it was the Travancore state that used low caste Catholics to oppose Protestant low caste claims to rights and, more subtly, to elaborate a more muscular form of Hindu state power. As spaces of caste purity became spaces of caste modernity, coastal Catholics went from being heathen Christians to nonmoderns. Religious inferiority registered as developmental deficit.

Protestant Anti-Catholicism in a Native State

When Protestant missionaries first arrived in Travancore, their deprecation of Indian Catholicism hinged on two main elements: the Catholic Church's approach to caste and its approach to native rule. In the nineteenth century, the Catholic Church's accommodation of native rule was harshly criticized by such Protestants as Bishop Caldwell, who, in his less generous moments, pronounced indictments of the entire Roman Catholic order: "The genius of Romanism is unfavorable to improvement. . . . Consequently it may not only be asserted but proved, to the satisfaction of every candid enquirer, that in intellect, habits and morals the Romanist Christians do not differ from the heathens in the smallest degree" (Pascoe 1901). Caldwell and his fellow evangelists saw Catholicism primarily as an accommodative force that failed to wield the message of the cross as a challenge to Hindu orthodoxy. That the Catholic Church functioned within the caste order of the Travancore kingdom was a clear sign to them of the resemblance of "bigoted Popery" to "Asiatic despotism." Many a travelogue by visiting Protestant missionaries to southern Travancore attested to the plight of Catholic converts, whose conversion seemed to have only Hinduized the faith. This excerpt from the travelogue of Reverend Claudius Buchanan of the LMS, writing of his travels in 1812, is exemplary in this regard.

> In passing through the Romish Provinces in the East, though the Author had before heard much of the Papal corruptions, he certainly did not expect to see Christianity in the degraded state in which he found it. Of the Priests it

may truly be said, that they are, in general, better acquainted with the Veda or Brama than with the Gospel of Christ. . . . What a heavy responsibility lies on Rome, for having thus corrupted and degraded that pure and ancient Church! (Buchanan 1812)

Following Buchanan in 1844, Elijah Hoole of the LMS similarly expressed his outrage at the depraved state of Christianity among native Roman Catholics.

The conformity to heathen practices which Dr. Buchanan found at Aroor, may be seen throughout the worship of the Church of Rome in India. At the principal Romish Mission Stations, it is usual for them to have a car, in imitation of those used by the Hindoos, on which the image is placed, and taken in procession on festival occasions. In the intervals, it stands near the church, under shelter of a thatched roof, which is removed when it is required; and then the car is adorned with drapery, banners, garlands of flowers, etc; and the attendance on the image is with a pomp as nearly like that of Heathenism as circumstances will allow. The procession is accompanied with the discharge of rockets and crackers; a practice which is also borrowed from the Heathen, but in the frequent use of which the Romanists now exceed them. And their worship is rendered the more imposing and attractive to the poor natives, by dramatic exhibitions, in which also they have imitated the Hindoos (Hoole 1844: 100).

To LMS missionaries, Catholic imitation of Hinduism was most visible in the attitude toward caste. Roman Catholic missionaries typically regarded the caste system as the given and religiously neutral structure of Indian society within which evangelization, understood as the conversion of natives without detaching them from their social context, might proceed (Ballhatchet 1998; Forrester 1980). The first mass conversions of the Paravar and Mukkuvar fisher castes were strongly influential in later Roman Catholic missionizing. Unlike Protestant orders, which held as sacred the model (if not the practice) of individual psychological transformation as the only possible standard of "true" conversion, Catholic missionaries continued to perform and even prefer the mass conversion of whole caste groups.

It was this dimension of Catholic practice in India that was initially singled out for the harshest criticism, as it was caste above all else that struck LMS missionaries as most at odds with the message of the gospel. Most of them were products of the missionary movement in nineteenth-century Britain, which was at the same time a social emancipation movement of an emerging lower middle class positioned on the periphery of European society (Forrester

1980; Kooiman 1989). Their own social background produced an abhorrence of caste hierarchy and fervent support for low caste uplift.[8] As much as the missionaries believed in the uplift of the oppressed through Christianity, however, they were wedded to the model of individual, as opposed to collective, conversion. They believed that it was only through the power to regenerate the individual that Christianity could regenerate society. This was especially important for a population whose race was seen as a natural barrier to civilization. Low caste converts could never lose the stigma of race; however, Christianity could provide individuals a step up on the ladder of civilization and minimize the detrimental influence of race. That the Catholic Church would allow for caste feeling was a clear sign of its disregard for gospel truth.

Despite their stated abhorrence of caste, however, LMS and CMS attitudes toward native Christians exhibited a caste logic. One of the key arguments deployed by the LMS and the CMS against native rule hinged on the condition of native Christians. Many a missionary traveler and proselytizer deplored the pitiable state of Travancore's Christian population, in particular, the Syrian Christians, whose role in the rituals of state were interpreted as the result of Hindu coercion. Even though the missionaries actively courted high caste Syrian Christians, going out of their way to win them over to the side of Christianity's battle against Hindu despotism, they were not quite so solicitous of low caste Catholics, whom they saw as wards of their church. Although some feeble attempts were made to convert Catholics from "papism" to "true" Christianity, Catholic low castes served a far more useful rhetorical role for the LMS and the CMS as exemplars of Catholic depravity. Throughout the first half of the nineteenth century, the historical "complicity" of Roman Catholicism with Hindu rule became a target of Protestant missionary ire.

Anti-Catholicism also provided occasion to deride the unenlightened conduct of Britain's imperial competition. For instance, Elijah Hoole castigated native Catholic clergy for their negligence and avarice, singling out Goa, the administrative heart of Portuguese India, for special mention.

> The Tamul Romish Missions are generally supplied with native Priests from Goa, who take little pains to acquire the language of the people, and whose character and education are very inferior. They are supported by the people among whom they reside; and the royal grant made to each of them from an endowment by a former King of Portugal, is generally assigned by them to the relatives they have left behind in Goa. Those endowments are now said to be the chief subsistence of that city. (Hoole 1844: 100)

Hoole and others associated Catholic patronage politics and bureaucratic mismanagement with Catholicism's inherent hostility to social progress and enlightened statehood.

However, mission critiques were by no means wholly representative of colonial opinion. Indeed, British Indian officialdom was divided on the question of native Christianity. That Christianity in Travancore was anything but an alien or persecuted faith came in for comment in several official surveys of the native states. For instance, Lieutenants Ward and Conner, who surveyed Travancore and Cochin from 1816 to 1820, noted that "Christianity is fully acknowledged by the chief authorities in those countries, and whether from their justice or indifference does not appear to have been exposed to persecution" (Ward and Conner 1863: 129). Others interested in annexation, however, offered counterinterpretations that dovetailed with missionary rhetoric.

In the petitions flying between mission, native state, resident, and the Madras Presidency in the 1850s, the tension between regime change and maintaining the status quo is palpable. Significantly, native Catholics became pawns in the negotiations over caste and native rule. As proof of state toleration of non-Hindus, residents who were unsympathetic to missionary activism pointed out that only the mission societies appeared to see the oppression of Christians everywhere. In 1855, the resident wrote to the Madras Presidency complaining of missionary hysteria, insisting that "from the great mass of the Christian population, from the Roman Catholics or Syrians, but few complaints are received and none on the score of persecution."[9] That native Roman and Syrian Catholics found no fault with native state authority, he argued, was proof of Travancore's "liberal" policies.[10]

In response to state and resident use of Catholic testimonies to counter its portrait of Hindu religious oppression, the LMS pointed to the ignorance of the Catholic laity, singling out low caste Roman Catholics but not high caste Syrian Catholics for this charge. The understanding of low caste Catholics as cowed by clerical authority and living in a state of ignorant submission was a standard trope in Protestant mission writings. Elijah Hoole's 1844 travelogue notes that "the successors of Xavier have not taken pains to afford Christian instruction to the numerous congregations under their care. The Scriptures have not been translated by them, nor are the people permitted to read the translations made by Protestant Missionaries. In their place, there are most stupid and incredible legends of saints, and trifling poems equally valueless" (Hoole 1844: 100). Marshalling evidence of lay Catholics' inability to challenge the institutional nexus between their church and the Travancore palace became a key strategy for privileging the testimonies of their own converts, who, the LMS claimed, had through conversion come to recognize and give voice to their oppression by Hindu rule. The case of Devasahayam (Daivasahayum), a Roman Catholic turned Protestant, became emblematic of how converting from "heathen" Catholicism to "true" Christianity allowed for freedom of will and conscience.

> Daivasahayum, the man who died from the effects of the torture inflicted on him inside the Fort, by order, and in presence of the Kariakaran of the Palace, was an inhabitant of Kundamunbagum, a few miles east of Trevandrum. He was formerly a Papist; but had come under Christian instruction, and attended on Lord's day the native service at the Protestant Chapel in the Cantonment. (Nagam Aiya 1906: v. 2)

Devasahayam's conversion and subsequent torture and death in the palace became a celebrated testament to Protestant enlightenment and to Hindu and Papist barbarism. It marked the low caste convert to Protestantism as a shining exemplar of moral virtue and antiestablishment zeal.

In carrying their ecclesiastical battle with Catholicism into Travancore, Protestant missions set up a distinction between Protestant and Catholic converts that hinged on certain key oppositions: faith as the outcome of conscience versus blind faith, civic virtue versus religious orthodoxy, and individual merit versus religious patronage. The transformation of southern Travancore into one of India's most active mission fields ensured the proliferation of these ideas, not just within mission circles but more widely. The LMS's vanguard role in private education was one of several avenues through which Travancore's emerging public sphere of rights politics was increasingly infused with a Protestant ethos. As argued earlier, this Protestant ethos was anything but antithetical to caste affiliation. In fact, it helped bolster claims to caste modernity among Protestant converts and others subscribing to the civic ideals associated with the LMS. Furthermore, it accorded low caste Catholics the status of wards of their church and state, a designation that native state officials, newly aware of the threat of Christianity to their historical privilege, used to their strategic advantage.

Muscular State Hinduism

One should not overemphasize the transformative role of the LMS to the exclusion of the mission's own changes during its tenure in Travancore. In many ways the LMS internalized a caste sensibility in dealing with its own congregants and other native Christians, preferring high to low caste converts and allowing for caste-specific churches to facilitate the spread of the faith. Furthermore, the missions were not solitary agents of social change; indeed, with the decline in colonial state support in the 1880s, they became increasingly dependent on the good will of the Travancore government to further their educational, entrepreneurial, and other goals.

In the postrebellion period, Travancore's *dewan*s also played a pivotal role in transforming the political space of the region. Typically, *dewan*s were selected by the maharaja and approved by the Madras Presidency, thus giving the colonial state considerable power in defining the contours of Travancorean administration. Starting with T. Madhava Rao, who assumed the post in 1858, a succession of *dewan*s schooled, in liberal English education by the Madras Presidency's British teachers, came to Travancore. It was during Madhava Rao's tenure that Travancore witnessed numerous changes, including the creation of educational and medical facilities through collaboration with the LMS and the CMS, the founding of a public works department to oversee road and public building construction, judicial reforms that brought in judges from outside the state, the abolition of various state monopolies in trade, and the granting of full ownership rights to peasant tenants of government land (Jeffrey 1976: 75–103). Madhava Rao's "enlightened" interventions in native government earned him the applause of the Crown and knighthood in the Order of the Star of India.

Under Madhava Rao (r. 1858–1872) and his successors, A. Seshaiah Sastri (r. 1872–1877) and V. Ramiengar (r. 1880–1887), Travancore's rulers initiated far-reaching changes to the economic and political landscape of the state. In part, this was to secure their place as "approved" sovereigns and ward off the threat of annexation or increased intervention in their affairs by the British. As Manu Bhagavan notes in his work on the princely states of Baroda and Mysore, the construction of the native princes as exemplars of traditional sovereignty did not release them from the critical scrutiny of colonial modernizers: "The language of modernity permeated the hierarchy of classifications designed for princely India, so that some states were labeled 'more progressive' than others" (Bhagavan 2003: 5). After the queen's 1858 proclamation of nonintervention, this set of classifications, matched as it was by an elaborate system of gun salutes and regalia to symbolize the exact position of princes in the imperial hierarchy, animated princely claims to a reformed, modern sovereignty that would elevate their position on the imperial ladder.

Travancore's maharajas and *dewan*s did not look favorably on missionary and imperial pressure on the state, especially because an increasing number of low castes had begun to assert themselves and reject received ideas of caste deference. At the same time, they were invested in proving themselves as moderns, and in this they actively collaborated with the Protestant missions in creating new schools, hospitals, and other institutions that came to define the modern public (Kawashima 1998; Kooiman 1989). The proliferation of Protestant church-run institutions, a trend that in the postindependence period paved the way for a regional explosion of nongovernmental institutions of all kinds, and the state's active patronage of both Christian and Hindu institutions of "social improvement" contributed to Travancore's reputation as a model native state. By the early twentieth century, the notions of progress and social uplift, which initially were mantras of the LMS, had been generalized as constitutive of a modern outlook.

At the same time that Travancore's *raja*s and *dewan*s actively adopted strategies of modernization, they, like other modernizer princes, rejected the equation of modernization with Westernization (Bhagavan 2003). Instead, they took on board liberal prescriptions and gave them a native flavor, often in order to argue for strengthened native sovereignty. A particularly interesting instance of this dates back to 1868, when John Lidell, the former acting commercial agent in the Travancore government, was jailed for theft of the state treasury. He contested the government's authority to jail him as a British subject, explicitly challenging an 1837 ruling subjecting European subjects residing in native territories to the laws of the princely states. Dewan Madhava Rao, otherwise an enthusiastic advocate of British-style liberal reform in Travancore, vehemently opposed the Madras government's intervention on Lidell's behalf on the grounds that Travancore's legal jurisdiction was "an inherent right of sovereignty" (Kawashima 1998: 39). Such battles over the precise terms of paramountcy were a frequent occurrence and underscore the importance of distinguishing between the initiation of liberal reforms to bring princely administration in line with British requirements and the relinquishing of native sovereignty.

Indeed, over the second half of the nineteenth century and into the twentieth century, precisely when the Travancore palace undertook the furthest-reaching reforms in compliance with British dictates, the Travancore palace issued numerous defenses of its sovereign authority. The state still claimed for itself a Hindu affiliation; unlike its eighteenth-century articulation, however,

Hindu sovereignty came increasingly to be defined in terms of a religious exclusivity that tied the interests of the state first and foremost to its Hindu subjects.

Rulers and *dewans* were aided in their self-defense against missionary critiques by the conservative turn in British imperial policy in the 1880s and 1890s. Unlike Macauley and his liberal compatriots, conservative opinion reinforced racial notions of difference and the impossibility of transforming Britain's Indian subjects into citizens of a liberal democracy. Rather than molding Indians into brown Englishmen, the colonial state determined that it was better suited to the purposes of empire to seek legitimacy through the mediation of the "natural leaders" of the distinct communities that constituted the Indian public (Metcalf 1995). This was especially so when it came to native India. It is in the period between 1880 and 1910 that conservative policy helped Travancore to reconstitute itself as a more muscular Hindu state. Indeed, the shift in the terms of paramountcy was dramatic enough to elicit strikingly different comments from LMS missionaries just three decades apart. Writing in 1871, Samuel Mateer noted that "though nominally an independent State," in reality Travancore "was a tributary to the British Government." By contrast, I. H. Hacker in 1907 stated that the maharaja "has his own administration . . . and . . . has perfect freedom in the management of his own affairs" (quoted in Kawashima 1998: 81).

Significantly, muscular Hinduism in Travancore also signaled a shift in state attitudes toward caste. From outright opposition to low caste rights, the state began to grant rights to Hindu low castes in its effort to arrest the decline in Hindu numbers as a result of conversion. New policies undercut the work of the Protestant missions as Hindu state ideology shifted from the incorporation of the ritually pure regardless of religion to the incorporation of low castes *as Hindus*.

Much of this shifting state attitude toward caste was provoked by the publication of the census. As in British India, the Travancore state census animated a politics of rights among newly enumerated populations of low castes and non-Hindus. It also generated acute anxiety for the state and its Hindu elites, who saw in their diminishing numbers the demise of caste authority and the erosion of Hindu sovereignty. Nagam Aiya, the census commissioner from 1875 to 1891, expressed this fear most starkly in the 1906 *Travancore State Manual*: "In Travancore, the Hindus form 69 per cent of the total population; in Mysore 92.5 per cent. Madras 89 per cent and in Hyderabad 89 per cent . . .

the conservative Hindu State of Travancore is much less Hindu than even the Mahomedan State of Hyderabad" (quoted in Kawashima 1998: 154). A new politics of demography finally succeeded in forcing the Travancore government to initiate legislative reforms demanded for decades by low castes.

The example of education policy offers an illuminating window onto the changing politics of caste. In 1866, the Travancore government remained staunchly opposed to opening its schools to low castes, expressing the opinion that "if the state, in present circumstances, throws the schools open indiscriminately to all castes, the practical alternatives offered to the high castes is either that they should forgo the advantage of state education or secure that advantage under serious violence to religious feelings. Both these alternatives are to be deprecated" (quoted in Kawashima 1998: 100). Instead of desegregating government schools, the Travancore government began issuing grants-in-aid to Protestant missions to educate Hindu and Christian low castes. By the 1890s, however, the government's education policy had shifted considerably. It started building schools for low castes, often locating them near mission schools in direct competition with the latter. In addition, the palace introduced new educational rules through which it would control the curricula, qualifications of teachers, state of buildings, accommodation, and sanitation of aided schools. As a result of the new stringent regulations—in particular, the restriction on religious instruction in schools—the number of privately aided mission schools dropped precipitously from 1,265 in 1896 to just 472 a year later. So dramatic were the changes in state support for low caste education that by 1906 Nagam Aiya would write in the *Manual*, "There is no village of any consequence in the whole State whose educational requirements have not been or are not being supplied directly by Government" (quoted in Kawashima 1998: 104). In 1909, the government followed with its most radical step yet and opened all government schools to all castes.

The use of the census to shore up claims to low caste and non-Hindu rights provoked other state interventions. In 1851, the Travancore government rejected missionary demands that Protestant converts be released from the disabilities of caste by insisting that the status of converts remain identical before and after conversion. Then-*dewan* Krishna Rao laid down as a general rule that, "though an Illoowen [Ezhava] becomes a Christian, he must not cease to be an Illoowen" (quoted in Kawashima 1998: 58). By contrast, in 1887, the instruction provided to enumerators in the state revenue handbook read:

It having come to the notice of Government that some officers, when they have to record the names of Christian converts who appear before them in connection with cases in which they are concerned, unnecessarily insist upon such converts giving their former caste designations besides their Christian names, it is hereby directed that no public officer shall demand of any Christian convert the caste to which he belonged except when such is relevant to the case or other matter in question, and that in all public documents, such as tax receipts, etc., in which the names of Christian converts have to be written, it is sufficient to enter their Christian names together with other usual particulars, such as place of residence, and trade or calling.[11]

Additional legislation sought to distinguish Christian from Hindu low castes. For instance, in 1937 the government decreed with reference to public education that "Hindu depressed people [ex-slave castes] should continue to get full fee concession but 85 per cent of converts from these people must pay full fees, and 15 per cent may get half-fee concession" (quoted in Kawashima 1998: 185).

This about-face denial of caste affiliation to Christian converts is best explained by situating it within the larger context of rights struggles. By isolating Christian converts as outside caste, the Travancore palace hoped to undercut the interreligious caste solidarities that underpinned the newly emergent political associations of the early twentieth century, deny compensation for historical disabilities to low caste Christians, *and* constitute them as a nonnative population. As I show later, it is for the last purpose that low caste Catholics came in most handy.

Nagam Aiya's Defense

In this turn-of-the-century context of proliferating state legislation hostile to Protestant missionizing and the British Crown's retreat from protections for the missions and their converts, the palace published the first Travancore state manual. Its author, V. Nagam Aiya, used it as a platform to address debates on Hindu state legitimacy and rights politics. Two key themes in his writings were the question of who belonged in a Hindu state and the relationship of caste to Christianity.

Nagam Aiya, who served as census commissioner under three maharajas, was especially gifted at rhetorically navigating between British paramount power and popular rights politics. Born, bred, and educated in Travancore, he oversaw the production and compilation of the 1875, 1881, and 1891 censuses and the 1906 *Travancore State Manual*. In 1904, he was selected for the post of *dewan* by Maharaja Sri Mulam but was rejected by the Madras Presidency, which considered him "quite unfit" for the post. Explaining the decision, the governor of Madras stated that "V. Nagam Aiya is a Travancorean, who has never been out of Travancore, and who has a very inflated idea of himself. He would not do as Diwan, as he is too intimately associated with local cliques, besides lacking the requisite ability" (quoted in Kawashima 1998: 46). Despite being denied the post of *dewan,* Nagam Aiya wielded considerable influence as the author of key government documents, using the *Manual* and the census as platforms to expound on a number of different subjects under debate in the state.

As a prominent member of Travancore's high castes, Nagam Aiya's commentaries on caste, Christianity, paramountcy, and native rule are especially revealing of changing elite attitudes in the state. One way that he staved off British pressure from without and missionary and low caste pressure from within was to craft a claim to benevolent rule on the basis of religious pluralism. In this particular defense of the Travancore palace, one can see the shifting terms of cultural integration, from the earlier organization of princely state power around ritual purity to late-nineteenth- and early-twentieth-century imaginings of a Hindu nation. Particularly noteworthy is the place of caste in these different state frameworks—the way caste is used to both incorporate Christians as part of a sovereign Hindu fold and circumscribe them as subjects without rights. Nagam Aiya takes caste sentiment among Christians as evidence of the state's Hindu cultural substratum; at the same time that he wields Christian caste feeling to justify Hindu sovereignty, he trivializes low caste rights claims as mere squabbling among subordinates for elevated social status. Particularly significant is the prominent place of Catholics in his elaboration of caste feeling.

The second state census, published in 1894, reflected the notion that Roman Catholicism was the religion of the uneducated masses. In the census report, Nagam Aiya had this to say about Travancore's native Catholics:

> One fact stands out conspicuously in these returns, I refer to the preponderance of the Roman Catholics. In the south the efforts of the early Portuguese Missionaries, who preceded the Protestant Missionaries by centuries, laid the sure foundation of this superiority in numbers, and there is much in the doctrines of Roman Catholicism which tends at the present day to make that the most palatable form of Christianity to the uneducated Hindus, from amongst whom the large majority of converts is taken.[12]

Two points of note emerge from this statement. The first is the success of Protestant missions in education so that their converts, by contrast to those of the Roman Catholic Church, now appear to be made up of "educated Hindus." In just forty years, then, low caste Protestants have become a different social class altogether from their Catholic counterparts. The second noteworthy aspect of the statement is the passing of Protestant anti-Catholicism into high caste common sense so that it now appears as the religion of the underclass. Although high caste derision toward the low-ranking is certainly not new, this denominational distinction among them certainly is.

Other comments by Nagam Aiya further suggest a differentiated attitude toward caste feeling among Protestants and Roman Catholics. First, Nagam Aiya takes the opportunity to lash out at Protestant missions. Against LMS claims to Christian egalitarianism, he highlights the persistence of caste among Protestants: "I have often noticed that these Christians maintain their caste distinctions with rigidity and even take pride in doing so." He then dwells pointedly on the differences between Protestantism and Catholicism, arguing for Catholicism as the more native of the two Christianities. Speaking through the figure of a native Christian "informant," whom, given the gist of his comments, we might understand to be a Roman Catholic, Nagam Aiya criticizes Protestant missionaries for attempting to "Europeanize Natives" by denying them caste belonging.

> One of them, a well-informed and intelligent Native Christian, writes to me that "it is an injury to the Native Christian communities (both Catholic and Protestant) to have entered them in the returns simply as Native Christians instead of adding a separate column for Caste." This definitely shows the unfortunate feeling that exists between the adherents of a faith whose cardinal tenet is "the brotherhood of all men and their perfect equality." He goes to the length of saying that "changes which are no improvements are to be deprecated, and the practice of denationalizing Native Christian converts in dress, mode of life, and manners is not worthy of encouragement. The great drawback of Christian work in India is the necessity insisted upon by the Protestant Missionaries of renouncing caste, and of tearing oneself away from one's kinsfolk and friends who are dear to his heart. Another source of fruitful evil is the attempt made by some zealous Missionaries to Europeanize Natives. Natives of India when they become Christians are and must be Asiatics still. The efforts of Missionaries to cast the Christian converts into a uniform European mould entails a mere waste of power, and destroys the vitality of the

original materials. Christian proselytism fails in India because it strives to make its converts English middle-class men."[13]

With this lengthy quote from a native Christian informant, Nagam Aiya does several things. First, he elevates the Travancore palace as an anticaste modernizer that tried in vain to eradicate caste among Christians by excising its mention in the census. This allows him space to comment on the "unfortunate feeling" of caste among Christians, offering as evidence his informant, who insists that Indian Christians must remain "Asiatics still" by maintaining their caste ties. We are left, then, with a stark image of the bind that conversion places Protestant converts in. Neither accorded full Christian status by their missionary patrons by virtue of their lingering caste identification nor able to be fully native because of the internalized imperative to renounce caste, they inhabit a cultural no-man's land, a suspended state between native and Christian. It is only with the comparison to Roman Catholics, however, that Nagam Aiya's distinction between native and deracinated Christians becomes clearer.

After consigning low caste Protestants to cultural limbo, Nagam Aiya takes up Roman Catholicism as more representative of a "national" Christianity, one still rooted in the cultural bedrock of caste. The sense of caste pride and attachment to "national sensibilities," he argues, is especially visible among Roman Catholic Christians. Quoting a decision of the Madras High Court in which Roman Catholics are referred to as "Roman Catholic Hindus," he insists that "the habits of the Roman Catholic Hindus had not changed since their conversion. In their dress, habits, and all circumstances of social life, they were in every respect the same as their non-Christian brethren." Indeed, Nagam Aiya concludes, once again quoting his informant, "In matters of inheritance, adoption, acquisition, enjoyment and devolution of property, the customs of the several families are rigidly followed. . . . In fact as regards these matters, the caste Christians are entirely governed by Hindu law."[14]

The argument for caste and Hindu law as the governing principles of Travancorean society places native Catholics within the fold of "national culture" while deracinating those, such as Protestant converts, who would step outside them. But it also signals a shift in state practice away from a commitment to overlapping sovereignties that allows for mutuality between Hindu kingship and a variety of other religious affiliations to a defensive posture on Hinduism that requires the incorporation of non-Hindus into an exclusive sovereignty. Although native Catholics are rhetorically affirmed as an integral part of the state, their appellation as Roman Catholic Hindus is ultimately a denial of their religious particularity. Ironically, it was only in the early twentieth century that the perceived subordination of Christian to Hindu by Protestant missionizing was addressed in Travancore state ideology. In one sense, this document validates the Protestant missionary view of Travancorean society as a collection of distinct, if not mutually hostile, religious communities. Furthermore, if caste feeling is the key determinant of nativeness, then the denial of caste to Travancore's Christians within the state census is ultimately a denial of cultural belonging. What do we make of Nagam Aiya's more positive estimation of Catholic caste feeling and his defense of the state's rejection of caste as a referent of Christianity in the census? I would argue that this seeming contradiction rests in his distinction between caste as feeling and caste as a vehicle for rights.

It is quite clear from Nagam Aiya's writings that caste affiliation is to be accommodated among Christians only insofar as it does not translate into a demand for caste rights. In this too Nagam Aiya distinguishes Protestants from Catholics, singling out Catholics for favorable mention as more native because their attitude to caste is not oppositional. When he does mention claims for higher status among Catholics, his tone rapidly becomes derisive, as in this section of the 1906 *Travancore State Manual*, where he comments on the battles over caste status raging among groups of coastal fishers.

Nagam Aiya derives much satisfaction from highlighting the internal squabbles among coastal fishers and their compulsion to write "memorials and counter-memorials and [start] discussions in the public prints" (Nagam Aiya 1906: 118). One such status conflict erupted between two groups of fishers, the *Elunttikar*s (the Seven Hundred) and the *Anjuttikar*s (the Five Hundred), over the 1901 publication of then resident Gordon T. Mackenzie's *Christianity in Travancore*. Nagam Aiya writes in the *Manual* that both parties addressed Mackenzie in their memorials, the *Anjuttikar*s taking the further step of writing to him with a warning not to give "undue importance" to their rival group "in an official document like the State Manual of Travancore."

> We have the honor to state that we lately sent a memorial to G. T. Mackenzie Esq., British Resident in Travancore and Cochin, with regard to certain class disputes between the seven hundred Christian community and ourselves, known as the Anjuticars, the occasion for this representation being the submission of a memorial to the British Resident by the former asserting that they are the descendants of the Thomas Christians. This was in reference to

certain statements made by Mr. Mackenzie relating to the Latin Catholics mentioned in his pamphlet re: Christianity in Travancore. We have fully disproved their ancestry in our memorial, and as we understand that you are the compiler of the Travancore Manual of which the British Resident's publication is a chapter on Christianity, we have taken the liberty to depute the bearer of this, Mr. E. W. Nigly, as our representative to interview you in our behalf and to do the needful in conformity to the object of our memorial (Nagam Aiya 1906: 120).

Nagam Aiya then proceeds to recount the claim made by the *Anjuttikars* to Syrian Christian affiliation, a group identity that they denied the rival *Eluntti-kars*. He notes that they make a point of distinguishing "two classes of fishermen": themselves, the Five Hundred, descended from the Thomas Christians and forced by the Portuguese to adopt the Latin Rite and fishing as their *occupation*; and their rivals, the Seven Hundred, converted by the Portuguese to Christianity and fishermen *by caste*. Nagam Aiya is clearly not a little amused, even embarrassed, by these efforts on the part of rival groups within a low caste to take "advantage of this occasion of the publication of Mr. Mackenzie's pamphlet to ventilate their grievances and press their claims for higher recognition." He ends his commentary in a tone dripping with condescension, noting that, although "these small differences are of vital importance in the opinion of the communities concerned and agitate their minds deeply," in truth "their contentions remind one of the Poet's lines, 'Strange all this difference should be, Twixt Tweedledum and Tweedledee'" (Nagam Aiya 1906: 121).

Significantly, Nagam Aiya is careful to address only conflicts between groups sharing a caste affiliation and not between different castes. He is also insistent on diminishing their importance by interpreting them as conflicts over small differences of status and not over the rights of low castes to inhabit public space or enjoy their share of public resources. He is also careful to avoid any mention of conflicts over status among *Hindu* low castes, perhaps to convey the irony that such petty squabbling is the prerogative of the supposedly casteless Christians. Naming caste conflict a *Christian* problem furthermore creates the illusion of a unified Hindu social body that rises above such pettiness. When we place the various statements together—the hypocrisy of Protestant missions on the question of caste and the deracination of their converts, Roman Catholic "nativeness" and the pettiness of status conflicts among low caste Catholics, and the valiant attempts of a modern state to school Christians in proper conduct through the census—we get a portrait of state paternalism, Protestant threat, and Catholic marginality. Protestants are placed outside the native fold primarily because of their claims to rights, making low caste rights politics itself inconsistent with cultural belonging. By contrast, Roman Catholics are situated within the native fold, but their aspirations to higher caste status are disparaged and belittled as the irrelevancies of low caste posturing. Ultimately, Nagam Aiya's writings endorse caste only as cultural belonging while rejecting it as the basis for political rights. Significantly, missionary charges of Hindu despotism similarly effaced caste difference as a key factor in determining the treatment of Christians by the state. As in the early-twentieth-century Travancore state, they too made religion the primary mode of social differentiation and affiliation.

Nagam Aiya was at his rhetorical best when claiming for Travancore a past of religious pluralism and using this vision of pluralist coexistence to critique "Christian England." It is worth quoting at length one of his remarkable expositions in the 1906 *Travancore State Manual.*

> The importance of the work of Christian evangelization in Hindu Travancore, which has prospered so well as to give His Highness the Maharajah today a population of 697,387 Christian subjects of all denominations, may be better understood if we bear in mind that the fact is of as much moment as, nay even greater than, if there were 8 millions of Hindus in England and Wales (which according to the Census of the 31st March 1901 returned a total population of 32 millions) distributed over every county, district, parish, owning 30,000 temples having endowments of lands and gardens attached to every one of them, and severally dedicated to Siva or Vishnu or the Goddess Bhagavati, and having close by numerous tanks and rivers provided with neat and spacious bathing-ghats which only a Hindu could rightly appreciate, and wells reserved for cooking and drinking purposes, and groves of the Figus religiosa and the Nim tree or their more congenial substitutes suitable to an English climate growing luxuriantly on their banks . . . all unmolested and unhindered, under the protection of the English police and the English magistrate, and let the reader fancy that this happy state of things has been going on in Christian England from A.D. 52, what would be the impression that the scene will produce on the prosaic European mind, and what testimony may this not mean to the wisdom and tolerance of former English administrations since the time of the Druids? The same credit may, I think, be justly claimed on behalf of this Native Government for the present prosperous condition of its numerous Christian population. (Nagam Aiya 1906: v. 2, 118)

The state's professed magnanimity toward Christian missionizing is especially striking when one considers that this treatise on the flexibility of "native government" followed on the heels of fierce battles between the Travancore palace and the LMS. Nevertheless, the history of mutual accommodation to which Nagam Aiya gestures is indisputable. The mutuality that structured the relationship between Travancore's rulers and such groups as the Syrian Christians (as noted earlier) was indeed a distinguishing feature of the region. By deftly fusing past and present, however, Nagam Aiya elides the critical factor of caste in shaping the fortunes of native Christians and the hostilities between Protestant missions and the state throughout the nineteenth century. Instead, we are given an impression of the Travancore state as a modernizing influence trying to eradicate caste among Christians, in part by officially recognizing only religious affiliations. In the process, religious pluralism becomes a mechanism to incorporate an unthreatening form of religious difference as represented by Roman Catholics, in part as a buffer against the challenge of caste rights.

Caste Modernity and Territorial Sovereignty

Together, low caste and Protestant missionary opposition to state sovereignty and state responses to such challenges moved Travancore onto new political terrain where the claim to modernity became the key determinant of sovereignty and rights. In the process, groups that did not participate in the inland battles of the nineteenth century, such as Catholic low castes, were increasingly consigned to the space of primitivism. Their incorporation by such Travancore state elites as Nagam Aiya into the fold of native culture as unthreatening social inferiors only marginalized them further, placing them outside the battles over political representation and territorial sovereignty that picked up pace in the early twentieth century.

By the late nineteenth century, struggles to expand access to ritually proscribed territories were joined by new demands: first, to end the upper caste monopoly over state institutions and then to create new representative institutions. Despite the colonial government's assurances that the princely states could chart their own course without having to abide by the constitutional reforms of British India, Travancore did experience some growth in representative politics and some expansion of state services.

Demands for political representation took a somewhat different form from the earlier street battles and processions. Typically, demands were made through a "memorial" presented to the ruler by a corporate body, usually a caste or religious association or, in later years, a political party. In addition to challenging the terms of access *to* government, the nature *of* government also became a heated topic of debate. The legitimacy of princely sovereignty—indeed, the very basis of divine kingship—came increasingly into question as new political actors argued over what constituted representativeness and what exactly was the relationship between democracy and indirect rule.

In response to more vocal collective demands for representation and in partial mimicry of processes in British India, Maharaja Sri Mulam Tirunal Rama Varma established new institutions of popular political representation that catalyzed action on an unprecedented scale among newly consolidated groups of Christians, Muslims, and low caste Hindus. Much of the political energies that had previously been devoted to contesting ritual boundaries were now poured into the struggle to expand representation in the state services and in these new representative institutions. The political space of Travancore was dramatically transformed by the rapid proliferation of new corporate associations putting forward collective demands for political reform. In the 1930s these associations collaborated in the establishment of new political parties. Whichever the subject of political rights—low caste, non-Hindu, or democrat—collective action in Travancore's political arenas increasingly assumed a bourgeois character. The language of democratic rights proliferated, even as the political arena was narrowed to accommodate only certain forms of political association. Increasingly middle class and educated, with a faith in a civic mode of cultural interaction, the activists of the early-twentieth-century agrarian and urban worlds of Travancore rejected the terms of princely sovereignty and ushered in a new way of doing politics with its own "outsides."

Analysts of late colonial Travancore have noted the increasing tensions between recently consolidated religious groupings in the battle over political representation and rights. It is certainly the case that the religious categories of the Travancore state census appeared to manifest themselves in rights politics almost seamlessly. The state was also refashioning itself quite consciously as a Hindu entity whose fate was entwined more with that of Hindus than with any of its other subject populations. However, these trends mask a significant phenomenon: the consolidation of caste modernity as the grounds for a politics of rights and the marginalization of "caste primitives" as outsiders to this agrarian-urban world of representative politics. The modernity of caste—the desire for "improvement," the claim to a unique history, an entrepreneurial spirit, and a legacy of political participation in the transformation of a princely state into a democratic one—had become the key determinant of political inclusion. In a capsule, caste modernity translated as the aptitude for sovereignty.

The coproduction of caste modernity and political space through the nineteenth and twentieth centuries was critical to the making of postcolonial Kanyakumari. Indeed, it would not be a stretch to characterize the reorganization of state space in this newly demarcated district as the assumption of sovereignty by caste subalterns turned moderns. The 1956 merger of the four southernmost revenue districts of Travancore with Tamilnadu as the district of Kanyakumari (see Map 1 on page xvi) threw into sharp relief the district's unique religious and caste demography, where Christians constituted more than 40 percent of the population. As for the demographic distribution of castes, the presence of Syrian Christians after the merger became negligible, because they were an overwhelmingly north Travancorean population, making Kanyakumari's Christians almost entirely low caste in composition. Similarly, upper caste Nairs and Brahmins were reduced to a minuscule percentage of the district's population, making low caste Nadars, Mukkuvars, and Dalits and high caste Vellalas the most populous castes, in that order. The Nadars emerged as the most politically powerful caste in the district. In addition to their numerical strength, their social and political ties to caste brethren across Tamilnadu elevated their political and social capital within Kanyakumari.

Cross-border ties between Nadars were shaped by state formation and reformation in the region. The liberalization of trade in the 1860s and the labor mobility that accompanied it took Travancorean Nadars to Ceylon or across the border to Tamil country, where they took up toddy tapping and agriculture, replacing other Nadars who had migrated to Ceylon for plantation work. This movement of people to and from the Madras Presidency generated a flow of ideas and practices, as seen in the new histories and political energies unleashed in the twentieth century. Christian missionizing formed yet another basis of cross-border solidarity (Hardgrave 1969; Kooiman 1989), knitting Nadars together in distinct caste churches that transgressed territorial boundaries. Ironically, the anticaste activism of the LMS and the CMS strengthened caste ties not only within Travancore but across the southern Indian region.

As for high caste Vellalas, their cross-border links with caste brethren hinged on participation in the Tamil literary revival of the nineteenth and twentieth centuries. For them, as for Nadars educated in the private mission schools that sprang up across southern Travancore in the nineteenth century, Tamil education became a key force of Tamil secessionism. Indeed, the beginnings of Tamil secessionist organizing began around the demand for a state-funded Tamil university in southern Travancore, and Travancorean Tamils received much financial support and publicity from Tamil newspapers and literary societies across the border in Madras Presidency.

When the four southern districts were joined with Tamilnadu as the district of Kanyakumari, these preexisting solidarities flourished. Together, those castes that came of age politically through the street and representational battles of the nineteenth and twentieth centuries exercised authority in a newly sovereign domain. Just as the territoriality of caste benefited Nadars and Vellalas, it hurt Mukkuvars. By contrast to Nadars and Vellalas, who were now united with caste brethren across Tamilnadu, Mukkuvars left the majority of their caste brethren behind in Kerala, rendering them even less politically visible than before. In contrast to the cross-border affiliations cultivated by Nadars and Vellalas throughout the nineteenth and early twentieth centuries that bore political fruit in 1956, Mukkuvar social and political power was further compromised with the merger. In addition, whatever Mukkuvar political representatives they had were based in northern Travancore. As a result, the merger left the church as the primary communal authority on the southwestern coast. The transformations of political space that brought Nadars and Vellalas to the forefront of district politics in Kanyakumari reinforced the exclusion of Mukkuvars, who wielded little power in shaping foundational power arrangements in the new district.

A number of factors point to the unevenness of social and political power in Kanyakumari today. The political class is drawn overwhelmingly from the Hindu and Protestant Nadar and Vellala castes. The representative power of different social groups is clearly seen in the drawing of political constituencies in the district. Whereas the boundaries of constituencies tend to enhance the demographic weight of agrarian and urban low castes, producing an effect akin to communal electorates, the coast has been carved up into a number of different political units. There is a stark contrast between the provision of public services—roads, buses, postal service, water, sanitation, schools—to agrarian and urban Kanyakumari and their provision to coastal Kanyakumari. Until recently, the only roads servicing coastal villages were those connecting villages to each other; hardly any roads led to inland agrarian pockets or to the district capital of Nagercoil. In a replay of ritual prohibitions, government buses forbade women fishmongers from carrying fish to local markets because they might "pollute" the public transport. Indeed, these prohibitions even cited the "immodest" garb of fisherwomen as cause, showing the entrenchment of caste-specific notions of bodily comportment among low caste moderns. To this day, clean water is scarce and drainage systems are almost nonexistent in coastal Kanyakumari. Most primary schools continue to be church run, and there is no high school on the coast. Indeed, when one looks at the institutional provision of services, it is the presence of the church and not the state that is felt most strongly on the coast.

In short, postindependence Kanyakumari reflects the reterritorialization of caste across a profoundly uneven social space. Although the social and political organization of power in the region has been radically reshaped over the nineteenth and twentieth centuries, these processes have produced new "insides" *and* "outsides." Oppositional terms have been transposed from Travancore to Kanyakumari, as the spatial divide between inland and coast is cast as that between democracy and religious autocracy. As I argue in later chapters, in this divide one can see the afterlife of indirect rule as the organization of power in territories of caste primitivism, where "traditional" authority inhibited the exercise of modern sovereignty.

Figure 3. Trawling boats. Courtesy of South Indian Federation of Fishermen
Societies, Trivandrum, Kerala.

3 Changing Developmentalisms

Spatializing the Artisan

A CENTURY OF POLITICAL CONVULSIONS in southwestern India made agrarian low castes into moderns and divine kings into modernizers. Out of this turbulence came inland modernity and a second, less noted artifact: coastal primitivism. Low caste fishers inhabiting Travancore's coastal belt found themselves sliding down the regional status ladder as their Catholicism and seafaring became synonymous with caste inferiority and the absence of a desire for improvement. In the twentieth century, these efforts at casting the coast and its fishers in a primitive mold intersected with new state imaginaries and interventions that came under the rubric of developmentalism.

Although southwestern fishers have been subjects of development since the early 1900s, the furthest-reaching changes to southwestern coastal harvest, ecology, and society were midcentury phenomena wrought by technocratic interventions of the postcolonial state. Compared to these interventions—in particular, the introduction of trawling technologies—preindependence encounters between fishers and states were arguably mild. Even so, marine fishers were in the crosshairs of state developmentalism a good fifty years earlier, when colonial and princely administrators together grappled with the fate of marine fishing in a world of rapid capitalist transformation. Contemporary understandings of artisanal fishing and fishers are owed in part to these earlier forms of developmental know-how and practice. Specifically, spatial imaginaries of coastal fishers—the set of ideas about culture and economy that map fishing populations onto geographic space—that informed colonial era developmentalism have filtered through to a wide spectrum of postcolonial institutions and practices with immediate consequences for fishers' lives.

Two spatial imaginaries of the southwestern coast have remained particularly resilient. The first image frames the coast as a bounded locality inhabited by subsistence fishers existing on the margins of an agrarian heartland; the second situates the coast within an oceanic world of trade, technological diffusion, and cultural exchange. These two warring images of resolute localism versus translocal interaction have informed state development intervention on the coast across successive sovereignties. Each has a jagged chronology that does not correspond neatly to a single form of rule, and each has been profoundly material in its effects.

In this chapter I track the relationship between these two spatial imaginaries and developmental interventions on the southwestern coast over the first five decades of the twentieth century. I show how a sense of space shaped material interventions and was in turn shaped by fisher engagements with these interventions. First, I consider how early-twentieth-century spatial understandings of the coast shaped the scale and scope of fisheries development. The debates that attended the beginnings of fisheries development in the Madras Presidency addressed the appropriate pace of socioeconomic change for marine harvesters and the historical destiny of the fisher. Although these debates are by no means characterized by consensus, they place fishers within a world imagined on an imperial scale. The perspectives of three administrators—Sir F. A. Nicholson, James Hornell, and B. Sundara Raj—on the fraught question of trawling help us to see overlaps and divergences among bureaucrats in a new arena of imperial development. This internal debate undercut consensus on the present and future of Indian fisheries and echoed parallel discussions in other arenas of development, such as forestry (Rangan 2001; Rangarajan 1996; Sivaramakrishnan 1999), irrigation (Mosse 2003), and wildlife conservation (Rangarajan 2005; Saberwal et al. 2001). The presence across the colonial bureaucracy of dissenters and iconoclasts, many of whose ideas and collaborative practices inform contemporary notions of alternative or appropriate development (Visvanathan 2001), invites a rethinking of late-nineteenth and early-twentieth-century empire as more fractured than coherent. Indeed, the collaborations across racial lines evident in some instances of dissenter development suggest continuities with C. A. Bayly's (1996) portrait of an eighteenth-century ecumene.

A dearth of sources on Travancore's fisheries in the early twentieth century weights this section heavily toward the Madras Presidency's Fisheries Bureau. There is also a more historical reason for this emphasis: The Madras bureau played a pioneering role in the southern region; as I show, its ideas and practices traveled to Travancore, motivating and guiding the establishment of a fisheries department in the princely state, and to the postindependence states of Tamilnadu and Kerala.

In the second part of this chapter I shift to postcolonial developmentalism and the remaking of southwestern fishing. The Tamilnadu Department of Fisheries inherited wholesale the administrative structure of its colonial predecessor; however, its developmental practices were reset to the prerogatives of an economy imagined on a national scale (Goswami 2004). One of the key questions of this chapter, then, is how fishing was respatialized by a developmental imaginary crafted to suit the imperatives of nation building.

Fish as Food: Early-Twentieth-Century Politics of Technology and Space

Imperial Localization

Fisheries came into view as a relevant sector of the Madras economy in the aftermath of Bengal's late-nineteenth-century famine. In 1899, Sir F. A. Nicholson, who was subsequently appointed honorary director of the Madras Fisheries Bureau, argued that

> the development of our fisheries is now absolutely essential in connection, whether direct or indirect, with our food-supply: when we despair of food independent of climate for a rapidly-increasing population, of industries for non-agriculturists, of manure for deteriorating soils, we may thank God that we have yet got the fisheries to develop. This all important subject has too long been neglected; the sea yields its harvests in enormous quantities wholly irrespective of droughts and seasonal catastrophes, and the food, being highly nitrogenous and concentrated, is of extreme value. . . . In this Presidency, where it has been recognized by Government that it will primarily be treated *not as a source of revenue, but as a means of increasing the food-supply*, the manurial resources, and the petty industries of the country, it is obviously the Agricultural Department which should deal with it. (Madras Fisheries Bureau 1915: 1, emphasis added)

Nicholson's championing of the inexhaustible marine resource, the sea's reliability relative to the contingencies of agrarian production, and its potential contribution to the famine relief effort proved fruitful, and in 1907 a bureau of fisheries was established as a subsidiary of the Agricultural Department.

The early distinction between food supply and revenue was a critical factor in shaping future understandings of marine fishing. Fish as food implied a radically localized economy whose practices were cued to subsistence needs rather than to the demands of trade and accumulation. Seeking only to fill the gap left by agriculture's waning contribution to the food supply, the Madras Fisheries Bureau eschewed an overhaul of the existing system of fish harvest in favor of incremental social measures to alleviate chronic indebtedness and to maintain steady food production. To be clear, this minimal intervention did not reflect an imperial sensitivity to coastal life and economy. Rather, it indexed how inconsequential the marine harvest was to the riches of empire. The only purpose of fishing to the British Raj was as a means to ameliorate the effects of a famine produced by colonial intervention in agriculture (Bose 1993; Davis 2002; Ranajit Guha 1963).

Late Victorian bureaucrats treated marine fish harvest in the colony as an anachronism that would be phased out by technological advance. At the same time, colonial fisheries administration took a largely conservative form that involved minimal technological intervention. When Nicholson first began his work as director, he considered the impending obsolescence of traditional fishing as a historical given. Writing in January 1905 after an initial investigation into the condition and needs of the coastal population, he insisted on the need for, and the inevitability of, industrial fishing.

> When the development of fisheries elsewhere is viewed historically and its economic conditions considered carefully, it is seen that progress has been and, in the present form of civilization, must be, from the independent fisherman with a single small boat and petty local trade to the capitalist-employer with his fleet of large boats and his wage-paid crews. (Madras Fisheries Bureau 1915: 36–37)

The inevitability of capitalist transformation for any fishery, Nicholson maintained, was even more so for India's fishing economy, because it was organized on a caste basis. An economy founded on caste, he wrote, could "by itself never provide the essentials of development" because its seafaring population is "born and not made." The incommensurability of caste and capitalism, or of ascriptive, precapitalist social identities and the "modern" identities of wage laborer and capitalist, would lead necessarily to the disappearance of the "independent boatman with his catamaran and canoe, the petty individual curer with his pinch of capital and half a dozen baskets of fish, the small market dealer or buyer, and the fresh-fish runner," or to their subordination "as the employees of capital" (Madras Fisheries Bureau 1915: 36–37).

These earliest statements on the inevitability of social transformation in accordance with universal principles of industrial capitalism appear in a more cautious, muted form in Nicholson's writings later in the decade. By 1909 he had become convinced of the need for a more gradual process of change. Revising his earlier stand on the necessity of rapid industrialization, he had begun to argue in favor of "the independent yet cooperative owner of the fishing smack and the petty factory rather than the capitalist-cum-laborer" (Madras Fisheries Bureau 1918a: 224). "In Madras," he wrote in 1915, "we have a vast existing industry worked for centuries in the most primitive fashion by a large population of ignorant but industrious men and one cannot ignore them and their interests, welfare and industrial conditions; we cannot jump at once from the catamaran to the steam trawler" (Madras Fisheries Bureau 1918a: 76). This kind of rapid technological advance, he warned, "could mean a revolution of the fishery system by bringing in the capitalist and reducing the fisherman to a paid hand" (Madras Fisheries Bureau 1918a: 76). Instead, Nicholson offered as a goal the gradual modernization of the existing production system, a "steady evolution rather than to attempt or even to suggest a revolution in fishery methods by even the experimental introduction of the latest western approaches" (Madras Fisheries Bureau 1918a: 223).

What do we make of Nicholson's change of perspective? It is clear that, for him, it was the technological and social backwardness of the Indian fishery that militated against the universal application of capitalist developmental strategies. The persistence of caste as a structuring principle of Indian society only reinforced his sense of its difference from the history and culture of Europe. The fact that the population assigned to him was coastal made him reject even more forcefully the universality of the principle of modern progress. He despaired of achieving even small-scale cooperative production because of the dearth of potential he saw in the community form of the fishing village. "Fishermen," he opined to the gathering at the 1909 Lahore Industrial Conference, "are far less united in corporate life than the inhabitants of an inland village, with their village administration, defined boundaries, rights and privileges, their corporate sentiment and communal and agricultural ties" (Madras Fisheries Bureau 1918a: 224). It was this lack of corporate sentiment, he continued, that made the harvester of the sea "less diligent and thrifty" than the cultivator of the soil. Nicholson worried that, given the difficulty of introducing new methods of production into agricultural villages, it would be nearly impossible to "develop the fisher folk by means which shall make and keep them independent yet cooperative, and to prevent their degeneration into mere laborers still more at the disposal of richer folk than they are now" (Madras Fisheries Bureau 1918a: 224).

This distinction between the corporate agrarian village and the more loosely structured yet oppressively hierarchical coastal village echoes reports of Nicholson's assistant director, V. Govindan. Govindan, previously an assistant to Edgar Thurston, the superintendent of ethnography of the Madras Presidency, was in charge of setting up village cooperative societies, inculcating a sense of "thrift" among the fishers, and convincing them to adopt "temperance" in their toddy (native liquor) consumption. His ethnographic expertise, culled from his experience in helping Thurston create an inventory of South Indian castes and tribes, made him Nicholson's main informant on coastal life. Nicholson regularly cited Govindan as a native authority on fisher culture, whose observations that fishermen were "not in touch with the civilized world" and that they "require[d] awakening and stimulating" formed the basis of the department's development strategy (Madras Fisheries Bureau 1918b: 133). This was a quintessential instance of the power of the native intermediary in shaping colonial social categories. As was the case in other contexts of colonial intervention, we see here the conjunction of native elite and colonial hierarchies of value in determining the fate of native subalterns.[1]

Govindan, who was given main charge of the social uplift of the fishing population, appears to have had a highly contradictory understanding of coastal life that rested on the superiority of the agrarian world. Writing after one of his visits to the coastal villages, Govindan commented that fishers "could hardly understand what co-operation was." On the very same page, he noted with enthusiasm "the influence of caste *panchayats* [village councils] in guiding special matters" (Madras Fisheries Bureau 1918b: 130). Govindan conveyed such conflicting observations to his superior as evidence of the backwardness of coastal society relative to the mores governing agrarian life. It appears that for Govindan, and by extension Nicholson, the distinction between fishing and agrarian castes was assumed: The very same *panchayats* taken as evidence of a corporate spirit among agriculturalists proved the opposite for fishers. The same was true of property ownership. In coastal villages, ownership of craft and gear typically followed a nuclear family model; ironically, this form of property cherished in the West as exemplary of civility was interpreted in the context of coastal India as a form of primitivism. Colo-

nial and postcolonial administrators alike railed against nuclear or individu-
ated forms of property ownership as the bane of traditional fishers that left
them vulnerable to the oppression of middlemen. Nicholson's insistence on
cooperative production as the only mechanism for fisher uplift was a lasting
legacy of fisheries development that was sustained through a century of significant changes.

These opposed senses of collectivity—agrarian corporatism versus fisher
primitivism—recalled spatialized notions of cultural difference that had crystallized over the nineteenth century across southern India. In the Madras
Presidency the contrast between civilized agrarian cultivators and threatening itinerant castes informed a colonial sociology of knowledge with far-
reaching consequences (Dirks 2001; Pandian 2005; Yang 1985). Although
fisher castes were not subject to the brutal forms of discipline meted out to
itinerant groups who in inland society were designated as criminal castes and
tribes, the coast constituted an external limit of settled agriculture and, by
extension, civil society. Nineteenth-century Madras witnessed an increasing
consolidation of agrarian caste power, in part through the instrumentaliza-
tion of colonial categories in security, development, and popular politics. The
line between civility and barbarism that crystallized in the late Victorian period separated not just East and West but also civilized and barbaric natives.

Ironically, the overarching classification of land and marine harvest as
agriculture only strengthened the distinction between agrarian and coastal
subjects of rural development. The same was true in neighboring Travancore,
where the pioneering role of the Madras Fisheries Bureau in the southern
region precipitated the establishment of the Travancore Department of Agriculture and Fisheries. As we saw in Chapter 2, similar processes of social
differentiation were under way in the princely state, where the consolidation
of agrarian caste power depended in part on the distinction between inland
moderns and coastal primitives.

Little material is available on Travancore's early-twentieth-century interventions in fishing, but what we do know reveals the influence of Madras. As
in Madras, Travancore's fisheries department was started as a subset of its Agriculture Department, and initially the primary goal of intervention was the
uplift of a "backward community" outside the pale of inland respectability.
The thrust of Travancore fisheries development was socioeconomic and not
technological; effort was put into helping marine fishers alleviate the burden
of debt by starting cooperative institutions that would help them to enhance
their productive power and undercut the power of middleman merchants.

What is especially striking about the classification of fishing activities in early-twentieth-century Travancore is the distinction carried over from Madras between trade and agriculture-related practices. Since at least the 1870s, Travancore had a thriving export trade in salt fish to British India and Ceylon that serviced the imperial armies and accounted for 1–2 percent of the princely state's total export revenue. Although the state did tax this trade, it by no means controlled it. Rather, it was run by enterprising merchants who linked coastal fishing populations to British and Ceylonese importers.

Mercantile power on the southwestern coast had increased with the integration of Travancore into the international commodities market. As we saw in Chapter 2, Travancore started to abolish a number of state monopolies in the mid-nineteenth century under pressure from European trading interests. In 1865, it joined the colonial system of free trade, adopted British Indian tariffs, and removed most of the duties on trade with British India. Fishing and agriculture were both commercialized in the nineteenth century. However, the remarkable advance in economic status experienced by Travancore's agrarian low castes as a result of the commercial trade in coffee, coir, and native liquor did not have a counterpart in commercial fishing, which, by contrast, did not change the fortunes of most fishers. Rather, it enhanced the power of a merchant elite.

By all accounts, Travancore was incredibly responsive to the demand for fish products. Travancore's fishers provided dried fish regularly for the laborers of coffee plantations (Day 1865, quoted in J. Kurien 1985). Once the British extended the railway into the states of Malabar and Cochin in 1854, the dry fish exports from Travancore doubled in a mere ten years (Day 1865, quoted in J. Kurien 1985). To promote this lucrative trade, the Travancore government favored the expansion of fish marketing and lifted the duties on salt.

Kurien notes that "such a quick response to international demand could only be undertaken with the initiative and drive of a merchant class open and responsive to profit opportunities" (J. Kurien 1985: A-71). This small class sucked up the profits generated by the export trade. In 1930, the Banking Enquiry Committee of Travancore commented on the sorry plight of the fisher: "Once the producer is indebted to the middlemen the tendency is that he is unable independently to market his commodity and the natural results are that he gets less prices and has to pay interest on loans. This cuts his small margin of profit clean" (Banking Committee Report 1930, quoted in J. Kurien 1985). It was this tiny minority of merchants among the Mukkuvars that appears to have accrued the benefits of the export trade in fish.

With the Banking Enquiry Committee report and the influence of the Madras Fisheries Bureau, the Travancore government did make attempts to break the hold of merchants. It encouraged the exchange of ideas with British India, and starting in 1912, students were sent to the Madras Fisheries Bureau for training in new methods of fish curing and canning (Madras Fisheries Bureau 1918b). As part of this process of exchange, beginning in 1917, the Travancore government also began to establish cooperatives of fish producers to curb merchant control over marketing. Through these cooperatives, the government tried to provide credit to redeem fishers from indebtedness, help them take control of processing facilities, such as curing yards, sell their fish collectively, and have collectively owned fishing equipment. By 1933, a third of Travancore's active fishermen were members of ninety-five cooperatives. Through the cooperatives, the government supplied fishers with food grains, cloth, and other essentials. It also introduced freezing technology for the preservation and storage of fish, established fish curing yards under the supervision of fishery officers to ensure a regular supply of salt and hygienic processing, and helped form the company West Coast Fisheries Ltd. to undertake exports (J. Kurien 1985: A-71). However, state commitment to curbing merchant power does not appear to have much helped the common fisher, and the divide between a merchant elite and an impoverished fisher population remained firmly in place.

The intermediary role of merchants only underscores the fact that Travancore fisheries were very much a part of a wider world of trade. When one looks at emerging Travancore state developmental classifications, however, this link between trade and marine fishing is severed. Instead, the exchange relations of the salt fish export trade are set apart from the labor of fishing, with fishing cordoned off as a form of subsistence harvest. The restricted mobility of fishing craft—their inability to work the deep sea, their need to land fish onshore every few hours because of the absence of refrigeration, and their lack of motorized technology—came to stand in more generally for the limited range of marine harvest. As in Madras, this classification obscured not just the high rates of fisher migration across the coastal belt in pursuit of a fugitive resource but also the centrality of trade, whether local, regional, or transregional, to the very organization of marine fishing. After all, fishers cannot live on fish alone and necessarily have to exchange their harvest for the basic staples of rice, grain, and greens. Their classification outside the category of trade obscured the position of marine fishers at the beginning of commodity chains stretching from coast to inland and from princely state to other sovereign territories. In short, emerging developmental classifications across the southern region increasingly constituted marine fishing as *local*.

The spatialization of South Indian marine fishing as local reinforced Nicholson's imperial geography, a radically uneven landscape in which Western technological advancements only highlighted pockets of atavism in the colonized world. During Nicholson's time as Madras Fisheries Bureau director, this racialized hierarchy of technological competence was "indigenized" through Govindan's agronormative sensibility and a colonial sociology of knowledge that privileged sedentary cultivation. With these conceptual apparatuses in tow, Nicholson advocated caution when handling fishers, whose ability to master new technologies was very much in doubt.

However, Nicholson's engagement with the southern fishery had another side. In effect, the pejorative view of southern fishers that underpinned his advocacy for gradual development produced a great variety of interventions for socioeconomic uplift, enhancement of fishers' productive capacity, and cautious experimentation with new technologies. The schemes begun during his tenure—cooperativization, canning, improvement of indigenous technologies—were developed through sustained interaction with fishers. By the eve of his retirement as fisheries director, Nicholson had refined his understanding of development: "I desire here to disclaim any idea either of measuring the success of the department by its balance sheet, or of narrowing its scope and objects by considerations of immediate departmental profit and loss. Its primary object is not revenue but development and progress; revenue is incidental and while welcome as a fiscal contribution and as a fund providing for further expenditure, is not a direct object save as an evidence of success in concrete fishery operations" (Madras Fisheries Bureau 1918a: 182). It is precisely Nicholson's enduring sense of the Indian coast as spatially, temporally, and culturally distinct from both the European coast and the Indian inland that opened his eyes to other perspectives on coastal life, livelihood, and development. To put it differently, it was Nicholson's pejorative sense of Indian fishers' cultural difference as an inferior, unassimilable otherness that led to a more enduring sensitivity to fisher welfare and made him, in practice, much more like his successor, James Hornell.

Imperial Translocality

At first glance, James Hornell's attitude toward Indian marine fishing and indigenous technologies could not be more different from Nicholson's. His tenure in the Madras Fisheries Bureau lasted less than a decade, but it was only a brief part of a much longer intellectual engagement with issues of marine ecology, technology, and resource use that covered stints as marine biologist, colonial administrator, fisheries advocate, and ethnographic researcher. Hornell's extensive analyses of the Raj's marine resources, coastal population, and fishing technologies display a passionate regard for indigenous crafts and skills. Both during and after his directorship, Hornell traveled widely and wrote extensive comparative analyses of indigenous technological developments in the empire's colonies. Hornell's exhaustive accounts of indigenous technologies go so far as to say that the fishermen of Madras had kept "full pace with the times" (Madras Fisheries Bureau 1918a: 49) and had developed technology "which would pass muster as very serviceable fishing boats in the waters of Northern Europe" (Madras Fisheries Bureau 1918a: 45). At times Hornell's healthy respect for the craft and techniques of Madras's marine fishers even brought out his poetic spirit: "No finer sight can be seen off our coasts than a fleet of these boats beating out to the roadstead in the face of a strong breeze. Heeling well over under the power of the great lateen that billows in graceful curve below its huge yard, these boats ride the seas in a manner that bespeaks the weatherliness of their model, and the skill of the helmsman" (Madras Fisheries Bureau 1918a: 51).

Both Nicholson and Hornell promoted small-scale fishing over industrial fishing, but Hornell's recognition of the valid and informed nature of the marine fishers' response to new technologies was in sharp contrast to Nicholson's dismissal of the coastal population as "conservative folk in an industry hitherto wholly untouched by progress or even by industrial thought" (Madras Fisheries Bureau 1915: 38). Hornell's developmental choices were often inspired by the activities of fishermen themselves. Unlike others who could see only stagnant primitivism, Hornell was keenly aware of the dynamism of marine fishing and that craft and gear on different parts of the coast were tailored to suit the local conditions. Hornell's admiration of the *kattumaram*, or catamaran, the craft that most often invoked horrified reactions from colonial modernizers, is a clear example of his attitude.

> Wherever heavy surf breaks on a long stretch of open coast unbroken by any shelter-giving headlands, the form and handling of the catamaran have been brought well nigh to perfection. In the effective simplicity of its design, in the safety with which it can be launched and brought ashore through the wildest

surf, in the ease with which its parts may be taken apart and carried up the beach and afterwards reassembled, the catamaran is certainly the most serviceable craft for use on a surf-beaten coast. (Madras Fisheries Bureau 1918a: 34–35)

After his fishery investigation of 1908, Hornell wrote of seeing a number of new craft designed by fisher "pioneers" and "innovators" that were ideal for offshore fishing and would "point the way for further development" (Madras Fisheries Bureau 1918a: 40). During Hornell's tenure, the Madras Fisheries Bureau's approach to technological experimentation closely followed the paths hewn by fishers themselves.

Over the period of his directorship, Hornell also drew on his understanding of "traditional" fisher authority in emphasizing the need for fisher representation in both local government and in policy making. His belief in the need for strong fisher organizations that would be in dialogue with the bureau seems to have become an article of faith during his trip to Norway and Denmark in 1920, where he witnessed the cooperation between governments and fishery councils made up of local fisher organizations. After returning from Europe, Hornell began to work toward the evolution of a similar system of departmental accountability in Madras. By 1923, as a result of "representations made by the department from time to time," representatives of fishing communities were nominated as members on several maritime revenue district boards and municipal councils of the Madras Presidency. A few were appointed as honorary magistrates, and one was nominated to a seat in the Madras Legislative Council (Madras Fisheries Bureau 1938: 30). In addition, a fisherman of the Paravar fisher caste, J. A. Fernandez, was appointed as a fisheries administrator, becoming the first of his caste to obtain such a high position in the Madras Presidency's bureaucracy (Madras Fisheries Bureau 1938: 31).

Nicholson and Hornell were quite distinct in their attitudes toward marine fishers, their technologies, and cooperative endeavors, but in other ways they shared an imperial vision of the world within which India was one of many colonial possessions with specific contributions to make toward imperial objectives. Manu Goswami maintains that British colonial state practices were part of an "imperial scale-making project" in that they reproduced a "globally organized British imperial economy" (Goswami 2004: 213). Nicholson was an example of someone whose evaluation of Indian fishers had everything to do with their insignificance to an economy elaborated on an imperial scale. At the same time, the marginal status of fisheries in colonial developmentalism gave the bureau under Nicholson license to experiment with gradualist strategies that echoed Hornell's concerns.

In Hornell we see how an imperial geography could also engender a sense of translocality. His travels and research were certainly facilitated by an imperial system organized around its own reproduction. Indeed, Hornell's work even after his tenure in imperial administration, when he took on fisheries advisory work in Sierra Leone, Mauritius, the Seychelles Islands, Malta, Palestine, Fiji, and Baroda, was arranged by the British Colonial Office. However, Hornell's mental map of the world was patterned as much by the flows of fishing technologies and harvest practices as by any top-down administrative optic. Following the movement of watercraft to corroborate his culture diffusion theory, Hornell went to places as a researcher unconnected to British officialdom: Cyprus, Egypt and the Nile, the Anglo-Egyptian Sudan, Uganda, the Gulf of Aden, and ports along the coasts of Kenya, Tanganyika, Madagascar, Mozambique, and Angola. He firmly believed that coastal societies were porous to oceanic influences and that small-scale fishing was a historically adaptive and dynamic enterprise.[2]

Hornell's interest in indigenous technologies for their histories of use, dispersion, and adaptation to specific ecological niches made his a minority opinion in a turn-of-the-century world suffused by white supremacist ideologies based on a belief in Western technological and scientific superiority. His fascination with technological diffusion and the malleability of cultural practice further distinguished him from a colonial mainstream committed to a framework of hierarchized parallel evolution. The major debates of the period pitted "racists" against "improvers," narrowing the range of acceptable opinion to those who rejected or avowed the ability of the colonized to effectively adopt superior Western science and technology. Michael Adas succinctly summarizes the tautology of this strand of late-nineteenth-century European thought: "Scientific and technological achievements were frequently cited as gauges of racial capacity, and estimates of racial capacity determined the degree of technical and scientific education made available to different non-Western peoples" (Adas 1989: 275). The power of Western technology to effect a "complete moral revolution" in India (Adas 1989: 225) was rarely in question; the only issue was whether Indians were prepared for such a transformation.

By contrast, Hornell subscribed to the idea that maritime cultures were in constant flux through ongoing histories of interaction. Hornell's travels

across the length and breadth of the British imperial system and beyond produced a wealth of ethnographic material on fishing craft, gear, and peoples.
As his biographers put it, "He was constantly seeking clues to the origins of
traditions and designs and looking for evidence supporting the diffusionist
theory of cultural spread" (Heppell and Sherman 2000: 43). Hornell's quest
for patterns of technology distribution and changing histories of use took him
to numerous global destinations.

Hornell's legacy shaped early interventions in marine conservation not
just in territories under his jurisdiction but also in neighboring Travancore,
where measures to conserve fish stocks through regulating the mesh size of
fishing nets were implemented in inland lake fishing. Hornell's initial survey
of the inshore ecology of Travancore's coastal zone prompted later research
on prawns and mullets aimed at assessing breeding patterns and life cycles.
Before and after his tenure as Madras Fisheries Bureau director, he also lent
his expertise to assessing marine ecosystems and advocating developmental
strategies in other princely states, such as Baroda, and in various other British
colonies. In a sense, one could think of Hornell as a cultural transmitter, carrying knowledge of marine fishing strategies across oceanic spaces that were
rendered less navigable by the British imperial system. His directorship did
hew new paths toward what would later be termed biodiversity conservation
and participatory development.[3] However, it was only later in the twentieth
century, after the resource depletion wrought by trawling, that others forging
new translocal imaginaries and conservation practices revived these aspects
of Hornell's legacy. In the interim, the ascendancy of territorial nationalism
and its technocratic imperatives scuttled whatever influence Hornell's oceanic imaginary had on southwestern fisheries development.

The similarities and differences between Nicholson and Hornell reflect tensions within British colonial ideology in the early twentieth century. Thomas
Metcalf points out that, beginning in the late nineteenth century, British administrative theory and practice were defined by both an acknowledgment of
the cultural similarity between Britain and India and an insistence on difference (Metcalf 1995). He argues that Henry Maine, among others, identified
India's "Aryan heritage" as evidence that

> India was implicated with Britain, somewhat paradoxically, in a common ori-
> gin, and yet was fundamentally different. In much the same way, the British
> were, in Maine's view, at once agents of 'progress,' charged with setting India
> on the road to modernity, and at the same time custodians of an enduring In-

dia formed forever in antiquity. . . . Throughout the later nineteenth century, as they constructed their 'India,' the British had always to negotiate this disjuncture: between an acknowledgement of similarity, and an insistence upon difference. The task was never to be easy, nor was the result to be a coherent ideology of rule. (Metcalf 1995: 66)

Nicholson and Hornell's collaboration bears testament to the "rule of difference" of late imperialism. Although widely divergent in their estimation of indigenous technologies and practices of marine harvest, they nevertheless overlapped in their cautious approach to coastal social change in the colony. Nicholson was typical of turn-of-the-century evolutionists. He espoused the universal truth of capitalist democracy yet denied the application of this principle to those outside the history and culture of Europe. Indian fishers, he maintained, could not be as productive or as capable of self-governance as European ones precisely because they were not European. Nicholson fell back on racial notions of India's enduring difference from Europe to deny Indians the ability to forge independent paths to progress or to imitate Europe's civilizational accomplishments. Hornell's directorship, on the other hand, more closely subscribed to a notion of cultural diffusion that acknowledged racial classification but not as a marker of evolutionary hierarchy. For Hornell, machines *were* "the measure of men" (Adas 1989), but European technological achievement did not determine the standard of measurement. Hornell's concern with origins and patterns of diffusion buttressed a conception of race as a complex product of history, geography, and biology. As the ethnographer in administrative clothing, Hornell was open to native practices, and his extensive studies of fishing technologies revealed a faith in the malleability of culture and the interconnections between seeming cultural isolates. As an ethnographer, he possessed a skepticism about universally applicable technical solutions and about the automatic superiority of modern over premodern techniques, a skepticism that was nevertheless rooted in the same notions of racial difference that helped Europeans manage the so-called Orient intellectually and politically.

Although Nicholson and Hornell were far apart ideologically, in practice their development interventions had a remarkable overlap. In the Madras Fisheries Bureau, Nicholson's caution about imposing superior Western technologies on a vulnerable and technologically backward population reconciled with Hornell's faith in the malleability of indigenous technological knowledge and use to produce an approach to fisheries development that was unique for its time. Even in colonial India, the Madras Fisheries Bureau stood apart from the bureaus of the Bombay and Bengal Presidencies in its privileging of community development over industrial production (Reeves et al. 1996).

Protonationalism in the Colonial Bureaucracy

When we compare Nicholson and Hornell with the Madras Fisheries Bureau's third director, B. Sundara Raj, their similarities become clearer. The issue of trawling in Indian waters served as a lightning rod for debates over the pace of fisheries development and the suitability of different harvest methods to both ecology and people. The general consensus before independence was that widespread introduction of trawlers was inappropriate, but there was considerable difference of opinion on why this was so. Parsing out these differences offers the best window onto distinct spatial imaginaries within the same administrative structure.

During his directorship and after, Nicholson continued to oppose trawling as unsuitable economically and socially for southern Indian fishers. His oft-repeated phrase—"Indian fisheries bear about the same relation to British fisheries as a catamaran does to a steam trawler"—encapsulated his perspective on the possibilities of trawlerization. For him, India with its caste structure, its rudimentary craft, and its traditional fishers militated against the rapid transformations associated with trawling.

Hornell's position on the trawling question was more experiential than culturalist. Hornell's objections to trawling were based on an understanding of fisher territoriality and understandings of the relationship between gear use and the marine ecology that cut across colonial contexts. He also put forward more strictly economic arguments against trawling. Writing in 1922, Hornell advocated the use of the Danish seine in place of the proposed steam trawl for exploratory surveys of offshore resources.

> My advocacy of a trial of the Danish seine . . . in preference to steam-trawling is due to an appreciation of four facts, viz:
> (a) that India, and Madras in particular, are not yet ready to consume greatly increased catches of fish owing to the lack of cold storage facilities at the ports where trawlers would have to be based;
> (b) that trawled fish cannot possibly be sold remuneratively at low rates, owing to the high running costs of this type of vessel;
> (c) that the only market capable of absorbing largely increased catches is the low-priced one—the better classes who demand prime fish and can afford good prices are very limited in this Presidency, and

(d) that the present methods of fishing are extremely economical because of the low standard of living of the fisherfolk and the cheapness, simplicity, and comparative efficiency of their gear.

It was lack of appreciation of these fundamental limitations that led the Bombay Government astray over their recent trawling experiments and landed them in a dead loss of three lakhs. (Madras Fisheries Bureau 1918a)

A third position on trawling, one that is representative of an emergent modernizer nationalist strain within colonial administration, was represented by B. Sundara Raj. When Hornell retired in 1923, Sundara Raj took over the Madras Fisheries Bureau as its first Indian director. In Sundara Raj's writings, one sees an incipient national developmentalism couched in arguments about territorial rights and Madras's place among various national fisheries. In this section I quote at length from Sundara Raj's writings to show how a national, as opposed to an imperial, spatial imaginary became tied to developmentalist arguments in favor of trawling. But first, a note about the relationship of nationalist imagination to territory.

Sundara Raj's writings are clearly nationalist in how they forge links between territory and economy and insist on the need to adopt particular policy measures to correct the unevenness of development investment in the imperial system and still remain competitive in an international community of nation-states. In this sense, Sundara Raj is representative of the move to rethink the economy in national terms and to shift policy away from an imperial scale of operation toward a national one. However, one key difference is apparent between the economic nationalists represented in, for instance, Manu Goswami's (2004) work and a person like Sundara Raj. Goswami depicts the territorial imagination of M. G. Ranade, R. C. Dutt, Dadabhai Naoroji, and others as faithful to the contours of British India, whereas the territory of Sundara Raj's nationalist imagination is regional. When Sundara Raj spoke of imperial unevenness, international competitiveness, economic self-sufficiency, or territorial rights, he was most often referring to the Madras Presidency and not British India. I would argue that Sundara Raj, like many others, represents a moment of openness in the late colonial period when nationalist imaginaries were yet to be yoked so definitively to a single form of territoriality. Second, this regional imagining of economy cannot as easily be seen as a by-product of the imperial system. Although one could argue that Madras as an administrative unit was as much an artifact of empire as India, it would be difficult to extend this argument to include the cultural dimensions of regionalism that arguably have a longer duration than the life span of British imperialism.

From his first report as director, Sundara Raj expressed clear opposition to the government's neglect of Madras fisheries and preference for conducting their development on the cheap. In 1923, Sundara Raj requested a trawler and a Danish cutter to explore offshore resources located between Madras and Ceylon. When his request was denied, he used the publication of the bureau's annual report to vent his frustration.

> Early this year the Ceylon Government have bought a trawler for pearl bank inspection and deep-sea fishing experiments in grounds untouched by Ceylonese fishermen, the most extensive of which is the "Wadge Bank" off Cape Comorin which properly belongs to this Presidency as it adjoins India and is about 18 hours steaming from Colombo. The newly formed Fisheries Department of Malay States have prepared an attractive exhibit for the British Empire Exhibition to display the opportunities that exist for the investment of capital and enterprise to develop the valuable Malay fishing grounds with the aid of modern appliances. In view of the great awakening in these sister States the initiation of experiments in deep-sea fishing on modern lines by the Madras Government who have been all along pioneers in developing the fishing industry in India was most opportune. With the acquisition of a full-sized trawler such as I had proposed for the transport of salt, and a new Danish cutter, the Madras Fisheries Department would have been behind no other in India as regards its equipment for deep-sea work. As it is, however, other Governments will exploit the Madras fishing grounds and the Department will be helpless having been deprived of the means of fishing the banks. (Madras Fisheries Bureau 1938: 34)

That Ceylon should have benefited at the expense of Madras, which held territorial rights to the Wadge Bank, was particularly irksome to Sundara Raj, as was the developmental advance of other British imperial fisheries beyond the scope of Madras. At this point, Sundara Raj was arguing very much within the framework of intra-imperial competition that was in full performative display at the British Empire Exhibition. His use of "sister States" such as Malaya was intended to throw into relief the competitive disadvantage of the Madras fishery while expressing the threat of other territorial states to what "properly belongs" to the Madras Presidency. We see here both his sense of imperial location and an understanding of territorial sovereignty that was scaled to the region. Sundara Raj insisted on technological development as a prerequisite not simply for more effective exploitation of marine resources but for the defense of sovereign property, because only deep-sea fishing would allow for the surveillance of the entire swath of the Presidency's marine territory. His frustration with the slow pace of technological advance in his bureau expresses a proprietary stake in Madras that is not echoed in the writings of either Nicholson or Hornell. Although Sundara Raj was fully cognizant of Madras's place within an imperial world, his sense of his own location and administrative purpose was clearly scaled to the territory of the Madras Presidency.

In 1930, Sundara Raj revisited the argument in favor of trawling by first echoing Nicholson's assessments of the Indian fisher, with an emphasis on the caste strictures placed on the developmental future of the industry.

> Fishermen in India are an extremely poor, ignorant and conservative caste. They consequently have neither the initiative nor the capital to develop the industry. The more enlightened and wealthy castes are precluded from entering the fishing profession which is not their parental occupation. Fishing craft and methods have, in consequence, remained extremely primitive in spite of the great strides made in other professions in recent times. The dug out canoe and the catamaran (a raft) are the only fishing craft in the country. On account of the small sized nets and appliances used and the total absence of mechanical power or labor-saving devices, the area fished by local fishermen is the strictly inshore belt of the sea up to an extreme limit of ten miles from the shore. (Madras Fisheries Bureau 1938: 4–5)

Unlike Nicholson's acceptance of the Madras fishery's primitive character, Sundara Raj uses his argument about the impossibility for self-directed development on the part of an inferior caste to oblige the state to intervene with trawlerization to develop the fishery beyond the capacity of its primitive practitioner.

> [The fisherman] now knows practically nothing about the contents and character of our seas outside the ten mile range. Unless similar knowledge regarding the deeper sea beyond is made available to the fisherman, he will obviously never be able by himself in his present state of ignorance and poverty to extend his field of operations or exploit deep-sea fisheries. The whole aim before the trawler is to obtain and make available such knowledge. So far as the department and the Government are concerned, this knowledge of the deep-sea fisheries is the only safe and sure foundation on which any

intelligent and useful scheme of fishery development can be based. (Madras Fisheries Bureau 1938: 1)

Sundara Raj's persistence finally won him his exploratory trawler in 1930. The considerable increase in financial allocation to fisheries that this trawler required elicited widespread criticism as an unnecessary burden on the state exchequer. However, in 1931, the exploratory deep-sea trawler discovered rich fishing grounds in offshore waters, eliciting from a triumphant Sundara Raj a fervent plea for the state to invest in the commercial development of the fishery.

> The fact, however, that the survey by the trawler in such short time should have disclosed fishery resources altogether unsuspected before, is proof sufficient of the appalling ignorance that now exists concerning the off-shore fishery resources of the Presidency. . . . Indications are not wanting that in the wake of the systematic survey of the off-shore fisheries which the trawler has set out to make, will follow momentous developments in the fishing industry which may rush to avail itself of the potentialities thereby disclosed, provided assistance and technical advice are afforded by the State. Such assistance is given even in advanced countries with enlightened, wealthy and enterprising fishermen and trade, and is indispensable in India for the development of the industry under the ignorance, poverty and conservatism prevailing among local fishermen. (Madras Fisheries Bureau 1938: 6)

The contrast between Sundara Raj's and Hornell's reactions to exploratory trawling is striking. Hornell responded with caution to the prospect of trawlerization by pointing to the understandable opposition of fishers to the trawling of inshore waters, and he even incorporated fisher councils into the administrative apparatus of the Madras Fisheries Bureau; on the contrary, Sundara Raj saw the coastal social milieu as one of "ignorance, poverty, and conservatism" that was nothing but a hindrance to the fishery. Here, we see his developmentalist logic scaled up to encompass all of British India and his pejorative assessment of Indian fishers as the obverse of the "enlightened, wealthy and enterprising fishermen and trade" of the "advanced countries."

By 1931, Sundara Raj's argument for greater financial investment in fishery mechanization had become a strongly worded indictment of colonial underdevelopment. Relying both on external references to countries beyond British dominion and on internal comparison with other parts of the empire, he made a protracted argument about the need for the Madras fishery to meet world developmental standards. During the Depression, he wrote:

The world-wide economic depression notwithstanding, the year under re-view has been one of the most eventful in the history of fishery development throughout the world. The modern trend in world development has impor-tant lessons for Madras. Intensive ocean research and exploration of fishery grounds are the outstanding features of the year in all leading countries. Japan has built a research ship "Hakuyo Maru" of 1,300 tons for fisheries training and research; America has launched a 410 tons research ship "the Atlantis" to explore the ocean floor; while the largest research vessel "Challenger" for fishery exploration and discovery of new fishing grounds has been launched by Great Britain. The "Challenger" is an oil-driven vessel of 1,400 tons and was built on the recommendations made by the Committee of Civil Research appointed in 1929, at a cost of 80,000 pounds, and her running expenses at 34,000 pounds a year have been sanctioned by the British Exchequer for the next five years. Further, the Empire Marketing Board in England in collab-oration with the Newfoundland Government has founded two new fishery research stations, the Bay Bulls station, St. Johns, Newfoundland, and Torry station, Aberdeen, Scotland, with their research trawlers, "Cape Agullas" and "City of Edinburgh" respectively, for fishery investigation and research in the northern Atlantic and the Arctic oceans. Besides these leading countries, the advance made by other nations during the year is equally significant. Russia has earmarked a milliard roubles for fishery development in her five years' pro-gram up to 1934; nearly half the amount (41½ million roubles) is to be spent on the construction of steam fishing vessels. Norway, in collaboration with the Ulster Government in Ireland, has launched the world's largest whaler "Kosmos II." Canada has established a new fishery research station at Prince Rupert, British Columbia, for research on the Pacific Halibut fisheries and for the survey of the Hudson Bay fisheries of the Atlantic coast; she has voted 65,000 dollars and the Dominion Government has chartered the sea trawler "Loubryne" for the purpose. The Union government of South Africa has built a new fishery survey and research vessel "Africana" at Aberdeen which was launched on the 23rd September 1930. Egypt has reorganized her Fisheries Department and has adopted for the first time motor-powered vessels on a considerable scale, for working her fisheries. Even Turkey has appointed Dr. J. J. Simpson, a well-known Zoologist who investigated in 1906 the Pearl fish-eries of the Murgui Archipelago for the Indian Government, as her fishery officer to advance her fishing industry and has established a fishery research station in the Sea of Marmora and has provided it with a research vessel. As much for the immediate development of the Madras fisheries, therefore, as for ensuring her steady progress on approved lines in conformity with the rest of the world, the continuance of the modest research that has been commenced by the trawler "Lady Goschen" seems to be the only course indicated and is to be strongly recommended. (Madras Fisheries Bureau 1938: 2)

With spirited indignation, Sundara Raj took pains to lay out the advance of various other countries—Japan, Egypt, Ireland, Norway, Russia, Canada, South Africa, "even Turkey"—over Madras, making pointed reference to the sizable outlay from the British exchequer for exploratory surveys of British seas. One cannot mistake the urgency in his tone: Madras is falling out of step with the rest of the world. This is a significantly different position on the status of Madras than that displayed by either the evolutionist Nicholson or the diffusionist Hornell. Sundara Raj's Madras was not the object of dispassionate scrutiny to be considered analytically alongside other places. Even as he mobilized detailed information on the exact processes of fisheries development being carried out elsewhere, his was ultimately an argument about rights—the rights of a new entrant into the community of nations. His charge against colonial underdevelopment echoed those of his nationalist contemporaries, although he made his passionate arguments from within the steel frame of the colonial bureaucracy.

Fish as Revenue: Technocratic Intervention in National Space

The Political Economics of Nationalism

Manu Goswami has forcefully argued that "in their attempt to envision a nationalist political economy . . . Indian nationalists assembled a strongly autarkic vision of the nation as the natural scale of capital accumulation (Goswami 2004: 280). Nationalists raged against the "drain of wealth" by colonial economic practices, but they also shared with their colonial adversaries a faith in the universalistic promise of development. The key task at hand was not to dismantle developmentalism altogether but to scale it to the nation. Economic practices, however localized, regional, or transoceanic, were to be given new meaning as part of national reconstruction.

As early as 1860, the Indian intelligentsia's hope that British rule would help industrialize and modernize India, building it into a mirror image of the imperial metropole, had given way to the belief that what colonialism had actually produced was the underdevelopment of India's economy. Even as they accepted modern industry as a vital component of national progress, early nationalists identified the colonial ideology of free trade as the primary cause of Indian underdevelopment. In opposition to nineteenth-century economic orthodoxy, which maintained that the unfettered circulation of capital was imperative to economic growth, nationalists argued that colonial free trade was the key *obstacle* to Indian development, which instead was ruining Indian handicrafts, transforming India into a source of raw materials, and forcing India's infant industries into premature and unequal competition with the large-scale industries of Britain.

The discursive production of an "Indian economy" crippled by the immoral overlay of colonialism was a key impetus to Indian nationalism (Goswami 2004). By the early twentieth century, the overwhelming majority of Indian leaders had joined the ranks of opposition to foreign capital, declaring with near unanimity that it would not encourage but rather replace and suppress Indian capital, keeping India in a state of eternal economic dependence on Britain. They argued that just as Britain had protected its industries in the early phase of industrialization, so would Indian development depend on self-rule by a state acting on behalf of the nation, not in the interests of empire. Only an independent Indian state would protect its indigenous industries until they were modernized and could stand up to foreign competition. Political independence, they maintained, must thus be buttressed by economic independence from the global capitalist economy. As part of the process of decolonization, a protectionist state would delink India's economy from world capitalism and lead the country to true economic development (B. Chandra 1993: 62–70).

This early emphasis on an economic nationalism founded on territorial closure and indigenous capitalist development was reflected in the planning process in the lead-up to independence. Toward the end of 1938, the Indian National Congress party instituted the National Planning Commission (NPC). By this time, however, the growth of socialist thinking within the Congress Party and the Gandhian emphasis on village democracy complicated any neat correspondence between political independence and state capitalism. The socialists decried the concentration of wealth inherent in capitalist development. The Gandhians insisted on prioritizing spiritual and moral values over ever-increasing standards of living and the growth of luxury.

The final developmental focus on industrialization was a victory for both the socialists and private industrialists in the NPC and a critical loss for the Gandhians. However, the Gandhian legacy was kept alive in planning for the rural sector. Agriculture was to be a space of relative autonomy from state control with its own self-governing institutions and cooperative petty-commodity production. Agricultural land, mines, quarries, rivers, oceans, and forests were defined as forms of national wealth, the ownership of which was vested in the people of India collectively. The cooperative principle was to be applied to the exploitation of these resources by developing collective and cooperative institutions. The state would encourage petty-commodity producers but divest agrarian capitalists and middlemen of their economic and social power (B. Chandra 1993; Frankel 1978). The Congress Party never intended to follow Gandhi to the extent of "villagizing" the administrative steel frame of the developmentalist state that it took over from the British Raj. However, to the degree that the Gandhian legacy did shape planning, the Community Development Program for rural reconstruction was its outcome.

Community Development

The Community Development Program represented the NPC's application of the Gandhian prescription for national reconstruction to rural India. It envisioned the uplift of rural Indians in their own localities, a process that would tap the organic solidarity of the village with its self-governing institutions and principles of "moral economy." The NPC's consensus on maintaining the village as the primary unit of rural development was by no means an easy one to reach. To Indian statesmen, village India represented organic solidarity and moral economy on the one hand and caste authoritarianism, feudal social relations, and a parochial mind-set on the other. These different views of the village split the development debate and polarized the national leadership. In the end, the accommodations of both the pro- and antivillage factional opinions within the Community Development Program made it a peculiarly contradictory set of impulses (Fox 1989; Kantowsky 1980).

Community development was finally formulated as a program that would actualize the potential of the Indian village in a way that colonialism had never permitted. Tarlok Singh, a member of the NPC and an influential advocate of the community approach, noted that the NPC recognized the persistence of caste and vested interests in the village as the "natural characteristics of a comparatively static rural society stagnating under alien rule" (Singh 1969: 21). India had been socially crippled, the NPC maintained, by the British distortion of caste rather than by anything essential to the caste system. With the end of village India's isolation, new social possibilities and avenues of change would be created that were not available during the colonial period.

These deliberations resulted in a community development approach that linked the transformation of the village to the building of the nation. The village would have to undergo changes commensurate with national progress even while remaining the cornerstone of the nation. This process would involve "select[ing] and revitaliz[ing] some of those elements in the existing situation which are capable of making a positive contribution" (Singh 1969: 21). The village community was therefore to be suitably "adjusted" through the establishment of a new scheme of institutions and incentives that would instill a dynamism in those "static" elements of rural society so that they could help meet the needs of national development.

Indian nationalists-turned-statesmen equated self-rule with the end of multiple forms of colonial unevenness: first, the unevenness of metropolis over colony; and second, the unevenness of urban India over rural India. Colonial rule had underdeveloped the Indian village and nation; self-rule would promote the interests of both. The postcolonial developmentalist assumption that India's villages were out of sync with national time and had to be effectively integrated into national space froze them into timeless localities. The Community Development Program followed a logic much like Henry Maine's: The Indian state was an engine of progress setting village India on the road to development; at the same time, it was charged with preserving the moral and social underpinnings of the village. Unlike an imperial imaginary of the village, however, the postcolonial state charged itself with eradicating the unevenness of colonial development by making the village a seamless part of the nation. In effect, postcolonial development spatialized the village as both within and outside the nation: distinct from a purported mainstream but within state territorial borders.

Fisheries Community Development

How, then, did the imagining of economy as properly national and of rural community as properly local shape postcolonial state intervention in fishing? It is in the promotion, transformation, and circumscription of fisheries community development from the 1950s through the 1960s that one sees most clearly a new postcolonial spatiality emerging for marine fishing. National fisheries policy, formulated at the NPC's 1946 gathering, contained all the contradictory impulses of the Community Development Program. Assessing the harvest potential of the Indian Ocean, a government expert committee determined that marine fishermen, whose technologies limited their range and efficiency of operation, harvested less than 20 percent of the marine resource. The committee recommended technological intervention by the state for several reasons: to increase the Indian fisherman's capacity to exploit offshore resources, to raise the fish output for domestic consumption, and to provide a cheap source of protein to the rural poor and to urban consumers. In addition, increasing harvest levels would allow for the export of fishery products and enhance foreign exchange earnings (Tamilnadu State Planning Commission 1972). With the submission of the committee's report, the NPC proposed a dramatic change in fishery technology that would boost catches to levels commensurate with the postulated wealth of the oceans, contribute to the economic development of the country, and help feed its burgeoning population. This was to be an all-India affair, promoted by the central government and adopted with variation in every coastal state.

The NPC's recommendation of rapid technological change for alleviating coastal poverty, raising the Indian fisher's standard of living, and increasing levels of production was justified by perceptions of the coastal population as culturally backward. In a tone strikingly similar to Nicholson's when he first took on the directorship of the Madras Fisheries Bureau, the NPC characterized the existing fishery sector as "largely of a primitive character, carried on by ignorant, unorganized and ill-equipped fishermen. Their techniques are rudimentary, their tackle elementary, their capital equipment slight and inefficient" (Shah 1948). The NPC determined that the poor productivity of indigenous fishing technologies was largely attributable to "coastal culture," itself a product of "social isolation." The incorporation of the coast into a national framework of development was to help in undermining those forms of coastal primitivism that were inimical to social progress.

This radically localized image of coastal fishing erased the world of interconnections Hornell had recognized. The coastal village of the NPC's modernist imagination was one whose parochial nature showcased the universal modernity of the developmental state. Although in some ways similar to Nicholson's portrayal of the coastal village, the NPC's imagined village was nonetheless substantially altered by its territorial container of the nationstate. The change is most clearly seen in the increasing levels of technological intervention since the mid-1950s. For the NPC, the principal charge of the postcolonial developmentalist state was to level the unevenness of colonial rule under a protective umbrella. Although the Community Development Program did invoke a spatial distinction between an industrializing mainstream and rural communitarianism, the aspiration to "a world-class fishery" eventually subordinated difference to sameness. To put it differently, although economic nationalists refused the ideologies of free trade in favor of protectionist development, their imagination of modernity was still global. The philosophy of delinking allowed partial autonomy from a global system of capital but not its associated hierarchies of value. Indian fisheries development was haunted by the specter of its Western counterpart and gradually reoriented around technological mimicry.

From the outset, fisheries community development was beset by tensions between socioeconomic and technological approaches to rural development, each with its own spatial logic. Initially, fisheries development policy followed Nicholson and Hornell in focusing on intracommunity social inequalities, singling out fisher indebtedness to merchants and moneylenders as the key source of fisher "backwardness." The First Five Year Plan (1951–1955) emphasized institutional reorganization toward the more efficient use of manpower as the basis of the Community Development Program. Accordingly, the Tamilnadu Department of Fisheries identified two priorities. First was the building of cooperatives, a scheme that carried over from the colonial Madras Fisheries Bureau and was intended to harness the power of the rural collective. As had been the intention during the days of Nicholson and Hornell, the department's fisheries cooperative societies, which numbered 259 by 1956, provided loans and marketing channels with a view to "eliminat[ing] middlemen" (Department of Fisheries 1962). Following in colonial footsteps, the postcolonial state targeted the middleman as "an alien intruder in the imagined timeless space of a central invention of the 'colonial sociology of knowledge,' that is, the traditional village republic" (Goswami 2004: 63). By exteriorizing the middleman, the state secured its imaginary of the ideal village as a self-contained locality. This did not mean, however, a commitment to village autonomy. The cooperative societies had the additional purpose of localizing the state. As David Ludden remarks in the case of colonial agriculture, "The 'removal of intermediaries' resonates with the language of Munro and Jones, who understood it to mean an increase in centralized state power and rationality. . . . Putting the peasant and state face to face, with no mediating institutions between them, did, however, imply that the state would become part of every farm's operation" (Ludden 1992: 275). Similarly, fisheries community development inserted the state into the everyday life of the fisher through the presence of the cooperative societies. Even in its socioeconomic emphasis, then, state developmentalism undercut the spatial autonomy of the village that the Community Development Program was meant to buttress. The coastal village was now both unquestionably local and only meaningful as a subset of the national state. The life of Henry Maine's "traditional village republic" (1871) depended on state intervention.

The second thrust of fisheries community development was technological. It is in the trajectory of technological development that the fisher artisan emerges as a spatially demarcated entity. Beginning in 1953, the Indian government partnered with the United Nations Food and Agriculture Organization (FAO) to reach the technical objective of fishery mechanization. It is here that we see the most enduring legacy of Victorian evolutionism, now blended with an emphasis on bridging the gulf between postcolonial and Western achievements. It is clear from postcolonial state efforts that technological change within Indian fisheries meant only one thing: the transfer of Western technology that had been tried and tested for efficiency and output. Despite Hornell's developmental legacy, other considerations, such as social and ecological compatibility, were blithely set aside.

The FAO's fish philosophy was neatly encapsulated in a statement at its second annual conference in 1946: "The fishing-grounds of the world are teeming with fish of all kinds. Fisheries are an international resource. In underdeveloped areas, especially, the harvest awaits the reaper" (Food and Agriculture Organization 1985: 63). The FAO's involvement began with the Indo-Norwegian Project for Fisheries Community Development, initiated in 1953 in Travancore-Cochin. The Indo-Norwegian Project was part of the United Nations Expanded Program for Technical Assistance, which had been established as an avenue for postwar reconstruction and development assistance to the newly independent developing countries. The success of the Marshall Plan in the reconstruction of the war-torn economies of Europe was a point of departure for "developed" economies to extend technical assistance in the form of machinery, aid, and expertise to "developing" ones. The UN's technical assistance program, started in 1950 after the report of the First World Food Survey undertaken by the FAO, became the main channel for the direct transfer of knowledge and technology on all aspects of fisheries development and management to the developing world. The tripartite agreement signed in New Delhi between the United Nations, the government of Norway, and the government of India, was the world's first development project of this kind (J. Kurien 1985: A-72). The FAO's intervention in Tamilnadu was the second. These two interventions initiated a general pattern of foreign intervention in fisheries of the global South, and international development assistance soon followed for the countries of Southeast Asia and Africa. By 1981, external assistance to the fishery sectors of developing nations totaled nearly $400 million, a 50 percent increase from 1974 (Bailey et al. 1986: 1269–1275; Food and Agriculture Organization 1954, 1955).

In 1953, FAO experts began work on new mechanized fishing craft for use in southwestern waters. Using two Danish boats, FAO naval engineer Paul Zeiner created a 26-foot mechanized boat prototype, the Pablo, in 1955. G. Illugason, another FAO expert, began experimenting with gear by substituting nylon for cotton thread to weave the gill nets (nets designed to catch fish at the gills by forming a weighted wall either on the seabed or suspended in the water) used by local craft. In 1956, the Pablos were outfitted with Illugason's nylon nets and were incorporated into the subsidy scheme. Anticipating a "mechanization fever" (Department of Fisheries 1956), Illugason recommended the building of an even bigger boat to increase catch volumes. In response, Zeiner built a 30-foot and then a 32-foot gillnetter in 1957, which came to be called the IB (the Illugason boat). In 1958, a third naval architect, P. Gurtner, arrived from the FAO and crafted a new 32-foot trawl boat named the Stern Trawling Boat, or STB. This trawler, designed to catch fish by scraping the sea bottom with a bell-shaped net to catch bottom-dwelling fish, promised a sharp increase in the efficiency of harvest.

In addition to Europeans coming to India, Indians also traveled far for training. To improve fish marketing, the FAO sent an officer of the Tamilnadu Department of Fisheries to undergo training in marketing organization, methods, and techniques at the International Training Center, Hong Kong, in 1954 (Department of Fisheries 1955). The department created a new post, propaganda assistant, to advertise its endeavors. The first person to occupy this post was sent to New Delhi to attend the International Industries Fair, where he could study the latest techniques used by foreign governments, other state governments, and private industrialists in the construction, decoration, and display of exhibits (Department of Fisheries 1962). Upon his return, the department made a concerted effort to publicize the new mechanization program. It began to publish a monthly newsletter in Tamil to educate fishermen on department activities and give them technical advice. The newsletter was distributed through the cooperative societies. The department also dispatched an audiovisual unit to tour the state and exhibit films on fisheries development and other issues of "national importance." This unit toured all the coastal districts and exhibited films in 157 centers; some of the films screened were *Tomorrow Is Ours, Marine Marvels, Fishing for Food, Wealth of Our Water, Project for Plenty, The Case of Mr. Critic, Health for Millions,* and *Villages and Works.* In a twist on the process by which colonized peoples were made objects of a colonial gaze (T. Mitchell 1991; Said 1978), these publicity stunts put modernization itself on display as a spectacle to be consumed and desired. The Tamilnadu Department of Fisheries kept meticulous notes on the size of audiences in different parts of the coastline and stepped up its publicity work in areas where the turnout was meager.

The Spatial Work of Technology

A striking aspect of postcolonial fisheries development was the accommodation of, even dependence on, Western technologies under the rubric of national self-sufficiency. The Tamilnadu Department of Fisheries promotion drive exemplified this approach. It was part of a pan-Indian push for technological modernization. In theaters and villages across India, governments lauded the promise of Western technology for lifting rural Indians out of penury. In this vision of development modernity, technology carried both universalist and culturally specific meanings. Its universality allowed its adoption by India's many social worlds without the taint of foreign dependence. It permitted the insistent claim to the spatial integrity of the village or the nation. On the other hand, it was precisely the foreignness, or Westernness, of the trawler or the dam or the tractor that invested it with national developmental promise. However, through its mediation of technology transfer, the state hoped to translate foreign commodity into national implement, thus maintaining its own centrality as the indispensable instrument of change. To the extent that rural India would engage with the world beyond the nation, it would be through the paternalistic guidance of the national state.

Until 1958, technology transfer was still conducted under the umbrella of cooperativization. All the craft designed by the FAO were to be distributed evenly across the coastal belt to the cooperative societies for collective use by fisher groups. Although the provision of modern scientific inputs for increasing production was a priority, primary emphasis was placed on initiatives for institutional change that could mobilize local manpower and resources for development. The Community Development Program promised to build cooperative institutions for the more efficient use of manpower, to undercut the power of local middlemen and merchants, and to instill an ethic of egalitarianism among fishers. In the final version of the First Five Year Plan, the problem of rural development was identified as the persistence of "certain inhibiting socio-economic factors which prevent the most dynamic forces of the economy from asserting themselves" (Frankel 1978: 95). The plan document argued that lower levels of output depended less on the absence of modern technology than on the exploitative social and economic relations that prevented more efficient use of existing labor-intensive production methods.

This scenario changed with the food crisis of the late 1950s. A comparison with the food crisis of the late nineteenth century is illuminating. Unlike the first crisis, in whose wake the Madras Fisheries Bureau was formed with a strictly non-revenue-oriented focus, the Indian Food Ministry's solution to the 1950s crisis was "a reorientation of agricultural policy to restore the priority for the introduction of scientific inputs over changes in organization as the foremost instrument of increasing agricultural productivity and surpluses" (Frankel 1978: 147). Without the growth of technology and the application of science on a large scale, natural resources, the ministry believed, could neither become fully known nor most effectively be put to productive use (Singh 1969: 339). Communities would have to be educated at the grassroots level and organized to place common and long-term objectives above individual and short-term interests. Education and technology proceeding apace, with education creating the desire for change and technology providing the means to fulfill it, would help preserve and enrich further "the heritage which a community receives in the form of its natural resources" (Singh 1969: 345).

Along with this embrace of technology came a shift from the First Five Year Plan's emphasis on comprehensive, extensive development to the Second Five Year Plan's emphasis on selective, intensive development. The impact of the First Five Year Plan's extensive Community Development Program agenda, planners believed, had been spread too thin and as a result had not gone far enough in developing the intrinsic resources that local communities could mobilize. For the quality of performance to improve in substantial measure, a period of consolidation and concentration of effort had become essential. Areas with favorable conditions for growth would serve first as "test cases" for speedy changes in organization and technology (Singh 1969: 312) and later as points of diffusion to other areas. Across Tamilnadu, the Department of Fisheries constructed training centers at test-case fishing centers to instruct fishermen in the use of mechanized craft and gear. At these centers, fishermen would learn:

(i) Elements of navigation including compass and its uses;

(ii) Upkeep and maintenance of marine diesel engines;

(iii) Fishing gear utility in different types of fishing and modes of operation;

(iv) Theoretical knowledge of fish habits, oceanography, fishing craft and boat building. (Department of Fisheries 1962)

These centers shifted the locus of knowledge from the experience of the fisherman to the scientific expertise of the state, which it had gained through a reconstituted international development regime. This shift reversed the flow of information, making scientific fishing the preeminent form of knowledge. Thus those who spent their daily lives at sea came to these centers to learn how to fish.

The shift from extensive to intensive development underpinned a new political economy of unevenness that, ironically, had been the very object of anti-imperialist critique. Within the rural-urban divide, there was a new division between test-case beneficiaries and rural others, with the test-case beneficiaries more effectively integrated into and representative of national developmental imperatives. However, it was not until the "pink gold rush" of the 1960s that the division between modern fishers and traditional artisans would become rigidly spatialized.

The Pink Gold Rush

What is particularly striking about state-led rural development is its conceit of territorial control that is belied by ongoing transnational experiments in rural development undertaken by missionaries, philanthropists, and other nongovernmental organizations (Sinha 2008). In addition to these not-for-profit transnational linkages unauthorized by the developmentalist state, entrepreneurial activity also transgressed national borders, sometimes cutting against state strategies and at other times paving the way for the state.

One particular entrepreneur catapulted the southwestern coast into global view and shifted the pace of fisheries development dramatically. In 1953, a private merchant in Kerala took the bold step of exporting 13 tons of frozen prawn to the United States. This was followed by a swift increase in American demand for frozen prawn to fill the vacuum left by lost access to China's exports after the founding of the People's Republic of China in 1949. By 1957, five more firms had joined the fray and had exported a total of 458 tons of frozen prawn to the United States. The success of private entrepreneurship and rapidly expanding market for prawn (see Table 1), first in the United States and subsequently in Japan, which had lost access rights to Mexican waters, led in 1956 to a collaboration between the Indo-Norwegian Project and the Central Marine Fisheries Research Institute for an assessment of the marine wealth of Kerala (Mathew 1986). The marine survey led to the discovery that Kerala's waters were some of the world's richest prawn grounds and to a radical shift in the Indo-Norwegian Project's goals to bottom trawling for prawn. From a commodity formerly used to provide manure for coconut palms, prawn rapidly became the "pink gold" of marine exports from India. In 1961, the beach price of prawn was only 240 rupees per ton—even less than the price of mackerel, which was considered the poor man's protein. In 1971, prawn prices reached 1,810 rupees per ton. Between 1971 and 1984, prices increased nearly sevenfold and reached 14,120 rupees per ton.

This rapid escalation in value happened at a time when foreign exchange was crucially needed (J. Kurien 1978: 1561). Through the first postindependence decade, the dearth of foreign exchange to finance India's import bill had remained a major concern, and the central government grasped every possibility to generate earnings. It therefore welcomed with open arms the sudden export potential of prawn. Immediately, the Ministry of Commerce formed what was to become a powerful institution in the fisheries field—the Marine Products Export Development Authority (MPEDA)—for the specific purpose of promoting the export of fish and fishery products.

Nurtured in every way by the state, the export of marine products from India exploded from a meager 15,732 metric tons in 1961 to 75,591 metric tons in 1980 and to 296,277 metric tons in 1995 (Marine Product Export Development Authority 1997: 60, cited in *Outlook*, January 17, 1996). In 1995, marine products were the fourth-largest category of foreign exchange earners in India after gems, cotton, and textiles and had reached an estimated value of more than US $1 billion (*Outlook*, January 17, 1996). By 1973, India emerged as the premier producer of prawn for the world market. Unlike other major producer countries, India exported 100 percent of the catch (Mathew 1986). By 1975, seafood, previously a negligible commodity, became one of India's ten most important exports. By 1983, it was the country's sixth-largest export, and prawn alone accounted for more than 60 percent of the total quantity and 85 percent of the total value of India's marine product exports.

In Tamilnadu, as across the Indian coastal belt, the pink gold rush signaled the subordination of cooperative development for domestic consumption to the export trade in prawn. The earlier emphasis on crafting "new but

Table 1 Export of frozen prawn from India

Year	To Japan			To the United States			Total		
	Quantity (metric tons)	Value (millions of rupees)	Price (thousands of rupees per metric ton)	Quantity (metric tons)	Value (millions of rupees)	Price (thousands of rupees per metric ton)	Quantity (metric tons)	Value (millions of rupees)	Price (thousands of rupees per metric ton)
1953		none		13	N/A	N/A	13	N/A	
1957		none					496	N/A	
1962*	9	0.1	8.9	2,055	9.8	4.8	2,238	10.8	4.8
1966	1,005	11.9	11.9	7,100	69.4	9.8	8,784	88.8	10.1
1967**	2,590	41.6	16.1	7,957	79.8	10.0	11,173	129.8	11.6
1971	11,575	205.3	17.7	9,504	86.7	9.1	23,181	313.3	13.5
1974	19,174	390.3	20.1	12,681	200.3	15.7	34,361	637.3	18.5
1979	36,583	1737.0	47.2	13,117	357.8	27.3	53,511	2,231.2	41.7
1982	37,713	2352.3	62.4	11,256	399.7	35.5	54,625	3,009.7	55.1

SOURCE: Kerala State Planning Board (1969) and Marine Product Export Development Authority (1978, 1984), all cited in Mathew (1986).

* In 1962, the rupee was devalued.

** In 1967, Japan became the main buyer of prawn.

traditional designs" (Department of Fisheries 1958) and building cooperative institutions was rapidly superseded by a new focus on trawlerization by
a government hungry for foreign exchange. The Tamilnadu Department of
Fisheries shifted emphasis to the rapid distribution of subsidized trawling
boats for prawn harvest. The pink gold rush restructured domestic fishing for
monocrop export-oriented production; this was a Blue Revolution to match
the Green Revolution in agriculture.

In accordance with the shift in Tamilnadu fishery policy toward trawlerization, the Indo-Norwegian Project, whose operations had catalyzed the
prawn rush in neighboring Kerala State, extended its operations to Tamilnadu. The project had made two key contributions to Kerala's economy: It
confirmed the existence of vast prawn grounds off the Kerala coast, and it
introduced 30–36-foot trawl boats for prawn capture. More indirectly, the
Indo-Norwegian Project brought Kerala's fishery and its resources into
sharper focus on the world market (Mathew 1986). As a result of the Indo-
Norwegian Project, prawn exports in Kerala took off, with the percentage of
exports to total catch increasing almost 200 times, from 2 percent in 1956 to
91 percent in 1970 (Mathew 1986: 25).

Witnessing the boom, the Tamilnadu government solicited the help of the
Indo-Norwegian Project. A Norwegian skipper conducted deepwater trawling off the Tamilnadu coast and identified rich prawn grounds, after which
the Indo-Norwegian Project took up the construction of trawl boats on the
eastern Coromandel Coast. The first three five-year plans witnessed the construction and distribution of 335 mechanized gillnetters, whereas during the
Fourth Five Year Plan period (1966–1970), the Tamilnadu Department of
Fisheries allocated 200 million rupees, of which half would be provided by
the central government, to increase the tempo of the development program.
The department set a construction target of 1,000 mechanized trawlers, to
be distributed at a 25 percent subsidy. An additional 275 trawlers were to be
built by the district fishermen cooperative federations and financed by the
Agricultural Refinance Corporation. The central government also allocated
38 million rupees for improving landing and berthing facilities and 62 million rupees for the construction of major fishing harbors at Madras and Tuti-
corin on the Coromandel Coast (Department of Fisheries 1971). (See Table 2
for budget data.)

Tamilnadu soon began to compete with Kerala's skyrocketing marine exports. In 1967, exporters shipped 5,438 metric tons of seafood products from

Table 2 Tamilnadu Department of Fisheries budget, 1951–1995

Five-year plan period	Budget outlay (average/year in millions of rupees)
First Five Year Plan, 1951–1956	0.63
Second Five Year Plan, 1956–1961	1.51
Third Five Year Plan, 1961–1966	5.15
Annual plans, 1966–1969	13.25
Fourth Five Year Plan, 1969–1974	21.57
Fifth Five Year Plan, 1974–1978	38.35
Annual plans, 1978–1980	30.66
Sixth Five Year Plan, 1980–1985	72.30
Seventh Five Year Plan, 1985–1990	98.27
Annual plans, 1990–1992	130.99
Eighth Five Year Plan, 1992–1997	207.97

SOURCE: Department of Fisheries, Madras (1988, 1994).

Tamilnadu's ports. By 1993, the volume had increased to 24,336 metric tons, which equaled 10 percent of India's marine exports. Over three decades, the main income earner continued to be prawn, accounting for 59 percent of the export volume and 87 percent of earnings in 1993 (Department of Fisheries 1994). In four decades, marine catches in Tamilnadu increased more than sevenfold, from an estimated total landings of 45,700 metric tons in 1952 to 337,552 metric tons in 1993 (Central Marine Fisheries Research Institute 1995, cited in Mathew 1986).

The prawn rush signaled the massive influx of private capital into fishing. Although regional governments certainly invested in trawlerization, state construction and distribution of trawl boats were soon overtaken in scale by private initiatives. Export merchants became key players in the manufacture, operation, and sale of trawlers. Ironically, they became even more powerful in the fishing economy than they had been before the initiation of postindependence fisheries development, the intention of which had been to undercut their control over India's indebted fisher population.

Development Spatialities

Prawn rapidly crystallized what had begun as a more tenuous spatial divide between villages slated for intensive development and other coastal localities. Trawlerization distinguished those who, through prawn harvest, were vertically integrated into the developmental nation and a world fisheries market from those who, by contrast, appeared ever more localized. The new modern trawling sector stood increasingly apart from fishermen who continued to fish using a wide array of what came to be seen as "artisanal" implements. With its rapidly expanding revenue base, trawling became the darling of state fisheries development, whereas coastal "artisans" remained objects of the Community Development Program. Reminiscent of the earlier colonial era distinction between trade and agriculture-related fishing activity, the unevenness of the coastal belt was now writ large through the association of the trawling sector with export trade and the further circumscription of all other marine fishing as artisanal production for domestic consumption.

The received spatial imaginaries of the coast as locality and oceanic trans-locality took on new meaning with the localization of artisanship and the nationalization of trawling. As it had previously, technological difference underpinned new spatialities, although now lines of spatial difference dissected the coastal belt, often separating artisans from moderns within populations with shared histories of labor, kinship, and faith. In the following chapters, we will see how the various space-making projects of church patronage, caste modernity, and fisheries development impinged on postcolonial Kanyakumari and set in motion new forms of contestation over belonging and rights.

II   Postcolonial Challenges

Figure 4. Women fish vendors on the shore. Photo by Ajantha Subramanian.

4 Community Development to the Blue Revolution

New Technologies, New Shorelines

THE CREATION OF KANYAKUMARI DISTRICT as a separate administrative unit coincided with the beginnings of postcolonial fisheries development. In 1949, the princely states of Travancore and Cochin were merged into one, only to be remapped and renamed in 1956 as part of the Linguistic Reorganization of States. With the reorganization, most of Travancore-Cochin became the Malayali-majority state of Kerala, and the four southernmost Tamil-speaking *taluk*s (revenue districts) were merged with neighboring Madras; the merged area was renamed Tamilnadu (Land of Tamils). These four *taluk*s formed the newly created district of Kanyakumari (see Map 1 on page xvi). With these shifting jurisdictions, the coastal belt of Kanyakumari inherited three spatial legacies: the centuries-long consolidation of church patronage; the making of an inland sphere of caste modernity through the rights struggles of Travancore's agrarian low castes; and the to-and-fro of colonial fisheries development and its competing senses of the coast as locality and translocality.

In this chapter I return to Kanyakumari and the local interplay of these legacies. I look at how the spatial imaginaries of postindependence fisheries development impinged on a landscape of caste difference and church patronage. How did Catholic fishers, rendered increasingly marginal to the consolidation of inland caste power, experience postindependence developmentalism? What did the transition to postcolonial rule mean socially and spatially in Kanyakumari? How did it elicit new articulations of rights?

On the one hand, the postcolonial transition catalyzed a process of incorporation that, in its reach and force, surpassed the scale of princely or colonial power. Although preindependence development brought the state to the coast in the new institutional forms of the cooperative, the fish processing plant, and the temperance officer, the marginality of fishing kept princely and colonial state revenue collection and associated projects of social control to a minimum. Indeed, to hear fishers tell it, one would think that the state was nonexistent on the coast before the 1950s. When I asked older fishermen and fisherwomen about the presence of the state on the coast, I heard little mention of Travancorean rule or of colonial Madras's developmental tutelage, either in positive or negative terms. This lack of intimacy with or even recognition of state officials and practices was in sharp contrast to fisher depictions of the postindependence state, the mention of which always elicited heated discussion. This difference gave me the impression that postcoloniality on the coast had been experienced as the sudden encroachment of the state into a social world previously outside its immediate sphere of influence.

As we saw in Chapter 3, postindependence fisheries development abandoned an oceanic perspective on the coast, preferring instead an image of bounded stasis that justified far more intrusive forms of state intervention. Even so, the first decade after independence witnessed a continuation of the more gradualist approach that characterized colonial fisheries policy. Although new technologies were disseminated, the preference for social over technological solutions to rural poverty ensured some continuity in development practice. It was only with the onset of trawlerization and the escalating value of prawn in the late 1960s that the spatial divide between coast and inland was joined by another shoreline dividing the modern from the traditional sector. As we will see, the state's own status as a developmental actor also hinged on this shift from the Community Development Program to the Blue Revolution in trawling technology.

In some ways, the processes that generated this new shoreline mirror those that made caste moderns out of inland low castes in the nineteenth and early twentieth centuries. Now as then, the entry of new authorities and capitalist transformation of the economy produced shifts in status and forms of social differentiation. However, one distinction between the two periods of change is crucial. In the 1960s, southwestern fishers became subjects of development and postcolonial citizens *at the same time.* The institution of universal franchise in 1947 dramatically expanded the electorate. In South India, enfranchisement had an electrifying effect on the public, with voting percentages reaching 60 percent as early as 1967. The raw data of electoral statistics cannot be taken at face value as an index of political transformation, but the numbers beg interpretive work. What did the franchise mean to people? How did the pairing of development and democracy play out on the coast? How did it alter the makeup of coastal space, in particular, the operations of caste difference and church patronage?

Within the disciplines of anthropology and South Asian studies it has been commonplace to interpret development as an alibi for the excess of state or corporate power or as the elaboration of a global disciplinary regime. A chorus of scholars charge development as imperialism by other means, as the extension of state power, or as the rule of technocrats (Alvares 1992; Apffel-Marglin and Marglin 1990, 1996; Chatterjee 1993; Cowen and Shenton 1996; Crush 1995; Escobar 1995; Esteva 1992; Ferguson 1994 [1990]; Nandy 1988; Parajuli 2001; Sachs 1992; Shiva 1989). Many of these radical critics of development are themselves South Asianists. For instance, Partha Chatterjee has argued that postcolonial state planning "emerged as a crucial institutional modality by which the state would determine the material allocation of productive resources within the nation: a modality of political power constituted outside the immediate political process itself" (Chatterjee 1993: 202). This notion of development as a form of technocratic power that is fundamentally antidemocratic—even antipolitical—obscures the intense political wrangling that goes into both the making of development policy and the elaboration of development practice. As we saw in Chapter 3, developmentalism throughout the twentieth century involved fierce debate over the role of technology in development, the distinction between revenue and social uplift in the definition of development, and the place of the artisan within a global capitalist economy. The course of development was anything but predetermined. Certainly losers and victors emerged in the debates that shaped development policy, but to equate postcolonial development with a derivative form of technocratic governance would surely be to write the victors' history.

Similarly, when we look at development *practice*, we see a highly charged, politically fractious process that, in the postcolonial period, was intimately tied up with the proliferation of new democratic institutions. Development and democracy—the intertwined key words of postcolonial state formation—were more than simply a cynical mantra for the consolidation of state power. As processes elaborated in tandem, they have an intimacy that far exceeds the ideological intentions of states and institutions of global governance (Rangan

1996; Sinha 2003; Sivaramakrishnan 2000). In Part 2 of this book I address this intimate relationship between postcolonial fisheries development, the expansion of institutions of representative democracy, and understandings of political participation.[1] The postcolonial Indian state certainly fused development and democracy rhetorically. But what did these terms mean locally? And to what extent did the two become conjoined for southwestern fishers and other coastal inhabitants?

More specifically, and in continuity with themes explored thus far, I consider the spatial dimensions of the interaction between development and democracy as it unfolded on a preexisting landscape of caste difference and church patronage. As we have already seen, regional histories of caste rendered locally meaningful emerging distinctions between inland moderns and coastal primitives in the preindependence period. Missionary, state, and popular deployments of caste strengthened the political charge of caste as a mode of social and spatial distinction. Catholic church patronage only reinforced notions of Mukkuvar primitivism and of fishers as a population at a spatiotemporal remove from inland society. As we will see, caste and church were equally significant in *post*independence developmentalism. Jim Ferguson, paraphrasing James Scott, notes that developmental states try to establish "national grids of legibility" within which to contain their subjects (Ferguson 2005: 379). These grids, however, are rarely rationalized to the point of total individuation. Mediating structures of authority, sociality, and even preexisting forms of sovereignty can persist within a developmental grid. In the southwest, caste and church were two such structuring principles through which developmental and democratic institutions were established. Indeed, it would be impossible to comprehend emergent meanings of technology, space, or rights without factoring in their mediations.

New Machines, Machineries, and Machinations

Whenever I asked fishers in Kanyakumari about how mechanized craft were introduced into the district, they would tell me the story of Lourdammal Simon and K. Kamaraj. A fairly typical rendition of the story, with a slight village-level twist, came to me from Antony Raj, an elderly fisherman of Manakkudy village.

> At that time, we used only *kattumaram*s and *vallam*s. Kamaraj Nadar was the Congress Chief Minister of Tamilnadu, and he knew the plight of Mukkuvars and wanted to help in changing their lives. So he spoke with Lourdammal Si-

mon, who was the Fisheries Minister in his government. Lourdammal Simon was from Manakkudy village so she first came here to ask whether we wanted trawlers. But we said no. Our parish priest also urged us to accept the government boats, but I think there was fear of what trawlers would bring. So then she went to Colachel, her marital village, and they said yes. That is how most of the trawlers went to Colachel, and it is now the richest village in the district. Maybe we should have agreed to the trawlers and gotten rich ourselves, but look at all the trouble now between Colachel and us. I don't know, I think we did the right thing.

Aside from the clear ambivalence over the pros and cons of trawling and the retroactive construction of a missed opportunity, one striking aspect of this oft-repeated story is its intimacy. Development, by this account, is anything but the impersonal dissemination of new technologies, institutions, or ideas by a distant state. Rather, it works through kinship and patronage, caste and religion—in short, the most localized forms of sociality. Furthermore, the state in these narratives is highly personalized in the figures of Kamaraj and Lourdammal and is held morally accountable to the lives and livelihoods of its constituents. That these two figures most clearly personified the state for Mukkuvars in the 1950s is especially significant and requires some elaboration.

Fishery mechanization was launched in Tamilnadu as part of the Second Five Year Plan (1956–1961) under the Congress Party–led government of K. Kamaraj. Kamaraj was emblematic of the Nadar caste's meteoric rise to social and political prominence in the south. Indeed, he was not only regionally prominent but also regarded as a kingmaker within the Indian National Congress. Narendra Subramanian (1999) observes that Kamaraj exemplified the Congress Party's style of "bureaucratic clientelism." He was an avid modernizer who distributed contracts and industrial licenses associated with Second Five Year Plan projects to habitual supporters and to win over other industrialists. When it came to rural community development programs, such as fisheries development in Kanyakumari, Kamaraj adopted a different tactic. He solicited the support of so-called traditional authorities who could sell the promise of the postindependence state and its programs of rural uplift. Rural India, deemed not quite ready for total transformation, was to engage with the new state through its old authorities. What resulted was a kind of embedded patronage—one could even call it a continuation of indirect rule—with the state overseeing the activities of intermediary patrons.

The general elections had been held just the previous year, and Kamaraj, in true clientelist style, had chosen Lourdammal Simon, a Catholic woman from an elite Mukkuvar family and a prominent member of the Catholic diocese of Kottar, as the Tamilnadu state fisheries minister. Local politicians explained Kamaraj's choice of Lourdammal as a keen electoral calculation. One politician from a rival party summed up sardonically that with this choice, Kamaraj "hit three birds with one stone: gender, caste, and religion."[2] After the 1956 Linguistic Reorganization of States, the Mukkuvars emerged as the second-largest caste group in Kanyakumari after the Nadars. Kamaraj's rivalry with Nesamony Nadar, a leader of the movement to merge Tamil Travancore with Madras State, had split the Nadar vote in the district, making it imperative that Kamaraj win over the coastal population. He therefore overrode Nesamony's own nominee and handpicked Lourdammal Simon for a ministerial post.[3]

Kamaraj's efforts won him the support of both the local and the regional Catholic clergy. Regionally, the Congress Party's promise of support for religious minorities helped assuage the fears of a church that was watching the rise of the "atheistic ideologies" of communism and Dravidianism with alarm. In both the 1957 and 1962 national elections, Catholics were asked by the Tamilnadu Catholic Bishops Conference to vote for the Congress Party— "the party of God" (Narchison et al. 1983: 95). This state-level clerical consensus was also reflected in Kanyakumari. Even before Kanyakumari's merger with Tamilnadu, the groundswell of support for the Communist Party of India in Travancore had set off warning bells in southwestern churches and had consolidated clerical support for the Congress Party. Kamaraj's selection of a Catholic minister only strengthened the Kanyakumari clergy's political allegiance to the party. On the eve of the 1957 elections, the bishop of Kanyakumari's Kottar diocese sent out a circular requesting the faithful to exercise their franchise by electing candidates who would fight for freedom of religion, for the rights of private schools and colleges run by minority religious institutions, and against birth control—in short, for the Congress Party (Narchison et al. 1983: 97).

The landscape of religious patronage into which the Congress Party entered in 1956 was also a caste landscape. On the Kanyakumari coast, Catholicism was inseparable from Mukkuvar caste affiliation, and the Congress Party's insertion into regional dynamics meant much more than the state's avowed protection for Indian religious minorities. For local elites, both lay and clergy, Lourdammal Simon's selection signaled Kamaraj's acknowledgment of Mukkuvars as a politically significant caste (*Then Oli*, 1956, cited in Narchison et al. 1983: 97). They interpreted the Congress Party's rhetoric of developmental patronage as the long-awaited integration of Mukkuvars into inland caste dynamics.

However, the development technologies that came to underpin notions of Mukkuvar caste uplift were far from even in their spread. Within the caste, family played a key role in spatializing development. Minister Simon set about implementing the mechanization program across Tamilnadu with particular attention to her home district of Kanyakumari. The original intention of fisheries community development was to ensure an even spread of subsidized craft. As Antony Raj noted, however, they were channeled mainly to the minister's marital village of Colachel, coincidentally also a natural harbor in an otherwise turbulent coastline that made it a good test case for the technology. At the time, Simon's husband, A. M. Simon, was president of the State Fishermen Cooperative Society. The year that Lourdammal Simon was elected fisheries minister, the Tamilnadu government decided to constitute the state fisheries advisory board. Of its four nonofficial members, A. M. Simon was one. He was succeeded as Colachel State Fishermen Cooperative Society president by a series of three Congress Party loyalists, which secured Colachel's reputation as the local darling of state fisheries developers.

The choice of Colachel as the district's test case for fisheries development was justified by the shift from extensive to intensive development in the Second Five Year Plan. The village's privileged place within the district and its unique relationship to the state gradually became evident. Kanyakumari District's Fisheries Training Center was opened in Colachel, in a part of the village that was newly named Simon Colony (after Minister Simon's husband). Soon after the opening of the center, the Tamilnadu Department of Fisheries also began planning for harbor construction in the village. Out of the twenty-one Illugason gillnetters allocated for intensive fishing operations in Tamilnadu as a whole, Colachel's cooperative society received two. In the same year, the Tamilnadu government decided to import nylon nets from Glasgow to distribute to fishermen at 25 percent off the original cost. Of the sixty-five nets received by the end of 1957, Colachel secured twenty-four. Also in 1956, the government bought "terylene" from a local branch of the British Imperial Chemical Industries as a cheaper alternative to Glasgow nylon; Colachel's cooperative society was the only one of the sixteen cooperative societies functioning in Kanyakumari to receive 25 pounds of the material. In 1957, the government distributed across Tamilnadu twenty-six Pablo boats with nylon gill nets at 25 percent off the original cost, of which seven boats went to Colachel (Department of Fisheries 1957, 1958).

Disseminating Technology, Demarcating Space

The escalation of hostilities between Colachel's trawler owners and coastal artisans in the 1990s has effectively obscured the gradual demarcation of spatial difference between mechanized and artisanal modes of harvest. To hear today's fisher artisans tell it, Colachel village was set apart from the rest of the coast from the first moment of its selection as state beneficiary. Furthermore, Colachel's local ascendance has come to encapsulate the regional state's easy alliance with the rich.

At the time, however, the spatial divide between Colachel and the rest of Kanyakumari's coastal villages and the perception of the state as aligned with the wealthy did not arise automatically from the village's role as the locus of intensive development. During the Community Development Program years (1958–1968), the state's emphasis on cooperative ownership of gillnetters, its antimerchant rhetoric and stated commitment to dismantling rural social hierarchies, and the relatively low market price for all fish ensured the perception of fisheries development as part of state welfare for the poor. On the Kanyakumari coast, tensions between the rhetoric of social equalization and the practice of shoring up existing forms of privilege had contradictory effects. Some elites, such as the local clergy and white-collar Mukkuvars, applauded state intervention for its *political* effects, but merchants reacted with alarm to its intended *economic* effects. The state's rhetorical targeting of the middleman merchant as a scourge on rural society had a decisive effect on merchant sentiment. They, at least, seem to have taken the state at its word as a force for wealth redistribution.

As did fishers within Colachel. The village's early exposure to mechanization as a test case of intensive development generated a high level of demand for the new technology. In 1958, when the Kanyakumari District Department of Fisheries first began distributing mechanized gillnetters, most applications came from Colachel, and approximately 70 percent of the craft went to this one village.[4] In addition, the location of the Fisheries Training Center in Colachel gave its villagers the advantage of physical proximity to training programs and district fishery outreach officers. Within the village, too, family had a lot to do with the pattern of distribution. I interviewed all the early recipients of gillnetters who were still alive in the late 1990s. All underscored the importance of kin networks in satisfying the five-person requirement for acquiring a gillnetter for collective ownership. Typically, fishermen would seek out relatives by blood or marriage to make up their five-person group. They would pool their resources to meet the required down payment of 500 rupees and then work out an arrangement for sharing use of the mechanized boat.

When I met them, the overwhelming consensus among these early beneficiaries of state development was that cooperativization had been a disaster. They narrated lurid tales of deceit, avarice, and neglect that destroyed their dream of social mobility. The most common story was of one or two among the owner group of five conspiring against the rest to secure full ownership of the gillnetter. Forty years hence, they contrasted their own failed aspirations with the successes of those who acquired individually owned trawlers in the 1960s and later, mostly from merchant capitalists and not from the state. The message was clear: Shared ownership, even within the parameters of extended family, was unworkable. As a departure from the prevalent coastal model of nuclear family ownership of fishing assets, shared ownership required new understandings of cooperation and trust that ultimately did not take root. All in all, these early beneficiaries represented themselves not as beneficiaries at all but as victims of a foolhardy, shortsighted state scheme. Indeed, most spoke of early state patronage as a liability. They described their situation as "fated" by the coincidence of state-led mechanization with the opposition of the merchant elite and the low price of fish.

It is when we put the two narratives together—the early failure of cooperative mechanized fishing and the hostility of one sector of the local elite—that we get a full picture of what the Community Development Program and the shift to the Blue Revolution meant on the coast. These ill-fated beneficiaries of the Community Development Program started operating their gillnetters in 1958. The substantial catches of the new craft generated considerable tension on the coast, which finally exploded in a clash at sea in 1959. On one side were the *kattumaram* fishermen of Pudur, the next-biggest fishing village east of Colachel, and Colachel's merchant elite; on the other side were the gillnetter owners of Colachel. During the clash, considerable damage was done to the new craft, but the battle was contained at sea. Who were these different groups of fishermen? And why did increased catch volumes lead to violence?

The picture that emerges of the southwestern coastal belt immediately before the onset of fishery mechanization is of a varied productive environment. This ecozone was characterized by the availability of a wide array of fish species, and in Colachel, at the western end of the district, nineteen major varieties of fish were caught up to 1956. Seven of these varieties were pelagic, or surface-dwelling, fish, and twelve were demersal, or bottom-dwelling, fish (Chacko et al. 1957). Harvesting the two types of fish depended on the use of different nets: the pelagic species caught with different surface-setting nets and the demersal species caught with weighted nets or hooks and lines.

The two craft that James Hornell noticed in the early twentieth century— the *kattumaram* (*kattu* = to tie, *maram* = wood) and the boat-canoe, or *vallam*—were the main craft used in the region (Madras Fisheries Bureau 1938: 152). The *kattumaram* is made by tying together three or four logs of light, rough wood with coir ropes. The boat is square at one end; the other end is curved into a conical shape that rises slightly above sea level and forms the stem of the craft. Being light and easy to launch, the *kattumaram* was the most practical craft for the six to eight months of rough seas in Kanyakumari. The *vallam* was used less frequently and was primarily restricted to the calmer season starting in mid-October. The main *vallam* used was the plank-built canoe, which was 26–35 feet in length, could accommodate a maximum of ten people, and was used for launching the *karamadi*, or shore seine net.

The diversity of gear was the most striking feature of the southwestern coast. According to the 1978 fishery census reports, more than forty varieties of nets were used in Tamilnadu (Department of Fisheries 1982). The nets were grouped into three basic types: seine nets, bag nets, and gill/drift nets. Apart from these nets, hook-and-line fishing was also widely prevalent and set this stretch of coast apart from those farther north. Each type of gear corresponded to a specific seasonal use and a particular organization of labor and level of capital investment. The *karamadi* is a drag net pulled from the shore; it cannot be used in the rougher season or on rocky patches of the seabed. It was therefore operated only from September to June, when the sea is calm, and only from parts of the shore off which the seabed is sandy. As noted in Chapter 1, *karamadi* fishing required the greatest number of fishermen— from sixty to a hundred—and the highest level of investment. The bag net, or *thattumadi*, was operated in the inshore areas up to 3 nautical miles, required seven to nine fishermen, and was used in the rough season of the year from the middle of April to October. This net required the second-highest level of investment. Aside from the *karamadi* and *thattumadi*, a wide range of (non-mechanized) gill nets were used, each designed to catch individual species. Gill net fishing was carried out year-round with a crew of two to four men as and when specific species appeared in the coastal belt of the village. Finally, *thoondil*, or hook-and-line, fishing was conducted whenever the sea was calm; it required the least investment and usually involved two or three men (Thomson 1989).[5]

All fishing operations were organized on the basis of shares of the catch and not wages, although the share system differed from one operation to the next. In *thattumadi*, gill net, and *thoondil* fishing, each worker got one share and the owner of the craft got two shares (one for his labor and one for his craft). The owner's share was far bigger for *karamadi* fishing; the owner secured a third of the catch and the workers shared the rest. Most of the village elite either owned *karamadi*s or were merchant middlemen who could rely on a steady supply of fresh fish by advancing loans to fishermen. They were usually closely linked to the parish church and were members of the local governing body, the *oor* (village/parish) committee. As we saw in Chapter 1, they were the village leaders who helped the priests with administrative tasks, and they determined the percentage of catch to be extracted from each production unit as the contribution to the church fund (Narchison et al. 1983; Thomson 1989; Villavarayan 1956).

When the mechanized gillnetters were first introduced through the Colachel Fisheries Cooperative Society, many of these old elites reacted with suspicion, not to the craft themselves but to the logic of collective empowerment behind cooperativization. *Kattumaram* fishermen had other reasons to be hostile. Their main contention was the unprecedented size of the gillnetter catches, which they presumed were emptying their own nets of fish. The first incidence of conflict occurred a year after the gillnetters began operations in Kanyakumari. Upon seeing the catch volumes of the new craft, Pudur's *kattumaram* fishermen decided to intervene. They did not act alone. From Colachel, Barnabas, now one of the wealthiest and most politically powerful trawler owners of the village, gave them his support. At that time, Barnabas was a fish merchant. He responded to the catch volumes of the mechanized gillnetters with alarm, anticipating a fall in prices because of the abundant harvests of the new boats. Merchants such as Barnabas feared that, with state support and access to a new technology, poorer fishermen, who were committed through indebtedness to sell their catch to the merchants, would use their new organizational base in the cooperative society to disobey middleman dictates. It appears that the antimerchant rhetoric of the 1950s state and its commitment to cooperativization did convey a threatening radicalism to rural elites such as Barnabas. Perhaps not surprisingly, it was these aspects of fisheries development that were superseded a decade later by an emphasis on individual private production for export.

After this first confrontation, most of Colachel's mechanized gillnetter owners shifted operation to the harbors of Quilon and Cochin on the west coast of Kerala and to Veerapandiapattanam on Tamilnadu's east coast. This was largely because of the lack of docking facilities in Kanyakumari. Because the district lacked a harbor, the gillnetter owners were forced to anchor their craft at sea and rely on the help of *kattumaram* fishermen to transport men and materials from the shore to the boats. The tensions created by gillnetting made such an arrangement impossible to uphold. Within a few years, many of the original mechanized gillnetter owners reverted to the use of *kattumarams* and *vallams*. The relatively low price at the time for all species of fish, the lack of infrastructural support for the new craft, and their inability to invest money in repairs spelled financial ruin for them. As a result, many owners who had acquired gillnetters through the cooperative society either lost their craft to disrepair or sold them to Kerala merchants and wealthier fishermen.

Other gillnetter owners, however, were able to make the shift to trawling in the late 1960s. These included the prosperous fishing families, merchants, and moneylenders who controlled fish marketing. Bottom trawling had begun in neighboring Kerala as early as 1961 under the auspices of the Indo-Norwegian Project, and Colachel's merchants who operated out of Kerala's harbors saw firsthand the profits from trawling for prawn. One of Colachel's wealthy trawler owners, who used to be a net salesman and merchant, reflected on his introduction to trawling: "In 1961, Velayudhan from Kochi came here to buy gill nets, told us about trawling, and insisted that we accompany him to Kerala. . . . When he left, he took eight of us with him back to Kochi. We were given trawl nets on advance by the export company named Thykudan John and Co. The company took this advance back over a period of profitable catches." This pattern of merchant capital catalyzing new forms of technological use that the state would then incorporate into its subsidy schemes was prevalent across the Indian coastal belt. As in Kerala, trawl net acquisition through loans from private exporters in Tamilnadu was established well ahead of the government's own initiation of trawl boat construction and distribution. Even after it was established, the state's participation in trawl boat manufacture and distribution lasted only until 1974, after which the business passed entirely into private hands. Beginning in 1974, the state took up infrastructure development, subsidy provisions, and some amount of marketing to support the burgeoning trawling sector. It also provided support for mechanization less directly by turning a deaf ear to artisanal fisher complaints of trawler aggression and resource depletion.

In some ways, then, the diversification of harvest and expansion of markets in the fishing economy was conducted much as it had always been: through private and community channels. Apart from its initial foray into boat manufacture, the state remained more an outside patron of the mechanized fisher than a participant in marine fish harvest. From a government-supported cooperativist scheme for the alleviation of poverty, mechanization quickly became a lucrative form of private investment endorsed by a revamped developmental state. As I detail later in this chapter, in the transition from the Community Development Program to the Blue Revolution, the very understanding of what the state was and who it was aligned with changed.

The shift to trawling was significant temporally and, by extension, economically. Trawling opened up the possibility of year-round fishing for prawn and other lucrative species. Unlike artisanal gear, which can catch prawn only during the monsoon months when prawn become a midwater, or semipelagic, species, trawl nets can effectively vacuum the seabed in active pursuit. Although the mechanized gillnetters did increase the efficiency of harvest by speeding up the pursuit of fish, they also were limited to the harvest of pelagic species. By contrast, the operation and mesh sizes of trawl nets, which are much smaller than those of surface nets, overcame the need for using different types of nets in harvesting fish and also permitted the harvest of both adults and juveniles of a variety of species.

As the price of prawn gradually rose throughout the 1960s, more of Colachel's elites, including those who had initially opposed the mechanized gillnetters, were drawn to trawling. By 1966, about thirty Colachel families owned trawl nets, which they operated mainly out of Kerala's harbors. Three years later, the Tamilnadu government's promotion and provision of subsidies for trawling, evidence of rich prawn grounds off the Kanyakumari coast, and the spread of trawl boats to centers on the east coast brought them back to their home sea for part of the year. By this time, opposition from Colachel's merchants, many of whom had in the meantime gone in for trawlers themselves, had died down, but other villagers, especially those for whom the sea adjacent to their villages was rich in prawn, were poised to strike. When Colachel's trawl boats first began operating in the inshore waters of

Kanyakumari District in 1967, twenty-four villages together registered a court case against them. However, A. M. Simon wielded his influence within Congress Party circles and managed to get the case dismissed. Having failed to get their grievances addressed through legal channels, the villagers finally orchestrated an attack on Colachel in early 1970. This second confrontation brought the fight onto the shore and identified Colachel village itself as the symbol of a newly emergent threat. Furthermore, the shift from attacks at sea to an attack onshore was highly significant. Instead of targeting specific forms of fish harvest perceived as undercutting equal rights to a shared resource, the 1970 attack targeted wealth accumulation itself. Artisans set upon the new homes and other possessions of trawler owners, who, caught off-guard, evacuated the coast and sought refuge inland.

Common Property and Violence

To better understand the reasons for the two attacks in 1959 and 1970, and the differences between them, we have to explore the village-level management system that dictated the terms of marine resource access and use and the challenges posed to it by state-led mechanization. Before postcolonial state intervention in fisheries development, the Kanyakumari fishery, like most artisanal fisheries around the world, was governed under the rubric of "common property" (Bavinck 2001b; Berkes 1985; J. Kurien 1991; McCay and Acheson 1987). McCay and Acheson (1987) trace the resurgence of the concept of common property in the literature on natural resource economics to the writings of Garrett Hardin in the 1960s. Hardin's "tragedy of the commons" located the source of ecological degradation in "common property," which he interpreted as the free and unregulated access to scarce resources (Hardin 1968). The basic thrust of Hardin's argument was that freedom becomes tragic: that open access to a natural resource base leads necessarily to its overexploitation because individuals would rather maximize their own use of a shared resource than protect it from overuse. The solution to this inevitable tragedy of the commons, Hardin argued, was privatization, because individuals can be expected to protect only their own property.

In their analysis of Hardin's work and influence, McCay and Acheson maintain that the individualistic bias of Hardin's approach led him and others advocating privatization to misrecognize the structure and practice of common property. The thesis of the tragedy of the commons, they argue, "fails to distinguish between common property as a theoretical condition in which there are no relevant institutions (open access) and common property as a social institution (the commons)" (McCay and Acheson 1987: 8). Common property, McCay and Acheson contend, is not the same thing as institution-free open access, and to equate the two ignores the presence of regulatory institutions that manage use of collectively shared resources. In actual common property situations, rights of use are determined by a variety of factors, such as technology use, residence, or social identity. Common property thus refers to an exclusive and an inclusive notion of the commonwealth involved. It refers to specified sets of use rights based on some degree of legal or customary agreement, which itself presupposes social concern and conflict over the use of common resources. McCay and Acheson pinpoint this misrecognition of the inclusivity *and* exclusivity of common property as the source of the assumption that common property users need the intervention of an external authority to facilitate the proper management of resources through the allocation of individual use rights. They conclude that the acceptance of the Hardin scenario by state planners and developmental policymakers alike has polarized local communities and states because states refuse to acknowledge and accommodate institutions and norms governing local access and use, preferring instead to superimpose a codified system of individual private property rights.

McCay and Acheson identify the absence of "community" as the key problem in Hardin's analysis. Hardin, they point out, assumed only a collection of individuals using a common resource. He did not recognize the existence of communities that dealt with conflicts and ecological problems associated with the commons by creating and enforcing rules about their use. John Kurien, an analyst of the southwest coast fishery of India, concurs. He points out that the premechanization code of common property governing the southwestern fishery had built-in barriers to access: technical barriers, such as the need to have fishery-specific skills and the need to use technologies acceptable to the collective of fishers; and social barriers, such as the caste basis of fishing, which prevented free entry of capital and individuals from outside fishing communities into the fishery (J. Kurien 1993).

Much as on other parts of the Tamilnadu coast (Bavinck 1997, 1998, 2001a, 2001b, 2003), the jurisdiction of marine space in Kanyakumari rested on an understanding of the relationship between village territory and marine space. A village's marine territory encompassed the section of sea adjacent to village land. This territory was an arena of village *governance* but not of village *ownership.* Because marine common property came under village jurisdiction, the parish council was authorized to dictate what kinds of gear could be used within its marine space; however, its authority did not extend to the outright denial of access. Typically, if a fisherman used gear considered harmful, he was charged a monetary fine and forbidden from continuing to use that particular gear by the governing members of the village committee. Such prohibitions were uniformly applied both to fishermen from the host village and to outsiders using the village's marine space. The universality of such rules underpinned a system of reciprocity that allowed fishermen in pursuit of mobile species to enter different village marine spaces without hindrance, provided that they obeyed the use rules of that particular village authority.

The Tamilnadu government's introduction of mechanized boats radically challenged the existing rule system governing the use of marine common property. With the goal of enhancing marine fish production, the state sponsored and subsidized the operation of a far more efficient and unaffordable technology of harvest. Furthermore, it misrecognized the fine-grained institutional mechanism already in place to govern the use of the marine resource. The spatial effects of such an intervention were profound. State sponsorship of trawling deterritorialized fishing by endorsing the unregulated mobility of trawlers across marine common property spaces governed by village-level authorities.

Why did postcolonial fishery officials take no measure of existing local institutions and the possibility of a hostile reaction to the new technologies? Several explanations emerge from conversations with Tamilnadu fishery officials. First, they expected that artisanship was a dinosaur that would become extinct with time. Second, they assumed that the allure of profits from trawling would hasten this outcome as artisans opted to join the mechanized sector, first as laborers and later as owners. Third, they expected that trawlers would ply waters beyond the reach of artisanal craft, thus preventing a head-on confrontation. As it turned out, however, their temporal and spatial assumptions were proved wrong. Artisanship persisted despite the introduction of trawlers, and some villages even banned the purchase of trawlers outright as a violation of local rules of gear use. Apart from the social and technological ills attributed to trawling, the suitability of *kattumarams*—virtually unsinkable, highly efficient for crossing the rough southwestern surf, and easily fitted with a variety of gear and other technical innovations—ensured their continued preponderance in the district.[6] And rather than travel into offshore waters, trawlers preferred to ply inshore waters rich in prawn and other valuable species.

In his analysis of changes undergone by the California fishery in the early twentieth century, Arthur McEvoy argues that mechanization fundamentally changed the character of fishing. "Fossil fuels," he points out, "enabled Californians to tap new fisheries resources whose wealth the . . . fishers of the late nineteenth century could scarcely have imagined" (McEvoy 1986: 124). McEvoy's analysis of California partly resonates with the postindependence fisheries revolution in Tamilnadu. As they did in California half a century earlier, fossil fuels and trawl nets did extend the range and harvest potential of fishing craft. These advantages permitted mechanized boat fishermen to seek out marine life in a larger expanse of sea and consequently to be less dependent on the resources of a particular water space. However, as McEvoy points out, another production requirement—regular access to prime fishing grounds—replaced the declining reliance on a small territory. If denied a significant proportion of the sea spaces they use, mechanized boat fishermen face serious economic trouble. In postcolonial India, these prime fishing grounds teeming with export species were located squarely within the inshore sea, *not* in the offshore waters accessible by mechanized craft. Trawler owners thus used their newfound mobility to travel not to offshore fishing grounds but across coastal inshore commons. Unregulated access to inshore resources became essential to mechanized fishermen's production needs and central to their political agenda. Initially and to the extent that they operated from harbors dominated by trawling craft, such access was not a problem. When they traveled to coastal areas of Tamilnadu and Kerala that were dominated by the artisanal sector, however, they found themselves subject to rules that ranged from outright bans on trawling to the application of rigid territorial and temporal restrictions on the use of trawl nets.

Maarten Bavinck (2001b) has shown that "'harm' is not a one-dimensional concept for artisanal fishers." Rather, artisanal fishermen "distinguish between three types or indexes of harm: harm to the fish stock, which in turn affects the survival chances of the fishing community in question; harm to the majority style of fishing; and harm to the community as a social entity" (Bavinck 2001b: 133). The first kind of harm relates to the use of gear that depletes fish stocks by causing the fish to flee (as opposed to leading to extinction), so that they no longer inhabit grounds within access to fishermen. The second kind of harm relates to harm caused by a minority style of fishing to the majority style in the context of a shared fishing ground. And the third kind relates to new technology that is perceived to injure the community as a whole, by exacerbating wealth differences and denying equal opportunity among fishers.

Bavinck's insights into the different types of harm defined by artisanal fisher rules of resource access and use on the southeastern Coromandel Coast are strikingly relevant to the Kanyakumari situation. Charles, a Pudur villager and one of the perpetrators of the 1959 attack, has retired from fishing and now runs a small store selling artisanal fishing implements such as hooks and nylon for nets. In the 1950s, he was a member of the village council and a *kattumaram* fisherman with a wife and three girls. Reflecting back on this distant incident, he said: "We attacked the boats mainly because the noise from the motors was driving away the fish. It was also the way they operated. Their gill nets would catch so much fish and leave the sea barren for the rest of us. We all have to eat, you know. Can one man take away what belongs to the whole community? Is that just?" Charles went on to elaborate his own family's particular circumstances as a way of explaining the ill effects of trawling on social relations in the village.

> Charles: At that time, my three daughters were 15, 13, and 10 years old. Everyone knows that your household wealth decreases with each girl child. It has become worse and worse here. Just the other week, a trawler owner from Colachel demanded a crore[7] in dowry. A crore! What are we poorer fishermen to do?
>
> Question: Can you just refuse to pay dowry?
>
> Charles: That is not an option. We'd never get our daughters married. The more trawlers there are, the higher the expectations. Now, even a *kattumaram* fisher demands a huge dowry with a VCR and TV and all kinds of other things. It used to be that teachers or government employees could ask for the most dowry, then anyone who worked in the [Arabian] gulf, then merchants, then everyone else. But now, even to get your daughter married to a poor fisherman, you have to sell your craft and gear. To be the father of a daughter now is to be a poor man. There was a time when people would fall back on the village for help. Now, no one cares because everyone is trying to keep their families fed. Honestly, if I were the father of a son, I would demand dowry too.

In his retroactive assessments of the impact of trawling, Charles knitted together ecological and social consequences. For him, amassing wealth from excessive harvest was corrosive of both resource and village "moral economy,"[8] which used to permit room for the poor. Although it is debatable whether southwestern coastal society ever assured comfort for the poor, fishermen like Charles now invoke the past as a moral template against which to diagnose the ills of the present.

The fishermen who carried out the 1959 attack recollected that they had first tried to impose sanctions at the village level against the new craft, but they finally had to resort to physical violence when the gillnetter owners persisted in using their superior technical power to outrun the *kattumarams*. By the time of the second clash (in 1970), the prawn boom had also established the superior economic power of the trawlers, the state's support for them, and the competition between artisanal and mechanized fishers for prawn in the inshore sea. Initially, with the guidance of their parish priests, the fishermen of the twenty-four villages decided "to obey state law" and seek the mediation of an external authority. However, when they were defeated in the courts by the political clout of Congress Party leader A. M. Simon, they decided to fall back on their superior numbers in the district. By making the unprecedented move of bringing the battle onto the shore, they matched their superior strength on land to the mechanized sector's superior strength at sea and forced the boat owners to flee the coast altogether and seek refuge in the town. Peter, one of the artisanal fishers who attacked the homes of trawler owners recollected the moment that signaled the spatial demarcation of Colachel from the rest of the coast: "We told them that only fisher law worked on the coast, and if they wanted to follow state law, they would have to go into the interior."

Veena Das argues that violence has the capacity to produce boundaries and hierarchies, to change the very language that people use to conceptualize themselves, the Other, and the relations between them. Where boundaries are indeterminate or fluid, violence has the capacity to render them rigid (Das 1990). However, there are different forms that violence can take, and these forms may or may not produce lasting divisions. A case in point is the difference between the attacks of 1959 and those of 1970. The first attack continued long-standing patterns of village-level governance through which perceived harm to resource and community was addressed. Although it identified the perpetrator and assigned a penalty, the first instance of punitive action did not create lasting social division between mechanized and artisanal fishers or spatially separate Colachel from surrounding villages. The second attack, however, had a more decisive sociospatial effect. It crystallized both a social and a spatial distinction that, in subsequent decades, would take on a more rigidly territorialized ecological form. As I show in Chapter 6, the territorialization of artisanal collectivity would ultimately obscure the difference between haves and have-nots *within* Colachel.

That said, even as early as 1970, Colachel was becoming the material and spatial representation of a new mode of production that was distinct from artisanship, and a new class of fishers emerged who stood apart from the wider coastal population. However, this gradual polarization expressed enmity toward an emergent class more than it did an ecological consciousness of community. None of the artisanal fishers who orchestrated the attacks of 1959 or 1970 had an understanding of the exhaustibility of the resource or of mechanized fishing as destructive to it. Rather, theirs was the expression of moral economy based on an opposition to the immoral material advance of a few at the expense of the majority. It was based on a notion of the common good that ruled out unfair competition, but not on a critique per se of technology or development.

Clerical Dreams

In Kanyakumari, the responses of both the Tamilnadu Department of Fisheries and the Catholic clergy to the attacks were remarkably similar. Like the Department of Fisheries, parish priests of coastal villages encouraged fishers to accept the mechanization program as a necessary means to social mobility. When the first attack occurred, they assumed it was orchestrated by middlemen and merchants and carried out by ignorant and jealous *kattumaram* fishers. However, unlike the Department of Fisheries, which condemned the attack, the clergy had a muted response because of the close ties between the church and the merchants. As one priest put it, "We recognized that the attack came out of jealousy, but we were living in coastal parishes where merchants had a lot of power and provided financial support to the church."[9]

Clerical dreams of Mukkuvar caste uplift and wholesale incorporation into the inland polity through state patronage were belied by the course of fisheries development. The question that arises is whether the clergy simply subscribed to state strategies of capital accumulation as the means to social mobility or whether they had a different interpretation of what Mukkuvar "uplift" entailed. Depending on the decade, this question elicits different answers. As we have seen, there were considerable differences between 1950s and 1960s fisheries development. What began in the 1950s as the fisheries community development program for domestic consumption and poverty alleviation became, a decade later, individual, private ownership for commodity export.

For many priests from elite coastal families, 1950s technological intervention signaled an end to coastal penury and a new means to compete with the upwardly mobile castes of the interior. These priests had themselves left fishing for the clerical life, and their theological training in centers far from the Kanyakumari coast had given them a new perspective on their home, one that starkly contrasted the Mukkuvar cultural world with that of upwardly mobile groups. Returning to the coast as religious leaders, they were an educated middle class who were from but no longer simply of the coast.

Over the course of my research, I spoke with many priests about what modern technology had meant to them in the first postindependence decade. I was struck by the centrality of caste to their assessment of the development project and, indeed, of postcoloniality itself. Father Joseph, who served in Kottar diocese from 1944 to 1954 and then again from 1974 to 1984, was particularly candid about how profoundly his experience as a seminarian shaped his attitude toward new fishing technologies.

> I went to the seminary in Pune from Nagercoil in 1938. It was a very difficult time for us, those of us from the coast, because there was a lot of caste prejudice. Most people thought that the fisherman community was too ignorant for the priesthood. It was amazing to me to meet these people who were preaching the gospel and would treat us like untouchables, their fellow seminarians. I suppose such hypocrisy is human. It was when I was there that I realized how little had changed for coastal folk and how much needed to be done. The church can only do so much, you know. When I was in Kottar in the mid-50s, the government finally decided to do something for Mukkuvars by distributing boats. Those of us who entered the priesthood at least have some education. The rest were still so ignorant, poor, and in debt. And they were also so insulated from the world. That's why most of the villages rejected the boats when Lourdammal Simon offered them. She was doing what was best for them but they reacted out of ignorance.[10]

Like Joseph, many Mukkuvar priests translated their own experiences of caste prejudice into support for such projects as fishery mechanization, which they saw as the state's long overdue commitment to fisher caste uplift. For them, education (through the priesthood or otherwise) and trawling were parallel paths to middle-class respectability. Furthermore, Lourdammal Simon represented Mukkuvars' arrival on the stage of representative politics. Another priest, Father Ignatius, commented, "Lourdammal made us feel like we weren't invisible anymore." When the state introduced the mechanization scheme, these priests were quick to identify it as a much needed catalyst for Mukkuvar integration into the national economic and cultural "mainstream" and the long-awaited counterpart in the fisheries sector to the commercialization of agriculture. The development program promised to level older hierarchies and provide an avenue of economic and social mobility for the community as a whole. The clergy therefore embraced the program, spoke of its necessity from the pulpit, and urged their fisher congregations to take up the new technology without hesitation. The development program was proof, they claimed, that the state was finally recognizing the needs of poor Catholics. At long last, poor fishers would experience the social opportunities that the district's Nadar caste had availed itself of over the past century.[11] Fishery mechanization would address coastal marginality by bringing coastal life into step with inland dynamics.

The clergy's equation of the new technologies with state-led caste uplift did several things. First, it mitigated the transnational thrust of the development initiative. Despite the fact that the technologies bore the names of foreign engineers—the Pablo, the Illugason—they were treated locally as state technologies. I most commonly heard the Illugason boat referred to as "*arasangatthoda* IB boat" (the state's IB boat) or "society boat," referring to the village fisheries cooperative societies' role in disseminating the technology. Second, it pegged development to changes in a caste landscape. Caste was the preeminent social category through which Mukkuvars, whether lay or clergy, experienced developmental promises and failures. Just as agrarian modernity translated as Nadar social mobility, so too fishery mechanization translated as Mukkuvar caste uplift. And third, clerical interpretation in the postcolonial period reworked caste mobility as national integration; in other words, the emergent middle-class beneficiaries of state developmentalism came increasingly to be seen by the clergy and by themselves as more nationally oriented than their artisanal counterparts. Western technology that was transferred to the Indian coast through international channels was thus indigenized in a variety of ways through clerical authority; it was linked to state beneficence, to national integration, and to regional caste mobility. By linking fishers to state, nation, and inland, clerical interpretation equated the new technology with coastal incorporation into wider cultural, economic, and political spheres.

Spatializing the State

The state's responses to the two clashes of 1959 and 1970 did have differences. In both moments, the Tamilnadu Department of Fisheries was quick to ex-

plain artisanal opposition to the mechanized gillnetters in terms that justified its development drive. The department's 1959 annual report states: "Although there had been sporadic protests about the use of this gear by persons
with vested interests supported by middlemen fish-merchants, there has been
a great awakening at all fishing centers about the use of this modern gear."
This report and subsequent reports contrast the benevolence of the state to
the oppression of the middleman and attribute resistance to mechanization to
middleman machination. Although it is indeed the case that merchants such
as Colachel's Barnabas were among those who opposed the new technology,
they did not orchestrate the protests as the Tamilnadu Department of Fisheries conveniently assumed to be the case. Unlike its colonial-era predecessor,
the Madras Fisheries Bureau, which recorded the existence of local rules governing resource use that were often deployed to challenge the introduction of
new technology on the grounds that it was disruptive to livelihood, the Tamilnadu Department of Fisheries chose to interpret the protests as animated by
ignorance, jealousy, and elite manipulation.

By the time of the second attack, however, the state's interpretation had
shifted. It was no longer elite manipulation and fisher jealousy that were identified as causes of violence but artisanal fisher resistance to change. Significantly, although the state recognized differences of power within the coastal
population during the early years of the Community Development Program
and saw the program as a means to undercut the power of middleman merchants over indebted fisher artisans, these differences were underplayed with
the onset of the Blue Revolution, whose beneficiaries included these very
elites. Instead, artisanal opposition to the state's investment in an export-
driven development drive became increasingly interpreted by state officials
as a sign of backwardness and resistance to change by fishers trapped in their
traditional ways.

Significantly, neither the Tamilnadu Department of Fisheries nor the
church in Kanyakumari acknowledged the difference between moral economies of harvest and merchant and middleman control over marketing. Unwilling to acknowledge the legitimacy of artisanal fisher opposition to specific
kinds of technological change, the Department of Fisheries and the church
dismissed the attacks as merchant orchestration. Neither the department nor
the church was willing to recognize that the protest could be the outcome of
deliberation based on customary laws that governed access to and use of the
marine resource. The existence of fisher regulation of resource use and access
was overlooked, partly because it was uncodified and therefore unrecognizable

as "law." Rather, the attack was read simply as a spontaneous and visceral reaction against modern technology by a premodern community.[12]

For state officials, the misrecognition of institutionally authorized punitive
action as spontaneous violence had to do in part with the sociology of caste
forged in the crucible of inland caste politics. Typically, Tamilnadu Department of Fisheries officials working in Kanyakumari district were members of
the Nadar or Vellala caste who came to the job of extension officer or department administrator well socialized in caste sentiment. For most, their role as
fishery bureaucrats only confirmed existing prejudices. One extension officer
who worked out of the Simon Colony Fisheries Training Center was a Protestant Nadar whose father had been active in southern Travancore's merger
movement. In a tone that vividly recalled missionary and developmental discourses of a previous era, he told me of his surprise upon visiting the coast.
"I knew that fishermen were cut off from development, but I had no idea to
what degree! It was even more shocking to me that these were Christians who
did not know how to conduct themselves in a civilized manner. One minute,
they are fighting each other to the death over some minor matter. The next,
they are like one extended family. It's difficult to know how to educate such
people about new technology or savings or even health."[13] Several Kanyakumari locals who served in the government bureaucracy admitted to me that
the fisheries sector was widely perceived as a "punishment post" because it
took people to the coastal periphery where they were outside their comfort
zone. Another official assigned to coastal savings-and-loans schemes told me,
"Here, you are at the mercy of their whims. You are on their territory so they
feel that they have the upper hand. It doesn't matter if you are an IAS [Indian
Administrative Service] officer, a fisheries scientist, or a party official. You
can't reason with them because they don't understand reason."[14]

In a 2002 article on how states come to be experienced as spatial enti-
ties, Akhil Gupta and Jim Ferguson argue that states commonly represent
themselves and are experienced through two images: verticality, or as being
"above" civil society, community, and family; and encompassment, as the out-
ermost circle within which those of family and community are encompassed
(Gupta and Ferguson 2002). Although I find their insight into state strategies
of incorporation relevant and useful, the comments of Kanyakumari District
Department of Fisheries officials point to another strategy that at first glance
seems at odds with state hegemony: the ability of the state to spatialize itself through absence. Official depictions of the coast as a space beyond rea-

son were a way of marking the absence of the state, or more to the point, a form of modern rationality represented by the state. Although Department of Fisheries officials served on the coast, often for decades at a time, they rarely spoke of fishers with familiarity. On the contrary, they seemed invested in maintaining the boundary between the state and its fisher subjects at all costs. Far from encompassment, their insistence that the coast and the state were antithetical spaces suggests other strategies and sentiments at play.

I submit that, at the most explicit level, their comments juxtaposed inland (state) modernity with coastal (nonstate) primitivism, but their arguments also indexed caste sentiment. The same officers who disparaged fishers for their lack of civility also talked to me of their own family histories, how a mere three generations ago, they were treated as untouchables by their caste superiors. "We struggled for our rights, we worked to better ourselves," the savings-and-loans official told me, "and this while the upper castes were kicking us down. My great grandparents were slaves to the Nairs. But nobody gave us our freedom. We won it through struggle. But these Mukkuvars, they don't even realize they are oppressed by their priests. They don't even realize how backward they are."[15] These other stories speak to the specific histories of regional modernity, histories of social mobility and emancipation that are narrated with reference to caste. Going back to Gupta and Ferguson's remarks on state spatiality, we see here how histories of caste service state spatial imaginaries by yoking the state to caste mobility. The Kanyakumari fisheries bureaucracy, then, is spatialized as "above" the coast not simply because of the modernist abstraction of the vertically integrated state but because it is the institutional location of specific upwardly mobile castes.

It is fairly clear that, for inland low castes who populated "the state," the caste divide between coast and inland mapped onto the divide separating the backward fisher from the modern state. To what extent was this spatial imaginary of the state as simultaneously above and absent from the coast shared by coastal inhabitants? Clerical accounts of the 1950s certainly do depict the state as an overarching authority whose power could elevate fishers out of their penury and backwardness. In this sense, the middle-class clergy shared the caste-based spatial sense of their inland compatriots. But how did fishers perceive the postcolonial state? And how did their perceptions of the state and its authority intersect with understandings of the church?

From talking to fishers about the beginnings of postcolonial development, I came to see that the perception and experience of the state and its power were slippery. To everyone, certain forms of state patronage were legitimate and other forms were illegitimate. Beyond that consensus, the fishers disagreed widely on what exactly constituted the state, where it was located, and what it did. The intervening forty years clearly had much to do with how people remembered the immediate postindependence state. To some, the state had always been a source of wealth in league with the wealthy, or quite plainly an extension of inland caste power. To others, it was a benign, distant force unable to contend with the corruption of local power. To yet others, it was an extension of church authority. Significantly, for everyone, the state as either an acultural bureaucratic apparatus or a universal authority just did not make sense. Rather, the state was always populated and always aligned with people and parties. Unlike the church, which they often described as a universal authority that transcended its particular institutional incarnations, the state was always situated socially and spatially.

Although fishers in the 1990s rarely mentioned particular church dictates from the 1950s, they certainly did remember that the clergy played an active role in shaping Mukkuvar attitudes toward the new political parties in their midst. Older Mukkuvar friends I spoke with described the Congress Party in particular as a force that was rendered meaningful only through the mediation of the church. Sitting around one afternoon discussing party politics, I asked a group of older Mukkuvar men what they remembered about the elections of 1957. Aloysius, a resident of Colachel and a retired *karamadi* laborer in his 70s, remembered them as both confusing and clear: "We had never voted before and there was a lot of confusion and chaos in Colachel about where we had to go, what we were supposed to do. I don't remember any choice, really. I just remember people saying, 'You have to vote for the hand [the symbol of the Indian National Congress].' So I did."

Aloysius's friend, John Vincent, added that the parish priest had told them to vote for the Congress Party because it was the only party that would protect Catholics. Older fisherwomen also had vivid recollections of parish priests making routine household visits that were usually used to request church donations or inquire into family matters. This time, however, it was to tell them to vote for the Congress Party.

From these and other recollections, it seems that the Congress Party first took root in the political consciousness of Mukkuvars as the party of the church. Indeed, for most who voted at the time, the Congress Party seemed inseparable from the church because the elites of the parish council embraced it as their party. To return to Gupta and Ferguson's spatial metaphors, the fishers' first sense of the postcolonial state seems to have been of an authority encompassed within the sovereign fold of the church. Congress Party politicians took care to work through existing church institutions and authorities: parish priests, elite-dominated village councils, and prominent villagers such as the Simons who enjoyed both class and religious power.

How did the shift from the Community Development Program to the Blue Revolution affect fisher perceptions of the state? Ironically, the mechanized sector's identity as the darling of the state and the significance of the spatial distinction between artisanal and mechanized sectors crystallized only in the 1970s, when state development intervention in trawling was waning. Although state support for trawling was never in question, private capital drove the mechanization drive far more than did state capital. As had been the case before 1957, the organization of marine fishing never really came within state control. While the Community Development Program years did see the state attempting to guide the transformation of the economy more closely, a mere decade later, control over technology and marketing had reverted to the merchants.

When mechanized fishers talked about the state, they described this shift from the Community Development Program to the Blue Revolution as a transformation in its nature from a poor man's state to a developmental actor. To them, this was a shift in *status*: Through its connection to a merchant elite, the image of the state had been favorably adjusted and its association with the fisher poor cleansed. This was a reciprocal arrangement. The state benefited from its association with merchant wealth, and, through the state, mechanized fishers anticipated the promise of caste modernity. As we will see in Chapter 6, this "expectation of modernity" (Ferguson 1999) continued to be constituted with reference to regional history, even when it took more overtly national forms.

As for fisher artisans, their sense of the state was one that gradually shifted from its particularization as an extension of church authority to a form of class and caste power to a more idealized depiction as an overarching moral umbrella. By the 1990s, artisanal fishers would rhetorically juxtapose the corrupt state that was socially and spatially instantiated in local power hierarchies with the moral state that transcended the vicissitudes of local politics. Indeed, as we will see in the Conclusion, their spatial imagery would eventually supplant the church with the state as the primary patron of the artisan.

Figure 5. *Vallam* with outboard motor. Courtesy of South Indian Federation of Fishermen's Societies, Trivandrum, Kerala.

5 Projects of Intermediacy

Regionalism, Artisanal Territory, Appropriate Technology

THE MOST COMMON REFRAIN I HEARD from fisher artisans in the 1990s when I asked about their attitude toward trawling was "As long as they stay outside our zone, it's fine. It's when they come within 3 miles of shore that there is trouble." Claiming the 3 miles closest to shore as artisanal territory has become a key ingredient of antitrawling politics since the 1983 Tamilnadu Marine Fisheries Regulation Act was introduced. The 3-mile zone, established at the regional state level, spatialized artisanship as a new form of territoriality rooted in common property.

Another common refrain from artisanal fishers when I asked about political party affiliation was "I vote for the ADMK." Like much of the rest of Tamilnadu State, the Kanyakumari coast in the late 1960s swung massively in favor of regional parties with roots in the Dravidian movement, a trend that has continued to this day. The DMK (Dravida Munnetra Kazhagam, or Party of Dravidian Uplift) and its offshoot, the ADMK (Anna Dravida Munnetra Kazhagam, or Anna's Party of Dravidian Uplift), are two regional parties that, with their message of caste uplift and regional sovereignty, successfully supplanted the Indian National Congress party and consigned national party politics to the wings of the electoral stage. Since 1962, Kanyakumari's fisher artisans have expressed their membership in a Dravidian polity at the ballot box, directly challenging church dictates to vote for the Congress Party.

Coinciding with the legal demarcation of an artisanal zone and following the political shift toward Dravidianism was a technological response to trawlerization. New motorized technologies—products of innovation in transnational circuits of exchange outside the purview of the state—spread rapidly across the southwestern coastal belt in the late 1980s and 1990s. Even as they expanded the parameters of artisanship, the motorized canoes reinforced artisanal claims to the inshore sea by technologically anchoring this domain of common property. In the 1990s, these canoes would take on vigilante operations in the 3-mile zone, becoming the policing arm of the artisanal sector.

In this chapter I argue that these three projects—the embrace of regional politics, the agitation for an artisanal zone, and the use of motorized technology—expressed the desire for intermediacy. Regionalism carved out ground between local and national political arenas and allowed Kanyakumari's fisher artisans to stake claims to supralocal belonging. The 3-mile zone elaborated a form of territoriality between the village and the open sea that anchored artisanship as a form of labor and sovereignty. The motorized canoe was a form of appropriate technology, neither traditional nor modern, that armed this emergent fisher class. Its production within networks that were both within and beyond the nation-state further underscored the intermediacy of this form. Together, all three projects—political, territorial, and technological— produced a supralocal political space that permitted new forms of maneuver.

Projects of intermediacy are but one alternative to the hegemony of national social logics. A more widely considered alternative within anthropology has been cosmopolitanism, the claim to a mobile, cross-border affiliation that eludes capture by national categories and forces (Clifford 1997; Ong 1999). Another anthropological favorite is localism, usually characterized as nonnational, antinational, or antistate in its forms of affective and organizational life (e.g., Escobar 2001; Esteva 1987). Yet another amalgam term is local cosmopolitanism, a blend of mobility and indigenization that allows the extranational, or outside, to become native, or inside, without passing through national parameters (e.g., Ho 2006).

Cosmopolitanism, localism, and local cosmopolitanism attest to the relatively recent and incomplete mode of social and political integration represented by the nation-state, but their privileging of scales other than the national scale often does not capture the real limitations and transformations generated by the nation-state system. By contrast, the three projects that I analyze in this chapter attest to the desire for a middle ground of maneuver motivated *by* the hegemony of the nation-state. There is no question that fishers, priests, and other coastal residents in the postindependence period were forced to grapple with the constraints and possibilities of the nation-state. As I show, however, these projects of intermediacy—regional politics, the reassertion of common property, and the forging of alternative development technologies—interrupted the seemingly predetermined historical trajectories of nationalism, privatization, and developmentalism and in the process expanded the parameters of political space.

A word on how I arrived at intermediacy as this chapter's umbrella term. Intermediacy is a term borrowed from the intermediate technology movement, which was inspired by economist and moral philosopher E. F. Schumacher. As stated on the website of the Intermediate Technology Development Group (ITDG), the outfit that Schumacher started in 1966, Schumacher saw "intermediate technology as belonging between the capital-intensive advanced technologies of the 'West,' driven by large scale production and profit, and the traditional subsistence technologies of developing countries."[1] But for Schumacher and others in the ITDG, intermediacy was not just about inhabiting technological middle ground; it also embodied a political aspiration to forge an alternative path to development that would meet the goals of poverty reduction, environmental conservation, and technology choice. The aspiration for a sociopolitical alternative to the poles of third world poverty and first world wealth drove the ITDG's technological innovation and was generative of that middle ground.

Initially, I had thought to use intermediacy as a framing idea only for the final section of this chapter, which deals specifically with technological innovation and with the ITDG in India. But then it struck me that the ideas motivating experimentation with intermediate technology in Kanyakumari resonated with those behind the embrace of regional politics and the crafting of an artisanal territorial zone. All three expressed the quest for a sociopolitical alternative to localism on the one hand and national or global homogeneity on the other. Building on the ITDG's moniker, then, in this chapter I elaborate on the three meanings of intermediacy: the political desire for an expanded space of rights; the processes through which such a space emerges; and the emergent space itself. In short, intermediacy here indexes aspiration, process, and spatiopolitical outcome.

Regionalism

In the elections of 1962 and 1967, fishers along the Tamilnadu coast voted overwhelmingly for the regional DMK, a political offshoot of the ethnonationalist Dravidian movement that swept the state of Tamilnadu in the 1960s (more on this later). In Kanyakumari, this phenomenon upset the hold of the national Congress Party on the district's electorate. Inland agrarian castes, such as the Nadars, remained staunch Congressites, but fishers threw their luck in with regional parties, once again distinguishing coastal from inland affinities. The sole exception to this new political geography was the village of Colachel. Through this upheaval, Colachel's villagers remained loyal to the national Congress Party—the party of Lourdammal Simon, the party of the Catholic Church, and the party that had provided them with the technological means to social mobility.[2]

Support for Dravidianism generated a new supralocal political arena. Significantly, Mukkuvars produced this space through existing parameters of patronage; this time, however, the chosen patron was not the church or the church's mandated political vehicle of the Congress Party but M. G. Ramachandran, or MGR, as he was popularly known, the rising star of the Dravidian movement. Their choice of MGR was generative of an intermediate political space where Mukkuvars could lay claim to regional belonging and state accountability, exceeding the bounds of church authority and caste marginality.

What was especially startling to those witnessing the coastal turn to Dravidianism was that fishers exercised a political choice at odds with their religious leadership. I spoke with N. Dennis, a Congress Party politician and son of Nesamony Nadar, one of the leaders of the merger movement, who confessed that this was a thoroughly unexpected turn in the electoral politics of the newly carved out district. "We never expected the coast to vote differently," he told me, "especially when the Kottar bishop was still very much a Congress man." In his next comment, however, Dennis dismissed the possibility that the artisanal fisher vote for the DMK could be read as the exercise of citizenship. "It was definitely part of the MGR craze. I suppose the fisherfolk saw MGR as their new savior!" With an amused shake of the head, Dennis conveniently recast fisher agency at the ballot box into simply another form of irrational devotionalism, reinforcing yet again the perceived incompatibility of coastal patronage and political sovereignty. For Dennis, MGR was a new patron who was able to step into the role historically occupied by the church, and the fisher vote by consequence was an act of submission to authoritarian power. When I suggested that perhaps Mukkuvars knowingly voted for someone who they thought might respond to their concerns, Dennis laughed and said, "What do coastal folk know about democracy? In their world, there is only prayer and fish!"[3]

The "MGR craze" marked the political ascendance of film star–politician M. G. Ramachandran to the center stage of Dravidianist politics. The Dravidian movement, which arose in the early twentieth century under E. V. Ramasami Naicker (popularly known as Periar, or Great Leader), had spread its influence throughout the Tamil country by articulating a politics of ethnicity that distinguished the "true" Dravidian sons of the Tamil soil from "outsider" groups, such as the Tamil Brahmins and resident North Indians. Periar launched the movement in the 1930s in response to the dominance of Brahmins in public arenas created during colonial rule, primarily English educational institutions, the bureaucracy, and the Congress Party. His Justice Party launched what Narendra Subramanian calls a "politics of heresy," which accorded the low caste Shudra—the fourth and bottom rung of the caste order described in Sanskrit scripture and mirrored in Anglo-Indian legality—primacy in the Dravidian community (N. Subramanian 1999).

With the formation of the DMK in 1949, Periar's critique of the Brahmin shifted to a critique of bureaucratic clientelism. As Subramanian shows, Dravidianists put forward a brand of "assertive populism" that incorporated groups marginal to the Congress Party patronage network. In contrast to the Congress Party's soliciting of traditional elites—such as landlord castes, religious authorities, and big industrialists—the DMK sought out emergent groups from among the middle strata of castes and tailored its agenda to their cultural identity and economic interests (N. Subramanian 1999).

MGR's appeal to groups whom the DMK's message of assertive populism did not reach was first noticed in 1963, after which his influence spread dramatically. Early in his film career, MGR chose such roles as dispossessed princes who regained their kingdoms to establish moral order, social bandits, mythic warrior-kings, and the heroic deities of lower caste groups. As he rose to political prominence in the DMK, he began to choose roles drawn more from everyday society and less from religious and historical mythology. These roles covered a wide spectrum of occupational and low caste groups, such as peasant, industrial worker, rickshaw puller, and fisherman. In these later films, MGR typically played either a hero who was from plebeian ranks or a wealthy person whose empathy with the poor led him to adopt some of their mores. He championed popular demands, including the provision of land, food, and clothing, protection from usury, provision of higher wages and lower prices, the formation of workers' cooperatives, the introduction of temperance through education and dry laws, and an end to violence against women and the poor. In line with the populist project, these needs were always fulfilled in the films without the enforced redistribution of property. Rather, the hero's victory normally led to the moral transformation of malevolent elites, who did not lose their wealth but recognized the validity of just norms and shared their wealth with the poor (Barnett 1976; Baskaran 1981; Dickey 1993; N. Subramanian 1999).

MGR is widely attributed with seducing the Tamil poor to Dravidianism. Among others, MGR brought fisher castes to Dravidianism. MGR's roles as a fisherman in the 1962 film *Padakotti* (Boatman) and in the 1977 *Meenavar Nanban* (Friend of Fishermen) are commonly thought to have consolidated fisher support for Dravidianism. Beginning in the early 1960s, MGR fan clubs sprang up across the Tamilnadu coast; his fans promoted his films, helped in election campaigns, and became informally affiliated with the DMK. Indeed, one of the first groups to flock to MGR were the fishers of Royapuram, a political constituency of Madras City, where some of the earliest MGR fan clubs were established.

The most common scholarly explanation for the Tamil poor's attraction to Dravidianism echoes the assessment of Congress Party politician N. Dennis. Pandian (1992), for instance, juxtaposes MGR's manipulation of popular cultural icons—his "image trap"—with his antipoor economic policies to argue that the Tamil poor were dupes of MGR's artful magic. Going by the theories of scholars and political elites, we might surmise that the MGR craze is the single reason for fishers' turn to Dravidianism. The logic seems impeccable: Fishermen love films; MGR appeals to them through his films; therefore fishermen vote for his party.

The political cleavage within the Dravidianist front in the early 1970s only reinforced the idea of MGR as the new patron whose hold over the poor in general and over the coastal poor in particular was essentially coercive and antidemocratic. N. Subramanian (1999) describes the tension that led to the 1972 split between the DMK and MGR's newly formed ADMK as that between "assertive populism," aimed at the middle classes, and MGR's "paternalist populism," which attracted poorer social groups. As the DMK had done to the Congress Party, MGR now charged the DMK with elitism and projected his ADMK as the party of the Tamil poor. In a five-year vilification campaign that finally won him the Tamilnadu government, MGR used populist imagery to brand the DMK as a middle-class party that had consolidated its base among socially powerful Tamils and was unconcerned about the plight of the masses.

By the time the ADMK came to power in 1977, riding a wave of support from the poor, MGR's rhetoric had split the meaning of Dravidianism into two: The DMK was the vehicle of middle-class self-assertion, and the ADMK was the party of the poor centered on the figure of a benevolent leader. As a result of this difference in rhetorical emphasis, Subramanian argues, "rivalries between the lower and intermediate strata in many parts of the state were played out in terms of alignments behind either the assertive or paternalist brands of populism" (N. Subramanian 1999: 179).

From the vantage point of political mobilization, MGR certainly did successfully cultivate an image of himself as the patron of the poor. This success, however, does not suggest a seamless mapping of party ideology onto voter subjectivity. Indeed, the notion of a craze or a trap suggests the innate irrationality of nonelite voters whose heads are easily turned by seductive images on the silver screen or by the empty promises of a self-appointed leader. This estimation of their political behavior translates the exercise of sovereignty involved in making an electoral choice into yet another form of social subordination. In the context of the Kanyakumari coast, it further reinforces the distinction between inland sovereignty and coastal patronage on which an inland politics of rights had been founded. Within such a framing, MGR stands in for the Catholic Church in the political arena as an undemocratic authority commanding the absolute loyalty of his fisher constituents.

To read fishers' intentions off political party platforms runs the risk of disregarding their own reasons for turning to Dravidianism and to MGR. Surely one should consider patronage "from below" as well to get the full picture. My own reading of coastal support for MGR does not have him pulling all the strings. Rather, I interpret the artisanal fishers' turn to the DMK and then to the ADMK as the continuation of a long-standing pattern of a coastal politics of patronage. Patronage can encode meanings and relations more complicated than the exercise of top-down authority circumscribing the agency of the client. As it did in the eighteenth and nineteen centuries, patronage can function more dialectically as a mechanism through which loyalty is conditional on the granting of specific rights and privileges. Whereas responses such as those of N. Dennis attempt to localize Mukkuvars as "coastal folk" ignorant of the workings of the world, in their embrace of Dravidianism, Kanyakumari's fishers were actively negotiating terms of engagement within an emergent political configuration. As I show, by supporting MGR, Kanyakumari's Mukkuvars contested their circumscription as mere locals and staked claims to a wider political arena. They set their sights on regional politics for both affective and strategic reasons that cannot be reduced to top-down patronage and, in the process, generated an intermediate space of maneuver.

It is quite clear from the iconography peppering the coast that MGR is the political figure closest to fisher hearts. A decade after his death, I frequently saw photographs of MGR hanging next to household shrines in an intriguing juxtaposition of political and religious devotion. I met Stephen, one of MGR's most fervent fans, in Kanyakumari. He had plastered his walls with film imagery of his hero, had a tattoo of MGR's party symbol, the *irattai elai* (two leaves), on his upper arm, and never tired of narrating MGR film plots and their sociopolitical significance. Stephen had joined the MGR fan club in his village because he loved MGR's films but also because, as he put it, "MGR plays a poor fisherman in his films, not a big boat owner or some other rich guy. Whenever rich people try to get away with something, he's there to tell them they're wrong." Listening in on our conversation, Stephen's friend Vincent, another MGR fan, pointed out that, even in the historical epics where MGR played a king, "he established a just rule where everyone prospered." Both of them agreed that, unlike MGR, Congress Party leaders "never bothered to understand us. They were with the priests, not with the people." Significantly, neither Stephen nor Vincent were of voting age or even politically active during MGR's lifetime. However, for them as for many others, the posthumous resurrection of MGR as action hero, savior, and just king has informed a politics of rights.

Like Stephen and Vincent, many other MGR fans in Kanyakumari adopted the ADMK as *yenge katchi* (our party). MGR's deft fusing of mythical past and political present in his films offered one reason for the allure of Dravidianism to Mukkuvars. Stephen put it this way: "Mukkuvars have always been part of *Dravida Naadu* [Dravidian nation]. You can see that in MGR's films. *Dravida Naadu* grew from the seashore, and fisherfolk were its custodians. We are the original sons of the soil. We were here before the farmers, and the kings, even before the bureaucrats!" Agathammal, a fish vendor in her 80s, echoed this narrative of origins in her response to a different question I asked about where Mukkuvars came from: "Came from? Nowhere! We've always been here, on this land. We don't have a high status but we are the original inhabitants of Tamilnadu." This claim to *Dravida Naadu* is especially striking given the perception of Mukkuvars by most other Tamils as belonging more to neighboring Kerala than to Tamilnadu because of their historical ties to Travancore and the presence of the overwhelming majority of the Mukkuvar caste on the southern Kerala coast.[4]

The sense of cultural rootedness, not just in the coastal locality but in *Dravida Naadu* was shared by many fishers I spoke with. I was curious about when and why this understanding of Dravidian belonging took root on the coast. I started a conversation about it with Father Tobias, a young Mukkuvar priest and a self-proclaimed Dravidianist who grew up in a coastal village, attended a seminary in Pune, and then returned to serve in his home diocese. He began with his own attraction to Dravidianism.

> For me, it means self-respect. We have always been a marginalized caste because of our livelihood and, frankly, because of how the church has historically behaved towards us. Dravidianism rejects the traditional power of high castes and reminds us low castes of our rightful place in the society. Plus, it gives us pride in being Tamil. I think this is why Mukkuvars are now Dravidian loyalists. It has given them a sense of caste pride that they never had before.

When I asked him why the Congress Party had not provided this self-respect, he said with a wry smile, "The Congress has always been the party of the elite, never the party of the people. It was only with the Dravidian parties that we finally felt part of a larger political community."

That even for a priest, the Dravidianist rhetoric of low caste inclusion should ring truer than the Congress Party's overtures to Mukkuvars as religious minorities is significant. For one, it suggests the primacy of caste as the mechanism of social inclusion and exclusion in the southwestern region, a form of social belonging whose parameters have shifted considerably over time but which nevertheless retains its political import. From the early days of their accession to power in Tamilnadu, Dravidian parties have recognized the centrality of caste to regional experiences of discrimination and privilege and addressed it through redistributive mechanisms, such as the implementation of caste-based affirmative action policies that have afforded fishing castes, among others, access to educational institutions and the state bureaucracy.

But I would argue that, for fisher artisans, the allure of Dravidianism was somewhat different from its attraction for their priests. Father Tobias's politics of caste pride comes very much out of experiences of discrimination within the clergy in seminaries still marked by past histories of caste exclusion. His and other priests' turn to Dravidianism is an attempt to carve out a space of maneuver within the priesthood that is underpinned by a middle-class pre-occupation with respectability and representative power as members of the district clergy. Tobias was one of several Mukkuvar priests who founded the journal *Kaniyam*, the term in classical Tamil literature used to refer to the coastal ecozone. *Kaniyam* addresses such themes as the responsibilities of Mukkuvar clergy to their caste congregants, the history of caste within the church and the diocese, and more specific social and political developments on the coast. Father Tobias and other younger Mukkuvar priests have been waging a pitched battle with Nadar and Vellala clergy for representative authority over coastal parishes that, in 1999, resulted in a dissection of Kottar diocese largely along caste lines. Unsurprisingly, and unlike the coastal parishioners whose rights they champion, most of these priests are staunch DMK (as opposed to ADMK) loyalists.

By contrast, it is the ADMK's brand of "paternalist populism," in particular, the party's continuing investment in MGR as patron, that seems to attract Mukkuvar fisher artisans. For Catholic artisans, the paternal authority represented by MGR was something both familiar and intimate. In this sense, Dravidianism represented both an expansion of political space beyond the parameters of coastal Catholicism and a continuity of its idioms and rituals of affiliation. To put it differently, although the choice of a new patron continued a long-standing pattern of coastal maneuver, the embrace of this particular patron (the leader of a political party) expressed a claim to a political space to which Mukkuvars previously had no direct access. Beyond the representational battle of claiming an identity as Dravidians, their link to MGR as film hero, political patron, and now saintly icon allowed fishers to mobilize his name in ways never anticipated by his party.

Let us turn to MGR's coastal fans to get a sense of what MGR meant to them and how they mobilized patronage within their own lives to lay claim to a wider polity. When I asked MGR fans whether MGR had actually done anything to better their lives, Stephen, Vincent, and several other MGR fans insisted that he had. Among the programs mentioned, the noon meal scheme, through which free lunches were provided for children in public schools throughout Tamilnadu, came in predictably for mention, as did the dry laws prohibiting liquor consumption.[5] Rather than seeing them simply as welfare handouts tying them to a benevolent leader, however, those who mentioned these measures offered more complicated understandings of what they meant socially and politically. Fisherwomen, in particular, had a lot to say about MGR's policies.

Therese Ammal, a supporter of the ADMK and a coordinator of one of the microcredit associations functioning in her village, spoke of how much the dry laws helped her battle her husband's drinking habit. "It was MGR who helped me stop my husband from drinking," she told me. Much to our amusement, Therese Ammal regaled me and the other women participating in the discussion with stories of how, when her husband returned home drunk, she would turn to MGR's portrait, beat her chest, and call upon him to reform her husband. With a twinkle in her eye, she recounted how she would wail, "'*Ayya, ayya* [master, master], forgive him. He is violating your law, save him from this sin.'" This plea for MGR's intercession in transforming her husband from a drunkard into a virtuous man attributed to him a near-divine authority, making MGR one of the various saints adorning Therese Ammal's household shrine.

Whatever MGR's actual powers, Therese Ammal's husband finally did succumb to her routine verbal battering and gave up his liquor. What is most noteworthy in her story, however, is how she and a number of other women, fed up with their drunken spouses, banded together and embarrassed the local ADMK party office into shutting down the liquor shop in their village. It was an uphill battle, she told me, "because the party office was getting a nice 'cut' from the liquor shop for looking the other way." Knowing full well that this was the case, the women nevertheless took up positions outside the party office and loudly called on the mortified cadre within to "implement MGR's law." Also noteworthy is Therese Ammal's shaky allegiance to her patron. She told me that, although she continued to vote for the ADMK "because my whole family does," she had parted ways with MGR after 1982 for two reasons: his government's repeal of the liquor ban and his muted response to Hindu nationalist attacks on the Kanyakumari coast that year. In a voice quivering with emotion, she said, "We were suffering so much then. The Hindus had attacked us, poured kerosene in our wells, everything was in chaos, and he barely glanced at us. We are his most loyal supporters, but when we suffered, he did nothing." With resignation, she ended with, "Finally, he was just a politician like so many others, but at least he got my husband to stop his drinking!"

Not only did it change the dynamics of her household, but Therese Ammal's persistent wielding of MGR against her drunkard husband was a stepping-stone to other kinds of supralocal involvements. Having secured her family finances against liquor, Therese Ammal went on to become an active member of a microcredit association functioning at the Tamilnadu state level. She is now one of the association's village coordinators, overseeing the savings schemes of numerous other women, and routinely participates in state-level gatherings where (national and international) microcredit funders, NGO office bearers, and village women hammer out the pros and cons of microcredit policy. Therese Ammal chuckled as she said, "If it weren't for MGR, I never would have fought my husband, and I would have no money to save!"

Yet another instance of mobilizing patronage from below as a means to claiming access to an intermediate political space came to me from Philomene Mary, one of the key organizers of a movement demanding public buses for fish vendors. The stigma attached to fish vending is perhaps the most graphic instance of Mukkuvars' subjection to caste norms that place them on a low social rung. The attitude displayed by inland castes, both high and low, toward Mukkuvar women fish vendors is reminiscent of the ritual taboos preventing inland low castes from entering sanctified upper caste social spaces. The spatial dynamics of women's work undercuts the structural autonomy from agrarian social relations that fisher*men* enjoy. As Kalpana Ram observes:

> Women's work . . . requires of them a continuous task of mediation between the community and the outside world. Older women, who form a small but significant minority of fish traders, work alongside men from other castes and communities in markets and auctions. Even as cooks and childcarers, and in their alliances of marriage and friendship, women's activities carry them not only outside the domestic dwelling but away from the coastal belt into the interior of the district. (Ram 1991: 77)

Compounding the inland caste aversion to the "polluting" labor of handling fish is the censure against fisherwomen for their transgression of gender norms. The stereotypes of women fish vendors as filthy, uncouth, argumentative, and lewd are ubiquitous. Not only are such pejorative assessments of their bodies and behavior insulting, but they also have had serious effects on coastal women's livelihood. Until their demand for special coast-to-market buses with racks for fish vessels was granted by MGR's government, women vendors were routinely denied passage on public transportation. Many older vendors recounted tales of daily struggle to get their fish to the market before it spoiled. Philomene Mary, one of the most outspoken vendors over the age of 45 whom I befriended, was particularly fond of mocking the horrified reactions of well-turned-out young women from the Nadar villages bordering the coast who traveled to Nagercoil for clerical work in the many church-related organizations or even more numerous STD/ISD/FAX (local calling, international calling, faxing) booths.

> If my *mundani* [the fold of the sari that wraps over the shoulder] slips even a little bit, or if my sari is too wet, they start to whisper! They are so young, even younger than my granddaughters. They wouldn't dare to say something to me directly or even look me in the eyes. But they have learned from their parents that they shouldn't be like us, that they are better than us because we have to sweat and carry a heavy load. But their mothers buy our fish to cook! What would they do without us? They would have to eat rice and lentils without any taste.[6]

Ironically, most of the young girls whom Philomene Mary spoke about in half-amused, half-bitter tones are the descendants of those Nadars who fought the famous breastcloth battles of the 1830s and demanded inland low caste women's right to cover their breasts. It is testament to the shifting line of social exclusion that these young Nadar women, aspirants to social respectability and mobility, deride older Mukkuvars for their own uncovered laborers' breasts.

In the early 1990s, Philomene Mary and a number of other women vendors decided to, as she put it, "push our way onto the bus." In doing so, they mobilized MGR's paternalistic rhetoric about Tamil motherhood, camping out in front of the district collectorate and chanting slogans such as "All mothers have rights," "Justice for fisherwomen," "The market is ours too," and "No buses, no fish." Philomene Mary spoke to me about what motherhood meant.

> What does it mean to be a mother? It means feeding your children, giving them life, helping them understand right from wrong. We are poor people. For us, life is a struggle. No one understands this. Motherhood is a struggle. MGR recognized how important mothers are in Tamil culture. Without us, there would be no Tamilnadu. Who would raise the children? Who would feed them? Other mothers can be mothers without struggling, but fisherwomen are different. Look, even the government doesn't want us to be mothers. How can we feed our children without selling our fish? Without getting to the market? They think we are dirty and just want to fight. But really, we just want to feed our children so we have to fight.

After two years of street demonstrations, petition writing, and market boycotts, MGR's party finally granted women vendors buses specially designed for the transport of fish. In granting these buses, the state not only extended new public services to the coast but also built special buses that recognized the unique needs of a coastal citizenry. For their part, women vendors such as Philomene Mary boarded these buses with a newfound sense of ownership. These were *their* buses provided to them by *their* hero's party. The layout of the buses—racks running along one side for the baskets and stainless steel vessels carrying fish and seats along the other side—linked these forms of modern transport unmistakably to a household trade marked by state modernizers for obsolescence.

These instances of mobilizing patronage from below helped carve out an intermediate space within which Mukkuvars enacted new social relationships and imagined new political outcomes. The sense of regional political belonging symbolized by the claim to *Dravida Naadu* fostered new forms of participation not only at the ballot box but also in credit associations and through demands for public services. However, the governmental measure most commonly invoked by both men and women to exemplify their connection to MGR was the 1983 Tamilnadu Marine Fisheries Regulation Act. As with the examples of Therese Ammal and Philomene Mary, this legislation had a double-sided character: From one angle, it looked like top-down patronage that simply reinforced the localization of Mukkuvars; from another, it was quite clearly the result of collective mobilization for rights by MGR fisher loyalists that gave them access to wider political networks.

Marine Territoriality

Coastal states whose marine fisheries have been plagued with inshore conflicts, most often between trawlers and artisanal craft of one kind or another, have resorted to a variety of management strategies, including outright bans on trawling, the creation of trawler-free zones, and the separation of gear groups in space or by time (Bavinck 1997, 1998, 2001a, 2001b, 2003; Mathew 1990; McCay and Acheson 1987). The demand for curbing the activities of the burgeoning trawling sector arose in India in the late 1970s when two decades of unregulated trawling began to result in falling catches. It rose particularly from the National Forum for Kattumaram and Country Boat Fishermen's Rights and Marine Wealth, a representative body of thirteen regional fishermen's unions formed in 1978. In response to the forum's agitations, the central government issued a marine bill in 1980 that established broad parameters permitting further notification by regional state governments. Well before the central government took action, however, Tamilnadu's fisher artisans called in the debt owed to them by the MGR government.

As mentioned, MGR's electoral triumph in 1977, won on the votes of the Tamil poor, is most often seen as a masterstroke by a canny politician adept at crafting his image for mass appeal. However, image makers rarely have complete control over their masterpieces. Four months after the ADMK formed the government in Tamilnadu, simmering tensions between artisanal and mechanized fishers exploded into large-scale riots that shook Madras city and thrust artisanal fishers into the spotlight.

Before and after his ascent to power, MGR had vilified the DMK's role in fisheries development. The DMK's 1967 electoral victory had coincided with the start of trawling in Tamilnadu and the rise in prawn prices in the international market for fisheries products. Once MGR came to power in June 1977, he highlighted the fact that many DMK leaders had bought trawlers with the generous loans granted to entrepreneurs during DMK rule, and he aligned himself in opposition with the artisanal sector.[7] The widespread feeling that the DMK government supported and had been supported by the mechanized boat owners, the steep drop in average artisanal earnings during the 1970s, MGR's opposition to the DMK, and his self-fashioned image as a champion of the poor all contributed to the final climax of sectoral tensions in October 1977.

The hostility between artisanal fishers and the DMK had gradually increased over the ten years since the party's ascent to power. The first statewide artisanal fisher organization was established in 1967 and was linked to the newly formed DMK government. By 1972, the growth in the number of trawlers and recognition of the government-endorsed impunity with which they operated led the organization to dissociate itself from the DMK and establish itself as an independent body. When the National Forum for Kattumaram and Country Boat Fishermen's Rights and Marine Wealth was formed in 1978, the organization joined it.

Even before they dissociated from the ruling party, fisher artisans of the organization began to hijack boats and set them on fire, in response to which trawler owners armed their crews and gave them license to retaliate. To manage the coastal crisis, the Tamilnadu government constituted district peace committees in 1968, which included government officers and representatives from both fisher sectors. A few years later, the Tamilnadu Department of Fisheries included a clause in the hire-*cum*-purchase agreement of boats that restricted their use to a zone beyond 3 nautical miles from shore. In 1972, the Marine Products Export Development Authority initiated a registration system for mechanized boats to make it easier to trace offenders. However, none of these regulations were enforced, and because they applied only to fishermen who had purchased their boats from the state fisheries department, they also left the growing number of privately manufactured trawlers unaccounted for.

The unregulated operation of trawlers led to the 1977 riots, when Madras city witnessed a series of violent clashes between artisanal and mechanized fishers, which finally climaxed on November 24. Unlike previous incidents in which artisanal fishermen clearly only meant to teach the mechanized boat fishermen a lesson, this time they seemed intent on destroying the boat sector as a whole. It was only police intervention that prevented this outcome (*The Hindu*, November 25, 1977).

The intensity of the intersectoral clashes, the active role played by MGR's fan clubs in the violence, and their invocation of MGR as an inspiration in their fight for economic justice reflected a new faith in the representative power of the ADMK. This faith forced the ADMK government to formulate an official policy on trawling that was based on the 1980 marine bill to regulate inshore fishing. In 1983, the Tamilnadu Marine Fisheries Regulation Act came into being. The conflicts of the previous decade largely defined its content. The act provided for "the regulation, restriction, and prohibition of fishing by fishing vessels in the sea along the whole or part of the coast line of the State." The two principal clauses of the act imposed spatial and temporal limits on mechanized fishing. The first clause directs that "no owner or master of a mechanized fishing vessel shall use or cause or allow to be used such fishing vessel for fishing operation in the sea within three nautical miles from the coast line of the State" (Section 5.3). The second clause, which is appended to the main body of the act in a schedule, determines that "the mechanized fishing vessel . . . shall leave the notified place of berth only after 5 a.m. and . . . report back at the notified place of berth concerned not later than 9 p.m."

The act explicitly allows for the possibility of further regulation by government notification. Sections 5.1 and 5.2 provide possibilities for such supplementary regulations. Section 5.1 empowers the government to introduce supplementary regulations on fishing activity in certain areas, during defined hours, or with certain kinds of fishing craft and gear. Section 5.2 specifies the main grounds for such regulations as follows: the maintenance of law and order, the need to protect the interests of a particular group of fishermen, and the conservation of fish stocks.

Territoriality and Property

By forcing themselves into the state's framework as a distinct category of producer requiring specific territorial rights and legal protections, fisher artisans rejected their own projected obsolescence. The 3-mile marker substituted a horizontal boundary for the vertical ones separating villages and became a marker of sectoral identity. The zone as a form of marine territoriality marked the exclusive rights of one set of fishers across the inshore sea, not just in the sea adjacent to their village shore, as had previously been the case. Furthermore, this form of marine territoriality corresponded not simply to village authority but also to state law. As noted in Chapter 4, artisanal attacks on trawlers within the inshore sea dated back to the 1960s. However, in those instances, fishers were continuing a long-standing practice of punishing those whose mode of fishing was forbidden by village authorities. Now, the juridical power to police the inshore sea derived not simply from such long-standing institutional mechanisms but also from state law. Increasingly, village councils adjudicating conflicts over use and access to marine resources incorporated the 3-mile rule into their deliberations. By the time I arrived in Kanyakumari in 1996, the territoriality of artisanship in the 3-mile zone was a fiercely defended right. What had a decade earlier been a relatively noncommittal state effort to address coastal law and order on paper had become an intrinsic ingredient of a spatially elaborated artisanal fisher collective.[8] Indeed, the state's assumption appears to have been that the conflicts would eventually die down as more and more artisans switched to trawling or joined the mechanized sector as laborers. In effect, however, the act exacerbated tensions between warring fishers. Everywhere, fisher artisans saw the 3-mile zone as their territory and therefore subject to their norms. Of course, such norms buttressing the rights of an entire sector had to be elaborated anew because the artisanal sector as a political subject was of a different order than the artisanal villager.

To what extent did the spatialization of artisanal fishing across the 3-mile zone intervene in the projected course of fisheries development? In a 2003 article, Maarten Bavinck offers an explanation for the "spatially splintered state" on the Tamilnadu coast. How, he asks, do we understand "the patchwork nature of state regulations in the marine fisheries sector"? The answer he finds is that, in the arena of marine fisheries, where the state has had a limited presence historically, the state "occupies a relatively weak position vis-à-vis local user groups, and strives to maximize its legitimacy by adapting to local political circumstances. The result is a legal patchwork with strong spatial connotations" (Bavinck 2003: 633).

Considering Kanyakumari as one node of what Franz von Benda-Beckmann calls a "geography of law" (cited in Bavinck 2003: 654), we see that the state has effectively absented itself from adjudicating conflicts by submitting to the outcomes of local negotiations over marine resource use. Although this may be due in part to the weakness of state machinery, I would argue that it is also the result of a lack of state will to take seriously artisanal concerns over resource depletion. State officials did not particularly care that law shaded into custom on the coast because, as far as they were concerned, this did not have a direct impact on capital accumulation. It was only in the 1990s with the escalation of coastal conflict beyond allowable limits that the state stepped in to elect a new peacekeeping authority.

Whatever the cause of state absence, the result was a strengthening of artisanal jurisdiction over the 3-mile zone, a form of territorial sovereignty that was enhanced with the development of intermediate technology. The absence of the state as a regulatory mechanism only enhanced artisanal fisher expectations that the zone was theirs, an arena of a reinvigorated common property that would be sheltered from trawler aggression. As before, access to the marine commons was to be limited to certain agreed-upon forms of technology. However, the zone territorialized artisanship in a way that made it both a more flexible and a more fixed mode of production. In the 1990s, when artisanal territoriality became a weapon in the trawler wars, the absolute distinction between artisanship and trawling made access to the inshore sea contingent on only a single factor: no trawling. This meant that innovations to artisanal craft and gear that may not have previously passed local regulation were permitted access to inshore waters.

But what did Tamilnadu fishery officials think about the pluralistic approach to marine fishing regulation? The architects of the 1983 act aimed to defuse the tension between artisanal and mechanized craft by separating the two groups of fishermen into distinct geographic zones: Artisanal fishermen would work the sea up to 3 nautical miles from shore, and trawlers would carry out operations only beyond this limit. The government's territorial approach to fishery regulation was framed primarily in terms of law and order, with resource conservation and the rights of fisher artisans as lesser priorities. Department of Fisheries officials paid no heed to artisanal fisher complaints of diminishing catches, suggesting official disregard for fishermen regulations and institutions. Department officials quite clearly thought that artisanal fisher codes of common property access and use were based on a mixture of superstition, jealousy, and conservatism and had no "scientific basis" whatsoever. Therefore, they saw no "objective" reason for codifying laws against what fisher councils perceived as destructive technology. The 1983 act, officials emphasized, was just a temporary peacekeeping measure.[9]

The distinction between fisher custom and the law of science, which in 1983 pointed to the inexhaustibility of the resource and the virtue of increasing production limits, is grounded in a perceived cultural difference between the "modern" department and the "premodern" community it governed. In my conversations with them, Department of Fisheries officials constantly invoked the cultural gulf separating them from the mass of fishers in a tone that was almost colonial in nature. They clearly felt burdened by the need to accommodate the volatility and temperamental ways of the fisher population and often referred to them in terms more befitting children. They also had strong opinions about the two-party system in Tamilnadu and its relationship to development. Most spoke bitterly about the 1980s decade of ADMK rule as the period when fisheries development was abandoned for fishermen welfare. R. Rajamanickam, the joint director of fisheries in Tamilnadu, explained that before 1979, all allotment of funds was for "productive schemes," but that in the 1980s, "funds for developmental activity started drying up for political reasons." Beginning in 1979, he said, the department witnessed a slow shift to an emphasis on socioeconomic measures, such as free housing, savings-cum-relief schemes for the lean fishing seasons, and insurance schemes for accidental deaths at sea. This, he stated dryly, "was a political maneuver for cheap popularity," a characteristic, he maintained, of ADMK rule.[10]

Like Rajamanickam, other fishery officials also complained that, after 1980, all "real development" was transferred to the private sector, leaving the Department of Fisheries with the "nonproductive" task of "appeasing poor fishermen with welfare handouts." Another official stated that "before 1980, we were in charge of developing new technology and improving the condition of the coast. Now it's the other way around, and we're just here to listen to the fishers' demands for everything, from money to buy a new net to vaccines for their children. We're all skilled engineers, and we're not using our skills anymore!"[11]

This articulation of a shift in focus from development to welfare, or from "productive" to "nonproductive" measures, obscures the fact that the Department of Fisheries continued to actively promote trawling through related branches, such as the Marine Product Export Development Authority, and to provide subsidies for the private purchase of trawlers, as it did in 1987, 1988, and again in 1992. Significantly, each of these years corresponded to a shift from ADMK to DMK rule. Although the ADMK came to be associated with welfare schemes for the poor and the DMK with production benefits for small capitalists, the DMK also continued to fund the schemes that the ADMK introduced. As Rajamanickam sarcastically put it, "No one dares to withdraw nonproductive schemes. When MGR introduced the noon meal scheme, the DMK opposed it as a cheap ploy to win over the poor. But when the DMK came back to power, they added an egg to the noon meal!"

Fishery officials clearly thought that the Tamilnadu Department of Fisheries deteriorated as a force of development after the mid-1970s. Connected to this feeling was their sense that MGR's rule emboldened artisanal fishers, who now felt entitled to make demands of the government. Not only was development hijacked by the turn to welfare, but also, they maintained, "cheap popularity" subjected the government to the mercy of fisher whims. Being beholden to the poor in this way, most argued, was detrimental to building a strong fishing industry.

In one sense, the complaints of Department of Fisheries officials were accurate. After 1977, artisanal fisher politics was more consolidated and acquired more definition, but this was in spite of and not because of the direction of governmental policy. MGR's various paternalist policies, the 1983 act, and the subsequent fisher welfare measures were intended to pacify artisanal fishers while continuing to pursue capital accumulation through trawlerization. Instead, the policies increased artisanal militancy. By reserving the 3-mile inshore area for the artisanal sector, the government unwittingly redrew territory in sectoral terms and subjected the inshore sea to the rule of a revamped common property. As we will see in Chapter 6, this new form of marine territoriality came to political fruition in the 1990s, when the discourse of environmentalism and judicial recognition of fisher artisans enhanced the militancy of artisanal politics.

The 3-mile zone is another instance of how artisanal fisher spatial practices, elaborated in the idiom of patronage, generated a space of intermediacy between the fishing village and the open sea, in the process changing relations of hegemony. By extracting state legal recognition and then acting on behalf of the state to regulate trawling, Mukkuvars changed the artisanal sector from a developmental subject slated for modernization into a legal subject authorized to defend its territory. In the process, artisans checked the developmental calculus that privileged the trawling sector as the only beneficiary of the state. Significantly, they interpreted the state as a moral umbrella distinct from its incarnate institutions of the Department of Fisheries, the revenue divisional office, and the collectorate. It was this distant state, embodied in MGR, to whom they were linked in relations of verticality, allegiance, and affect—and it was in its name that they acted.

Liberation Technologies

The 3-mile zone was a triumph for fisher artisans, not because it came with governmental teeth but because it established artisanship as a permanent feature of the fisheries landscape, not something to be naturally phased out through industrialization. Furthermore, it anchored the collective of artisans territorially. But the sociolegal classification of the inshore sea as artisanal territory came without enforcement. In part, this was due to the intended decentralization of management written into the language of the 1983 act. More important, however, was the lack of state will. Although the act served as an alibi for the government when faced with artisanal fisher complaints of trawler aggression and dwindling catches, officials did little to actually establish a surveillance system for the 3-mile zone.

By the 1990s, however, fisher artisans were policing the zone themselves. This was largely a result of the widespread use of a new motorized technology developed under the auspices of the church. This "appropriate technology" constituted the third project of intermediacy. The notion of appropriate technology signaled a global disquiet with the trajectory of development modernization, in particular, the vaunting of capital-intensive technologies that exacerbated existing differences in socioeconomic power. Opposition to the state's drive for technological modernity grew in a number of different social spaces, but it took particular form within the Catholic Church. In Kanyakumari, a section of the Kottar clergy with firsthand experience of the widening wealth gap on the coast and exposure to Latin American liberation theology and the Indian communist movement, spearheaded changes in the church's relationship to state developmentalism. Intermediate technology became a fruitful arena for reworking a practical theology. Through their entry into a translocal development arena, Kanyakumari's diocesan clergy tried to challenge state and church orthodoxies by constructing an ethical standard by which to gauge the value of development and ministry.

Indigenization Redux

Although the Dravidianist challenge to national party rule reshaped the political future of the Congress Party in Tamilnadu, the Catholic Church was facing challenges of its own. The 1960s and 1970s marked a period of structural and ideological change for the global church and for the diocese of Kottar. In 1962, the Second Vatican Council began in Rome. Out of this conference came three important documents that reflected the changing perspective of the church. The first, *The Constitution on the Church*, considered the identity of the church. It redefined the church not in terms of its hierarchy of bishops, priests, and religious but as the church of the people of God. It emphasized the equality of its members and the duty of its officers to serve, not be served. Older hierarchies, the document underscored, were not suitable to modern times, neither that raising clergy above laity nor that subordinating the clergy of the poorer nations to those of the more prosperous. The second document, *The Church in the Modern World*, underscored the need to rethink the relationship of the church to civil society and to people of other religions and ideological persuasions. Significantly, the document defined the church not as an institution dedicated solely to spiritual matters but as a body concerned equally with material reality and questions of economic justice. The third document, the *Sacrosanctum Concilium*, addressed liturgical renewal and the need for the adaptation of liturgy to different cultural contexts. It set the guidelines for translating the canon into vernacular languages and for the "inculturation" of Christian worship.

Immediately after the Second Vatican Council, the Catholic Bishops' Conference of India (CBCI) took up the task of liturgical renewal. At its 1966 general meeting, the CBCI set up the Commission on Liturgy. Three years later, at the Second All-India Liturgical Meeting in Bangalore, commission members produced a common declaration: "Our Liturgy should be closely related to the Word of God, the Indian cultural and religious tradition, and actual life situations" (Catholic Bishops Council of India 1969: 242). They sent a twelve-point program for introducing "an Indian atmosphere in worship" to the CBCI and Rome's Consilium for the Implementation of the Constitution on Sacred Liturgy. The program was approved by Delhi and Rome on April 25, 1969.

Why was the CBCI's emphasis on Indianization any different from the church's previous accommodations of native culture? As we saw in Chapter 1, the Catholic Church in India was reputed to be an institution that was, if anything, too accommodating of local norms. From Robert de Nobili, who accepted caste hierarchy as a part of India's "religiously neutral" social structure, to the seminarians who agitated for the ordination of more Mukkuvar priests, caste was accommodated as part and parcel of the Indian Catholic Church. In fact, the creation of Kottar as a native diocese that drew its clergy from within the boundaries of the district represented the success of this earlier moment of Indianization.

But although caste was an accepted part of Indian Catholicism, *class* had remained a nonissue. The key shift in the post–Vatican II climate was the combination of an emphasis on "inculturation of the faith" with that on the "option for the poor." Only in the 1960s did the class question emerge as a key factor in Catholic ministry. The option for the poor called for a different kind of inculturation, one that contradicted the church's long-standing attitude toward native culture. In the Indian context, the key shift in perspective was the choice to identify the poor rather than the elite as representative of India.

Although the Second Vatican Council provided a global mandate for institutional change, it merely lent legitimacy to processes that were already under way. Kanyakumari's Kottar diocese was only one example of a church that had begun to challenge its own forms of ministry and relationship to the laity. Kottar bishop Agniswami's decision in 1954 to terminate the *kuthagai* system, through which the church extracted a certain portion of the daily catch from fishers through the services of an outside contractor, was the first sign of a new, critical approach to the church's feudal role on the coast. By 1960, others had begun to push the church toward opting for the poor.

One of these innovators was Belgian James Tombeur, a priest of the Society of Auxiliaries for the Missions (SAM). SAM was started by Vincent Lebbe in 1925 for the purpose of sending European priests to mission countries to serve under native bishops. Tombeur was the second Samist to travel as a diocesan priest to India, where he arrived on October 3, 1950. By the time I met him in 1996, Tombeur, or Babuji, as he was affectionately called by friends and followers, was a frail man suffering the final stages of Parkinson's disease. I lived for a time in Thirumalai Ashram, a center for activist and clerical organizing. Tombeur had founded the ashram in the 1970s, and it was where he lay bedridden, resolved to die in his adopted country where he had worked in so many ways and for so many years. Our friendship was largely a one-sided conversation, with me narrating the excitements and frustrations of my coastal research to his twinkling eyes. Every once in a while, he would struggle to respond to my queries, but his words were rarely intelligible. It was clear, though, that he delighted in my fascination with fishing and would smile broadly whenever I brought along his autobiography and pointed to sections that I found particularly revealing. Babuji died in 2002, was buried on the grounds of the ashram, and remains one of the most significant figures in the local church and in local fisheries activism.

Tombeur grew up a child of middle-class parents in Belgium where, as he describes it, "the capitalist system in which I was born and educated was not questioned. Rather, it was highly valued and taken for granted. The only other alternative which we knew was atheistic communism which was branded as materialist and anti-religious" (Tombeur 1997: 113). Hard work and competition, Tombeur reflected, were the defining characteristics of this middle class and what set it apart from both the proletariat and the aristocracy. Lebbe's equation of work with service to the poor shook Tombeur's early social education. His arrival in India disrupted it further. By 1985, after nearly four decades of work among the low castes of Kanyakumari, Tombeur was writing as a Christian socialist.

> The present capitalist society is blatantly the opposite of the way of life given by Jesus. It has to be transformed according to an ideology which would respond to the call of Jesus, a society where people would not be divided into classes of oppressors and oppressed, where everyone would be allowed to develop himself/herself fully, where concern for the others would be a reality of daily life. This new society cannot be based on a capitalist ideology; it is better expressed in what we now call "socialism." (Tombeur 1997: 120)

Reading Tombeur's writings, it is clear that he saw development "praxis" as his contribution to building the "true church of Christ." Despite opposition from local leaders and the Kottar priests' conviction that "these people are damned to be drunkards and illiterate" (Tombeur 1997: 43), Tombeur finally convinced a hesitant bishop of the wisdom of starting the Kottar Social Service Society (KSSS).

The KSSS signaled the church's option for the poor. Its primary purpose was to take up development projects among the Catholic poor who fell by the wayside of the state's developmental agenda. However, for most clergymen and -women, this was not an explicitly political calling. Although they affirmed the option for the poor, this did not necessarily translate as a challenge to the structural dynamics that created poverty. Rather than questioning the role of state power and capitalist development in generating class differences, they simply took poverty as a given and directed their attention to providing services for the poor. For them, the KSSS was a religious institution that would extend Christian charity to fill the development gaps left by the state. Their task was to supplement state intervention toward community uplift, not challenge the state's role in creating a class divide. In effect, this perspective maintained the evolutionary bias of development and the value neutrality of technology.

For others among the clergy, however, the KSSS was a vehicle for examining and challenging the power structures of the day, in particular, the nexus between the church, the state, and a trawler elite. This group interpreted the Second Vatican Council's call for the interaction of spiritual and material goals as an invitation to enter into dialogue with previously "forbidden fruit," such as the social critiques of Marxism. By the early 1970s, the circulation of Marxist ideas among an increasingly vocal clerical minority acquired definition. Edwin, a Mukkuvar priest serving in the parish of Kodimunai, started the Kottar Pastoral Orientation Group in 1972 to discuss the positive values in Marxism. He was joined by others such as Pierre Gillet, a Belgian priest and engineer who followed Tombeur to Kanyakumari, and Amirtharaj, a Nadar priest recently returned from his doctoral studies in France. Together, they grappled with church history, the collusion of the church with colonial and native structures of domination, and the meaning and purpose of ministry in a society stratified by class and caste.[12] The experiments they generated ran the gamut from the setting up of basic Christian communities along the same lines as in Latin America, to joining the Communist Party of India, to innovating with new fishing technologies.

Indigenizing Development

In his autobiography, *Led By God's Hand*, James Tombeur describes the work of the KSSS from its founding in 1963 to 1985, when it began distributing motorized canoes from its Boat Building Center, as a process of "indigenizing" development. For him, as for others who entered the development arena in the 1960s, indigenization meant adopting the perspective of the poor as the definitive lens through which "development," and "India" for that matter, was to be understood. In practice, it meant a wide range of choices, from using

Indian instead of English words to name local organizations to involving fishers in the formulation of development projects. It also involved a redefinition of community not in terms of religion or caste but in terms of class.

At the same time, however, clerical critiques of class power did not immediately translate as a critique of technological modernization. Although they questioned the role of the state's Community Development Program in producing class stratification, the clergy sought to correct the class divide primarily through the distribution of capital-intensive technology to those who could not afford it themselves. Tombeur was appointed full-time executive director of KSSS in 1974. Even before his appointment, he took up the directorship of the society's first coastal endeavor: the Indo-Belgian Fisheries Project (IBFP).

In 1963, the KSSS had received the services of a Belgian technician. On the insistence of his fellow priests and nuns, Tombeur and the technician began formulating a plan to experiment with new technologies on the coast. The technician got an old outboard engine and a rubber boat from a private source, and together the two of them began to regularly visit villages, inflate the boat with its 10-horsepower engine, and operate it along with the *vallam*s and *kattumaram*s. Seeing interest among the fishers, they designed a project for engine distribution and repairs to be based in the coastal village of Muttom. To fund this project, the Belgian technician contacted the UN Food and Agriculture Organization (FAO) and the Belgian Freedom from Hunger Campaign. These efforts culminated in 1968 in the second bilateral fisheries development project, the IBFP.

The IBFP took up the unrealized goals of the FAO: introducing nylon nets, motorizing *kattumaram*s, and designing a beach-landing craft. With the help of the Freedom from Hunger Campaign, which paid the customs duty, the IBFP imported a hundred engines from Belgium. One hundred fishermen, each owning a *kattumaram* and a set of nets, received three weeks of special training in use of the motors. A Belgian director, master fisherman, and outboard technician were invited to oversee the training and trials. In economic terms, the project was successful. A 1970 study of fifty motorized and fifty nonmotorized *kattumaram*s revealed that, in one year, the gross income of the fishermen with motorized boats was three times higher than that of the fishermen with nonmotorized boats, and the net income was nearly double. The study attributed these increases to the greater mobility of the fishing craft and the excellent prawn catches that year (Gillet 1979).

However, by 1972, the motors were no longer in use, relations between the fishermen of Muttom and the project staff were tense, and the project was in disarray. A KSSS study of the project sought to understand why. Project goals were derailed, the study argued, because it "failed to take into account the social structure of Muttom and the marketing system" (Gillet 1979: 4). The fishermen's name for the IBFP—the *velleikaran* [white man's] project"—provides the first clue as to why it created such tensions in Muttom. The project was partly staffed with foreign technicians and funded from abroad. Because the engines were issued free of cost, fishermen conveniently overlooked the condition that they pay back the customs duty. The affluent lifestyles of the foreign project staff only strengthened their resolve. One fisherman who was given a motor argued his case by saying, "Why should we have paid them back? Giving money to a white man is like adding a drop of water to an ocean!"[13] Second, the decline in prawn catches after the first two years of the project's operations, coupled with the steep rise in the cost of fuel, the high cost of spare parts, and the unnecessarily high horsepower (18 hp) of the motors produced diminishing returns that eventually led many fishermen to sell their motors to the highest bidder. Finally, the tug of war over the image of the IBFP played havoc with project goals. In place of the Belgian project manager who joined the FAO, the Belgian Freedom from Hunger Campaign appointed an advocate from Bombay. The interference of the Belgian organization in project operations offended the Tamilnadu government, which wanted to appoint its own manager. Finally, the situation was hastily resolved by giving the KSSS responsibility for selecting a manager from a panel offered by the Tamilnadu Department of Fisheries. The KSSS, with active pressure from the department, selected Captain Fernando, a Catholic from the Paravar fisher caste, to head the IBFP. Religion and caste concerns lay at the heart of the governmental choice. Naming a Catholic Paravar manager was one way for the department to signal community participation in the development process without allowing actual fishers to help structure IBFP goals. It was the government's way of "indigenizing" the project.

These various strains brought the IBFP to a close in December 1973. Tombeur's own personal assessment of the project offers a critique of its methods and goals in terms of indigenization. Successful development, in his view, involved the indigenization of processes and technologies, the cultural molding of a development agenda to suit the local context. He clearly did not approve of the government's own efforts at indigenizing the IBFP through caste representation. For Tombeur, effective indigenization had to be preceded by a structural critique of society and shaped by class concerns. The experience of the IBFP brought Tombeur to the recognition that development could be indigenized only by adapting to the needs and perspectives of the poorest. On this basis, Tombeur identified three key problems with the project: first, the imposition of new production norms on the fishermen, which then coexisted with older cultural patterns and social structures; second, the inability to change the existing social structures; third, the failure to incorporate the fisherman into the decision-making process. Tombeur concluded by arguing that "it is not enough to offer better working conditions. The people should evolve into a social force. New leadership has to emerge out of their own group . . . we cannot speak of development if people themselves are unwilling to take their situation in their own hands" (Tombeur 1997: 70). It was this idea of self-directed development that Tombeur tried to make the basis of IBFP's successor, the Fisheries Development Project.

The IBFP was wholly taken over by the KSSS in 1974 and became known simply as the Fisheries Development Project. This time, Tombeur tried to incorporate the lessons learned from the earlier initiative. The goals of the new project were to form fishermen *sangam*s (cooperative societies), which would double as savings banks and marketing bodies, establish a boat-building center as logistical support to those *sangam*s that chose to attempt motorization, and start a research center for appropriate technology.

In certain key respects, the Fisheries Development Project operated as a challenge to statist development in a way that the IBFP never did. Cooperativization was one arena in which this challenge was most directly posed. The KSSS started new cooperative societies as substitutes for the government's fisheries cooperative societies, which had been monopolized by merchants and trawler owners. As Mariadasan, the former president of the first KSSS *sangam* started in the coastal village of Mel Manakkudy, put it, "The government societies didn't help the poor, only the people the officers knew." The tainted history of cooperative societies in the district required a change in name. "It was important not to call these new village organizations 'societies,'" Mariadasan explained, "because people associated them with the government societies. So Lucas[14] came up with the name '*sangam*' as a substitute, both because it is an alternative to 'society' and because it is an Indian word which showed our intention to make it address community and not state concerns."[15] The terms of membership also distinguished the *sangam*s from the societies. Membership was restricted to owners of *kattumarams* and *vallams*; trawler owners and merchants were denied entry.

The *sangams* were a direct outcome of clerical and not lay activism and, as such, were at first seen by fishermen as an extension of the IBFP. However, fisher faith in the *sangams* increased when the coastal merchants consolidated their power to oppose the new institutions. The first *sangam* was started in the village of Mel Manakkudy, where the parish priest, Father Dionysius, recognized the need to challenge the financial bondage of the majority of villagers to middlemen and merchants who charged extortionist rates of interest on loans. Dionysius was himself from the coast and was one of the priests who were beginning to question the church's collusion with existing social hierarchies. On Dionysius's insistence, a group of four priests and a lay activist called a village meeting, as a result of which a *sangam* was started with seven village members, the only ones who did not have outstanding debts to local middlemen or merchants. As a push for the new body, Bishop Agniswami's successor, Arockiasamy, contributed 200 rupees to its savings fund.

At first, merchants refused to buy fish from *sangam* members and prevented the members from selling their fish in both Kanyakumari and the neighboring district of Tirunelveli. The first three weeks resulted in heavy losses for the *sangam*, but the fourth was profitable. At this point, the merchants changed their strategy by purchasing all the *sangam*'s fish and delaying the payments. This tactic had unexpected results. The village united against the merchants, forcing them to pay more than 20,000 rupees. Having failed at the village level, twenty-nine merchants approached the new bishop and threatened to end their financial contributions to the church if he did not shut down the *sangam*. They accused the *sangam* of putting them out of business, disturbing the peace and equilibrium of the village, and causing the breakdown of the "moral economy" that permitted the circulation of loans and fish within the village. The bishop refused their request, and soon after, four more *sangams* were started in four other coastal villages.[16]

As a second step in its coastal development agenda, the KSSS opened the Boat Building Center (BBC) in Muttom village. The original goal of the BBC was to build gillnetters and trawlers, although at a cheaper rate than those supplied by the FAO and the Indo-Norwegian Project and only for distribution to the newly started *sangams* to operate on a cooperative basis. In effect, the BBC wanted to revive the Nehruvian Community Development Program that was derailed by the onslaught of the prawn rush. Rather than rethink development entirely, the BBC aimed to fulfill the state's original goal of co-operativist capital-intensive production.

This second coastal experiment was helped along by another Belgian priest, Pierre Gillet, who arrived in Kanyakumari in 1973. Tombeur describes his meeting with Gillet in prophetic terms: "A turn toward the right 'Appropriate Technology' was made when I met a priest-engineer, fiber-glass specialist, boat-builder and a lover of the Bible, all in one person" (Tombeur 1997: 97). Gillet put it differently, and far more modestly. He explained that he did not arrive in India armed with the gospel of appropriate technology. Instead, it took a slow learning curve over fourteen years in South India for him to reach an awareness of the politics of technology. "I came initially to build gillnetters and trawlers," he recollected, "because the government was extricating itself from fisheries development without having served the majority of fishermen."[17] At that time, the KSSS's main concern was correcting the uneven effects of the state's development program by making mechanized technologies available to the poor.

At first, the KSSS Boat Building Center produced two fiberglass trawlers that were beyond the means of artisanal fishers. Gillet took over their management for three years and finally sold them outside the district to avoid their procurement by local merchants. The BBC then built three 21-foot gillnetters. These too were beyond the means of *sangam* members, and so the BBC decided to give them for cooperative use to the *sangam*s. However, because they were collectively owned, no single fisherman would take the responsibility of managing them, and they eventually fell into disrepair and had to be abandoned.

Frustrated by his lack of success, Gillet resolved to return to Europe to pursue a course in the United Kingdom in fisheries management. But he was discouraged by activist friends from neighboring Kerala, who insisted that what he needed instead was not further training in "European" science but a better grounding in "Indian" social science. After some consideration, Gillet decided to follow their advice, and, in 1977, he went to the Indian Social Institute in Bangalore for a three-month course on social analysis. Alongside the course, Gillet and seven of his fellow students formed a working group on Indian fisheries to come to a better understanding of the history of state intervention in fishing.

That same year, intersectoral violence broke out in Madras city, and Gillet was forced to contend with the fallout of state intervention not simply in theory but through witnessing large-scale violence. A field trip to the Madras coast revealed disturbing facts. Gillet learned that, in 1978 alone, 106 trawlers had been attacked and destroyed by artisanal fishers. Some fishers had been imprisoned. Others were demonstrating in front of the Tamilnadu Department of Fisheries against the operation of trawlers in the inshore area. This trip was an ideological turning point for him. In an analysis of his experiences in South India, he wrote: "The starvation in some fishing *kuppams* (slums) was appalling and I could recall myself my previous experience as trawler manager: how much immature fish are destroyed when you catch prawns with bottom trawl nets. It is no surprise that nothing was left for the small fishers" (Gillet 1979: 29). By the time Gillet returned to Muttom, he had abandoned trawler production altogether and had turned to innovating with local craft.

In *Small Is Difficult: The Pangs and Successes of Small Boat Technology Transfer in South India* (1985), Gillet's analysis of the Muttom BBC's operations, Gillet describes the difficulties of rethinking the flow of influence from that of technology on society to that of society on technology. Failure took on new meaning for him; he no longer understood it in terms of the ability of social groups to adapt themselves to technology but rather in terms of using technology to address social needs and therefore be found necessary. As is evident from the title of his book, Gillet and the BBC project drew inspiration from E. F. Schumacher's *Small Is Beautiful: Economics as If People Mattered* (1973). There was also a more direct link between the two. Beginning in the mid-1970s, the BBC began working with London's ITDG. The ITDG's statement of purpose reads:

> Whereas the conventional approach to industrialization takes technology as a *given* factor in development, as if it were an unchangeable force to which all other factors must adapt themselves, the new approach starts by considering technology as an important *variable* which can and should be adapted so as to work in harmony with the economic, social and cultural environments of developing countries.[18] (italics in the original)

ITDG's emphasis on fulfilling the direct needs of the communities they engaged, rather than following an abstract developmental trajectory, resonated with Gillet's new understanding of coastal goals. The KSSS and the ITDG embarked on technological experimentation fueled by a new vision of community as the collective of artisans.

The Spread of an Intermediate Technology

In 1982, the BBC and the ITDG successfully completed the prototype of a plywood canoe that was built to be fitted with an outboard motor. The substitution of plywood for the rarer and more costly *chilla* wood that was first used drastically reduced the cost of the canoe, and after 1987 its use began to spread along the coast. After the prototype's initial success, orders for plywood canoes began pouring into the BBC, making the workload for the moderately sized establishment overwhelming. Finally, in 1987, the BBC decided to transfer the technology and prototype to the South Indian Federation of Fishermen Societies (SIFFS) in Kerala, an umbrella body of fishermen's *sangams*. The technological experimentation conducted at SIFFS bears testimony to the long history of development and the complex genealogies of its multiple strands. SIFFS has reprinted and circulated many of the writings of the Madras Presidency's fisheries director, James Hornell, and its engineers routinely turn to his meticulously reproduced designs of craft and gear from across the British imperial landscape for inspiration.

Motors made fishermen less subject to the whims of the wind, increased their radius of operation, and considerably reduced the time taken for trips to and from the sea—all factors that made the new canoes desirable. Seeing the success of the canoe, other private boatyards also began building a version of the canoe and making *kattumarams* that could be fitted with motors. At first, the cost of these craft was prohibitive for artisanal fishers. But this changed after 1985, when as part of the Seventh Five Year Plan, the Tamilnadu government introduced a new subsidy scheme for outboard motors (Department of Fisheries 1990). By 1995, the total number of motorized plywood *vallams* operating in Kanyakumari District had skyrocketed to 504. Adding motorized *kattumarams*, the number of motorized craft reached 815 (Kanyakumari District Fishermen Sangams Federation 1995).

In some ways, the spread of motors across the coast signaled the incorporative logic of capitalism (Meynen 1989). Artisanal fishers availed themselves of this more costly technology in hopes of going into deeper waters in search of new fishing grounds. However, going to new depths meant a significant rise in operating costs, without a reduction in the uncertainty of catching fish produced by their unfamiliarity with deeper water fishing grounds. Confronted with this situation, most fishermen were left with the single option of continuing to fish in the coastal waters for longer periods of time. To compensate for the rise in investment costs, some fishermen began to innovate with new, more destructive gear (such as nets with smaller mesh sizes that caught juvenile fish), changes that increased tensions among artisanal fishers.

In other ways, however, motorization posed a real challenge to trawler activity and its excesses of capital accumulation and resource depletion. Furthermore, the tensions brewing among artisans around the use of motors were largely offset by their unified opposition to trawler activity, which produced a collective identification reinforced by the 1983 act's territorialization of sectoral identity. Although motors made it far easier for *vallam* and *kattumaram* fishers to travel farther than the 3-mile inshore zone reserved for them by the act, most continued to fish within this zone using passive gear that limited their catch volumes to levels far below those of the trawlers. Most important, as we will see in Chapter 6, motorized craft assumed a new role in the intersectoral drama that legitimized their presence in the eyes of non-motorized fishers. Motors increased the speed of the craft, making possible confrontations with trawlers at sea. When trawlers transgressed the 3-mile boundary or when damage was caused by the trawl net to either the craft or gear of artisanal fishers, a chase and retaliation followed. In the absence of a government coast guard, motorized craft took on vigilante activity to ensure trawler compliance with the 1983 act. When trawlers did not do so, they faced violent retribution.

Intermediacy and Rights

The 1970s and 1980s was a period of intense political activity, not just on the Kanyakumari coast but across India. In various ways and through a variety of projects, people questioned the givenness of national space that was a material and ideological product of anti-imperialist nationalism and postcolonial state formation. On the Kanyakumari coast, where the nation was a latecomer to the drama of spatialization, these decades witnessed an explosion of projects that challenged the hegemonies of nationalism, developmentalism, and capitalist accumulation. I have argued in this chapter that regionalism, artisanal territoriality, and alternative technology were space-making projects guided by an ethic of intermediacy. Each project produced political space through material practices of voting, fishing, and technological innovation. By voting for the ADMK, fisher artisans generated a space of regionalism inclusive of the coast. In plying the 3-mile zone in their artisanal craft, they carved out a space of common property proscribed to trawling technology. The appropriate technology project was generative of a translocal space reminiscent of Hornell's spatial imaginary. This was a space of technological innovation, diffusion, and adaptation involving a variety of social actors linked by their commitment to "alternative development."

In the next chapter, I follow these three space-making projects into the last decade of the twentieth century, a period dominated by the global processes of neoliberalism and environmentalism. I look at how these projects of globe making intersected with ongoing politics of caste, patronage, and technology on the southwestern coast.

Figure 6. Chinnamuttom harbor. Courtesy of International Collective in Support of Fishworkers, Chennai, India.

6 Locality and Nation
Respatializing Rights Under Neoliberalism

IN 1991, THE INDIAN GOVERNMENT opened its 200-mile Exclusive Economic Zone to foreign capital ventures. Prompted by a balance-of-payments deficit and a clause in the 1982 Law of the Sea requiring states to liberalize access to territorial waters if they are unable to fully exploit their own marine resources, the government introduced a new, far-reaching deep-sea fishing policy. According to the new policy, deep-sea resources would be tapped through joint ventures between foreign and Indian private companies. The incentive package offered to the foreign partners included easy financing and the supply of diesel fuel at international rates; license to export their entire catch, processing it onboard at sea; and license to use a foreign port as the base of operation. In return for these inducements, the Indian government would receive 12 percent of the foreign exchange earnings of the enterprises and the Indian partner would benefit from the transfer of technology (Sharma 2001; A. Subramanian and Kalavathy 1994; A. Sundar 1999).

That same year, the National Fishworkers Forum (NFF) responded by launching an opposition campaign.[1] The organization joined hands with its erstwhile adversary, the Indian trawling sector, to demand state protection for domestic producers. In October 1993, the NFF and the Small Mechanized Boat Operators of India jointly submitted a memorandum to the prime minister demanding the revocation of all new licenses issued to joint ventures in deep-sea fishing and the enactment of a deep-sea fishing regulation act that would encourage the harvest of deep-sea resources by domestic fishers (National Fishworkers Forum 1993; *Indian Express*, October 25, 1993). The following year, the NFF and thirty-one other organizations and trade unions from nine maritime states called for a one-day all-India fisheries strike. On February 4, most of the mechanized and artisanal fishers struck work and generated a total boycott of harbors and fish markets (*The Hindu*, February 5, 1994; *Indian Express*, February 5, 1994; Sharma 2001). In July 1994, the two sectors along with export merchants and the owners and workers of fish-processing, ice production, and net-making industries formally came together as the National Fisheries Action Committee Against Joint Ventures (NFACAJV) (*The Hindu*, July 18, 1994; *Indian Express*, July 18, 1994; National Fishworkers Forum 1994).

The NFACAJV's argument against joint ventures hinged on a few key points. First, even before the announcement of the policy, the catch per vessel had gone down in all sectors and, in contrast to the Commerce Ministry's estimation, the UN Food and Agriculture Organization's own 1992 study of the Indian Ocean fishery suggested that the commercially viable fish available in the deep sea could be caught by existing domestic fleets if their operations were diversified (J. Kurien 1995; Sharma 2001). Second, past experiments with deep-sea fishing in the Indian Ocean had generated heavy losses, making it clear that the only way for joint-venture vessels to reap a profit would be to encroach on the resource-rich territorial waters, thus adding to the vulnerability of domestic fishers. Third, the license to process fish onboard without ever landing them onshore denied a participatory role for laborers in the Indian fish-processing industry.

In July 1994, the NFACAJV called for a "Black Day," when fishers across the country hoisted black flags on their boats and staged marches and demonstrations to demand an end to joint ventures. This was followed in November 1995 by a two-day national fisheries strike and a week-long hunger fast in May 1995 by Catholic priest Thomas Kocherry, chair of the NFF and convener of the NFACAJV, that was supported by relay fasts by fishers across the country. In response to the protests, the Indian government announced that it was temporarily suspending the issue of licenses, and it appointed a committee to study the problem, which submitted a report upholding the 1991 policy. The committee's report generated another protest on November 23 and 24, during which fishers struck work and fishing in the maritime states came to a virtual standstill. About 1 million people boycotted work at sea and in processing plants and fish markets as a show of protest against the policy. The government then constituted another committee, headed by P. Murari, that was composed only of government officials. The NFACAJV organized yet another agitation and in May 1995, Thomas Kocherry went on an indefinite hunger strike in Porbundar, the birthplace of Mahatma Gandhi. When the press and opposition parties came out in unanimous support of the fishers, the government finally agreed to expand the Murari committee to include six representatives from the fisheries sector, including Kocherry. In February 1996, after a comprehensive tour and survey of coastal states, the Murari committee submitted its recommendations, which included the total cancellation of all joint-venture licenses, the provision of training and subsidies to enable small- and medium-scale fishers to harvest the deep sea, and mandatory consultation with the fishing community on all fishery legislation and policy. When the government hesitated to implement the committee's recommendations, Kocherry began another hunger fast in Bombay on August 7, 1996, with support actions across the country carried out by the central trade union federations, the National Center for Labor, and the National Alliance of People's Movements. On August 10, fishers and dockworkers began an indefinite blockade of all major harbors, as a result of which the Ministry of Food Processing Industries agreed to stop issuing licenses and to begin implementing the recommendations. After another round of harbor blockages in March 1997, the Indian government agreed to cancel all licenses and issue no additional ones. It was a remarkable victory against globalization.

The collaboration against the deep-sea fishing policy reflected a notion of community that encompassed the fisheries sector as a whole, undifferentiated by sector, region, or class and extended to national scale. The NFACAJV called on the developmental state to renew its commitment to this community of fishers rather than to foreign capital. In a conversation about the antiglobalization protests, Thomas Kocherry pointed out the reasons for this unusual collaboration between the adversaries of the domestic fishing economy: "Initially, the entire struggle was around the contradiction between traditional fishing and trawlers, but when they realized that there was a bigger threat to face, they came together spontaneously. Previously the struggle was at the regional level; now it has acquired national dimensions."[2] Kocherry explained that the reorientation of the struggle around opposition to global capital necessitated a reframing of community in national terms.

This particular instance of a resurgent late capitalist nationalism is notably at odds with millennial expectations of the nation-state's demise. In the late 1990s, the striking consensus across the political spectrum in the U.S. academy and popular press over the interpretation of neoliberalism as a rupture with previous forms of territorial power and affiliation (e.g., Appadurai 1996; Bhagwati 2004; Friedman 2000; Hardt and Negri 2000) obscured the continuities in nationalist and state-centered responses to globalization. By contrast, analysts of grassroots opposition to global capitalism in India and elsewhere have noted that activists and their supporters articulated a combined defense of national self-sufficiency *and* local resource rights (C. T. Kurien 1994, 1996; McCarthy 2005b; Patnaik 1995a, 1995b). In India, many of the 1990s social movements with broad ecological platforms that arose among tribal, fisher, and farmer populations called for the strengthening of the state as a barrier to unfettered transnational capital while articulating localized rights claims in terms of national political belonging. The symbolism of an earlier anti-imperialist nationalism informed such movements, which represented their cause as a second independence struggle, this time for the poor. Pinpointing economic self-reliance as a founding tenet of postcolonial state formation, antiglobalization activists argued that neoliberal restructuring was a betrayal of the promise of national independence.

In fisheries, the juxtaposition of state-led neoliberal deterritorialization and the opposition's call for a robust national territorial sovereignty suggests a shift in both economic policy and political organizing away from the projects of intermediacy in the 1970s and 1980s. Then, fisheries politics was juxtaposed against the national, bringing coastal fishers, the regional state, the transnational church, and other international migrants together in ongoing negotiations over the meaning of polity, economy, and community. For Dravidian fishers, communist priests, and Belgian engineers, the problem of national developmental hegemony and domestic capitalism had occupied center stage. It appeared that in the current situation the space of intermediacy carved out by these earlier negotiations had been eclipsed by a new emphasis on anti-imperialist *nationalism*. Through its mobilizations across the Indian coastal belt, the NFACAJV produced a space of national sovereignty as the ground of struggle.

Yet, when we turn back to Kanyakumari, a more complicated picture emerges. The 1990s was the decade of the most sustained antitrawling activity. Even though antiglobalization brought artisans and trawler owners together in campaigns across Indian city centers, in Kanyakumari, artisanal village after village passed resolutions against inshore trawling, engaged in pitched battles with trawlers at sea, harangued politicians to address the impact of trawling on marine resources, and mobilized in collective protests in strategic inland locations. Indeed, one could tell a very different story about the southwestern fishery in the last decade of the twentieth century from that which begins this chapter.

This other story would most likely highlight two other pivotal events. In 1990, the government of Tamilnadu opened Kanyakumari's first harbor in Chinnamuttom village at the eastern end of the district to serve primarily as a berthing and launching pad for mechanized craft. Within a few years, the number of trawlers in Chinnamuttom and the adjoining village of Kanyaku-mari grew from three in 1987 to almost a hundred in 1995. Thus the district had two trawling centers—Chinnamuttom in the east and Colachel in the west—separated by a number of villages with artisanal majorities.

In 1993, the Indian Supreme Court reached a verdict in favor of the Kerala state government's 1989 decision to ban trawling during the monsoon months of June, July, and August. After the 1989 ban, the Kerala Trawlnet Boat Opera-tors' Association had registered a case against the Kerala state government in the High Court of Kerala's capital city of Trivandrum, arguing that the ban was a violation of their right to livelihood as well as a detriment to the coun-try's foreign exchange earnings from the export of prawn and other valuable species. When the Boat Operators' Association won a stay from the High Court that allowed them to renew operations during the monsoon months, the Kerala union affiliated with the NFF took the case to the Supreme Court. The protracted struggle between the Kerala trawling sector and the artisanal union finally ended with the 1993 verdict in support of the monsoon trawl-ing ban. In his verdict, Justice Jeevan Reddy gave a decisive statement about development.

> We are of the opinion that the Government of Kerala is perfectly justified in adopting the attitude that the public interest cannot be determined only by looking at the quantum of fish caught in a year. In other words, production alone cannot be the basis for determining public interest. The government is perfectly justified in saying that it is under an obligation to protect the eco-nomic interest of the traditional fishermen and to ensure that they are not deprived of their slender means of livelihood. Whether one calls it distribu-tive justice, or development with a human face, the ultimate truth is that the object of all development is the human being. There can be no development for the sake of development. Priorities ought not to be inverted nor the true perspective lost in the quest for more production.[3]

This verdict encapsulated the NFF's stance against capitalist development and recast development in terms of distributive justice. It signaled the court's recognition of artisanal fishers as producers with a right to protection by the state against the excesses of private capitalism. On a more practical level, the verdict increased the duration of trawler activity in Kanyakumari, because trawlers that used to fish from Kerala's harbors began coming to Kanyakumari during the monsoon months to escape the ban. Kanyakumari's trawler owners returned to their district sea with great apprehension. The Supreme Court verdict signaled a threatening consolidation of a fisher politics of territorial closure. In response to the militancy of Kerala's artisanal fishermen, Kerala's mechanized fishers had begun to police the entry of other trawlers into Kerala seas. Kanyakumari's mechanized fishers realized that, with increasing restrictions on their mobility, it was time to make a more strident claim to the resources of their home sea.

A decade ago, China historian Arif Dirlik pointed out the centrality of "the local" to contemporary political discourse. "It would seem by the early nineties that local movements, or movements to save and reconstruct local societies, have emerged as the primary (if not the only) expressions of resistance to domination" (Dirlik 1996: 22). The concern with the local as a site of resistance and liberation, he continued, is intimately linked to the emergence of a global capitalism. Dirlik connected the political centrality of the local to the renewed importance of "place" in millennial social movements. "The challenge," he reflected, "is how to recapture places for politics (and use-value) against their consumption into postmodernist privatization, where one place is scarcely distinguishable from another in an unending change of exchange-values" (Dirlik 1997: 6). Ecological movements, he argued, engage in a "critical localism" that recognizes that localities have been worked over by processes of historical transformation but still need to be appropriated from the onslaught of new, even more pervasive forms of capitalist modernization.

Like Dirlik, a number of writers have linked the symbolic valence of locality in the 1990s to a globalizing capitalism in a dialectic of power and resistance. But as mentioned, in Kanyakumari, as elsewhere on the Indian coast, opposition to global capitalism was expressed primarily through an anti-imperialist nationalism. What, then, did the turn to locality express? Long-time Kerala fishery activist A. J. Vijayan echoed Dirlik's notion of a critical localism in his assessment of southern fishery activism. "In spite of the national collaboration, the same contradictions and animosity continue to exist locally. In fact, I would say that they've even gotten stronger."[4] When I asked him why, he said, "We've realized more and more that the sea could become a desert. We see the urgency of conservation now more than ever before and the need to defend local resources against overfishing. Ecological sustainability has become the most important issue for us." One could certainly argue that this expression of environmental ethics is the quintessential localist response to global capitalism. However, I would argue that for Vijayan, environmentalism provided not so much the tools to rethink globalization as the tools to reassert locality against national capitalism. Ultimately, the emphasis for him was on continuing the struggles against domestic capital through the postindependence period and engaging regional and national states to secure artisanal rights. In other words, mediating scales of society and state were crucially important to crafting a critical localism.

Spaces and Idioms of Protest

To what extent can we characterize the 1990s as having ushered in a shift in political imaginaries and practices? What do we make of the difference between late-twentieth-century expectations of an unmediated local-global encounter and the lived politics of mediation?

In some ways, the deep-sea fishing campaign presents a conundrum. Narrowly framed as a campaign of opposition to foreign capital intervention in the Indian fishery, it was wildly successful. More broadly conceived as opposition to all unsustainable fishing, whether foreign or domestic, it was less so. Furthermore, in Kanyakumari, a much broader consensus on antiglobalization than on antitrawling had developed. Writing about the parallel campaigns against deep-sea fishing and inshore trawling, political scientist Aparna Sundar comments that "in contrast to the struggle against trawling, the deep-sea fishing campaign in Kanyakumari district was conducted formally, in sites commonly agreed upon as 'political'—meeting halls, the Collectorate. . . . For all that the deep-sea fishing campaign was a 'campaign' and by definition time-bound, intense, and concerted, in Kanyakumari it nonetheless reflected a state of 'normal' or 'routine' politics" (A. Sundar 1999: 107–108).

In my own participation in the campaign against deep-sea fishing in Kanyakumari, this routinization of politics was palpable. Although it was through my involvement in this campaign that I was first drawn to researching the history of the coast, it was evident to me even then that foreign vessels did not convey the same immediacy of threat that local trawlers did. Much of the antiglobalization campaign was organized and orchestrated by social workers, church volunteers, and interlopers such as myself. We wrote letters to government officials, toured fishing villages to speak about the government's neoliberal turn, and wrote articles for the popular press on the resilient national opposition to the new fishing policy. The shared currency of nationalism paved the way to meetings with members of the government and press.

Returning to the coast for my research two years later, I was once again struck by the relative complacency of artisanal fishers in mobilizing against globalization. Far more commonly, they had to be encouraged by parish priests to attend protests held in front of the district collector's office, where we would gather under a covered area set up for protesters, shout slogans, and then disperse at a predetermined time. The discipline of these protests and their authorization by the police gave them an aura of predictability. I was left with the sense that the deep-sea fishing campaign was a trickle-down politics that lost meaning as it traveled to the Kanyakumari shoreline.

The distance between the campaign against globalization and the everyday reality of resource depletion was also reflected in the disintegration of the NFF in Kanyakumari. During my time in the district, the NFF was in disarray. Meetings were difficult to sustain, villagers had to be coerced into attending, and there was a constant turnover in leadership. Indeed, the immanent threat of foreign industrial fishing in the deep sea seemed of little immediate relevance to most fishermen and fisherwomen I spoke with. It was only when the national leadership of the NFF arrived in Kanyakumari for rallies and campaigns that its mass base would materialize.

On the other hand, antitrawling politics was fierce and spontaneous. Talk of trawler transgressions on the part of artisans was the stuff of daily conversation. Here, too, capital and community were in hostile conflict. However, here, both capital and community were spatialized as local, and it was precisely contestation over the cultural and political contours of locality that generated such hostility.

In the rest of this chapter, I take up these two trajectories in 1990s fishery politics: nationalization and localization. I consider who engaged in each space-making project, what tools they used, and to what ends. I argue that, rather than a rupture with fishery politics of the previous decades, antiglobalization in Kanyakumari provided new tools for domestic adversaries in the trawler wars of the 1990s. The language of ecology, locality, and nation circulated by the campaign against deep-sea fishing offered new ways to generate space and claim rights in the district's fishery.

Nationalizing the Artisan

Producing the artisanal fisher as a national political subject was a project of the NFF. Excavating a genealogy of naming offers some sense of the changes wrought to the organization's mandate and membership over time. At the time of its founding in 1978 as the National Forum for Kattumaram and Country Boat Fishermen's Rights and Marine Wealth, the forum included artisanal fisher organizations from the three regional coastal states of Tamilnadu, Kerala, and Goa, where the battle against trawling was most intense. By 1983, the forum had expanded to include thirteen major regional fishermen's unions and was renamed the National Fishermen's Forum. In 1985, the forum was registered as a trade union. The final change of name occurred at the forum's annual meeting in 1989, when an opposition walkout by women members of the organization resulted in a serious rethinking of gender exclusivity. The choice of fish*worker*, however, was guided by other considerations too. Nalini Nayak, a longtime activist with the NFF who has been a key figure in bringing fisherwomen's concerns to the table, told me of the lengthy discussions that went into replacing *fishermen* with *fishworker*.

> The existing trade union movement didn't want to have anything to do with us because we weren't part of the industrial proletariat. They couldn't understand where we fit because the majority of artisanal fishermen own their own craft and gear. Then, within the NFF, there was the added sidelining of women's issues seen in the very choice of fisher*men* for the name of the organization.[5]

Fishworker signaled the place of fisher artisans within a national working class, checking both the romantic localism of *fisherfolk* and the gendered exclusivity of *fishermen*. It indicated a collective class identity that transcended the particularities of caste, region, and gender.

But things changed in the late 1980s. In 1989, the NFF organized a national demonstration called the Protect Waters, Protect Life March that culminated in Kanyakumari. The march brought together fisher groups and supporters from across the country who were opposed to the depletion of marine resources, and signaled the crystallization of a national ecological movement in the fisheries sector. The use of ecology as a rallying cry was a significant change in the NFF's mobilization activity because it reflected a shift from a primarily class-based stance against unequal access to technology, to a recognition that mechanized fishing and the intersectoral competition that it produced was leading to both economic and biological overfishing (National Fishworkers Forum 1989).[6] NFF ideologues now pointed to the inadequacy of class as a category for analyzing the dynamics of an economy characterized by natural resource harvest, common property, and private ownership of the means of production.

The deep-sea fishing campaign nationalized the artisan in a way that previous mobilizations had not. Through opposing the "new imperialism," the NFF was able to spatialize its artisanal constituency as national. At the same time, however, the discourses of ecology, nation, and locality that proliferated in this newly constituted national space were taken up by others for their own projects. I turn now to these projects within Kanyakumari.

Nationalizing the Church

The deep-sea fishing policy brought together erstwhile adversaries in the domestic fishery in an uneasy and episodic truce. It also elicited the censure of the Catholic Bishops' Conference of India (CBCI) and strong words from the newly appointed chairman of its labor commission, Leon Dharmaraj, a native of Kanyakumari District. Dharmaraj had succeeded Arockiasamy as bishop of Kottar in 1990. After 1991, he mobilized the national church against the deep-sea fishing policy wholeheartedly. Locally, opposition to the policy also provided him with a means to unite the warring factions of his fisher congregation and to highlight the church's patriotism at a time when Hindu nationalism was ascendant.[7]

Bishop Dharmaraj appears to have wanted to take Kottar diocese in a decidedly socialist direction, a goal that comes out clearly in several of the circulars he issued beginning in 1991. Immediately after the announcement of neoliberal economic reforms by the ruling Congress Party, Dharmaraj issued a circular to coastal parishes that included a statement on communism and capitalism.

> The collapse of the Communist system in so many countries certainly removes an obstacle to facing the problems of marginalization and exploitation in an appropriate and realistic way, but it is not enough to bring about their solution. Indeed, there is a risk that a radical capitalistic ideology could spread which refuses even to consider these problems, in the a priori belief that any attempt to solve them is doomed to failure, and which blindly entrusts their solution to the free development of market forces. (*Kottar Newsletter*, July 1991)

Dharmaraj's response to the deep-sea fishing policy continued this line of reasoning. In another circular issued on November 15, 1994, Dharmaraj invited religious and lay members of the diocese to "promote social justice in a Christian spirit" by protesting peacefully against the "invasion of our seas by foreign fishing vessels." He urged all fishers to participate in the strikes organized by the NFF by not catching, selling, or consuming fish on strike days. In yet another letter he issued to the CBCI in his capacity as head of its labor commission, Dharmaraj called on bishops in coastal dioceses to "motivate their flock to join the protest meetings. . . . By giving solidarity to this action," he concluded, "we indeed are preaching the Gospel" (Catholic Bishops' Conference of India 1994).

For both warring factions of the Kanyakumari fishery, the deep-sea fishing policy signaled a betrayal by the state, and they responded to the bishop's plea by jointly participating in some of the NFF's campaigns. However, their collaboration was tenuous. The frequency of intersectoral clashes on the Kanyakumari coast had risen sharply since 1993 as a result of several interlocking factors, including the successful spread of the Muttom Boat Building Center's motorized canoes, the construction of the new harbor at Chinnamuttom, and the entry of the NFF into the district. All these factors contributed to a more aggressive opposition between artisanal and mechanized fishers and each group's more strident articulation of sectoral identity. New terms—ecology, science, locality, and nation—accrued political weight and anchored the territorial polarization of sectors in the district.

Using the momentum provided by the 1989 Protect Waters, Protect Life March, the NFF began canvassing support in Kanyakumari's coastal villages for a district-level artisanal union. A section of the Kottar clergy responded to the NFF's work with a mixture of caution and alarm. The increasing militancy of fisher politics in Kerala and the participation of a vocal section of Kerala's Catholic clergy in the artisanal fisher campaigns had set off alarm bells in the Kottar church. This was the case despite the fact that Kottar Social Service Society (KSSS) work in *sangam* formation and intermediate technology had reflected an expanded sense of religious ministry that included the "secular" work of technological development. The bulk of the clergy had understood the KSSS's work simply as their way of filling a development gap left by the state. Rather than a direct challenge to reigning paradigms of development and authority, they promoted the KSSS as the effort by a benevolent clergy to secure a place for the poor in a modernizing nation.

Unionization, on the other hand, was a step that most of the clergy could not countenance. Parish priests from twenty of the forty-four coastal villages of the district took the matter before Bishop Dharmaraj. They alleged that Fathers Thomas Kocherry, Arulanandam, and Francis de Sales, the three priests spearheading the NFF's unionization effort, were fomenting violence on the coast in the name of the empowerment of the poor. They denied the validity of unionization as clerical activity by distinguishing technological innovation, which *could* be accommodated as religious work, from unionization, which took clerical activity wholly into the realm of the secular. Rather than an expansion of the religious domain, they charged that union formation obliterated religiosity altogether.

Why were the priests who had encouraged the church's turn to development work now so resistant to unionization? A key reason appears to have been the threat of fisher autonomy. A union independent of church authority signaled a challenge to clerical leadership in a way that the KSSS *sangams* never had. Second, the formation of unions threatened to further escalate the violence on the coast by negating the possibility of common ground among fishers using different forms of technology.

In response to the clerical standoff, Bishop Dharmaraj invited the three priests to argue their case for unionization. Using the Second Vatican Council document *The Church in the Modern World,* which defined the church as an institution dedicated to both spiritual matters and material reality, Fathers Kocherry, Arulanandam, and Sales argued that institutions promoting social justice for the poor continued the work of Christ. Community, they maintained, could no longer simply be equated with a religious collective shepherded by priestly authority. Rather, the true Catholic community, the church of Christ on earth, was the community of the poor, and the clergy was morally obliged to subject itself to their struggle, not as leaders but as followers. They stated strongly that the mechanized sector was undermining the coast's moral economy by monopolizing and depleting the resource for personal profit. By flourishing at the expense of the lives of the wider community and of the sea on which they depended, they had placed themselves outside the bounds of the community of Christ.[8]

Despite a lack of resolution, Bishop Dharmaraj gave his support to the three priests and allowed unionization to continue. As the bishop of Kottar and the head of the CBCI's labor commission, he pronounced his support for the fisher poor and entrusted the NFF with the "Christian goal of ensuring the dignity of labor," which, he insisted, could not be compromised in favor of private property.[9] In his circular of May 11, 1991, Dharmaraj defined his position on the local conflict by stating, "The right to private property has been understood by Christian tradition as situated within the broader context of the right common to all to use the goods of the whole of creation: the right to private property is subordinated to the right to common use, to the fact that goods are meant for everyone" (*Kottar Newsletter,* May 1991).

This statement in support of common over private property, which sounded remarkably like the NFF's own language, sealed the bishop's vote in favor of the NFF and alienated a number of the Mukkuvar clergy, who continued to see the NFF's work as a threat to the church and a source of divisiveness within a caste that was already disempowered. These priests would, in the mid-1990s and with the urging of state officials, embark on a peacekeeping mission that sought to both reinforce their authority over the coast and bring the warring factions of the fisher Catholic population together under the banner of caste and faith.[10]

Artisanal Militancy and the Production of Locality

For fisher artisans, the 1990s was a period of consolidation. Previous projects of intermediacy and the newly circulating discourse of ecology grounded a sense of local moral community that excluded trawler owners who shared the same caste and faith. This reconstituted community had a territorial basis (the 3-mile zone), a technological basis (artisanal craft and gear), and an ecological basis (a symbiotic relationship with the marine resource). Most important, it was the assertion of belonging to a locality. Consider this statement by Constantine, a district leader of the NFF: "Trawlers can go anywhere to fish, but we have to rely on our local sea and protect it for our children. Who else will do it? Certainly not the state or the church! We have to because *kadalamma* is our mother and without her, we will die." This striking convergence of an older sense of the sea as an unpredictable, all-powerful force with a more recent recognition of its vulnerability contributed to artisans' sense of collective destiny—even a new kind of caste status—as the protectors of the sea against the threat of trawling.

Apart from being a threat *to* the sea, trawler ownership now signaled an uprooting *from* the sea and, by extension, from community. This reconstitution of community is expressed strongly in this explanation provided by Selvaraj, a fisherman who participated in the firebombing of a trawler owned by a friend's relative. When I asked him how a population sharing caste and faith came to be so divided, he explained, "It's because the trawler owners have forgotten who they are and what they know about the sea. You see, anyone can use a trawl net—a farmer, a teacher, even a bureaucrat! But when we go out to sea, we have an instinctive sense of where the fish are. We can read the water like others read the land. It's this shared sense of the sea that makes us a community."

Opposed to a new moral community expressed through what Liisa Malkki (1995) has called a "sedentarist metaphysic" was the trawling class, characterized in artisanal fisher discourse as mobile, accumulative, and profiteering. Although artisanal fishers also have historically migrated to other parts of the coast to fish during their local lean season and continue to do so, they now affirmed a rootedness in locality that they claimed trawler owners had lost. Connected to trawler mobility was their privileging of personal gain over social responsibility and of private wealth over marine wealth. I was told several times that as trawler owners grew richer, they contributed less and less to the church fund from which the needs of the village poor were met. This social irresponsibility was expressed further in their immoral neglect of the future of the resource.

As early as 1987, the demand for a monsoon trawl ban in Kerala began to be echoed in Kanyakumari. That year, the *kattumaram*-dominated village of Kanyakumari, at the eastern end of the district, decided to take matters into its own hands. In the presence of a Tamilnadu Department of Fisheries official, the village council forced the approximately ten trawler owners in the village to sign an agreement containing two clauses: (1) to observe a monsoon trawl ban of five months in order to protect fish stocks during the spawning season and (2) to leave the shore after 6 a.m. and return before 6 p.m. to promote the visibility of their operations and reduce the chance of damage to the gear and craft of artisanal fishers. When the mechanized boat owners argued that these rules were at variance with the rules framed in the 1983 Tamilnadu Marine Fisheries Regulation Act, council members pointed out that the act does allow the issuing of local notifications to prohibit the catching of fish in any period (Section 5d) as well as for the determination of other fishing times (Section 5e). The Department of Fisheries official present was content to support the informal agreement without giving it any legal status, which appeared to him to be the best way of solving the law and order problem.[11]

In general, and in keeping with the parameters of the 1983 act, the Tamilnadu Department of Fisheries continued to promote the simultaneous development of both sectors and to resort to local agreements to deal with their increasingly more conflictual relationship. As V. Raman, the secretary of the Department of Animal Husbandry and Fisheries of the government of Tamilnadu, explained to me, "We believed in integrated development that promotes both sectors. Each has its own range; each has a different level of operation. In the inshore area, the goal is to motorize traditional craft in order to improve efficiency and increase catches. Beyond the 3-mile zone, trawlers need to be encouraged. So we envision encouragement and coexistence of both."[12] The Department of Fisheries chose to ignore the visible signs of stock depletion and the dire need for resource management, opting instead to interpret artisanal militancy as a sign of "ignorance and superstition." As several department officials indicated, standing by local agreements was simply the quick and easy way of dissipating tensions on the coast and of assuaging the volatile passions of fisher artisans. Even when they agreed that resource management was needed, they were quick to assure me that this recognition was in no way spurred by artisanal fisher activism against trawling, which was driven purely by "jealousy" and had no "scientific basis" whatsoever.[13]

In tune with its commitment to "integrated development," the Tamilnadu Department of Fisheries increased its subsidies for motors at the same time that it began construction of a new harbor in Chinnamuttom village at the eastern end of the district in 1989. The Chinnamuttom harbor facilitated the launching and berthing of mechanized boats, so that they would no longer have to travel to Colachel's natural harbor at the western end of the district (Department of Fisheries 1990). By 1991, one year after the harbor was opened for operations, the number of trawlers in the two villages nearest the harbor alone had increased exponentially from a mere ten in 1987 to approximately one hundred. In addition, the number of trawlers in and around Colachel continued to increase, so that trawlers were concentrated on the eastern and western ends of the district's coastal belt.

The first appropriation in 1987 of the Tamilnadu Marine Fisheries Regulation Act for enforcing a local agreement to curb trawling set the stage for future actions at the village level. Increasingly, the terms adopted by artisanal villagers in appropriating the act reflected the language politicized by the NFF. Interestingly, even though the NFF's own unionization work moved in fits and starts and was met with a lukewarm response, its message of artisanal fisher rights and the link it made between artisanal fishing and marine resource conservation did circulate and spurred activity in different fisher organizations. As in Kanyakumari village, the councils of other villages with an artisanal majority became focal points of sectoral consciousness and began exercising their authority to curb trawlers. In addition, another organization—the Kanyakumari District Kattumaram Vallam Meen Pidi Thozhil Pathukappu Sangam (Association for the Protection of Kattumaram and Vallam Fishing)—was formed in 1993 at the initiative of motorized *vallam* fishers with the express purpose of protecting artisanal fishing from trawler aggression. This association was backed by the Communist Party of India (Marxist), which heralded its emergence outside clerical initiative as the much-awaited sign of "genuine class consciousness" on the coast.[14]

The turning point for artisanal activism was 1993, when the militancy spurred by the NFF's discourse of ecology was further strengthened by another material factor. Beginning in the mid-1980s, the price of cuttlefish had been slowly rising in the world market for fishery products, with Japan leading the charge as its main importer. As had happened earlier with prawn, the Kanyakumari sea was discovered to be rich in cuttlefish, which were found mainly in the region just around the 3-mile boundary that separated the inshore zone reserved for artisanal fishers from the offshore zone. This coincidence—one might call it the agency of the cuttlefish in nesting in a particular section of ocean space—sealed the class polarization. As its price rose and cuttlefish became the most coveted species caught off the Kanyakumari coast after prawn, the NFF, the Association for the Protection of Kattumaram and Vallam Fishing, and an increasing number of village councils began to independently demand trawler regulation. The terms in which they made their demands marked a shift from a moral economy argument based mainly on distributive justice to one framed in the language of ecology. Trawling must be regulated, they argued, not only because of the economic disparity between the mechanized minority and the larger community of fishers and the damage that trawl nets caused to artisanal fisher craft and gear, but also because of the need to preserve the marine resource for future generations. Even though *vallam* and *kattumaram* fishers began using more ecologically destructive fishing techniques—nets with smaller mesh sizes and fuel-intensive motors—in order to compete with one another and with trawlers for a diminishing resource, they invoked an ecological sense of community to contest trawler activity.

A series of clashes took place between 1993 and 1995, all during the months of August and September, when cuttlefish was found in abundance in the inshore area.[15] Once again, Kanyakumari's village council provided the leadership. In 1995, Kanyakumari's trawler owners submitted a petition to the district collector of Kanyakumari arguing that their craft were idle for fear of artisanal attacks and that artisanal craft should remain within the 3-mile inshore zone and not cross into the zone for mechanized craft.[16] The collector forwarded their demand[17] to the commissioner of fisheries in Madras, who dismissed it, stating that the 1983 act reserved a zone only for artisanal and not for mechanized craft.[18] In response, the trawler owners of Kanyakumari and Chinnamuttom decided to challenge the commissioner, the district collector, and the assistant director of fisheries in Kanyakumari in the Madras High Court.[19] The Madras High Court gave an interim injunction staying the order of the commissioner of fisheries for two weeks, within which time the local parties were to come to a new agreement. On the day before the two-week period expired, the trawler owners proceeded to fish armed with the court order and police protection. In reaction, artisanal villagers caused serious damage to their houses and literally evicted them from the coast.[20] Once again, both factions met with the district collector and the assistant director of fisheries and came up with a new agreement that reduced the trawl ban period from five months to three and a half months. Even though the agreement was not legally notarized by the Department of Fisheries, the village council members took it upon themselves to literally carve the text of the agreement on a stone tablet, which was then placed in front of the village's Lady of Ransom Church. As G. Stephen, one of the village councillors, remarked: "We didn't need the government to endorse the agreement; we had Mother Mary as our witness. We know best what is just: where to fish, how to fish, and how to protect the sea."

These recent discursive trends of appealing to the Virgin and expressing collectivity in terms of a highly localized—indeed naturalized—notion of ecological subjectivity suggest a form of spatial and cultural self-enclosure that reproduces the hegemonic divide between coast and inland. However, the stone tablet's references to the 1983 act and the repeated efforts by artisanal village after village to seek state recognition for their agreements make it clear how internal the state had become to their sense of political collectivity.

This expression of artisanal rights constituted a new moral economy of the artisan. However, this reconstituted moral order was by no means distinct from the state. Indeed, many of Kanyakumari village's fishermen and fisherwomen invoked none other than the figure of M. G. Ramachandran (MGR) as the moral authority behind their cause. Significantly, they made a point of distinguishing between the district state officials whom they encountered in their local negotiations with trawlers and the idea of a moral state as exemplified by the years of MGR's rule, using the figure of MGR to criticize state embeddedness in local power relations. But they did so to articulate an ideal relationship to the state rather than to assert their autonomy. Artisanal fishers' use of state laws such as the 1983 act and of state authorities such as MGR in redefining community exhibits their sense of themselves as a population very much in dialogue with the state if not wholly within its parameters. As I show in the final section, by the mid-1990s, artisanal fishers began to explicitly express this intimate link to the state in the language of citizenship.

Kanyakumari village's reinforcement of the monsoon trawl ban caused a chain reaction. Beginning in August 1993, village after village began to target trawling boats. In August 1993, motorized *vallam* fishers belonging to the Association for the Protection of Kattumaram and Vallam Fishing burned three of Colachel's trawlers, which they claimed had come into the 3-mile zone and destroyed two cuttlefish nets. In August 1994, motorized *vallam* fishers from Muttom village, which had the highest concentration of motorized craft, seized seven Colachel boats and took them to Muttom. In 1995 came the biggest conflagration of all. In August, then Tamilnadu fisheries minister Krishnakumar visited Colachel to survey the shore for the proposed construction of a harbor. In anticipation of his visit, Colachel's boat owners anchored their boats at sea. News of the minister's visit and the proposal to construct yet another harbor in the district created an uproar among artisanal fishers. To register their protest against this sign of collusion between state and mechanized sector interests, motorized *vallam* fishers from the villages of Muttom, Enayamputhenthurai, and Kadiapattanam spirited away four boats to Muttom. In retaliation, Colachel's boat workers caught two *vallam*s and fifteen *kattumaram*s and locked up fifty-two fishermen in the boat union office in Colachel. It took a meeting with the superintendent of police, the collector, and the Kottar bishop for each group to release its captured people and craft. Despite the mutual compromise, tempers were running high. Two days later, Colachel boats damaged the hooks and lines of two *vallam*s, which were fishing at the 3-mile border. In response, *vallam* fishers from seven different villages joined hands and burned fourteen boats anchored offshore in the sea adjacent to Colachel. In a final retaliation, Colachel boat workers turned on neighboring Kodimunai village, which was seen as complicit in the attack, and caused extensive damage to houses and artisanal craft. When three priests arrived to try to intervene, Colachel trawl boat workers took the unprecedented step of locking them up in the church. It was only then that the police arrived in force and ended the fighting with a display of gunfire that claimed the life of one *vallam* fisherman.[21]

Trawler Defense and Discourse of Science

Although they signed the 1995 agreement, Colachel's boat owners were incensed at this instance of what they perceived as the "tyranny of the majority" endorsed by both the state and the church. Their suggestions for alternative agreements, such as a three-three arrangement—each sector fishes three days of the week, with Sunday as a day of rest—which held in districts further north on the east coast, or the month-and-a-half trawling ban held in Kerala, had been shot down by the *vallam* and *kattumaram* fishers. In addition, the prospect of being hemmed in between an aggressive artisanal sector in the inshore area and foreign vessels beyond territorial waters caused even greater anxiety.

The Indian government's decision to license foreign vessels was especially devastating for the mechanized fishers, who had adopted the local self-image as representatives of national development. Beginning in 1987, in response to a rise in artisanal militancy, mechanized fishers embarked on a strident politics of representation as a modernizing force that would elevate their community from premodern obsolescence to national prominence. They began to speak of themselves as part of a modernizing middle class defined by its commitment to development. Many of Colachel's mechanized fishers diversified their investments, buying land as well as more trawling boats. The ownership of property away from the coast brought them into greater contact with interior caste groups and gave them a new affiliation with other economically mobile communities. Interestingly, they began to describe their own set of changing values by using the primitivizing language used by inland castes and government officials to distinguish coastal from agrarian culture. A disposition to save money rather than spend it rashly on liquor, to foster an ethic of cleanliness, to resolve conflict through dialogue and not force, and to give up insular thinking to foster ties with other communities are some of the ways that they characterized their cultural transformation from primitive to modern Mukkuvars. Consumption practices also changed dramatically. Big concrete homes, motorcycles, and cars became more common sights in Colachel and with these came a sharp rise in dowry rates. By the early 1990s, the dowry demands in Colachel were the highest in the district as a whole, reaching an upper limit of 10 million rupees. Along with lavish homes and exorbitant dowry rates, women's domestication also became a symbol of household status. These markers of "civilization" further insulated Colachel from other artisanal villages.

In response to artisanal redefinition of the marine commons in terms of the moral economy of artisanship, Colachel's mechanized fishers invoked national citizenship as the basis of *their* right to the resource. Faith in modern technology was pivotal to this identity. Their crusade as an embattled coastal minority committed to national development depended on the reverse image of a tyrannical artisanal majority manipulated by regressive local forces. One means that trawler owners adopted in expressing their opposition was the written word. The Colachel Boat Union printed and widely distributed pamphlets discrediting the mobilization work of their artisanal adversaries. One such pamphlet, "Boat Work and Fishermen's Development: The Real Story," is representative of their overall message and begins with a strong statement in favor of modernization.

> It is not wrong for people practicing traditional methods to change with the times and adopt new ones. This is evolutionary growth. People who used to walk now travel in vehicles. People who lived in caves now live in mansions. They used to use leaves to cover themselves; now they wear colorful clothes and live in sophisticated surroundings. They ate raw meat and now they eat cooked food. In agriculture, single cropping has given way to cultivating the land three times a year.
>
> But: It is a mystery that the fishermen who used *kattumaram*s and *vallam*s are still not accepted by many when they start using mechanized boats to catch fish. Are these people living in this century? Are they regressing? Are they being kept from developing by others?

The pamphlet distinguishes a generic "people's" natural evolution to modernity from the artisanal fishers' manipulative regression "by others." Significantly, *kattumaram* and *vallam* fishers are not even attributed with the capacity to be self-willed because if that were so, the pamphlet implies, then they too would "naturally" believe in evolution. As it stood, however, they were "regressing" and being "kept from developing." We learn from other pamphlets that this regressive force is the clergy, who "instead of preaching and tending to religious matters march on the streets like Communists and incite ignorant fishermen to violence." These pamphlets denounce the un-Christian values of the artisanal sector, which "only practices violence while the trawlers multiply the fish just as Jesus did." In contrast to these "bad" fishers and priests are the trawler owners, who "contribute financially to Catholic festivals and to the upkeep of parish churches" and have "given the Mukkuvar caste a national name."[22] Through these publications, Colachel's mechanized fishers underscored the greater contribution of trawler over artisanal fishing to the building of caste, church, and nation.

Significantly, the spatial polarization of Colachel from surrounding villages by sectoral affiliation produced a discursive erasure of class within the mechanized sector. As Colachel came to be known as the boat village, the owners and laborers (or coolies, as they are called in Kanyakumari) within the mechanized sector came to be defined collectively as the boat fishers. Even within Colachel, villagers refer to the collective of boat owners and coolies as the village's majority, although there are many more owners of artisanal than of mechanized craft. This erasure of class was made possible by several factors. First, the polarization of Colachel and artisanal villages and the increasing violence against trawl boats and coolie laborers at sea produced an identification of boat coolies with their employers. Second, despite a decisive shift in the mode of production, boat work continues to be structured in many of the same ways as artisanal production. For instance, the term *thozhilali*, or worker, is still used to refer to both owners and coolies in the boat sector, even though an increasing number of boat owners are now absentee capitalists who no longer participate in fishing. Also, boat fishing is organized as a share system and not as a wage system, which generates a different experience and consciousness of work. Although the distribution of shares—65 percent for owner and 35 percent for coolies—is far more hierarchical than in most forms of artisanal fishing—where owners get only one more share than the coolies—coolies leap to the defense of boat owners and argue that the share system allows them to accumulate savings and eventually invest in a boat of their own. Rarely does a coolie speak of the distribution of shares as unfair. They all point to the level of investment required as justification for the owner's far higher share.

Boat workers fall into two groups. One group consists of older fishers who lost their craft and gear to debt or dowry[23] and turned to coolie work on the boats. The second, rapidly expanding group consists of young men between the ages of 14 and 30. Most of their fathers were either artisanal fishers with their own craft and gear or recent members of the village coolie workforce. Although many of them have *kattumaram* and *vallam* fishers in their families, these young men, who grew up on a polarized coast, consider artisanal work beneath them. Rather than learn the painstaking skill of artisanal fishing from their fathers or uncles, they prefer to work on the boats with an eye open for making the move from worker to owner. An added deterrent to their participating in artisanal work is the fact that, from time to time, the coastal tensions between Colachel and surrounding villages have translated into attacks on the *vallam* and *kattumaram* fishers *within* Colachel.[24]

What Colachel has experienced, in effect, is a deskilling of the labor force, as more and more boat owners are opting for employing coolies in the 20 to 30 age range who are far less skilled than the older group trained in artisanal fishing. Advanced technology has thus allowed for the absorption of unskilled youth in the only occupation where they are competitive and can assert traditional or caste rights. Although a number of young men spoke of having changed boats often in reaction to "employer greed" and work conditions, their lack of artisanal fishing skills, the much higher profits of boat work, and the difficulty of mobility into other sectors of the economy keep them from leaving the mechanized sector altogether.

With the escalation of violence in the 1990s, Colachel's young boat workers began to form their own associations. Significantly, and despite the fact that many of them did suffer from poor wages and working conditions, these associations were not labor unions and never claimed to be. These were essentially institutionalized gangs that acted as muscle for boat owner–employers. Interestingly, most of these associations carried saints' names, such as the Antoniar Sangam (St. Anthony's Association) and the Kuzhanthai Yesu Sangam (Baby Jesus Association), and claimed to be working for "village uplift."[25]

In response to the combined threat of artisanal fishers on one side and foreign vessels on the other, both owners and workers in the mechanized sector began to selectively deploy ecological discourse, combined with a heavy dose of nationalism. Interestingly, their arguments against the Indian federal government's decision to license foreign vessels ran parallel to those of artisanal fishers against the Tamilnadu state government. These statements from boat owners and workers in Colachel reflect some striking similarities with artisanal arguments against trawling.

They are not allowed to fish here; only in the deep sea. But they violate the permit and come to the inshore where local fishermen fish. For us, this is very damaging. Where we cast our nets, they do pair trawling with two vessels and one net. Because of this, we get absolutely nothing. After coming back with empty nets over and over, we finally gave a report to the Fisheries Dept saying "foreign vessels are trawling close to the shore and this is damaging our livelihood so please restrict their operations." They took no action.

They have a zone. If they stay there, there's no problem. Most of us have taken out loans from the bank to purchase fishing boats. If the resource is destroyed, what'll we do? We have to meet loan payments, interest payments, and already our wives have no gold in their ears or around their necks. What'll we do?[26]

Even while arguing that foreign vessels transgressed into the territorial sea reserved for domestic craft and depleted the national resource, mechanized fishers insisted on the sustainability, indeed the *necessity*, of trawling. Most vehemently denied the applicability to their own work of the ecological arguments they themselves used against foreign vessels. Consider the following statements that are broadly representative of the way boat owners and workers characterized the nature of boat work:

> Only if we trawl is there catch for others. With the trawl net, we bring up plants for small fish and then cuttlefish gather to eat the fish. Without trawling, small fish would just hide.
>
> Fish life is very short so we need to catch them before they die. Prawn has to be caught within five months. *Kattumaram* and *vallam* fishers don't let us trawl close to shore, but they're not able to catch these prawns so they just die.
>
> The monsoon trawl ban is rubbish. I don't believe that eggs are destroyed by trawling, or that the catch will go down or is going down. Only with mechanized boats operating can India's annual income grow.
>
> There will always be fish here. More fish come as we catch them. It's just a question of the tide coming in and going out.[27]

This infighting within the fishing community was a distraction, they insisted, from the *real* problem of globalization, which was the actual reason why fish stocks were being depleted.

Nationalizing Trawling

The 1995 attack on Colachel damaged the craft of many boat owners and reflected new heights of artisanal militancy. In particular, it hurt the assets of Selvanayagam, a prosperous Mukkuvar who owned five trawlers, was a private seafood exporter to Japan, and had a net-manufacturing factory inland where more than 50 percent of the employees were Hindu Nadar women. After some deliberation, a group of Colachel's boat owners led by Selvanayagam decided to seek out S. P. Kutty, the Tamilnadu state secretary of the Hindu nationalist Bharatiya Janata Party (BJP; Indian People's Party) and its sister organization, the Swadeshi Jagaran Manch (SJM; Movement for Economic Self-Reliance), both offshoots of the Rashtriya Swayamsevak Sangh (RSS; National Volunteers' Organization).

As mentioned briefly in the Introduction, the RSS and the Vishwa Hindu Parishad (VHP; World Hindu Council) achieved coastal notoriety in the early 1980s by orchestrating a series of attacks on the coast. In early 1982, from March to May, activists from Hindu nationalist organizations and Hindu low caste agriculturalists whose lands bordered the coast clashed repeatedly with Mukkuvar Catholics. Tensions between Hindus and Christians were not new. They had arisen as early as the 1930s, when the southwestern region first witnessed political mobilization along religious lines. However, the crucial factor distinguishing this phase of Hindu nationalist mobilization from previous ones was the focus on space. As Catholic fisher artisans and trawler owners were making territorial claims of their own over land and sea, Hindu nationalists began to highlight the importance of Kanyakumari in the sacred geography of the "Hindu nation." To "liberate" this landscape from "imperial" Christianity, Hindu activists embarked on a project of reclamation. Hindu idols and other iconography would "appear" at church sites and along public thoroughfares that activists would then claim as part of a national sacred geography. These acts of appropriation were for the most part unaccompanied by physical violence, but this ended with the siege of the coast in 1982. Over a period of two weeks, vigilante Hindu squads attacked coastal fishing villages, burning churches and leaving Hindu symbols standing in their place, leveling homes, destroying fishing craft and gear, and literally driving Catholics into the sea. The attacks embodied the worst excesses of orchestrated mob violence, but they were framed in terms of a spontaneous nationalist defense against an alien faith. Within Hindu nationalist discourse, Catholicism had been transformed from a faith tradition with a long history of engagement with coastal dynamics into an aggressive residue of European colonialism, and the coast had been transformed from a borderland of a pluralist nation into a space of extraterritorial loyalties. Hindu majoritarianism negatively affected Christians across the district during that period, but the geographic isolation of Catholic fishers made them a particularly easy target. Existing discourses of Catholic primitivism, particularly Catholics' outsider status in relation to agrarian modernity, rhetorically buttressed their scapegoating.

After that initial spate of violence in 1981 and 1982, overt clashes ended, although religious hostilities persisted in more everyday form. Most insidiously, notions of Catholic foreignness acquired new political purchase. It was therefore particularly significant that Colachel's trawler owners sought the support of the very Hindu nationalist organizations responsible for the anti-Catholic pogroms a mere decade earlier. Selvanayagam explained his reasons for seeking Hindu nationalist support.

> We sought their support for two reasons. One, the BJP is the only party not involved with the artisanal sector. They also have no support at all in the coastal areas because we're all Christians. So it helped them to get the support of the mechanized sector. Second, if the *kattumarams* and *vallams* attack Colachel, then those fishermen can't go inland because they have to pass through the Hindu Nadar villages which are controlled by the BJP and the RSS.

Selvanayagam's astute territorial logic mirrored Hindu nationalist strategy in the clashes of 1982. Just as they did, he fell back on the geographic location of communities to orchestrate a Hindu invasion of the coast. Because the "Catholic coast" is literally hemmed in by the "Hindu interior," Selvanayagam explained, the BJP was the best answer to artisanal fisher aggression. On a more personal level, an alliance with the RSS and the BJP also ensured protection for his inland net factory, which he feared would be an easy target of artisanal anger.

The BJP's S. P. Kutty provided his own interpretation of Colachel's turn to Hindu nationalism.

> Colachel people have joined the BJP because their rise in financial position and education has caused them to revolt against the Christian hierarchy. One young man said to me "As long as we are poor and uneducated, we did not know what priests were doing. But now we know after having gotten some status. Now we understand how these fathers behave. In this district, it's a common saying that when fishermen are at sea and on shore drinking arrack and unconscious, their womenfolk are at the mercy of the priesthood. This has been happening for hundreds of years."[28]

Kutty's reasoning follows the logic of Sanskritization, a term used by anthropologist M. N. Srinivas to describe the adoption of upper caste practices by upwardly mobile low castes: With material "status," Christian fishers had begun to reject the symbols of their cultural inferiority and aspire to a cultural identity that was commensurate with their newfound social capital. Hinduism provided them with the cultural status that was missing within the Christian fold and served as a weapon against their clerical oppressors. This interesting reversal of the nineteenth- and twentieth-century conversion narratives, with Hinduism providing the escape from the cultural hierarchy of Christianity, was especially striking because Colachel's fishers did *not* convert to Hinduism. Speaking of the presence of Christian fishers within the BJP, Kutty explained that conversion was not a goal of the party.

> They were considering conversion but I said, we don't want you to convert. Don't come to the Hindu fold; just understand your country. Ninety-nine percent of Christians and Muslims think BJP is a Hindu party. But we just say that there won't be any appeasement, that we'll only give you clean government. But if you feel you've come from Pakistan or Rome, we won't tolerate it.[29]

In his defense against "church poison" about the BJP forcing conversions, breaking mosques, destroying churches, and taking away minority rights, Kutty countered that the party had every intention of enforcing a common civil code in place of the existing personal laws for religious minorities but that this goal was a mark of the party's secularism. Referring to a 1995 Supreme Court judgment on Hindutva,[30] the term coined by Hindu nativist ideologue V. D. Savarkar for political Hinduism, he exclaimed, "Even the Supreme Court has given the verdict that Hindutva is a way of life. It doesn't mean Hindu religion. It is Bharatiya culture. BJP stands for Indian culture. But in Christianity and Islam, the preaching is that wherever you live, you are under Pope and Prophet." Kutty was careful to distinguish the BJP's position on conversion from that of its sister organization, the VHP. "The VHP is a religious organization while we are a political party," he explained, adding quickly that the VHP also did not conduct conversions; it only helped minorities "find their way back to Hindu culture through reconversion." Indeed, Kutty proclaimed, "The BJP believes in religious tolerance. We don't expect all our members to be Hindus. They can follow whatever religion they wish, as long as they are patriotic to Bharat and its Hindu culture."[31]

This restatement of Hinduism in assimilative, cultural nationalist terms that rejected the need for religious conversion clinched the BJP's arrangement with Colachel's mechanized boat owners and workers. On their part, the fishers from Colachel who approached Kutty admitted to considering conversion initially as a way of striking out at the state, the church, and their artisanal adversaries. They cited the instance of an earlier revolt in 1964 against the Catholic Church in Idinthikarai, a coastal village in neighboring Tirunelveli

District. During that revolt fishermen converted to Hinduism under the guidance of the VHP to escape the church's fish tax (see Sivasubramanian 1996). However, Colachel's fishers ultimately decided that conversion was too far a step to take, and, besides, the RSS and the BJP had not made their support conditional on conversion. In speaking of their decision to collaborate with the BJP, most of Colachel's boat owners and workers referred to their decision not to convert as evidence that they had done only what was absolutely necessary to ensure their livelihood and protection against more violence. As Sahaya Antony, the Colachel fisherman nominated as president of the newly formed BJP fishermen *sangam*, stated:

> We only voted for the BJP. We didn't change our religion. And also, it's only after joining the BJP that I see that it's not them who are religious fanatics. It's the church! In fact, the fathers were behind the problem. If they had taken steps, this trouble would not have gotten so bad. They should be neutral and for peace, but they are on one side. Our own Christian leaders support and encourage trouble so why shouldn't we go to the BJP? We didn't change religion or anything. But because of the BJP, we were safe.[32]

In simultaneously defending their faith while disavowing the church, Colachel's trawler owners spoke of two kinds of spatialized majority-minority dynamics, one local and the other national. Speaking of the local situation, they expressed their sense of being a threatened "coastal minority" that was besieged by the combined forces of artisanal aggression and religious orthodoxy. To defend their minority status on the coast, they explained, they had to turn to a national majoritarian force that could curb the local power of the church and artisanal fishers. In effect, this was a restatement of federalism in which a local economic minority took recourse to the protective force of Hindu nationalism to ensure their economic rights in the face of local religious power. The national situation, they maintained, would humble the coalition between artisanal fishers and clergy, because at the national level, they were minorities both economically and culturally. In delineating "community" from "nation," Colachel's mechanized fishers actually pointed to a line between coast and inland where, they stated, community ended and nation began. Significantly, nation was equated with the absence of the church and the presence of inland castes. If the *vallam* and *kattumaram* fishers attacked Colachel, they strategized, "we can escape to the interior Hindu Nadar villages which are controlled by the BJP and the RSS. The Bishop is scared now because he knows that, if they attack us, we have the RSS on our side. The church can't tell us what to do anymore. We're with the BJP now."[33]

Sahaya Antony and other mechanized fishers characterized fisher activism in Kanyakumari as communitarian and political, which they contrasted to artisanal fisher activism in Kerala, which was "valid" because it was scientifically grounded and nationally recognized. "It's only because *vallam*s and *kattumaram*s are the majority here," they complained, "that this agreement has been forced on us. In Kerala, the ban is for a valid reason—to protect spawning—and the national government has recognized it. Here we have a ban only because there is majority rule." John Rose, a Colachel boat owner who became the cashier of the BJP fishermen's *sangam*, declared that communism was the ideology behind this community-based majority rule and the clergy's weapon against the rise of a lay coastal leadership.

> Priests are responsible for all this fighting—Father Sales, Father Kocherry. Our community has many illiterates. When money is available, they send children for education. Especially in Colachel, there are many educated people now. Before we used to just be quiet. Now we answer back, and the church doesn't like that. That's why the parish priests have gone communist and say that the trawlers are destroying fish eggs. So we boat owners opposed the church and joined the BJP. BJP didn't look for votes like other parties that answer to the artisanal majority. The BJP and SJM are more interested in the right to work for all citizens. That's why they oppose the foreign vessels and support us also. They understand that no one has right to stop work.[34]

In addition to the RSS's paramilitary strength and the BJP's political support, the SJM's particular variant of economic nationalism was a crucial attraction for Colachel's boat owners. Like the NFF, the SJM opposed the Indian government's 1991 deep-sea fishing policy. But unlike the forum's opposition to both foreign and domestic capitalization of the fishery, the SJM advocated the more rapid spread of trawling technology across the Indian fishery. In 1995 the SJM undertook an awareness campaign among fishers by conducting a *jala yatra*, or water pilgrimage, from Somnath on the west coast to Vishakapatnam on the east coast. In SJM national co-convener S. Gurumurthy's words, "The pilgrimage sought to unify the national mind against the threat of foreign capitalist vessels.[35] Upon reaching Vishakapatnam, SJM, BJP, and RSS leaders organized a conference on the deep-sea fishing policy. In his message to the participants, D. B. Thengadi, RSS member and founder of the SJM, defined

Swadeshi as a call for "envisaging globalization on the principle of Hindu economics. Our task is to project a philosophy of globalization on the principle of
Vedic guidance for International Trade" (Swadeshi Jagaran Manch 1995).

Within the SJM framework, the Hindu nation is composed of concen-
tric circles of family, group, caste, and community functioning organically
through the operation of the unifying principle of *dharma* (duty). From this
perspective, the state is not the force of nation building; rather, the nation
predates the state and provides its cultural ethos. Interestingly, because the
cement of society is the "duty" that binds people who inhabit different kinds
of social relationships, the integrative and redistributive functions of the state
are deemed irrelevant. Rather, society appears as an organism functioning according to essential cultural principles, outside the purview of the state.

However, this vision of society as a cultural organism functioning outside
state machinery does not preclude the crucial role played by capitalism. Interestingly, unlike socialism, which is defined as completely outside the cultural framework of Hinduism, SJM leaders maintain that capitalism *can* be
indigenized and indeed that Indian capitalism is easily reconciled with the
functioning of *dharma*. Speaking of this indigenized capitalism, Gurumurthy explained: "We will have capitalism, but nationalist capitalism like Japan
does. Indian capitalists will not be greedy. They will spend large amounts for
Dharmic purposes." Within this vision, indigenous capitalism will flourish,
and Indian capitalists will contribute to the overall uplift of the country as a
part of their patriotic duty.[36]

The SJM's articulated commitment to the capitalist development of domestic fisheries provided Colachel's fishers with the assurance of support
against both local environmentalism and global capitalism. Against the artisanal sector's claim to common property, trawler owners and workers asserted
their right to private property as a means to developing the national resource.
Against the church's local religious authority, they asserted their national citizenship. This reliance on the nation—and a particular class perspective on the
nation—secured their alliance with Hindu nationalism.

Enforcing Locality

Colachel's turn to Hindu nationalist support signaled an exacerbation of
coastal tensions and threatened a repetition of the Hindu-Catholic clashes
that had inflamed the coast in 1982, only this time with Colachel on one side
with the BJP, RSS, and SJM, and the Catholic Church and artisanal fishers on

the other. Once the clashes subsided, the two officials in charge of maintaining law and order in Kanyakumari District—the collector and the revenue divisional officer—and the assistant director of fisheries for the district called on the Catholic Church to act as a mediating force between the warring fishers and between community and state.

All three state officials explained their decision to approach the church as a necessary measure to deal with a population that recognized religious authority above state authority. Significantly, they distinguished coastal peace-keeping in Kanyakumari from that in other parts of the Tamilnadu coastal belt where the fisher population is Hindu or multifaith in character. "Here, they are not integrated into the wider society," the collector explained, "and so we have to deal with them more carefully. They're like a sea tribe; they don't understand the laws that govern the rest of the society. They're very volatile and superstitious, and they don't respect state authority. Only the church can tell them what to do."[37] Along the same lines, the revenue divisional officer, who organized several peace talks between artisanal and mechanized fishers, also protested that the fishing community respected only church authority. "If you want to attract their attention," she said in an exasperated tone, "you only have to ring the church bell and they'll come running. And if the *government* requests them to attend a meeting, they won't move an inch!"[38] Most telling was the reaction of the assistant director of fisheries, who had worked with coastal populations for more than three decades. In the middle of a conversation, he confessed that the Kanyakumari fishers were a group that he just "cannot relate to." When pushed on why a population of fishermen and fisherwomen would seem so alien to a fisheries official, he finally answered that it was because they were "even more inward-looking than other fisher communities."[39] Although these officials acknowledged that the emergence and spread of lay institutions on the coast represented competing representative authorities, they assured me that all such secular institutions were ultimately subject to the sway of clerical power and therefore could function best when brought under the umbrella of the church.[40] In effect, their answer was to devolve more responsibility to the "natural leaders" of the coast and fall back on the "traditional" identities of caste and religion to mitigate the class tensions generated by development modernization.

This raises the question of why, after forty years of development intervention, state officials continue to characterize Catholic fishers as an insulated community outside the parameters of state power. Why do they see coastal conflicts as problems of intracommunity law and order when artisanal fishers have consistently demanded that the state intervene in the local fishery to regulate trawling?

The state's willful disregard of its imbrication in the makeup of coastal community through forty postindependence years is a mode of bureaucratic practice that has hardened in the postliberalization period. As Partha Chatterjee (1993) has argued, the developmental state has long exhibited the propensity to distinguish the spaces of policy and politics. For most Tamilnadu Department of Fisheries officials, artisanal activism is simply community politics and cannot be used as a means to craft state policy. As should be clear from the discussion of the Community Development Program era in Chapter 4, this attitude toward the targets of state developmentalism is of earlier vintage. However, I would argue that the recourse to community in the 1990s in Kanyakumari also signaled a departure from the 1950s understanding of community. One key difference was in the privileging of religious authority and not state mediation in resolving rural social ills. The 1950s developmental state recognized rural social hierarchies as a problem to be solved by state intervention, but the wealth generated by the Blue Revolution obscured increasing coastal conflict and inequality. In the 1990s, law and order became a much more pressing concern than wealth redistribution, and, in this cause, church mediation was enlisted. The purpose of church mediation was to respatialize Mukkuvar artisans as resolutely local by binding them to a single, spatially circumscribed authority. In turning to the church, district officials sought to use clerical patronage to curb artisanal maneuver. To put it differently, "community" came to serve as a means for the liberalizing state to protect the conditions for capital accumulation and disregard distributive justice.

This disregard, even dismissal, of social policy in favor of a narrowly defined economic policy is symptomatic of a more general disaffection in the postliberalization period with the role of the state as an engine of social change. Significantly, this growing disregard for the social dimensions of state policy has coincided with the call for decentralized management of resources and devolution of authority to the community.[41] One would expect that the valorization of devolution would provoke a reappraisal of the rigid divide between policy and politics and between state and community. What we see instead is a hardened stance against local politics. Most fisheries officials contrast fisher politics, which they regard as whimsical and reactionary, with "real" development and conservation work, which they locate firmly within the domain of science. This instinct to rationalize development as a neutral zone set apart from the vicissitudes of political life echoes James Ferguson's (1994) characterization of development as "an anti-politics machine." As several department officials indicated, for them devolution meant standing by local agreements, which was simply the quick and easy way of dissipating tensions on the coast and assuaging the volatile passions of the fisher population. Even when they agreed that resource management was needed, they were quick to assure me that this recognition was in no way produced by artisanal fisher activism against trawling.

What this has meant in Tamilnadu is that the political ramifications of developmental intervention are systematically placed outside the boundaries of state responsibility. This negligence is seen in every dimension of the government's approach to its fishery, despite its purported commitment to resource management. Unlike the Kerala government, which has responded to pressure from the substantial numbers of mobilized artisans in its largest industry, commissioned scientific studies of resource depletion, and legislated regulatory measures to curb stock depletion, the Tamilnadu government has done next to nothing to look into artisanal fisher complaints of stock collapse and increasing social vulnerability. Rather, the Tamilnadu Department of Fisheries has counted on the steady rise in value of fisheries products and the increasing number of species in demand for export and has remained complacent and unresponsive on the issue of resource management. It has not responded to artisanal activism to determine ceilings for the number of mechanized boats in any fishing port or for the state as a whole. Trawl net mesh size, which determines whether juvenile fish are caught, also remains unregulated. Finally, the linchpin of the 1983 Tamilnadu Marine Fisheries Regulation Act—the prohibition of mechanized boat fishing within 3 nautical miles from shore—is also basically unenforced because patrolling capacity is limited. All in all, mechanized boat fishing in the state remains fundamentally unregulated and subject to the local agreements made with artisanal fishermen.

To some extent, the argument of fisheries officials that fishermen are best left to decide fishing rules through local agreements has merit. Officials argue that any effort to impose formal laws would have no effect because fishermen will simply not respect them. However, there are several problems with this argument in favor of localized, informal regulation. First, because such agreements have no legal status, they can and are overridden by state courts, to which trawler owners have routinely turned. Second, as I have argued, the state's willingness to turn over regulation to the local level stems from its understanding of conflict as a problem of law and order rather than one of resource conservation and social justice. For fisheries officials, local regulation is a quick fix for coastal turbulence but should in no way be confused with the science of conservation. This attitude has allowed the Tamilnadu Department of Fisheries to relinquish authority over the course of fisheries development to the free market just when the negative fallout of development is most acutely felt. Finally, in Kanyakumari the church's role in overseeing informal agreements has increased fisher frustrations over their lack of access to the state. As I show in the next section, these frustrations expressed by both artisanal and mechanized fishers have led not to the rejection of the state but to a rejection of church mediation, which they have increasingly experienced as a limit on their rights of citizenship.

The Coastal Peace and Development Council

In November 1995, at the behest of the assistant director of fisheries, the district collector, and the revenue divisional officer, the Kottar church established the Coastal Peace and Development Council. Although the council was established as a "coastal people's body," it came under the jurisdiction of the church and had a clerical leadership. The council's general body consisted of one representative from each coastal village, three representatives from each of the three trade unions, one parish priest from each six-village zone, a priest appointed by the bishop to be the director of the council, a coordinator from the fishing community who was not an active fisherman, the vicar-general of the diocese, and a set of four nominees selected by the bishop. The assistant director of fisheries was an invited guest at the council and was requested but not required to attend. Significantly, it was Father Selvaraj, the priest reputed to be sympathetic to the boat sector, who was chosen as director. Although most artisanal fishers resisted this decision, the bishop thought that Selvaraj's presence was necessary to inspire the mechanized sector's confidence in the council and bring them to the table. Equally significant was the hierarchy of goals elucidated by the council: It was intended primarily to be a peacekeeping force, with a secondary concern for resource management.

The council wielded three key shared elements in its efforts to foster coastal peace: religion, caste, and nationalism.[42] Father Jesudoss, an older Mukkuvar priest who has served in coastal parishes for more than forty years, often began council meetings with a prayer for peace. He spoke of Christian forgiveness, the community of Christ, and the natural advantage that Kanyakumari's fishers had over others who did not share the same faith. "You are all one community," he reminded the gathered fishers, "and have always been one community. We have always been able to work out our differences as a family. Surely we can still do that?"[43] The language of sin and redemption was a crucial ingredient in council discussions. Hearing the clergy slide back and forth between using cost-benefit analysis and using the language of sin and redemption to address fisher grievances, one got the distinct sense of the flexibility of church authority over its fisher congregation and the state's role on the coast as mere onlooker onto dynamics internal to a bounded community.

The call for Christian community in the face of divisive influences was buttressed by shared caste status. For the Mukkuvar clergy, the council provided an arena in which to address caste concerns and ultimately to consolidate caste power within the church. Those who had witnessed Nadar ascendance to power in the 1960s with resentment saw in the council an opportunity to secure representative authority over the coast and to wield this authority in staking a greater claim to church resources. The council was to provide a corrective to the imbalance of caste power between Nadars and Mukkuvars in the district as a whole, an imbalance that they believed also structured the church. It was to be the voice of the Mukkuvar community as a consolidated low caste Catholic population. In council meetings and during interviews afterward, the clergy repeatedly invoked caste uplift as a reason for reconciling sectoral differences. When I asked about the resource question and the parallels between the intersectoral violence in Kanyakumari and in other districts, I was told, "We are a backward caste and have always been one. This *sahodarar yudham* [war of brothers] is not helping us achieve a respectable standard of living. First we must stop the war; then we can turn to other issues like resource management."[44]

The council's emphasis on strengthening community ties to foster peace was a return to the turbulence of the early days of mechanization. As they had then, the Mukkuvar clergy associated with the council urged fishers to think of themselves in cultural, not class, terms. Although the clergy did not laud mechanization as the answer to the underdevelopment of the community, as they had in the 1950s and 1960s, they did warn that class war would be to the detriment of the community as a whole. The explicit invocation of caste in their articulation of community was also a shift from the 1960s. As part of their council work, the clergy underscored the need for caste uplift and representation at a time when other low castes were benefiting from affirmative action and increased participation in the Indian public sphere. Both locally and nationally, they pointed out, Mukkuvars needed to make their mark on India and become a visible part of the national mainstream.

The Breakdown of Peace Talks

Three months later, in September 1996, almost exactly a year after the 1995 clash, the uneasy truce that had been maintained since the establishment of the Coastal Peace and Development Council broke down. Five boats from Colachel and one each from the nearby villages of Vanniyakudi and Chinnavalai that were operating within the 3-mile zone were captured by approximately 200 *vallam* fishermen and taken to the Muttom village shore, where four boats were burned and three were sunk. Some of the boat fishermen onboard were beaten severely.[45]

Immediately after the clash, the Coastal Peace and Development Council called an emergency session. The meeting was in an uproar. Fathers Selvaraj and Jesudoss began the session by distinguishing between the actions of the two factions. Although blame must be placed on both sides, they asserted that there was no justification for the attacks on the boats and for the financial loss incurred by the owners because of the destruction of their craft. The actions of the fishermen on the boats did not warrant the severity of the punishment they received at the hands of the *vallam* fishermen. The fishermen on the boats had committed a *kuttram* (sin), but the *vallam* fishermen had committed a *maha kuttram* (great sin).

After days of negotiation, no resolution was found for the 1996 clash. The *vallam* fishermen were unwilling to compensate the boat owners for their loss, and the boat fishermen refused to work toward a new agreement without compensation. Bernard, the DMK Legislative Assembly member for the Colachel constituency, also attended the meetings and tried to wield his political influence and image as a lay representative of the community to foster good will between the two sides. But neither side was willing to budge, and each side found fault not only with the other but also with the church.

After the breakdown of talks, Colachel's boat owners argued that they could not trust the council to arrive at a reasonable solution to the impasse because of the church's role in precipitating the crisis. They pointed out that it was the church's role in development that first began the motorization drive and the ensuing violence. The church was not neutral, they complained, because the influence of communism on the clergy limited their ability to see the significant contribution that boats had made to the development of both community and nation.[46]

On their part, *vallam* and *kattumaram* fishermen expressed their frustration and resolved to seek alternative channels to address their concerns. The council, many stated resolutely, had made it more difficult to get justice. They found that when they tried to meet state officials directly to express concerns over livelihood, their complaints were deflected to council director Father Selvaraj. Voicing his frustration about this growing trend, Bergmans, the president of the Association for the Protection of Kattumaram and Vallam Fishing, exclaimed, "We are not interested in being in the Council any longer. I spoke out strongly last year. This year, because I've been incorporated into the Council, I've been silenced. Previously, the Collector would call me to discuss issues. Now he doesn't. If we approach the Collector or Revenue Divisional Officer with a complaint, they tell us that they'll only talk to Fr. Selvaraj!"[47] Bergmans and other *vallam* fishermen pointed to the process in Kerala as an ideal to emulate: "There, the government listens to fishers, and the church has no say in fishing matters. Why is the church interfering here? The priests don't have the power to do anything anyway. Every time we demand punishment for the boats, they say, 'The Council cannot punish, so go to the government.' Well, we'll just forget about the priests then and go straight to the government!"[48]

However, *vallam* and *kattumaram* fishermen admitted to also being frustrated by the state's discrepant treatment of the two sectors. They pointed out that, in the negotiations that followed the clashes of 1995 and 1996, the boat owners had been allowed to represent themselves before the ADMK representative, the revenue divisional officer, and the collector, whereas these state officials had requested the presence of the parish priests of the artisanal fisher villages involved in the conflict. This, they concluded, meant that the state did not consider the NFF or the Association for the Protection of Kattumaram and Vallam Fishing adequate to the task of representing their members.

Third, many of the *vallam* and *kattumaram* fishers thought that the emphasis on peacekeeping meant that, most often, their attacks on trawlers were interpreted as a worse sin than the more subterranean violence of resource depletion committed by the trawlers. They pointed to the reactions of the clergy to the 1996 clash as evidence. "Why were we the only ones to blame?" a few members of the Association for the Protection of Kattumaram and Vallam Fishing exclaimed. "It was the boat owners who committed the first wrong by breaking the 1995 agreement!" One of the fishers ended the conversation by stating emphatically, "It is time for war, not peace. So what if we're all brothers? We'll attack the trawlers if we think they're not obeying the rules of the coast!"[49]

The breakdown of peace talks was not even resolved by a dramatic incident that occurred the following month. In early October, artisanal and mechanized fishers operating near the Chinnamuttom harbor caught three foreign vessels poaching in territorial waters. They surrounded the vessels, climbed aboard, forced the vessels to anchor near the shore, and took catch and sailors hostage. In a statement to the press, the mechanized fishers of Kanyakumari village drew attention to the depletion of the marine resource by foreigners and the suffering of Indian fishers. "We were forced to catch the vessels," they stated, "because the government refused to heed our complaints and take action. It was only then that our community people all gathered together and decided that we somehow have to catch a foreign vessel. Only then would the government take proper steps" (*The Hindu*, October 15, 1996). The Coastal Peace and Development Council tried to capitalize on this "heroic defense of the national resource" (*Kottar Newsletter*, November 1996) by both artisanal and mechanized fishers in order to reinitiate regular council gatherings. However, both sectors expressed their increasing suspicion and disillusionment with clerical mediation and resolved to address their concerns through independent channels.

The power that the council continued to assume over the coast, despite a growing disillusionment with the peacekeeping process, culminated in an unprecedented step taken by fisher artisans in June 1997. Artisans from Kovalam village launched an attack on trawling boats, after which the boat owners approached the council for justice. Father Selvaraj called a meeting during which a decision was reached by all present to forbid Kovalam's artisans from fishing for a week. This provoked an outraged response from the village council, whose members approached the Kanyakumari District Fishermen Sangams Federation for help. After discussions with the South Indian Federation of Fishermen Societies, the federation's apex body in Kerala, Kovalam's villagers and the federation board decided to wield secular law against their religious leadership and take the council to court. "We needed to teach the church a lesson," explained Vincent, one of Kovalam's councillors, "so the priests realize that they can't stop us from fishing. Let them stay behind the pulpit where they belong!"[50]

By making the unprecedented move of taking the church to court, Kovalam's villagers signaled a wholesale rejection of the compact between state and church that upheld the church as the main representative authority of the coast. For the first time in the history of the coast, Catholic fishers wielded state law against their religious leadership, accused the clergy of overstepping the limits of their authority, and demanded their right as citizens to oppose church decrees. If the church worked against the poor, they asserted, it could no longer be the moral backbone of the Catholic community.

In their petition, they called on the state as benefactor of the poor and patron of the artisan to recognize and protect their rights as custodians of the local sea and to regulate trawling. Significantly, the village councillors who drafted the petition on behalf of fifteen artisanal fishing villages made a point of distinguishing between the district officials whom they encountered in their negotiations with trawlers and the state as a moral umbrella that, unlike the church, transcended the vicissitudes of local politics. At the same time, the petition also held the state to a higher standard. Cataloguing the many transgressions of justice enacted by church and state in support of Kanyakumari's trawler owners, the petition called on the court to bring justice to artisans by reinstating "MGR *rajyam*" (MGR rule). By claiming a privileged link to this moral state through the figure of MGR and by using the courts to stage their protest, artisanal fishers expressed a demand for justice—indeed, for equal citizenship—that fused patronage and rights.

Conclusion

ON DECEMBER 26, 2004, the Asian tsunami struck the Indian coast, causing catastrophic destruction of life and livelihood. The southern coastal belt was the worst affected. Among southern districts, Kanyakumari faced the worst losses after Nagapattinam: 1,500 fisher lives, 7,800 coastal homes, and more than 10,000 boats, 1,000–1,500 motors, and 30,000 nets. It was a disaster of overwhelming proportions, particularly for a population whose lifeline is the sea. Some of the most poignant testimonies from fisher survivors spoke of their sense of betrayal and fear, how fishing nets and boats became death traps for many fleeing the waves, their bodies entangled in nets and thrown against boats. "The nets that fed us have killed us," one coastal villager said; another spoke of the tsunami as *kadalamma*'s (goddess of the sea) vengeance for profligate resource exploitation.

In some ways, the outpouring of concern and support for coastal inhabitants was a notable departure from the historical negligence of coastal problems. The disproportionate harm experienced by fishers put them in the spotlight like never before. Aid flooded in. Newspaper coverage of the coast was sympathetic and highlighted the suffering of fisher families and the collaboration of civil society organizations and individual citizens in cleanup, housing construction, and distribution of food. I have not been back to Kanyakumari since the tsunami, but I have followed the rehabilitation process from a distance through conversations with friends and through the many publications put out by the Tamilnadu government, nongovernmental organizations, and activist movements in the fisheries sector.[1] In what follows, I address some of the concerns raised by fisher artisans and their activist supporters that reflect many of the problems associated with the political economy of fishing and cultural perceptions of coastal populations.

One of the main concerns was the assessment of loss and compensation. Did compensation mean giving back to each family what they had lost: a two-story house for a two-story house and a hut for a hut, a trawler for a trawler and a *kattumaram* for a *kattumaram*? Or did reconstruction mean a move toward equality and trying to ensure that new assets were more equally distributed? Who would be given priority? Would the rich get their boats first and then, with whatever money was left, *kattumaram*s be provided to other fishers? Or would the poorest get what they had lost and only after would the well-to-do get their losses covered? What about laborers who had no assets of their own?

In most instances, it quickly became clear that existing social hierarchies of class and caste were giving shape to the rehabilitation effort. First was the class question. Fishing assets have always been privately owned, usually by nuclear family units, although many owners in both artisanal and mechanized sectors employ laborers on their craft. Unlike in the artisanal sector, however, where individuals shift status from owner to laborer depending on whether they are operating their own or someone else's craft, the division between owner and laborer on trawlers is fairly rigid. I have yet to encounter a trawler owner who labors on another's craft, although trawler laborers are sometimes owners of artisanal craft. After the tsunami and depending on the coastal region, laborers who previously had no fishing assets of their own were either given boats indiscriminately (more on this later) or were prevented from receiving boats by their trawler owner–employers, who feared losing a captive labor force. In some areas, such as parts of Nagapattinam District, trawler laborers formed their own unions to demand equal treatment as an affected population in their own right. In other areas, such as Kanyakumari, where the sectoral divide had ensured the more effective subordination of a trawler proletariat to owners, the needs of trawler laborers failed to be adequately addressed.

Second was the caste question. In Kanyakumari, where low caste fishers constituted the overwhelming majority of coastal dwellers, there was less opportunity for caste discrimination. However, farther north, Dalit inhabitants (the former untouchable castes who occupy the lowest rung of the caste ladder) were often disregarded in favor of fisher castes whose claim to coastal resources was assumed to take precedence. A starker form of caste stigma also came into play. In relief shelters, caste segregation was prevalent, with fisher castes permitted to physically separate themselves from Dalits. Indeed, such stigmatization was not limited to tsunami victims. Government bodies overseeing the relief effort also employed Dalits for some of the most menial tasks associated with "polluting" labor, such as the cleanup of corpses, reproducing long-standing understandings of how caste, labor, and status are tied.

The trend of privileging fisher castes was exacerbated by the Tamilnadu government's choice of dominant local organizations to administer coastal relief: in the north, fisher *panchayat*s, and in the south, the Catholic Church. In line with what Tania Li calls neoliberal "governance through community" (Li 2007), the assumed isomorphism between territory, authority, and community resulted in the overlooking of internal coastal schisms of class, caste, and family. In some cases, adequate oversight ensured checks on the unevenness of relief. In Nagapattinam, for instance, the South Indian Federation of Fishermen Societies (SIFFS) coordinated the relief effort out of the district collectorate alongside the Social Needs Education and Human Awareness nongovernmental organization (NGO). Together, the two organizations, one a fisher activist organization and the other a broader social organization, formed the Resource Center for Tsunami Relief through which money and effort were channeled. By contrast, in Kanyakumari, responsibility for coastal recovery was predictably relegated to the Catholic Church. The diocesan Kottar Social Service Society (KSSS) served as the coordinating body for setting up refugee camps for displaced fisher families, distributing food and clothing, and organizing housing construction. Significantly, it was not just the government that delegated authority to the church. Organizations working on the coast that have been critical of the church's representative monopoly, such as SIFFS, also decided to work under its auspices to ensure better coordination of the relief effort. Although the KSSS appears to have operated transparently, a number of fishers and NGO groups I corresponded with perceived the choice of the church as yet another instance of state neglect.

Coastal land expropriation was another key concern in the aftermath of the tsunami. Coastal land is prime real estate coveted by the tourism, aquaculture, and other industries. Customary rights to coastal land and livelihood have long served as a partial barrier to corporate takeover of seashore property. After the tsunami, these industries set their sights on the evacuated shoreline. As Naomi Klein (2007) noted in her book on disaster capitalism, the tsunami was seen by many corporate investors as an opportunity to open up common property previously out of reach to private investment. This was especially the case in Sri Lanka, where the alienation of coastal land occurred at a precipitous pace. In Kanyakumari, by contrast, the presence of the Catholic Church as a long-standing institutional authority appears to have prevented privatization. This does not mean, however, that incentives to evacuate the coast were not on offer. Understandably, fishers and other coastal dwellers in southern India expressed fear at the prospect of another tsunami and living with that sense of vulnerability. Information about the infrequency of tsunamis could have gone a long way toward dispelling such fears, allowing coastal inhabitants to make a more informed choice about rehabilitation. However, in most instances government officials conveniently assumed that permanently relocating inland would be preferred by coastal dwellers, an assumption that rested on the desire to free up coastal land and on sedimented beliefs about a coastal culture of poverty and backwardness. The Tamilnadu government did not make relocation away from the coast mandatory, but its incentive package of land and $3,388 for housing construction in the inland was a serious push factor, especially compared with the absence of any financial assistance to rebuild on the coast. Although the Tamilnadu government insisted that its relocation scheme was intended purely for the safety of fisher families and not to make coastal land available to other industries, suspicions remained alive and well that alienated land would quickly be siphoned off by the far more powerful hotel or aquaculture lobby.

The way that rehabilitation schemes were elaborated gave little consideration to the specificities of fishers' relationship to coastal land: first, that living on the shore, even in vulnerable thatched huts, was a great convenience for their livelihood; second, that coastal inhabitants belong to a population with strong historical attachments to place; and finally, that rehabilitation schemes that sought to shift fishers inland disregarded the importance of coastal land as an asset, particularly for the most marginalized. Land ownership on the Tamilnadu coast is a tenuous business, with most coastal land officially classified as *poromboke* (government land), but in practice the coastal land comes under the jurisdiction of customary authorities of one kind or another. Although such land is recognized as having use but not exchange value, people commonly build houses and "sell" the land valued at the cost of the house. With the increase in coastal wealth over the last forty years, families with marriage-age girls and no other assets will often sell their land in this way to meet dowry demands. The alienation of coastal land thus hits at the most vulnerable among fisher populations.

The most serious concern raised by fisher artisanal organizations was the flood of capital investment into the Tamilnadu fishery. Immediately after the tsunami struck, the unprecedented volume of aid targeted at affected populations rapidly became evident. Some of this funding, much of it from the European Union, was for fishing assets. India has a long history of experiments with inappropriate technology transfer that have resulted in class division and the depletion of particular marine fish species. In light of the preponderance of evidence that technology transfer needs regulation, the Coalition for Fair Fisheries Agreements (CFFA), based in Brussels, has insisted that the minimum standards for vessel transfers should include compliance with local requirements and adherence to genuine needs assessments rather than to European Union demands, compliance with local development priorities for job creation and for improving average income levels and working conditions, and assurance that vessel and gear transfers have positive social and environmental impact. In the posttsunami recovery, however, the influx of fishing assets was permitted without regard to these criteria.

The unregulated distribution of boats for the sole purpose of enhancing the productive capacity of fishers provoked an immediate response from fishery activist organizations. They pointed out that Tamilnadu's marine fishery had reached overcapacity in the 1980s, after which fishing craft recorded steadily decreasing catch volumes. This would be the time, they insisted, to rethink the developmental trajectory of the fishery and shift it in a more ecologically sound direction. This meant refusing technology transfers that were unsuitable for a multispecies tropical fishery dominated by artisanal beach-landing craft and incapable of supporting the larger capital-intensive craft that required harbor facilities. It also meant a serious commitment to diversifying employment options for coastal dwellers so that they did not have to rely on a dwindling resource for their livelihood. However, the governmental response was fairly typical. Instead of appointing a commission to look into fishery management issues, the Tamilnadu government embraced the influx of boats and authorized their distribution. Not only has this exacerbated existing problems of overcapitalization, but the poor quality of the boats has also further threatened the safety at sea of a population whose security is ostensibly of paramount importance in the rehabilitation process.

These aspects of posttsunami rehabilitation reproduced key problems faced by Kanyakumari's fisher artisans: their circumscription as religious subjects, the threat to resource sustainability and livelihood of an overcapitalized economy, and the assault on common property, both shore and inshore sea, by processes of privatization. They point to the enduring legacy of historical processes of coastal primitivization and capital accumulation that have made it easy for governments to distinguish the particular claims of fisher artisans from universal questions of citizenship rights and sustainable development.

Arguments

In this book, I have made three key arguments. First, I have highlighted the importance of prior histories of claim making as the grounds for postcolonial democracy. Contemporary fisher rights politics has clear continuities with past forms of political maneuver, in its use of patronage as an idiom of rights, in the significance given to caste as a form of political collectivity, and in the centrality of space in making claims. Fisher politics, I have argued, suggests the need for greater attention to sedimented forms of power and protest that give meaning and shape to the practice of rights in any given context. Furthermore, fisher politics shows the processual character of rights—how rather than deriving from a fixed juridical order, the practice of making claims is itself constitutive of rights. Such an understanding of rights as emergent cuts against a perspective on rights shared by both modernists and antimodernists in which postcolonial democracy is a derivative modernity echoing a European original. I have argued instead that we need to think about democracy as a politics rather than as a historical condition, one with continuities into regional pasts of claim making.

Recently, anthropologists inspired by the work of Giorgio Agamben (1998) have emphasized the resurgence of a form of sovereign power that reduces political subjects to "bare life" (e.g., Biehl 2004; Caton 2006; Fassin and Vasques 2005; Feldman 2007; Hoffman 2007; N. Sundar 2004). Some scholars focus on the transformation of society into a camp where the rule of force substitutes for the rule of law, whereas others follow Agamben in arguing that rights today have been emptied of any meaning or force. This scholarly response to contemporary excesses of power, most notably seen in the global "war on terror," is understandable, but the faithful application of Agamben's framework threatens to substitute a theory of power for an ethnography of politics when we most need to attend to the resilience of political aspiration and practice.

Jacques Rancière's critique of Agamben and Hannah Arendt is instructive in this regard. In his essay "Who Is the Subject of the Rights of Man?" (2004), Rancière takes issue with Arendt and Agamben for, each in his or her own way, depoliticizing rights through a form of "consensus." Rancière argues that Arendt, in her *Origins of Totalitarianism* (1951), limits real rights to the rights of the citizen, in the process emptying anything beyond the sphere of citizenship of political meaning. Rights are rendered tautological in her account: "The rights of the citizen . . . are the rights of those who have rights" (Rancière 2004: 303). Arendt thus "anthropologizes" the subject of rights by giving him social flesh and predetermines the domain of politics as the domain of normative citizenship. By contrast, Agamben's *Homo Sacer* (1998) identifies the sovereign as the ultimate arbiter of rights. In focusing on the ability of the sovereign to step outside the law and reduce the citizen to bare life, Agamben predetermines the domain of politics as that of sovereign power. He makes rights void: "The rights of the citizen are the rights of those who have no rights" (Rancière 2004: 303).

Rancière maintains that both Agamben and Arendt establish a consensus between law and fact that does not allow for the play of politics. Both writers foreclose the possibility of investing political life with new meanings and of claiming political belonging and entitlement in terms that expand the parameters of rights. By contrast, Rancière argues for "dissensus," or the openness of political process and the ongoing formation of the political subject. To quote him again: "The very difference between man and citizen is not a sign of disjunction proving that rights are either void or tautological. It is the opening of an interval for political subjectivization" (Rancière 2004: 304). Against Agamben and Arendt, Rancière argues that politics is not a *sphere* but a *process* driven by the dialectic of the human and citizen through which the parameters of rights are consistently redrawn.

In this book, I have taken up Rancière's call for treating rights politics as a process of political subjectivization rather than as a standoff between a circumscribed sphere of objectified, exclusive rights and excluded subalterns, or as an obsolete form of consciousness. The idioms and practices that fishers use to lay claim to rights demand a more elastic framework that does not preemptively close off the dynamics of subject formation. It requires seeing the horizon of rights as open and generative of politics. Fishers did not simply reject or insert themselves into statist rights discourse. In the interplay of fisher claims and state responses, we see give on both sides. Mukkuvars' use of idioms of relationality has pulled state actors into new obligations. At the same time, as self-proclaimed clients of the state, Mukkuvars now think of themselves as political subjects of new communities of affinity extending beyond coastal lines. This is by no means a closed universe; rather, new political currents render fluid the terms of negotiation, the idioms of rights, and the forms of political subjectivity.

A second argument that runs through this book is about space and hegemony. Artisanal fisher rights politics in Kanyakumari exemplifies the spatial unfolding of a Gramscian notion of hegemony. Space making has been an instrument of both rule and rights, with sovereigns and subalterns mobilizing geographic imaginaries and practices in their political projects. In the southwest, a cultural common sense has been elaborated through the production of geographic distinctions, lending culture an environmental cast. However, it is equally the case that the meaning of space is not fixed. Indeed, the struggle over rights in the region has been a battle over competing forms of space making. Understanding the dialectic of rule and opposition in terms of the production of space allows me to both denaturalize the link between culture and geography and see how space itself is an essential ingredient in struggles for rights.

Fisher rights politics was not simply a form of negotiation *within* spaces of power; it also generated political geographies. Fisher Catholics produced new spaces—of regionalism, common property, alternative technology, and fisher citizenship—that challenged the circumscription of the coast as a domain of religious patronage antithetical to a politics of rights. As I have shown in Part 2, each of these space-making projects opened up the coordinates of coastal space and of fisher political subjectivity. By embracing a regional political imaginary, fishers laid claim to a polity that exceeded the spatial and temporal limits of coastal locality. In invoking filial links to Tamil state populists, Mukkuvars carved out a political space of regionalism that contravened a scalar model of encompassment privileging the church as the primary intermediary between coast and state. Similarly, they appropriated state managerial dictates to reinvigorate forms of marine common property. As the class war on the coast escalated, the Tamilnadu state government sought to contain this "law and order" problem by territorially separating artisanal and trawling craft. Artisanal fishers were relegated to the 3 miles closest to shore, whereas trawlers were to ply offshore waters. Instead of submitting to territorial containment, however, Mukkuvar artisans claimed the 3-mile zone as a fishing commons materially underpinning a new legal subject: the artisanal sector. By the 1990s, both territory and artisan had exceeded the bounds of the 3-mile zone to stand in for a global marine commons and the conservationist national subject.

Mukkuvar politics of space making suggests a rethinking of cultural difference as the quintessential expression of nonelite politics. The assumption that elite power works through a claim to universality, whereas subalterns contest power through a politics of difference, informs much social theorizing on subalternity. Within the literature on space, this equation of subalternity with alterity finds echoes in the notion of "place" (e.g., Basso 1996; Escobar 2001; Ramaswamy 2004; Tuan 1977). Although space is typically represented as a modality of power, by contrast place is an ethics of resistance. Space symbolizes the sweep of a rationalized, modernist imagination that disregards the particularities of experience. Place, by contrast, is intimate and personal and resists generality. Even in Marxist scholarship that typically resists notions of alterity, one finds an equation relating place to an anticapitalist politics (Dirlik 1997; Harvey 1997).

This distinction between space and place threatens to reinscribe the opposition between the universal and the particular, society and community, or reason and feeling. Furthermore, it obscures the role of nonelites and oppositional movements not only in claiming *place* but also in reconceptualizing *space*. Opposition to state power or social exclusion does not always involve a simple claim to difference, to particularity, or to localized autonomy. As I have shown through the example of fisher spatial practices, the most particularistic expressions of community can also express an encompassing vision of changing both the polity as a whole and the terms of participation in it. In other words, subaltern politics can make universal claims and, in doing so, change relations of hegemony.

Finally, I have argued for an understanding of subalternity in relational, processual terms. Rather than see fishers as nonmoderns inhabiting a bounded world of affect and hierarchy or as moderns captured by a statist logic, I have argued for the need to see how they constitute themselves as subjects of rights in a dialectical relationship with existing hegemonies. In the postcolonial period, one can see this dialectic playing out clearly in the arena of development. What is most interesting to me about the development process is that, despite the state's effort to render it an antipolitics machine, it has created a charged political arena that is constantly reworked by competing meanings and demands. Rather than producing docile subjects or insurrectionary Others, then, the state system actually opens up new spaces for the articulation of subaltern rights and sovereignty. This suggests that we need to understand state and community as mutually implicated and postcolonial citizenship not as a derivative, juridical construct that is a less authentic expression of cultural subjectivity but as a dynamic, locally constituted process through which people understand their relationship to territory, community, nation, and state.

What does this mean for resource conservation? As I hope to have shown, an approach to conservation simply as state science or as community practice is inadequate for sustainable resource use. The thorough implication of states and communities through the development process suggests that any effort to redress the ills of development has to be a joint one. The efforts by both artisanal and mechanized fishers to draw state actors and institutions into their resource conflicts suggest that they are more than willing to recognize a role for the state in regulating the fishery. The question remains, however, whether the state is willing to recognize the knowledge and practices of local actors as a valuable contribution to the conservation effort and whether it is willing to challenge the current emphasis on capital accumulation to seriously address the goal of conservation. At the moment, the Tamilnadu state government is far from committed to marine resource conservation, as evidenced in its convenient interpretation of coastal conflict as a problem of intracommunity law and order and its approach to posttsunami reconstruction. However, the increasing number of social movements in Tamilnadu that articulate citizenship rights in terms of resource rights may just force the government to pay more than lip service to the idea of resource renewal. At its core, resource renewal envisions new priorities: of the livelihoods of small producers over production for profit and of domestic consumption over the rapidly expanding export trade in fish.

Reference Matter

Notes

Introduction

1. To protect their anonymity, I have changed the names of all my informants except for those who spoke in an official capacity as representatives of the district clergy, of state administration, of political parties, or other political organizations.

2. In its attention to space as a mechanism of power and politics, my work is indebted to a rich literature in anthropology, geography, and history that includes Agnew (1987, 1997), Basso (1996), Brenner (2004), Brenner et al. (2003), Caldeira (2000), Craib (2004), Edney (1997), Gold and Gujjar (2002), Gordillo (2002, 2004), Goswami (2004), Gupta and Ferguson (1997, 2002), Harvey (1973), Lefebvre (1991), Massey (1994), McCarthy (2005a, 2005b), Mitchell (2003), Moore (1996, 1998, 2005), Raffles (2002), Robbins (2004), Scott (1998), Skaria (1999), Smith (1984), Smith and Godlewska (1994), Trouillot (2003), Tsing (1993, 2006), Williams (1973), and Winichakul (1994).

3. Some scholarly work on Tamil fishers derives their social status from the hierarchical ordering of physical landscapes in Tamil Sangam literature (first to sixth century A.D.) where the *naital* (seashore), is placed just above *palai* (wilderness) and below *marutam* (cultivated land), *mullai* (forested pastoral land), and *kurinci* (hill tract). I bracket this mapping of literary categories onto lived geographies in favor of a less culturalist, more historical analysis of fisher marginalization.

4. There is a long and distinguished development studies literature that has exhaustively documented the inequalities generated by development in South Asia and beyond. On fisheries development, such work includes Alexander (1982), Bavinck (1984), Bhushan (1979), Blake (1977), Firth (1966), Galtung (1969), J. Kurien (1978, 1985, 1991, 1993, 1996), J. Kurien and Achari (1990), J. Kurien and Mathew (1982), Mathew (1990), Meynen (1989), Nayak (1993), Nayak et al. (2002), Platteau et al. (1985), Sider (1986), Somasundaram (1981), Stirrat (1988), A. Sundar (1999), and Thomson

(1989). On inequalities generated by other processes of rural development, a noteworthy example is Epstein (1973).

5. Even in instances where the marketization of a fishery enacts a certain form of enclosure by making it difficult for poorer fishers to purchase harvest quotas, the marine resource itself is not privatized.

6. Founded in 1925, the Rashtriya Swayamsevak Sangh drew on the cultural experiments of earlier Hindu revivalists and reformers and was directly inspired by the writings of V. D. Savarkar, who coined the term *Hindutva* as a shorthand for political Hinduism. Christophe Jaffrelot notes that "Savarkar's Hindutva was conceived primarily as an ethnic community possessing a territory and sharing the same racial and cultural characteristics, three attributes which stemmed from the mythical reconstruction of the Vedic Golden Age" (Jaffrelot 1996: 27). For Savarkar, Christians and Muslims were external to the nation because of cultural, not racial, difference. "Mohammedan and Christian communities," he wrote, "possess all the essential qualifications of Hindutva but one and all that is that they did not look upon India as their holyland. . . . Their holyland is far off in Arabia and Palestine. . . . Their love is divided" (quoted in Jaffrelot 1996: 31). The RSS's second leader, M. S. Golwalkar, gave the organization a more explicit ideological framework. His was a less assimilationist perspective and more one that clearly identified Hindus as *the* nation in India. By extension, Muslims and Christians were alien invaders who were a "foreign body" lodged in Hindu society. Although both Savarkar and Golwalkar opposed their cultural nationalism to the universalistic notion of territorial nationhood, territory was by no means absent in their formulation of a Hindu nation. Rather, the territory of the nation was sacralized and made indivisible.

The Sangh Parivar, or Hindu nationalist family of organizations, now includes the RSS and its various offshoots, including the Vishwa Hindu Parishad (VHP, or World Hindu Council), the Swadeshi Jagaran Manch (SJM, or Movement for Economic Self-Reliance), and the Bharatiya Janata Party (BJP, or Indian Peoples' Party).

7. Indeed, the denial of political self-determination to postcolonials by virtue of their nonmodernity or political immaturity persists to the present day. A recent articulation of the colonial argument that the colonized were trapped in a time lag came from French president Nicolas Sarkozy, who, in his July 26, 2007, address at the University of Dakar, asserted that "the tragedy of Africa is that the African has never really entered into history."

8. Started in 1982, the Subaltern Studies Collective has had a transformative effect on South Asian historiography, postcolonial history and anthropology, and historical methodology more broadly. An exhaustive list of Subaltern Studies volumes (currently numbering twelve volumes), additional writings by the collective's authors, and other essays on subaltern studies can be found at http://www.lib.virginia.edu/area-studies/subaltern/ssmap.htm.

Chapter 1

1. A similar kind of primitivism outside history has long been attributed to tribal and forest peoples in other parts of the subcontinent. As Sumit Guha (1999) shows, western Indian forest peoples were in touch with the Dutch, Portuguese, Marathas, and Mughals and were a constituent part of the larger power structures. In another postcolonial setting, Christine Walley (2004) illustrates how the residents of Tanzania's Mafia Island, longtime participants in circuits of Indian Ocean trade, have more recently been recast as quaint isolates.

2. For an incisive analysis of how history is produced with its resonances and silences, see Trouillot (1995).

3. File on Mel Manakkudy Village, 1935–1950, Bishop's House Archive, Nagercoil, Kanyakumari District.

4. File on Pallam Village, 1935–1960, Bishop's House Archive, Kottar Diocese, Nagercoil, Kanyakumari District.

5. Such conflicts occurred across the southwestern and southeastern coastal belts up to the abolishing of the fish tax by successive dioceses from the mid-1950s through the late 1960s. Frequently, fishers would threaten religious conversion in the face of church authority and as a preemption of excommunication. One particularly interesting case of conversion that occurred in Idinthikarai village, Tirunelveli District, is dealt with by Sivasubramanian (1996).

6. File on Pallam Village, 1935–1960, Bishop's House Archive, Kottar Diocese, Nagercoil, Kanyakumari District.

7. File on Mel Manakkudy Village, 1935–1960, Bishop's House Archive, Kottar Diocese, Nagercoil, Kanyakumari District.

8. File on Keezh Manakkudy Village, 1935–1960, Bishop's House Archive, Kottar Diocese, Nagercoil, Kanyakumari District.

9. File on Mel Manakkudy Village, 1935–1960, Bishop's House Archive, Kottar Diocese, Nagercoil, Kanyakumari District.

10. File on Mel Manakkudy Village, 1935–1960, Bishop's House Archive, Kottar Diocese, Nagercoil, Kanyakumari District.

11. File on Keezh Manakkudy Village, 1935–1960, Bishop's House Archive, Kottar Diocese, Nagercoil, Kanyakumari District.

12. File on Pallam Village, 1935–1960, Bishop's House Archive, Kottar Diocese, Nagercoil, Kanyakumari District.

13. File on Pallam Village, 1935–1960, Bishop's House Archive, Kottar Diocese, Nagercoil, Kanyakumari District.

14. File on Pallam Village, 1935–1960, Bishop's House Archive, Kottar Diocese, Nagercoil, Kanyakumari District.

Chapter 2

1. Indeed, as Susan Bayly (1999) has argued, the importance of status within low caste rights politics forces us to rethink the distinction between a modern rights politics and traditional status conflicts.

2. The LMS was established in 1795 by Congregationists, Presbyterians, and Methodists and started work in south Travancore in 1806. The CMS was started by Evangelicals in the Church of England in 1799 and started working in north Travancore in 1816. Although the CMS played a critical role in northern Travancore, my historical synopsis here primarily addresses dynamics in the south, the region from which Kanyakumari District was eventually carved out.

3. Colonel J. Munro, letter to the Government of Madras, March 30, 1818, quoted by Yesudas (1980: 245).

4. The relationship of East India Company officials to missionary societies was not always one of mutual cooperation. Many missionaries expressed severe discomfort with officials, such as Munro, whose support for their work seemed to them to be driven entirely by "political motives." Furthermore, the mediating role played by Travancore's residents in facilitating relations between mission and palace gave them a free hand to determine mission policy and practice, something that many missionaries deeply resented.

5. Historically, the Nadar caste tended the palmyra tree, a type of palm. From the flowering stem at the top of these palms, Nadars extracted the sweet juice that was made into jaggery, fermented into toddy, or distilled into arrack.

6. There is a sizable literature on the end of matriliny in southwestern India and its impact on social and political change. See, for example, Arunima (2003), Jeffrey (1976), and Saradamoni (1999).

7. The rate of literacy rapidly increased from 10 percent in 1891 to 28.9 percent in 1931 to 55 percent in 1941. Predictably, the benefit of education was not evenly distributed; in 1931, 40.8 percent of men were literate compared to 16.8 percent of women, and 29 percent of Christians were literate compared to 12 percent of Muslims.

8. For comparisons with Protestant missionizing in other British colonial contexts, see Comaroff and Comaroff (1991), Turner (1982), and Viotti da Costa (1994). For comparisons with Protestant missionizing among national subalterns, see Burdick (1998) and Chang (2005).

9. Excerpt of letter from British Resident to the Madras Government, dated July 3, 1855, quoted in letter from Reverend F. Baylis to Reverend J. Cox, LMS Neyoor Mission, August 27, 1855.

10. Even Protestant missionaries, in less guarded moments, were known to acknowledge the unique historical relationship of Travancore's rulers and Christians. For instance, J. Knowles, an LMS missionary, stated in 1898 that "the Travancore

State has been conspicuous by its toleration of non-Hindu religions" (quoted in Kawashima 1998: 27).

11. Circular, November 21, 1887, quoted in Krishna Row (1889: 6).

12. *Census of Travancore, 1891*, Kerala State Archives, Trivandrum, Kerala, 1894, v. 1, p. 376.

13. *Census of Travancore, 1891*, Kerala State Archives, Trivandrum, Kerala, v. 1, p. 391.

14. *Census of Travancore, 1891*, Kerala State Archives, Trivandrum, Kerala, v. 1, p. 391.

Chapter 3

1. Shahid Amin (2007) remarks on a similar dynamic between native upper caste informants and colonial officials within the Linguistic Survey of India.

2. A selection of titles from among Hornell's numerous articles published in fields as varied as anthropology, marine zoology, natural history, and seamanship offers a sense of the range and orientation of his ideas; see, for example, Hornell (1918, 1920a, 1920b, 1921, 1924, 1928, 1933, 1934, 1945, 1946, 1947). Most of these essays speak to the central place of technology in Hornell's geographic imagination and sense of global interconnectedness. The 1928 and 1945 essays examine other traveling forms—the game of cat's cradle and the Christian Passion play—that similarly suggest a perspective on cultural history as a series of transmissions and indigenizations.

3. Although official power allowed Hornell to shape colonial fishing policy and practice, his nascent conservationism predated his tenure in the Raj's administrative services. Before his travels East, Hornell established the Jersey Aquarium and Biological Station on the island of Jersey in the English Channel with naturalist and amateur archeologist Joseph Sinel. The station opened in 1893, and Hornell and Sinel hoped to achieve two goals with it: satisfying the public's enthusiasm for wonders of the deep and providing scholars with a research facility. There was also a more pressing local reason for public education on marine ecosystems: the depletion of the local oyster and lobster fisheries as a result of overdredging. Despite the enthusiasm and dedication of the two founders, the Jersey station floundered for lack of government support. Hornell and Sinel's arguments that funding would allow them to investigate the life cycle of various larval crustaceans and perhaps even revive Jersey's defunct oyster and lobster fisheries for the benefit of local fishermen fell on deaf ears.

It took his relocation to Britain's southern Asian colonies for Hornell to finally realize his dream of well-funded marine research with practical teeth. Hornell was tireless in his search for a means to pursue and implement his research, sending proposal after proposal to the British government, even suggesting that he be assigned to the then nonexistent post of superintendent of fisheries of Jersey. Finally, an opportunity did open up, not in his native Scotland or England but in Ceylon, as assistant to his mentor, Professor Herdman, in investigating the pearl fisheries. Hornell's Ceylon tenure was checkered. As marine biologist to the government of Ceylon and director of the Galle Marine Laboratory, Hornell was able to pursue his research without shortage of resources; his work in and outside the colony won him the recognition of the Linnean Society, to which he was elected a fellow in 1904. While in Ceylon, Hornell's reputation grew and he was asked to lend his fisheries expertise to setting up a pearl fishery in the subcontinental princely state of Baroda. However, Hornell suddenly resigned his Ceylon post in 1907; his biographers opine that it was "probably because the Government ignored his recommendations and sold the pearl fishery concession to an American syndicate" (Heppell and Sherman 2000: 6). This was not the only instance in which Hornell the marine biologist and anthropologist took precedence over Hornell the imperial administrator and revenue collector. In 1915, the *Times of India* assessed Hornell's monograph on the sacred chank (conch shell) thus: "A report upon a subject like this is not usually of interest to anyone outside a somewhat restricted circle. We are therefore agreeably disappointed by this charming monograph which is full of out-of-the-way lore of all kinds. . . . Mr. Hornell's original objective was to report on the commercial possibilities of the chank trade. He has incidentally produced a treatise of the greatest value to students of Indian folklore and art" (quoted by Heppell and Sherman 2000: 8).

Chapter 4

1. In considering the relationship between development and democracy, my work builds on the growing critical literature on development that emphasizes the role of development in animating rights claims. These works include Agrawal (2005), Agrawal and Sivaramakrishnan (2000), Baviskar (1995, 2002, 2003, 2004, 2007), Bose and Jalal (1997), Brosius (1997), Cooper (2002), Cooper and Packard (1997), Edelman (1999), Ferguson (1994, 1999, 2005, 2006), Fox (1984, 1985), Gow (1997), Gupta (1997, 1998), Klein (2007), Leve (2007), Li (1999a, 1999b, 2000, 2007), Mbembe (2001), Moore (1996, 1998, 2005), Mosse (2003, 2005), Neumann (1992, 1995), Peet and Watts (1996), Peluso (1992, 1993), Rangan (1996), Rangarajan and Saberwal (2003), Roy (2007), Scott (1979, 1985), Sharma (2001), Sinha (2003, 2008), Sinha and Herring (1993), Sinha et al. (1997), Sivaramakrishnan (1995, 2000), Sivaramakrishnan and Agrawal (2003), Sivaramakrishnan and Cederloff (2005), Starn (1992, 1995, 1999), A. Subramanian (1994, 2002, 2003a, 2003b, 2003c), A. Sundar (1999), Trouillot (1988, 1990), Tsing (1993, 1999, 2006), Walley (2004), Washbrook (1997), Watts and Peluso (2001), and West (2005).

2. Interview with M. C. Balan, ex–Dravida Munnetra Kazhagam Member of Legislative Assembly, Nagercoil, Kanyakumari, Padmanabhapuram, August 1996.

3. Interviews with N. Dennis, Indian National Congress, member of Parliament, Nagercoil; and M. C. Balan, ex–Dravida Munnetra Kazhagam Member of Legislative Assembly, Padmanabhapuram, Kanyakumari, August 1996.

4. Mechanization scheme records from the district Fisheries Department office, Nagercoil.

5. I also gleaned much of this information from informal conversations with fishermen in a variety of coastal villages.

6. Indeed, according to the 1993 Tamilnadu Department of Fisheries report *Endeavors and Achievements: Fisheries Statistics*, Kanyakumari remained the district with the highest number of unmechanized traditional craft in the state.

7. In 1997, a crore, or 10 million Indian rupees, was worth approximately US $276,500.

8. I use the notion of moral economy as elaborated by E. P. Thompson (1971) to suggest not a precapitalist cultural code that persists unchanged into the contemporary period but a historically contingent framework for interpreting the ethical parameters of economic activity. In this sense, the moral economy of the artisan is a moving target that encapsulates different meanings at different times, from outright opposition to capitalist accumulation at one moment to partial accommodation at other times. Furthermore, as I show in Chapters 5 and 6, the assessment of economic activity as moral or immoral often has to do as much with the people engaged in it as with the activity itself.

9. Interview with Father Jacob Lopez, Colachel parish priest, 1957–1967, Trivandrum, Kerala, April 1996.

10. Interview with Father A. J. Joseph, Kottar parish priest, 1944–1954 and 1974–1984, Nagercoil, Kanyakumari, April 1996.

11. Interviews with Father A. J. Joseph, Kottar parish priest, 1944–1954 and 1974–1984, Nagercoil, Kanyakumari, April 1996; Father Jacob Lopez, Colachel parish priest, 1957–1967, Trivandrum, Kerala, April 1996; Father A. Dionysius, Colachel deacon, 1957–1960, Colachel, Kanyakumari, May 1996; and Father R. Servatius, chaplain of the Young Christian Workers, Nagercoil, Kanyakumari, May 1996.

12. Interview with ex-minister Lourdammal Simon, Chennai, June 1996.

13. Interview with John Pandian, Extension Officer, Fisheries Training Center, Simon Colony, Colachel, April 1997.

14. Interview with D. Daniel, Savings and Loans Officer, Kanyakumari District Department of Fisheries, Nagercoil, Kanyakumari, April 1997.

15. Interview with D. Daniel, Savings and Loans Officer, Kanyakumari District Department of Fisheries, Nagercoil, Kanyakumari, April 1997.

Chapter 5

1. The website for the Intermediate Technology Development Group, now known as Practical Action, is http://www.itdg.org.

2. Interviews with N. Dennis, Indian National Congress, Member of Parliament, Nagercoil, Kanyakumari, August 1996; M. C. Balan, ex–Dravida Munnetra Kazhagam member of legislative assembly, Nagercoil, Kanyakumari, August 1996; S. S. David, Coastal Peoples' Organization, Nagercoil, Kanyakumari, May 1996; Lourdammal Simon, ex–minister of fisheries, Chennai, June 1996; and M. A. James, advocate and

ex-president of the Colachel Mechanized Boat Owners Welfare Society, Nagercoil, Kanyakumari, May 1996.

3. Interview with N. Dennis, Indian National Congress, Member of Parliament, Nagercoil, Kanyakumari, August 1996.

4. Another surprising shift has been the alignment of Kanyakumari's inland Nadars with the Congress Party despite early overtures toward Dravidianism during the years of the merger movement. As I showed in Chapter 2, in the 1930s and 1940s, inlanders embraced the idea of a Dravidian homeland with Tamil as its language because it validated their demand to merge Travancore's four Tamil-dominated *taluk*s with the neighboring Madras Presidency. After the 1956 merger with Tamilnadu, however, Dravidianist loyalties shifted coastward, whereas the inland remained loyal to the Congress Party.

5. Interview with Father Tobias, Nagercoil, Kanyakumari, August 1996.

6. The supply of food, housing provision, pension schemes, unemployment doles, writing-off of unpaid agricultural loans, and agrarian subsidies were combined strategically to maintain support for the ADMK. MGR also supported his film images through sporadic acts of donorship, especially at times of distress for the poor. He would distribute clothes, slippers, and cooking utensils and contribute in money and kind when huts were destroyed by tidal waves or hurricanes. Significantly, he would hand out these articles himself to ensure that he was acknowledged as the source of the gifts. In keeping with MGR's advocacy of temperance in his films, the ADMK introduced dry laws soon after assuming power. By the end of the ADMK's first term in office in 1980, a three-month term of rigorous imprisonment and a fine of 3,000 rupees were mandated for those who so much as smelled of liquor. However, these policies caused a considerable fall in tax revenue and led to the relaxing of dry laws in the early 1980s. The abandonment of dry laws was widely unpopular, especially among women and poorer groups. To offset the damage to its paternalist image, the ADMK regime introduced a free lunch scheme in 1982. This scheme initially covered 6 million children between the ages of 2 and 9 who attended public schools and child-care centers. By 1984, the program was extended to children in the first ten school grades, nonschool-going children under the age of 15, pensioners, military veterans, and destitute widows. The number of beneficiaries increased to more than 8 million by 1985 and to 12 million, one-fifth of Tamilnadu's population, by 1986. Aside from the beneficiaries, about 200,000 people were employed to implement the scheme, with preference given to widows and Scheduled Castes. The scheme was called the Chief Minister's Nutritious Noon Meal Scheme, and it was publicized with photographs of MGR sharing a meal with children. It was highlighted in news programs produced by the state government; the programs were screened before all feature films in movie theaters. Government propaganda films even went so far as to splice shots from MGR's films

in which the hero provides food for the hungry into documentary footage of children eating their free lunches (N. Subramanian 1999).

7. Interviews with F. M. Rajaratnam, ADMK ex-member of legislative assembly, Nagercoil, Kanyakumari, April 1997, and with members of the MGR fan clubs, Chennai and Kanyakumari, January–April 1997.

8. A similar argument about a subaltern politics of rights that mobilizes official documents is made by Amita Baviskar (2002) about villagers' use of an 1886 forest settlement report to contest limits on their use of forest resources in the Great Himalayan National Park.

9. Interviews with R. Rajamanickam, joint director, marine fisheries, Tamilnadu Department of Fisheries, Chennai, April 1997; and P. Ravindran, assistant director of fisheries, Nagercoil, Kanyakumari, March 1997.

10. Interview with R. Rajamanickam, joint director, marine fisheries, Tamilnadu Department of Fisheries, Chennai, April 1997.

11. Interview with P. Ravindran, assistant director of fisheries, Nagercoil, Kanyakumari, March 1997.

12. Interviews with M. J. Edwin, August 1996 and January 1999; V. Amirtharaj, January 1997 and January 1999; and Pierre Gillet, March 1997, Nagercoil, Kanyakumari.

13. Interview with P. Mariadasan, ex-president, Kanyakumari District Fishermen Society Federation, Manakkudy, Kanyakumari, January 1999.

14. Lucas was a fisheries activist who went on to start Santidhan, a nongovernmental organization that worked primarily on microcredit for fisherwomen.

15. Interview with P. Mariadasan, ex-president, Kanyakumari District Fishermen Society Federation, Manakkudy, Kanyakumari, January 1999.

16. Interviews with D. Thomas Mohan, coordinator, Kanyakumari District Fishermen Sangam Federation (KDFSF), Nagercoil, Kanyakumari, March 1997 and January 1999; Antony Adimai, president, KDFSF, Nagercoil, Kanyakumari, March 1997; P. Mariadasan, ex-president, KDFSF, Kadiapattinam, Kanyakumari, January 1999; J. Lucas, ex-coordinator, KDFSF, Nagercoil, Kanyakumari, March 1996; Archbishop V. Arockiasamy, Madurai, Tamilnadu, January 1999; Father R. Tobias, January 1997, Nagercoil, Kanyakumari; and Father A. Dionysius, Colachel, Kanyakumari, November 1996.

17. Interviews with Pierre Gillet, Nagercoil, Kanyakumari, November 1996 and January 1999.

18. http://www.itdg.org.

Chapter 6

1. As I discuss later, the National Fishworkers Forum is the current name of what used to be the National Forum for Kattumaram and Country Boat Fishermen's Rights and Marine Wealth in 1978 and the National Fishermen's Forum in 1983.

2. Interview with Father Thomas Kocherry, Nagercoil, Kanyakumari, June 1996.

3. Supreme Court of India, Civil Appellate Jurisdiction, Civil Appeal No. 4222 of 1993 with Civil Appeal Nos. 4223–26 of 1993, *Kerala Swathanthra Matsya Thozhilali Federation and Other Appellants v. Kerala Trawlnet Boat Operators' Association and Other Respondents.*

4. Interview with A. J. Vijayan, Kerala Swatantra Matsya Thozhilali Federation, Trivandrum, April 1997.

5. Interview with Nalini Nayak, Trivandrum, April 1997.

6. To quote John Kurien, "Economic overfishing occurs when marginal costs of an additional unit of fishing effort are higher than marginal revenues. Biological overfishing occurs when the marginal yield of an additional unit of fishing effort is negative. At such a level of effort, the fish population stock is prevented from generating its maximum sustainable yield. In tropical multi-species fisheries, biological overfishing may occur even when total catch is still increasing because the decline in yield—or complete extinction—of one or several species may be compensated through higher yields of other species" (J. Kurien 1993).

7. I say more about the regional rise of Hindu nationalism later in this chapter.

8. Interviews with Fathers Francis de Sales, Arulanandam, and Thomas Kocherry, Kanyakumari, April–June 1996.

9. Interview with Bishop Leon Dharmaraj, Nagercoil, Kanyakumari, February 1997.

10. Interviews conducted between January 1996 and April 1997 with Sister Philomene Mary, secretary, NFF; Sister Lieve, manager, Thirumalai Ashram; Father Thomas Kocherry, chairperson, NFF; Father C. Arulanandam, parish priest, Periavilai village, and member of the NFF; Father R. Tobias, president of the Kottar Social Service Society; Father R. Servatius, chaplain of the Young Christian Workers; and Father Pierre Gillet, engineer, Muttom Boat Building Society.

11. Interview with G. Constantine, Keezh Manakkudy, Kanyakumari, October 1996.

12. Interview with R. Selvaraj, Muttom, Kanyakumari, April 1997.

13. Interviews with P. Siluvai, former assistant director of marine fisheries, Kanyakumari District; N. Pathinathan, president, Boat Owners Association, Kanyakumari and Chinnamuttom villages; and G. Stephen and P. George, members of the village council, Kanyakumari village, March–April 1996.

14. Interview with V. Raman, secretary, Department of Animal Husbandry and Fisheries, Madras, April 1997.

15. Interview with R. Rajamanickam, joint director of marine fisheries, Government of Tamilnadu, Madras, April 1997.

16. Interview with C. Jelastine, advocate and member of the Communist Party of India (Marxist), Nagercoil, Kanyakumari, October 1996.

17. Letter from R. Rabindranath, Revenue Divisional Officer, Nagercoil, to District Collector, Kanyakumari District, April 5, 1995, Government of Tamilnadu, Rec. No. 3093/95, Kanyakumari District Collectorate Archive.

18. Letter from the Kanyakumari Chinnamuttom Mechanized Boat Fishermen and Owners Association to the District Collector, Kanyakumari, March 20, 1995, Government of Tamilnadu, Kanyakumari District Collectorate Archive.

19. Telex Message SR 111 647-1/95, Government of Tamilnadu, Public Department, March 17, 1995, Kanyakumari District Collectorate Archive.

20. Letter from Commissioner of Fisheries, Madras, to the District Collector, Kanyakumari, April 12, 1995, Government of Tamilnadu, Ref. C2/15735/95, Kanyakumari District Collectorate Archive.

21. High Court of Judicature at Madras, Writ Petition No. 7742 of 1995, June 6, 1995, *Kanyakumari Chinnamuttom Mechanized Boat Fishermen and Owners Association v. Commissioner of Fisheries, Madras, Assistant Director of Fisheries, Kanyakumari, District Collector, Kanyakumari.*

22. Letter from R. Rajagopal, Collector of Kanyakumari, to the Secretary to Government, June 19, 1995, Government of Tamilnadu, Rec. No. Z3-20395/95, Kanyakumari District Collectorate Archive.

23. Letter from R. Rajagopal, Collector of Kanyakumari, to District Magistrate, September 11, 1995, Government of Tamilnadu, Rec. No. Z2/423/95, Kanyakumari District Collectorate Archive. Letter from Jyothi Nirmala, Revenue Divisional Officer, Padmanabhapuram, Kanyakumari, to the Collector of Kanyakumari, November 19, 1995, Government of Tamilnadu, Ref. B3.13504/95, Kanyakumari District Collectorate Archive. Statement of Velusamy, Deputy Superintendent of Police, Colachel, September 29, 1995, Government of Tamilnadu, Kanyakumari District Collectorate Archive.

24. From pamphlets circulated by the Kanyakumari District Mechanized Boat Operators Welfare Union.

25. An alarming number of Colachel's boat workers over age 40 explained to me that dowry was the key reason for their loss of craft and gear. Those with young girls not yet of marriageable age spoke fatalistically about the day when they too would have to sell their means of production to take up coolie work on the boats. Exorbitant dowry demands have become as characteristic of Colachel as a whole as have the lavish houses of the boat owners. One 50-year-old boat worker spoke of the trickle-down effect of dowry. "Now, even *kattumaram* fishers are demanding more dowry," he exclaimed, "because you can't live in Colachel and ask for as little as people do in other villages!"

26. There are three *vallam* and *kattumaram sangams* in Colachel that are units of the Kanyakumari District Fishermen Sangams Federation. Each of these *sangam*

units has experienced violence at the hands of young boat workers, who interpret their work as a sign of their silent support for Colachel's adversaries.

27. Interviews with members of the Antoniar Sangam and the Kuzhanthai Yesu Sangam, Colachel, Kanyakumari, June 1996.

28. Interviews with trawler boat owners and workers in Colachel and Chinnamuttom, Kanyakumari, February–May 1997.

29. Interviews with boat owners and coolies, Colachel, Kanyakumari, June 1996 to May 1997.

30. Interviews with Captain S. P. Kutty, Nagercoil, Kanyakumari, April 1996 and October 1996.

31. Interviews with Captain S. P. Kutty, Nagercoil, Kanyakumari, April 1996 and October 1996.

32. In 1995, the Supreme Court of India ruled that the concept of Hindutva, which had been used to garner votes in an election, was not a religious doctrine but a way of life. It ruled that the use of the term does not amount to corrupt practices during an election, because no interpretation can confine the meaning of Hindutva to the narrow limits of religion alone or equate it with fundamentalist Hindu religious bigotry. Hindutva, stated the Court, denotes the content of Indian culture and heritage. For counterarguments that point out that the attack on minorities is a constituent element of Hindutva, see Cossman and Kapur (1996) and Nauriya (1996).

33. Interviews with S. P. Kutty, Tamilnadu State Secretary, Bharatiya Janata Party, Nagercoil, Kanyakumari, in March 1996, July 1996, and April 1997.

34. Interview with Sahaya Antony, president, Kanyakumari District BJP Fishermen Sangam, Colachel, Kanyakumari, June 1996.

35. Interview with Sahaya Antony, president, Kanyakumari District BJP Fishermen Sangam, Colachel, Kanyakumari, June 1996.

36. Interview with John Rose, cashier, Kanyakumari District BJP Fishermen Sangam, Colachel, Kanyakumari, June 1996.

37. Interview with S. Gurumurthy, national co-convener, Swadeshi Jagaran Manch, Chennai, April 1997.

38. Started in November 1991, the Swadeshi Jagaran Manch defines itself as part of the movement to establish a Hindu nation. The SJM's culturalist response to global capitalism—its insertion of capitalism into a nativist mold—draws directly on new cultural discourses on capitalism produced in East Asia. Like the East Asian articulation of native culture into a capitalist narrative, the SJM constructs its own narrative of Hinduism as a conduit for an indigenized capitalism that will release "the Indian mind from its ideological prison." The SJM's vision of a return to civilizational glory through economic liberalization is linked to the establishment of a militarized state.

Swadeshi, or economic self-reliance, as spelled out by the SJM, is the promise of a return to civilizational glory through internal economic liberalization, a process that will be promoted by a militarized state that can effectively protect the integrity of its territorial borders.

39. Interview with R. Machendranath, district collector, Kanyakumari, May 1997.

40. Interview with Jyoti Nirmala, revenue divisional officer, Thuckalay, Kanyakumari, November 1996.

41. Interview with D. Sivagurunathan, assistant director of fisheries, Kanyakumari, October 1996.

42. Interviews with D. Sivagurunathan, assistant director of fisheries, Colachel, Kanyakumari, October 1996; N. Machendranath, Kanyakumari district collector, Nagercoil, Kanyakumari, May 1997; and Jyoti Nirmala, revenue divisional officer, Thuckalay, Kanyakumari, November 1996.

43. For work on the recently elevated role of community in resource conservation, the ideological grounds for the valorization of community, and the ramifications of this trend in conservation policy, see Agrawal (2005), Agrawal and Gibson (2001), A. Subramanian (2003a), N. Sundar and Jeffrey (1999), and Walley (2004).

44. I attended the Coastal Peace and Development Council meetings occasionally from February 1996 to April 1997 and received other impressions of the council's conflict management process from the council's minutes book.

45. From my notes on the proceedings of the Coastal Peace and Development Council meetings.

46. Interview with Father A. Selvaraj, director, Peace and Development Council, Kanyakumari, April 1996.

47. Letter from Revenue Divisional Officer, Padmanabhapuram, Kanyakumari, to the District Collector, Kanyakumari, October 4, 1996, Government of Tamilnadu, Rec. No. J3/22992/95, Kanyakumari District Collectorate Archive.

48. Interviews with members of the Kanyakumari District Mechanized Boat Operators Welfare Union, Colachel, September 1996.

49. Interview with R. Bergmans, Kadiapattinam, Kanyakumari, September 1996.

50. Interview with *vallam* fishermen, Nagercoil, Kanyakumari, September 1996.

51. Interview with members of the Association for the Protection of Kattumaram and Vallam Fishing, Nagercoil, Kanyakumari, October 1996.

52. Interviews with M. Vincent, councillor, Kovalam, Kanyakumari, June 1997; D. Thomas, coordinator, Kanyakumari District Fishermen Sangams Federation, May 1997; and Antony Adimai, president, Kanyakumari District Fishermen Sangams Federation, May 1997 and January 1999.

Conclusion

1. I have gathered information on posttsunami rehabilitation in Tamilnadu from publications of the South Indian Federation of Fishermen Societies, the National Fishworkers Forum, the International Collective in Support of Fishworkers, the Tamil Nadu Science Forum, and the Social Needs and Human Awareness Organization.

Bibliography

Achari, Thankappan. 1986. *The Socio-Economic Impact of Motorization of Country Craft in Purakkad Village: A Case Study.* Trivandrum, India: Fisheries Research Cell, Program for Community Organization.

Adas, Michael. 1989. *Machines as the Measure of Men: Science, Technology, and Ideologies of Western Dominance.* Ithaca, NY: Cornell University Press.

Agamben, Giorgio. 1998. *Homo Sacer: Sovereign Power and Bare Life.* Stanford, CA: Stanford University Press.

Agnew, John. 1987. *Place and Politics: The Geographical Mediation of State and Society.* Boston: Allen and Unwin.

———, ed. 1997. *Political Geography: A Reader.* London: Arnold.

Agrawal, Arun. 2005. *Environmentality: Technologies of Government and Political Subjects.* Durham, NC: Duke University Press.

Agrawal, Arun, and Clark Gibson, eds. 2001. *Communities and the Environment: Ethnicity, Gender, and the State in Community-Based Conservation.* New Brunswick, NJ: Rutgers University Press.

Agrawal, Arun, and K. Sivaramakrishnan, eds. 2000. *Agrarian Environments: Resources, Representations, and Rule.* Durham, NC: Duke University Press.

———, eds. 2003. *Regional Modernities: The Cultural Politics of Development.* Stanford, CA: Stanford University Press.

Alexander, Paul. 1982. *Sri-Lankan Fishermen: Rural Capitalism and Peasant Society.* Monograph on South Asia 7. Canberra: Australian National University Press.

Alvares, Claude. 1992. *Science, Development, and Violence: The Revolt Against Modernity.* Delhi: Oxford University Press.

Amin, Samir. 1976. *Unequal Development: An Essay on the Social Formations of Peripheral Capitalism.* New York: Monthly Review Press.

Amin, Shahid. 2007. "Making of the Linguistic Survey of India, c. 1890–1920." Talk given at Harvard University South Asia Initiative, October 11.

Anderson, Michael R., and Sumit Guha, eds. 2000. *Changing Concepts of Rights and Justice in South Asia.* SOAS Studies on South Asia. New York: Oxford University Press.

Apffel-Marglin, Frédérique, and Stephen Marglin, eds. 1990. *Dominating Knowledge: Development, Culture, and Resistance.* New York: Oxford University Press.

———, eds. 1996. *Decolonizing Knowledge: From Development to Dialogue.* New York: Oxford University Press.

Appadurai, Arjun. 1996. *Modernity at Large: Cultural Dimensions of Globalization.* Minneapolis: University of Minnesota Press.

Arendt, Hannah. 1951. *The Origins of Totalitarianism.* New York: Harcourt Brace.

Arunima, G. 2003. *There Comes Papa: Colonialism and the Transformation of Matriliny in Kerala, Malabar c. 1850–1940.* Delhi: Orient Longman.

Asad, Talal. 1993. *Genealogies of Religion: Discipline and Reasons of Power in Christianity and Islam.* Baltimore: Johns Hopkins University Press.

———. 2003. *Formations of the Secular: Christianity, Islam, Modernity.* Stanford, CA: Stanford University Press.

Bailey, Conner, Dean Cycom, and Michael Morris. 1986. "Fisheries Development in the Third World: The Role of International Agencies." *World Development* 14(10/11):1269–1275.

Ballhatchet, Kenneth. 1998. *Caste, Class, and Catholicism in India, 1789–1914.* London: Curzon Press.

Barnett, M. R. 1976. *The Politics of Cultural Nationalism in South India.* Princeton, NJ: Princeton University Press.

Baskaran, Theodore. 1981. *The Message Bearers: Nationalist Politics and the Entertainment Media in South India, 1880–1945.* Madras, India: Cre-A.

Basso, Keith. 1996. *Wisdom Sits in Places: Landscape and Language Among the Western Apache.* Albuquerque: University of New Mexico Press.

Bavinck, Maarten. 1984. *Small Fry: The Economy of Petty Fishermen in Northern Sri Lanka.* Amsterdam: Free University Press.

———. 1997. "Changing Balance of Power at Sea: Motorization of Artisanal Fishing Craft." *Economic and Political Weekly* 32(5):198–200.

———. 1998. "'A Matter of Maintaining Peace': State Accommodation to Subordinate Legal Systems—The Case of Fisheries Along the Coromandel Coast of Tamil Nadu, India." *Journal of Legal Pluralism and Unofficial Law* 40:151–170.

———. 2001a. "Caste Panchayats and Regulation of Fisheries in Tamilnadu." *Economic and Political Weekly* 36(13):1088–1094.

———. 2001b. *Marine Resource Management: Conflict and Regulation in the Fisheries of the Coromandel Coast.* New Delhi: Sage.

———. 2003. "The Spatially Splintered State: Myths and Realities in the Regulation of Marine Fisheries in Tamil Nadu, India." *Development and Change* 34(4):633–657.

Baviskar, Amita. 1995. *In the Belly of the River: Tribal Conflicts over Development in the Narmada Valley.* Delhi: Oxford University Press.

———. 2002. "States, Communities, and Conservation: The Practice of Ecodevelopment in the Great Himalayan National Park." In Vasant Saberwal and Mahesh Rangarajan, eds., *Battles over Nature: Science and the Politics of Wildlife Conservation.* Delhi: Permanent Black, 267–299.

———. 2003. "Between Violence and Desire: Space, Power, and Identity in the Making of Metropolitan Delhi." *International Social Science Journal* 175:89–98.

———. 2004. "Between Micro-Politics and Administrative Imperatives: Decentralization and the Watershed Mission in Madhya Pradesh, India." *European Journal of Development Research* 16(1):26–40.

———. 2007. "The Dream Machine: The Model Development Project and the Remaking of the State." In A. Baviskar, ed., *Waterscapes: The Cultural Politics of a Natural Resource.* Delhi: Permanent Black.

Bayly, C. A. 1996. *Empire and Information: Intelligence Gathering and Social Communication in India, 1780–1870.* Oxford, U.K.: Oxford University Press.

Bayly, Susan. 1981. "A Christian Caste in Hindu Society." *Modern Asian Studies* 15(2):203–234.

———. 1984. "Hindu Kingship and the Origin of Community: Religion, State, and Society in Kerala, 1750–1850." *Modern Asian Studies* 18(2):177–213.

———. 1989. *Saints, Goddesses, and Kings: Muslims and Christians in South Indian Society, 1700–1900.* Cambridge, U.K.: Cambridge University Press.

———. 1999. *Caste, Society, and Politics in India: From the Eighteenth Century to the Modern Age.* Cambridge, U.K.: Cambridge University Press.

Berkes, Firket. 1985. "The Common Property Resource Problem and the Condition of Limited Property Rights." *Human Ecology* 13(2):187–208.

Bhabha, Homi K. 1994. *The Location of Culture.* London: Routledge.

Bhagavan, Manu. 2003. *Sovereign Spheres: Princes, Education, and Empire in Colonial India.* Oxford, U.K.: Oxford University Press.

Bhagwati, Jagdish. 2004. *In Defense of Globalization.* Oxford, U.K.: Oxford University Press.

Bhushan, Bharat. 1979. "Technological Change in Fishing in Kerala: 1953–1977." M. Phil. thesis, Center for Development Studies, Trivandrum, India.

Biehl, João. 2004. "Life of the Mind: The Interface of Psychopharmaceuticals, Domestic Economies, and Social Abandonment." *American Ethnologist* 31(4):475–496.

Blake, B. A. 1977. "Cultural Adaptation and Technological Change Among Madras Fishing Population." In M. E. Smith, ed., *Those Who Live from the Sea.* San Francisco: West, 97–110.

Bose, Sugata. 1993. *Peasant Labor and Colonial Capital: Rural Bengal Since 1770.* Cambridge, U.K.: Cambridge University Press.

———. 1997. "Instruments and Idioms of Colonial and National Development." In Frederick Cooper and Randall Packard, eds., *International Development and the Social Sciences: Essays on the History and Politics of Knowledge.* Berkeley: University of California Press, 45–63.

Bose, Sugata, and Ayesha Jalal, eds. 1997. *Nationalism, Democracy, and Development: State and Politics in India.* New York: Oxford University Press.

Boxer, C. R. 1969. *The Portuguese Seaborne Empire, 1415–1825.* London: Hutchinson.

———. 1978. *The Church Militant and Iberian Expansion, 1440–1770.* Baltimore: Johns Hopkins University Press.

Brenner, Neil. 2004. *New State Spaces: Urban Governance and the Rescaling of Statehood.* Oxford, U.K.: Oxford University Press.

Brenner, Neil, Bob Jessop, Martin Jones, and Gordon MacLeod, eds. 2003. *State/Space: A Reader.* Malden, MA: Blackwell.

Brosius, Peter. 1997. "Prior Transcripts, Divergent Paths: Resistance and Acquiescence to Logging in Sarawak, East Malaysia." *Comparative Studies in Society and History* 39(3):468–510.

Brown, Vincent A. 2008. *The Reaper's Garden: Death and Power in the World of Atlantic Slavery.* Cambridge, MA: Harvard University Press.

Buchanan, Claudius. 1812. *The Works of Rev. Claudius Buchanan, LL.D., Comprising His Christian Researches in Asia, with Notices of the Translation of the Scriptures into the Oriental Languages, His Memoir on the Expediency of an Ecclesiastical Establishment for British India, and His Star in the East, with Three New Sermons.* New York: Whiting and Watson. Available from the Oriental and India Office Collection, British Library.

Buchanan, Francis. 1807. *A Journey from Madras Through the Countries of Mysore, Canara, and Malabar.* London: T. Cadell and W. Davies.

Burdick, John. 1998. *Blessed Anastácia: Women, Race, and Popular Christianity in Brazil.* New York: Routledge.

Caldeira, Teresa Pires do Rio. 2000. *City of Walls: Crime, Segregation, and Citizenship in São Paulo.* Berkeley: University of California Press.

Callon, Michel. 1986. "Some Elements of a Sociology of Translation: Domestication of the Scallops and the Fishermen of St. Brieuc Bay." In John Law, ed., *Power, Action, and Belief: A New Sociology of Knowledge.* London: Routledge and Kegan Paul.

Catholic Bishops' Conference of India. 1969. *Church in India Today.* Delhi: CBCI Press.

———. 1994. *Report of the Commission for Labor.* Delhi: CBCI Press.

Caton, Steven. 2006. "Coetzee, Agamben, and the Passion of Abu Ghraib." *American Anthropologist* 108(1):114–123.

Chacko, P. I., S. George, and P. P. Krishnaswamy. 1957. *Census of the Sea Fisherfolk and Fishing Crafts and Gear in Madras State, 1957.* Madras Fisheries Statistics Report 53. Madras, India: Department of Fisheries.

Chakrabarty, Dipesh. 1992. "Postcoloniality and the Artifice of History: Who Speaks for 'Indian' Pasts?" *Representations* 37:1–26.

———. 2000. *Provincializing Europe: Postcolonial Thought and Historical Difference.* Princeton, NJ: Princeton University Press.

———. 2002. *Habitations of Modernity: Essays in the Wake of Subaltern Studies.* Chicago: University of Chicago Press.

Chandra, Bipan. 1993. *Essays on Indian Nationalism.* New Delhi: Har-Anand.

Chang, Derek. 2005. "Brought Together upon Our Own Continent: Race, Religion, and Evangelical Nationalism in American Baptist Home Missions, 1865–1900." In Karen Isaksen Leonard, Alex Stepick, Manuel A. Vasquez, and Jennifer Holdaway, eds., *Immigrant Faiths: Transforming Religious Life in America.* Walnut Creek, CA: Alta Mira Press, 39–66.

Chari, Sharad. 2004. *Fraternal Capital: Peasant-Workers, Self-Made Men, and Globalization in Provincial India.* Stanford, CA: Stanford University Press.

Chatterjee, Partha. 1993. *The Nation and Its Fragments: Colonial and Postcolonial Histories.* Princeton, NJ: Princeton University Press.

———. 1997a. "Beyond the Nation? Or Within?" *Economic and Political Weekly* 32(1):30–34.

———. 1997b. "Religious Minorities and the Secular Nation-State: Reflections on an Indian Impasse." *Public Culture* 8:11–39.

———. 2004. *The Politics of the Governed: Reflection on Popular Politics in Most of the World.* New York: Columbia University Press.

Chaudhuri, K. N. 1985. *Trade and Civilization in the Indian Ocean: An Economic History from the Rise of Islam to 1750.* Cambridge, U.K.: Cambridge University Press.

Chiriyankandath, James. 1992. "'Democracy' Under the Raj: Electoral Politics and Separate Representation in British India." *Journal of Commonwealth and Comparative Politics* 30(1):39–63.

———. 1993. "Communities at the Polls: Electoral Politics and the Mobilization of Communal Groups in Travancore." *Modern Asian Studies* 27(3):643–665.

Clifford, James. 1997. *Routes: Travel and Translation in the Late Twentieth Century.* Cambridge, MA: Harvard University Press.

Comaroff, Jean, and John Comaroff. 1991. *Of Revelation and Revolution.* Chicago: University of Chicago Press.

Cooper, Frederick. 1997. "Modernizing Bureaucrats, Backward Africans, and the Development Concept." In Frederick Cooper and Randall Packard, eds., *International Development and the Social Sciences: Essays on the History and Politics of Knowledge.* Berkeley: University of California Press, 64–92.

———. 2002. *Africa Since 1940: The Past of the Present.* Cambridge, U.K.: Cambridge University Press.

———. 2005. *Colonialism in Question: Theory, Knowledge, History.* Berkeley: University of California Press.

Cooper, Frederick, and Randal Packard, eds. 1997. *International Development and the Social Sciences: Essays in the History and Politics of Knowledge.* Berkeley: University of California Press.

Cossman, Brenda, and Ratna Kapur. 1996. "Secularism: Bench-Marked by Hindu Right." *Economic and Political Weekly,* September 21, 2613–2630.

Cowan, Jane, Marie-Benedicte Dembour, and Richard A. Wilson, eds. 2001. *Culture and Rights: Anthropological Perspectives.* Cambridge, U.K.: Cambridge University Press.

Cowen, M. P., and R. W. Shenton. 1996. *Doctrines of Development.* London: Routledge.

Craib, Raymond B. 2004. *Cartographic Mexico: A History of State Fixations and Fugitive Landscapes.* Durham, NC: Duke University Press.

Crush, Jonathan, ed. 1995. *Power of Development.* London: Routledge.

Daniel, D. 1985. *Struggle for Responsible Government in Travancore, 1938–1947.* Madurai, India: Raj.

———. 1992. *Travancore Tamils Struggle for Identity, 1938–1956.* Madurai, India: Raj.

Das, Veena, ed. 1990. *Mirrors of Violence: Communities, Riots, and Survivors in South Asia.* Delhi: Oxford University Press.

Das Gupta, Ashin. 2001. *The World of the Indian Ocean Merchant, 1500–1800: Collected Essays of Ashin Das Gupta.* Delhi: Oxford University Press.

Das Gupta, Ashin, and M. N. Pearson. 1999. *India and the Indian Ocean, 1500–1800.* Oxford, U.K.: Oxford University Press.

Davis, Mike. 2001. *Late Victorian Holocausts: El Niño Famines and the Making of the Third World.* New York: Verso.

Day, Francis. 1865. *The Fishes of Malabar.* London: Bernard Quaritch.

De Lannoy, Mark. 1997. *The Kulasekhara Perumals of Travancore: History and State Formation in Travancore from 1671 to 1758.* Leiden, Netherlands: Leiden University Press.

Department of Fisheries, Madras. 1955. *Administrative Report of the Department of Fisheries, 1954–55.* Madras, India: Government Press.

———. 1956. *Administrative Report of the Tamilnadu Department of Fisheries, 1955–56.* Madras, India: Government Press.

———. 1957. *Administrative Report of the Tamilnadu Department of Fisheries, 1956–57.* Madras, India: Government Press.

———. 1958. *Administrative Report of the Tamilnadu Department of Fisheries, 1957–58.* Madras, India: Government Press.

———. 1962. *Administrative Report of the Tamilnadu Department of Fisheries, 1961–62.* Madras, India: Government Press.

———. 1971. *Administrative Report of the Tamilnadu Department of Fisheries, 1970–71.* Madras, India: Government Press.

———. 1982. *Administrative Report of the Tamilnadu Department of Fisheries, 1981–82.* Madras, India: Government Press.

———. 1988. *Administrative Report of the Tamilnadu Department of Fisheries, 1987–88.* Madras, India: Government Press.

———. 1990. *Administrative Report of the Tamilnadu Department of Fisheries, 1989–90.* Madras, India: Government Press.

———. 1994. *Administrative Report of the Tamilnadu Department of Fisheries, 1993–94.* Madras, India: Government Press.

Dickey, Sara. 1993. *Cinema and the Urban Poor in South India.* Cambridge, U.K.: Cambridge University Press.

Dirks, Nicholas B., ed. 1992. *Colonialism and Culture.* Princeton, NJ: Princeton University Press.

———. 2001. *Castes of Mind: Colonialism and the Making of Modern India.* Princeton, NJ: Princeton University Press.

Dirlik, Arif. 1996. "The Global in the Local." In R. Wilson and W. Dissanayake, eds., *Global/Local: Cultural Production and the Transnational Imaginary.* Durham, NC: Duke University Press, 21–45.

———. 2001. "Place-Based Imagination: Globalism and the Politics of Place." In R. Prazniak and A. Dirlik, eds., *Places and Politics in the Age of Globalization.* New York: Rowman & Littlefield, 15–51.

Dubois, Laurent. 2006. "An Enslaved Enlightenment: Rethinking the Intellectual History of the French Atlantic." *Social History* 31(1):1–14.

Edelman, Marc. 1999. *Peasants Against Globalization: Rural Social Movements in Costa Rica.* Stanford, CA: Stanford University Press.

Edney, Matthew H. 1997. *Mapping an Empire: The Geographical Construction of British India, 1765–1843.* Chicago: University of Chicago Press.

Epstein, Scarlet. 1973. *South India, Yesterday, Today, and Tomorrow: Mysore Villages Revisited.* New York: Holmes and Meier.

Escobar, Arturo. 1995. *Encountering Development: The Making and Unmaking of the Third World.* Princeton, NJ: Princeton University Press.

———. 2001. "Culture Sits in Places: Reflections on Globalism and Subaltern Strategies of Localization." *Political Geography* 20:139–174.

Esteva, Gustavo. 1987. "Regenerating Peoples' Space." *Alternatives* 12(1):125–152.

———. 1992. "Development." In Wolfgang Sachs, ed., *The Development Dictionary.* London: Zed, 6–25.

Fabian, Johannes. 1983. *Time and the Other: How Anthropology Makes Its Object.* New York: Columbia University Press.

Fassin, Didier, and Paula Vasques. 2005. "Humanitarian Exception as the Rule: The Political Theology of the 1999 Tragedia in Venezuela." *American Ethnologist* 32(3): 389–405.

Feldman, Ilana. 2007. "Difficult Distinctions: Refugee Law, Humanitarian Practice, and Political Identification in Gaza." *Cultural Anthropology* 22(1):129–169.

Ferguson, James. 1994 [1990]. *The Anti-Politics Machine: "Development," Depoliticization, and Bureaucratic Power in Lesotho*. Minneapolis: University of Minnesota Press.

———. 1999. *Expectations of Modernity: Myths and Meanings of Urban Life on the Zambian Copperbelt*. Berkeley: University of California Press.

———. 2005. "Seeing Like an Oil Company: Space, Security, and Global Capital in Neoliberal Africa." *American Anthropologist* 107(3):377–382.

———. 2006. *Global Shadows: Africa in the Neoliberal World Order*. Durham, NC: Duke University Press.

Firth, Raymond. 1966. *Malay Fishermen: Their Peasant Economy*. London: Routledge and Kegan Paul.

Fisher, Michael H. 1991. *Indirect Rule in India: Residents and the Residency System, 1764–1858*. Delhi: Oxford University Press.

Food and Agriculture Organization of the United Nations. 1954. *Activities of the FAO Under the Expanded Technical Assistance Program, 1953/54*. Rome: FAO.

———. 1955. *Activities of the FAO Under the Expanded Technical Assistance Program, 1954–55*. Rome: FAO.

———. 1985. *FAO, the First 40 Years: 1945–85*. Rome: FAO.

Forrester, Duncan. 1980. *Caste and Christianity: Attitudes and Policies on Caste of Anglo-Saxon Protestant Missions in India*. London: Curzon Press.

Fox, Richard G. 1984. "Urban Class and Communal Consciousness in Colonial Punjab: The Genesis of India's Intermediate Regime." *Modern Asian Studies* 18:459–489.

———. 1985. *Lions of the Punjab: Culture in the Making*. Berkeley: University of California Press.

———. 1989. *Gandhian Utopia: Experiments with Culture*. Boston: Beacon Press.

———, ed. 1991. *Recapturing Anthropology: Working in the Present*. Santa Fe, NM: School of American Research Press.

Frank, Andre Gunder. 1975. *On Capitalist Underdevelopment*. New York: Oxford University Press.

Frankel, Francine. 1978. *India's Political Economy, 1947–77: The Gradual Revolution*. Princeton, NJ: Princeton University Press.

Freitag, Sandria B. 1989. *Collective Action and Community: Public Arenas and the Emergence of Communalism in North India*. Berkeley: University of California Press.

Friedman, Thomas L. 2000. *The Lexus and the Olive Tree*. New York: Anchor Books.

Galtung, J. 1969. *Development from Above and the Blue Revolution: The Indo-Norwegian Project in Kerala*. Working Paper 2-12. Oslo: Peace Research Institute.

Gillet, Pierre. 1979. *Ten Years of Involvement with Fisheries and Fishermen in Kanyakumari District*. Nagercoil, India: Kottar Social Service Society.

———. 1985. *Small Is Difficult: The Pangs and Successes of Small Boat Technology Transfer in South India.* Nagercoil, India: Centre for Appropriate Technology.

Gilmartin, David. 1988. *Empire and Islam: Punjab and the Making of Pakistan.* Berkeley: University of California Press.

Gold, Ann Grodzins, and Bhoju Ram Gujjar. 2002. *In the Time of Trees and Sorrows: Nature, Power, and Memory in Rajasthan.* Durham, NC: Duke University Press.

Gordillo, Gaston. 2002. "Locations of Hegemony: The Making of Places in the Toba's Struggle for La Comuna, 1989–99." *American Anthropologist* 104(1):262–277.

———. 2004. *Landscapes of Devils: Tensions of Place and Memory in the Argentinean Chaco.* Durham, NC: Duke University Press.

Goswami, Manu. 2004. *Producing India: From Colonial Economy to National Space.* Chicago: University of Chicago Press.

Gow, David D. 1997. "Can the Subaltern Plan? Ethnicity and Development in Cauca, Colombia." *Urban Anthropology* 26(3–4):243–292.

Gramsci, Antonio. 1972. *Selections from the Prison Notebooks,* Quintin Hoare and Geoffrey Nowell Smith, eds. New York: International.

Guha, Ramachandra. 1983. *The Unquiet Woods: Ecological Change and Peasant Resistance in the Himalaya.* Delhi: Oxford University Press.

Guha, Ranajit. 1963. *A Rule of Property for Bengal: An Essay on the Idea of Permanent Settlement.* Paris: Mouton.

———. 1983. *Elementary Aspects of Peasant Insurgency in Colonial India.* Delhi: Oxford University Press.

Guha, Sumit. 1999. *Environment and Ethnicity in India, 1200–1991.* Cambridge, U.K.: Cambridge University Press.

Gupta, Akhil. 1997. "Agrarian Populism in the Development of a Modern Nation (India)." In Frederick Cooper and Randall Packard, eds., *International Development and the Social Sciences: Essays on the History and Politics of Knowledge.* Berkeley: University of California Press, 320–344.

———. 1998. *Postcolonial Developments: Agriculture in the Making of Modern India.* Durham, NC: Duke University Press.

Gupta, Akhil, and James Ferguson, eds. 1997. *Culture, Power, Place: Explorations in Critical Anthropology.* Durham, NC: Duke University Press.

———. 2002. "Spatializing States: Toward an Ethnography of Neoliberal Governmentality." *American Ethnologist* 29(4):981–1002.

Hardgrave, Robert L. 1969. *The Nadars of Tamilnadu: The Political Culture of a Community in Change.* Berkeley: University of California Press.

Hardin, Garrett. 1968. "The Tragedy of the Commons." *Science* 162:1243–1248.

Hardt, Michael, and Antonio Negri. 2000. *Empire.* Cambridge, MA: Harvard University Press.

Harvey, David. 1973. *Social Justice and the City.* Baltimore: Johns Hopkins University Press.

———. 1996. *Justice, Nature, and the Geography of Difference*. Cambridge, MA: Blackwell.

———. 2001. *Spaces of Capital: Towards a Critical Geography*. Edinburgh: Edinburgh University Press.

———. 2006. *Spaces of Global Capitalism: A Theory of Uneven Geographical Development*. London: Verso.

Haugerud, Angelique. 1995. *The Culture of Politics in Modern Kenya*. Cambridge, U.K.: Cambridge University Press.

Heppell, David, and Mark Sherman. 2000. "Tribute to James Hornell, 1865–1949." *Bulletin of the International String Figure Association* 7:1–56.

Ho, Engseng. 2006. *The Graves of Tarim: Genealogy and Mobility Across the Indian Ocean*. Berkeley: University of California Press.

Hoffman, Danny. 2007. "The City as Barracks: Freetown, Monrovia, and the Organization of Violence in Postcolonial African Cities." *Cultural Anthropology* 22(3):400–428.

Hoole, Elijah. 1844. *Madras, Mysore, and the South of India: Or, a Personal Narrative of a Mission to Those Countries: from MDCCCXX to MDCCCXXVIII*, 2nd ed. London: Longman, Brown, Green, and Longmans.

Hornell, James. 1918. "Further Evidence of Ancient Indian Trade with the Persian Gulf." *Modern Review* 24(5):492–493.

———. 1920a. "The Common Origin of the Outrigger Canoes of Madagascar and East Africa." *Man* 20:134–139.

———. 1920b. "The Origin and Ethnological Significance of Indian Boat Designs." *Memoirs of the Asiatic Society of Bengal* 7(3):139–256.

———. 1921. "Catamarans and Reed Rafts as Evidence of Former Race-Continuity from the Mediterranean Eastward to South America." *Man in India* 1(2):144–148.

———. 1924. "Marine Fish-Traps in South India and Brazil." *Man* 24:51–53.

———. 1928. "Cat's Cradles, the World's Most Widespread Game." *Discovery* 9(100):111–115.

———. 1933. "Had Viking Ships and South Seas War Canoes a Common Ancestry?" *Yachtsman and Motor Boating* 80(2180):382–383.

———. 1934. "The Origin of the Chinese Junk and Sampan." *Mariner's Mirror* 2:39–54.

———. 1945. "A Passion Play Staged by Indian Fishermen." *Man* 45:84–87.

———. 1946. "Primitive Types of Water Transport in Asia: Distribution and Original." *Journal of the Royal Asiatic Society of Greater Britain and Ireland* 2:124–141.

———. 1947. "Naval Activity in the Days of Solomon and Rameses III." *Antiquity* 21(82):66–73.

Houtart, Francois, and Genevieve Lemercinier. 1981. *Genesis and Institutionalization of Indian Catholicism*. Louvain, Belgium: Université Catholique de Louvain.

Houtart, Francois, and Nalini Nayak. 1988. *Kerala Fishermen: Culture and Social Organization.* Trivandrum, India: PCO Center.

Jacob, J. A. 1990. *A History of the London Missionary Society in South Travancore, 1806–1959.* Nagercoil, India: Diocesan Press.

Jaffrelot, Christophe. 1996. *The Hindu Nationalist Movement in India.* New York: Columbia University Press.

Jeffrey, Robin, 1976. *The Decline of Nair Dominance: Society and Politics in Travancore, 1947–1908.* Delhi: Vikas.

———, ed. 1978. *People, Princes, and Paramount Power: Society and Politics in the Indian Princely States.* Delhi: Oxford University Press.

Kantowsky, Detlef. 1980. *Sarvodaya, the Other Development.* Delhi: Vikas.

Kanyakumari District Fishermen Sangams Federation. 1995. *Annual Report 1994–95.* Nagercoil, India: KDFSF.

Kawashima, Koji. 1998. *Missionaries and a Hindu State: Travancore, 1858–1936.* New York: Oxford University Press.

Kent, Eliza. 2004. *Converting Women: Gender and Protestant Christianity in Colonial South India.* New York: Oxford University Press.

Klein, Naomi. 2007. *The Shock Doctrine: The Rise of Disaster Capitalism.* New York: Metropolitan Books.

Kooiman, Dick. 1989. *Conversion and Social Equality: The London Missionary Society in South Travancore in the Nineteenth Century.* Delhi: Manohar.

———. 1995. *Communities and Electorates: A Comparative Discussion of Communalism in Colonial India.* Comparative Asian Studies 16. Amsterdam: VU University Press.

———. 2002. *Communalism and Indian Princely States: Travancore, Baroda, and Hyderabad in the 1930s.* Delhi: Manohar.

Krishna Row, Mayaveram R. 1889. *A Revenue Hand Book, Containing All the Unrepealed Regulations, Rulings, and Proclamations Relating to the Revenue Administration of Travancore.* Madras, India: Addison.

Kurien, C. T. 1994. *Global Capitalism and the Indian Economy.* Tracts for the Times 5. Delhi: Orient Longman.

———. 1996. *Economic Reforms and the People.* Delhi: Madhyam Books.

Kurien, John. 1978. "Entry of Big Business into Fishing: Its Impact on Fish Economy." *Economic and Political Weekly* 13(36):1557–1565.

———. 1985. "Technical Assistance Projects and Socio-Economic Change: Norwegian Intervention in Kerala's Fisheries Development." *Economic and Political Weekly* 20(25/26):A70–A87.

———. 1991. "Ruining the Commons and Responses of the Commoners: Coastal Overfishing and Fishermen's Actions in Kerala State, India." Discussion Paper. Geneva: United Nations Research Institute for Social Development.

————. 1993. "Ruining the Commons: Overfishing and Fishworkers' Actions in South India." *Ecologist* 23(1):5–12.

————. 1995. "Joint Action Against Joint Ventures: Resistance to Multinationals in Indian Waters." *Ecologist* 25(2–3):115–119.

————. 1996. "On Development and Public Action: A Reflection on the Kerala Experience." In Sunil Bastian and Nicola Bastian, eds., *Assessing Participation: A Debate from South Asia*. Delhi: Konark, 212–241.

Kurien, John, and Thankappan Achari. 1990. "Overfishing Along Kerala Coast: Causes and Consequences." *Economic and Political Weekly* 25(35/36):2011–2018.

Kurien, John, and Sebastian Mathew. 1982. "Technological Change in Fishing: Its Impact on Fishermen." Unpublished paper prepared for Indian Council of Social Science Research. Trivandrum, India: Center for Development Studies.

Latour, Bruno. 1988. "To Modernize or Ecologize? That Is the Question." In B. Braun and N. Castree, eds., *Remaking Reality: Nature at the Millennium*. London: Routledge.

————. 2005. *Reassembling the Social: An Introduction to Actor-Network Theory*. Oxford, U.K.: Oxford University Press.

Lefebvre, Henri. 1991. *The Production of Space*. London: Blackwell.

Leve, Lauren. 2007. "'Failed Development' and Rural Revolution in Nepal: Rethinking Subaltern Consciousness and Women's Empowerment." *Anthropological Quarterly* 80(1)(winter):127–172.

Li, Tania. 1999a. "Compromising Power: Development, Culture, and Rule in Indonesia." *Cultural Anthropology* 40(3):277–309.

————, ed. 1999b. *Transforming the Indonesian Uplands: Marginality, Power, and Production*. London: Taylor and Francis.

————. 2000. "Articulating Indigenous Identity in Indonesia: Resource Politics and the Tribal Slot." *Comparative Studies in Society and History* 42(1):149–179.

————. 2007. *The Will to Improve: Governmentality, Development, and the Practice of Politics*. Durham, NC: Duke University Press.

London Missionary Society. 1887. *Annual Report of the Travancore District Committee in Connection with the L.M.S. for the Year Ending Dec. 31, 1886*. Nagercoil, India: London Mission Press, and London: Methodist Missionary Archive, School of Oriental and African Studies.

————. 1888. *L.M.S. Minute Book, 1875–1888, Minutes of the Annual Meetings of the Travancore District Committee*. London: Methodist Missionary Archive, School of Oriental and African Studies.

————. 1889. *Annual Report of the Travancore District Committee in Connection with the London Missionary Society for the Year Ending Dec. 31, 1888*. Nagercoil, India: London Mission Press, and London: Methodist Missionary Archive, School of Oriental and African Studies.

———. 1897. *L.M.S. Minute Book, 1889–1897, Minutes of the Annual Meetings of the Travancore District Committee*. London: Methodist Missionary Archive, School of Oriental and African Studies.

Ludden, David. 1992. "India's Development Regime." In Nicholas B. Dirks, ed., *Colonialism and Culture*. Comparative Studies in Society and History Book Series. Ann Arbor: University of Michigan Press, 247–288.

———, ed. 2001. *Reading Subaltern Studies: Critical History, Contested Meaning, and the Globalization of South Asia*. Delhi: Permanent Black.

Madras Fisheries Bureau. 1915. *Papers from 1899 Relating Chiefly to the Development of the Madras Fisheries Bureau*, v. 1, bull. 1. Madras, India: Government Press.

———. 1918a. *Annual Reports of the Madras Fisheries Bureau, 1908–1917*, Bulletin 1. Madras, India: Government Press.

———. 1918b. Letter from Sir F. A. Nicholson, K.C.I.E., Honorary Director of Fisheries, 25th June, 1912. In Madras Fisheries Bureau, *Annual Reports of the Madras Fisheries Bureau, 1908–17*, Bulletin 10 (pt. 2 of Bull. 1). Madras, India: Government Press.

———. 1929. *Report of the Commission on Fisheries in Madras*. Madras, India: Development Department, Government Press.

———. 1938. *Madras Fisheries Bulletin, 1918–1937*. Madras, India: Government Press.

Mahadevan, Raman. 1991. "Industrial Entrepreneurship in Princely Travancore, 1930–1946." In S. Bhattacharya, ed., *The South Indian Economy: Agrarian Change, Industrial Structure, and State Policy c. 1914–1947*. Delhi: Oxford University Press, 159–207.

Maine, Henry. 1871. *Village Communities in the East and West: Six Lectures Delivered at Oxford*. London: J. Murray.

Malkki, Liisa. 1995. *Purity and Exile: Violence, Memory, and National Cosmology Among Hutu Refugees in Tanzania*. Chicago: University of Chicago Press.

Mamdani, Mahmood. 1996. *Citizen and Subject: Contemporary Africa and the Legacy of Late Colonialism*. Princeton, NJ: Princeton University Press.

Massey, Doreen. 1994. *Space, Place, and Gender*. Minneapolis: University of Minnesota Press.

Mateer, Samuel. 1871. *The Land of Charity: A Descriptive Account of Travancore and Its People*. London: John Snow.

———. 1883. *Native Life in Travancore*. London: W. H. Allen.

Mathew, Sebastian. 1986. "Growth and Changing Structure of the Prawn Export Industry in Kerala, 1953–83." M. Phil. thesis, Center for Development Studies, Trivandrum, Kerala, India.

———. 1990. *Fishing Legislation and Gear Conflicts in Asian Countries*. Brussels: International Collective in Support of Fishworkers.

Matory, James Lorand. 2005. *Black Atlantic Religion: Tradition, Transnationalism, and Matriarchy in Afro-Brazilian Candomblé*. Princeton, NJ: Princeton University Press.

Mbembe, Achille. 2001. *On the Postcolony.* Berkeley: University of California Press.

McCarthy, James. 2005a. "Commons as Counterhegemonic Projects." *Capitalism, Nature, Socialism* 16(1):9–24.

———. 2005b. "Scale, Sovereignty, and Strategy in Environmental Governance." *Antipode* 37(4):731–753.

McCay, Bonnie J., and James M. Acheson. 1987. *The Question of the Commons: The Culture and Ecology of Communal Resources.* Tucson: University of Arizona Press.

McEvoy, Arthur. 1986. *The Fisherman's Problem: Ecology and Law in the California Fisheries, 1850–1980.* Cambridge, U.K.: Cambridge University Press.

Menon, Dilip. 2004. *Caste, Nationalism, and Communism in South India: Malabar, 1900–1948.* Cambridge, U.K.: Cambridge University Press.

Merry, Sally Engle. 1996. "Legal Vernacularization and Ka Ho'okolokolonui Kanaka Maoli, The People's International Tribunal, Hawai'i 1993." *Political and Legal Anthropology Review* 19(1):67–82.

———. 2005. *Human Rights and Gender Violence: Translating International Law into Local Justice.* Chicago: University of Chicago Press.

———. 2006. "Transnational Human Rights and Local Activism: Mapping the Middle." *American Anthropologist* 108(1):38–51.

Metcalf, Thomas R. 1995. *Ideologies of the Raj.* Cambridge, U.K.: Cambridge University Press.

Meynen, Wicky. 1989. "Fisheries Development, Resources Depletion, and Political Mobilization in Kerala: The Problem of Alternatives." *Development and Change* 20:735–770.

Mitchell, Don. 1996. *The Lie of the Land: Migrant Workers and the California Landscape.* Minneapolis: University of Minnesota Press.

———. 2003. *The Right to the City: Social Justice and the Fight for Public Space.* New York: Guilford Press.

Mitchell, Timothy. 1991. *Colonising Egypt.* Berkeley: University of California Press.

———. 2002. *Rule of Experts: Egypt, Techno-Politics, Modernity.* Berkeley: University of California Press.

Moore, Donald. 1996. "Marxism, Culture, and Political Ecology: Environmental Struggles in Zimbabwe's Eastern Highlands." In R. Peet and M. Watts, eds., *Liberation Ecologies: Environment, Development, Social Movements.* London: Routledge, 125–147.

———. 1998. "Subaltern Struggles and the Politics of Place: Remapping Resistance in Zimbabwe's Eastern Highlands." *Cultural Anthropology* 13(3):344–381.

———. 2005. *Suffering for Territory: Race, Place, and Power in Zimbabwe.* Durham, NC: Duke University Press.

Mosse, David. 2003. *The Rule of Water: Statecraft, Ecology, and Collective Action in South India.* Oxford, U.K.: Oxford University Press.

———. 2005. *Cultivating Development: An Ethnography of Aid Policy and Practice.* London: Pluto Press.

Nagam Aiya, V. 1906. *Travancore State Manual.* Trivandrum, India: Kerala State Archives.

Nandy, Ashis, ed. 1988. *Science, Hegemony, and Violence: A Requiem for Modernity.* Delhi: Oxford University Press.

Narchison, J. R., V. Paul Leon, E. Francis, and F. Wilfred. 1983. *Called to Serve: A Profile of the Diocese of Kottar.* Nagercoil, India: Assisi Press.

National Fishworkers Forum. 1989. *Annual Report, 1988–1989.* Trivandrum, India: NFF.

———. 1993. *Annual Report, 1992–1993.* Trivandrum, India: NFF.

———. 1994. *Annual Report, 1993–1994.* Trivandrum, India: NFF.

Nauriya, Anil. 1996. "The Hindutva Judgements: A Warning Signal." *Economic and Political Weekly,* January 6, 10–13.

Nayak, Nalini. 1993. *Continuity and Change in Artisanal Fishing Communities: A Study of Socio-Economic Conditions of Artisanal Fishing Communities on the South West Coast of India Following Motorization of Fishing Crafts.* Trivandrum, India: PCO.

Nayak, Nalini, Aliou Sall, and Michael Belliveau. 2002. *Conversations: A Trialogue on Power, Intervention, and Organization in Fisheries.* Chennai, India: ICSF.

Neumann, R. P. 1992. "Political Ecology of Wildlife Conservation in the Mt. Meru Area of Northeast Tanzania." *Land Degradation and Rehabilitation* 3:85–98.

———. 1995. "Local Challenges to Global Agendas: Conservation, Economic Liberalization and the Pastoralists' Rights Movement in Tanzania." *Antipode* 27:363–382.

Oddie, Geoffrey A., ed. 1997. *Religious Conversion Movements in South Asia: Continuities and Change, 1800–1900.* Surrey, U.K.: Curzon.

———, ed. 1998. *Religious Traditions in South Asia: Interaction and Change.* Surrey, U.K.: Curzon.

Ong, Aihwa. 1999. *Flexible Citizenship: The Cultural Logics of Transnationality.* Durham, NC: Duke University Press.

Ouwerkerk, Louise. 1994. *No Elephants for the Maharaja: Social and Political Change in the Princely State of Travancore (1921–1947).* Delhi: Manohar.

Palmié, Stephan. 2002. *Wizards and Scientists: Explorations in Afro-Cuban Modernity and Tradition.* Durham, NC: Duke University Press.

Pandey, Gyanendra. 1990. *The Construction of Communalism in Colonial North India.* Delhi: Oxford University Press.

Pandian, Anand. 2005. "Securing the Rural Citizen: The Anti-Kallar Movement of 1896." *Indian Economic and Social History Review* 42(1):1–39.

Pandian, M. S. S. 1992. *The Image Trap: M. G. Ramachandran in Film and Politics.* Delhi: Sage.

Parajuli, Pramod. 2001. "No Nature Apart: Adivasi Cosmovision and Ecological Discourses in Jharkhand, India." In Phil Arnold and Ann Gold, eds., *Sacred Landscapes and Cultural Politics: Planting a Tree*. Aldershot, U.K.: Ashgate, 83–113.

Pascoe, C. F. 1901. *Two Hundred Years of the SPG: An Historical Account of the Society for the Propagation of the Gospel in Foreign Parts, 1701–1900*. London: SPG Office.

Patnaik, Prabhat. 1995a. "Nation-State in the Era of 'Globalization.'" *Economic and Political Weekly* 30(33):2049–2053.

———. 1995b. *Whatever Happened to Imperialism and Other Essays*. Delhi: Tulika.

Peet, Richard, and Michael Watts. 1996. "Liberation Ecology: Development, Sustainability, and Environment in the Age of Market Triumphalism." In Richard Peet and Michael Watts, eds., *Liberation Ecologies: Environment, Development, Social Movements*. London: Routledge, 1–45.

Peluso, Nancy. 1992. *Rich Forests, Poor People: Resource Control and Resistance in Java*. Berkeley: University of California Press.

———. 1993. "The Political Ecology of Extraction and Extractive Reserves in East Kalimantan, Indonesia." *Development and Change* 23:49–74.

Platteau, Jean-Philippe, Jose Murickan, and Etienne Delbar. 1985. *Technology, Credit, and Indebtedness in Marine Fishing: A Case Study of Three Fishing Villages in South Kerala*. Delhi: Hindustan Publishing.

Povinelli, Elizabeth. 2002. *The Cunning of Recognition: Indigenous Alterities and the Making of Australian Multiculturalism*. Durham, NC: Duke University Press.

Prakash, Gyan, ed. 1995. *After Colonialism: Imperial Histories and Postcolonial Displacements*. Princeton, NJ: Princeton University Press.

Raffles, Hugh. 2002. *In Amazonia: A Natural History*. Princeton, NJ: Princeton University Press.

Rai, Mridu. 2004. *Hindu Rulers, Muslim Subjects: Islam, Rights, and the History of Kashmir*. Princeton, NJ: Princeton University Press.

Ram, Kalpana. 1991. *Mukkuvar Women: Gender, Hegemony, and Capitalist Transformation in a South Indian Fishing Community*. Delhi: Kali for Women.

Ramaswamy, Sumathi. 2004. *The Lost Land of Lemuria: Fabulous Geographies, Catastrophic Histories*. Berkeley: University of California Press.

Ramusack, Barbara N. 2004. *The Indian Princes and Their States*. Cambridge, U.K.: Cambridge University Press.

Rancière, Jacques. 2004. "Who Is the Subject of the Rights of Man?" *South Atlantic Quarterly* 103(2/3):297–310.

Rangan, Haripriya. 1996. "From Chipko to Uttaranchal: Development, Environment, and Social Protest in the Garhwal Himalayas, India." In R. Peet and M. Watts, eds., *Liberation Ecologies: Environment, Development, Social Movements*. London: Routledge, 371–393.

———. 2000. *Of Myths and Movements: Rewriting Chipko into Himalayan History*. London: Verso.

Rangarajan, Mahesh. 1996. *Fencing the Forest: Conservation and Ecological Change in India's Central Provinces, 1860–1914*. Delhi: Oxford University Press.

———. 2005. *India's Wildlife History: An Introduction*. Delhi: Permanent Black.

Rangarajan, Mahesh, and Vasant Saberwal, eds. 2003. *Battles over Nature, Science, and the Politics of Conservation*. Delhi: Permanent Black.

Reeves, Peter, Bob Pokrant, John McGuire, and Andrew Pope. 1996. "Mapping India's Marine Resources: Colonial State Experiments, c. 1908–1930." *South Asia* 19(1):13–35.

Report of Justice P. Venugopal Commission. 1986. *The Commission of Inquiry to Enquire into the Firing Incidents on the Clashes Between Christians and Hindus at Mandaikadu in Kanyakumari District on 1-3-1982 and 15-3-1982*. Madras, India: Government of Tamilnadu Press.

Robbins, Paul. 2004. *Political Ecology: A Critical Introduction*. London: Blackwell.

Roche, Patrick. 1984. *The Fishermen of the Coromandel: The Social Study of the Paravas of the Coromandel*. Delhi: Manohar.

Roy, Srirupa. 2007. *Beyond Belief: India and the Politics of Postcolonial Nationalism*. Durham, NC: Duke University Press.

Saberwal, Vasant, Mahesh Rangarajan, and Ashish Kothari. 2001. *People, Parks, and Wildlife: Towards Coexistence*. New Delhi: Orient Longman.

Sachs, Wolfgang, ed. 1992. *The Development Dictionary: A Guide to Knowledge as Power*. London: Zed Books.

Said, Edward. 1978. *Orientalism*. New York: Pantheon.

Saradamoni, K. 1999. *Matriliny Transformed: Family, Law and Ideology in Twentieth Century Travancore*. Delhi: Sage.

Schumacher, Ernst Friedrich. 1973. *Small Is Beautiful: Economics as If People Mattered*. London: Blond and Briggs.

Schurhammer, Georg. 1977. *Francis Xavier: His Life, His Times*, v. 2. Rome: Jesuit Historical Institute.

Scott, James C. 1979. *The Moral Economy of the Peasant: Rebellion and Subsistence in Southeast Asia*. New Haven, CT: Yale University Press.

———. 1985. *Weapons of the Weak: Everyday Forms of Peasant Resistance*. New Haven, CT: Yale University Press.

———. 1998. *Seeing Like a State: How Certain Schemes to Improve the Human Condition Have Failed*. New Haven, CT: Yale University Press.

Shah, K. T. 1948. *National Planning Commission: Animal Husbandry, Dairying, Fisheries, and Horticulture*. Bombay: Vora.

Shaikh, Farzana. 1989. *Community and Consensus in Islam: Muslim Representation in Colonial India, 1860–1947*. Cambridge, U.K.: Cambridge University Press.

Sharma, Mukul. 2001. *Landscapes and Lives: Environmental Dispatches on Rural India*. Oxford, U.K.: Oxford University Press.

Shiva, Vandana. 1989. *Staying Alive: Women, Ecology, and Survival in India*. New Delhi: Kali for Women.

Sider, Gerald. 1986. *Culture and Class in Anthropology and History: A Newfoundland Illustration*. New York: Cambridge University Press.

Singh, Tarlok. 1969. *Towards an Integrated Society*. Bombay: Government Press.

Sinha, Subir. 2003. "Development Counternarratives: Taking Social Movements Seriously." In Arun Agrawal and K. Sivaramakrishnan, eds., *Regional Modernities: The Cultural Politics of Development in India*. Stanford, CA: Stanford University Press, 286–312.

———. 2008. "Lineages of the Developmentalist State: Transnationality and Village India, 1900–1965." *Comparative Studies in Society and History* 50(1):57–90.

Sinha, Subir, Shubhra Gururani, and Brian Greenberg. 1997. "The 'New Traditionalist' Discourse of Indian Environmentalism." *Journal of Peasant Studies* 24(3):65–99.

Sinha, Subir, and Ronald Herring. 1993. "Common Property, Collective Action, and Ecology." *Economic and Political Weekly*, July 3–10, 1425–1432.

Sivaramakrishnan, K. 1995. "Imagining the Past in Present Politics: Colonialism and Forestry and India." *Comparative Studies in Society and History* 37(1):3–40.

———. 1999. *Modern Forests: State Making and Environmental Change in Colonial Eastern India*. Stanford, CA: Stanford University Press.

———. 2000. "Crafting the Public Sphere in the Forests of West Bengal: Democracy, Development, and Political Action." *American Ethnologist* 27(2):431–461.

Sivaramakrishnan, K., and A. Agrawal, eds. 2003. *Regional Modernities: The Cultural Politics of Development in India*. Stanford, CA: Stanford University Press.

Sivaramakrishnan, K., and G. Cederloff, eds. 2005. *Ecological Nationalisms: Nature, Identity, and Livelihood in South Asia*. Seattle: University of Washington Press.

Sivasubramanian, A. 1996. "'Fin-Levy' (*Thuvik Kuthagai*) Agitation in Idinthakarai, Tamilnadu, 1964–67," A. R. Venkatachalapathy, trans. *South Indian Studies* 2(July–December).

Skaria, Ajay. 1999. *Hybrid Histories, Forests, Frontiers, and Wildness*. Delhi: Oxford University Press.

Smith, Neil. 1984. *Uneven Development: Nature, Capital, and the Production of Space*. New York: Blackwell.

Smith, Neil, and Anne Godlewska. 1994. *Geography and Empire*. London: Blackwell.

Somasundaram, R. 1981. "Mechanization of Fisheries in Tamilnadu." Master's thesis, Department of Fisheries, Madras, India.

Spivak, Gayatri C. 1988. "Can the Subaltern Speak?" In Cary Nelson and Lawrence Grossberg, eds., *Marxism and the Interpretation of Culture*. Urbana: University of Illinois Press, 271–313.

Starn, Orin. 1992. "'I Dreamed of Foxes and Hawks': Reflections on Peasant Protest, New Social Movements, and the Rondas Campesinas of Northern Peru." In Arturo Escobar and Sonia Alvarez, eds., *The Making of Social Movements in Latin America*. Boulder, CO: Westview Press, 89–111.

———. 1995. "To Revolt Against the Revolution: War and Resistance in Peru's Andes." *Cultural Anthropology* 10:547–580.

———. 1999. *Nightwatch: The Politics of Protest in the Andes*. Durham, NC: Duke University Press.

Stirrat, Robert L. 1981. "The Shrine of St. Sebastian at Mirisgama: An Aspect of the Cult of the Saints in Catholic Sri Lanka." *Man* 16(2):183–200.

———. 1982. "Caste Conundrums: Views of Caste in a Sinhalese Catholic Fishing Village." In D. B. McGilvray, ed., *Caste, Ideology, and Interaction*. Cambridge, U.K.: Cambridge University Press, 8–33.

———. 1988. *On the Beach: Fishermen, Fishwives, and Fishtraders in Post-Colonial Lanka*. Delhi: Hindustan Publishing.

Subrahmanyam, Sanjay. 1993. *The Portuguese Empire in Asia, 1500–1700: A Political and Economic History*. New York: Longman.

———. 1996. "Noble Harvest from the Sea: Managing the Pearl Fishery of Mannar, 1500–1925." In S. Subrahmanyam and B. Stein, eds., *Institutions and Economic Change in South Asia*. New Delhi: Oxford University Press, 134–172.

Subramanian, Ajantha. 1994. "Is Development Just a Red Herring? Indian Fishworkers, Multinationals, and the State." *South Asia Bulletin* 14(2):108–114.

———. 2002. "Community, Place, and Citizenship." *Seminar* (Shades of Green: A Symposium on the Changing Contours of Indian Environmentalism), 516(August).

———. 2003a. "Community, Class, and Conservation: Development Politics on the Kanyakumari Coast." *Conservation and Society* 1(2)(July–December):177–208.

———. 2003b. "Modernity from Below: Local Citizenship on the South Indian Coast." *International Social Science Journal* 175(March):135–144.

———. 2003c. "Mukkuvar Modernity: Development as a Cultural Identity." In Arun Agrawal and K. Sivaramakrishnan, eds., *Regional Modernities: The Cultural Politics of Development in India*. Stanford, CA: Stanford University Press, 262–285.

Subramanian, Ajantha, and M. H. Kalavathy. 1994. "Between the Devil and the Deep Sea: The Dilemma of Artisanal Fisherpeople." *Frontline Magazine*, November 18.

Subramanian, Narendra. 1999. *Ethnicity and Populist Mobilization: Political Parties, Citizens, and Democracy in South India*. Delhi: Oxford University Press.

Sundar, Aparna. 1999. "Sea Changes: Organizing Around the Fishery in a South Indian Community." In Jonathan Barker, ed., *Street-Level Democracy: Political Settings at the Margins of Global Power*. Toronto: Between the Lines Press, 79–114.

Sundar, Nandini. 1997. *Subalterns and Sovereigns: An Anthropological History of Bastar, 1854–1996*. New Delhi: Oxford University Press.

————. 2004. "Toward an Anthropology of Culpability." *American Ethnologist* 31(2):145–163.

Sundar, Nandini, and Roger Jeffrey, eds. 1999. *A New Moral Economy for India's Forests: Discourses of Community and Participation.* Delhi: Sage.

Swadeshi Jagaran Manch. 1995. *Souvenir: All India Convention on Deep Sea Fishing Policy, 23 April 1995.* Vishakapatnam, India: SJM.

Tamilnadu Department of Fisheries. 1993. *Endeavors and Achievements: Fisheries Statistics.* Madras, India: Government Press.

Tamilnadu State Planning Commission. 1972. *Towards a Blue Revolution.* Madras, India: Government Press.

Thompson, Edward P. 1971. "The Moral Economy of the English Crowd in the Eighteenth Century." *Past and Present* 50:76–136.

Thomson, K. T. 1989. "The Political Economy of Fishing: A Study of an Indigenous Social System in Tamilnadu." Ph.D. dissertation, Madras Institute of Development Studies, Madras, India.

Tombeur, James. 1997. *Led by God's Hand: Reflections on My Faith Experience and Pastoral Ministry.* Chunkankadai, India: FCRT Publications.

Trouillot, Michel Rolph. 1988. *Peasants and Capital: Dominica in the World Economy.* Baltimore: Johns Hopkins University Press.

————. 1990. *Haiti, State Against Nation: The Origins of Duvalierism.* New York: Monthly Review Press.

————. 1995. *Silencing the Past: Power and the Production of History.* Boston: Beacon Press.

————. 2003. *Global Transformations: Anthropology and the Modern World.* New York: Palgrave Macmillan.

Tsing, Anna. 1993. *In the Realm of the Diamond Queen: Marginality in an Out-of-the-Way Place.* Princeton, NJ: Princeton University Press.

————. 1999. "Becoming a Tribal Elder and Other Green Development Fantasies." In Tania Li, ed., *Transforming the Indonesian Uplands: Marginality, Power, and Production.* Amsterdam: Harwood Academic, 159–202.

————. 2006. *Friction: An Ethnography of Global Connection.* Princeton, NJ: Princeton University Press.

Tuan, Yi-Fu. 1977. *Space and Place: The Perspective of Experience.* Minneapolis: University of Minnesota Press.

Turner, Mary. 1982. *Slaves and Missionaries: The Disintegration of Jamaican Slave Society, 1787–1834.* Urbana: University of Illinois Press.

Villavarayan, J. M. 1956. *The Diocese of Kottar: A Review of Its Growth.* Nagercoil, India: Assisi Press.

Viotti da Costa, Emilia. 1994. *Crowns of Glory, Tears of Blood: The Demerara Slave Rebellion of 1823.* Oxford, U.K.: Oxford University Press.

Visvanathan, Shiv. 2001. "On Ancestors and Epigones." *Seminar* (Through the Ages), 500(April).

Viswanathan, Gauri. 1996. "Religious Conversion and the Politics of Dissent." In Peter van der Veer, ed., *Conversion to Modernities: The Globalization of Christianity.* New York: Routledge, 89–114.

———. 1998. *Outside the Fold: Conversion, Modernity, and Belief.* Princeton, NJ: Princeton University Press.

Wallerstein, Immanuel. 1992. "The Concept of National Development, 1917–1989: Elegy and Requiem." *American Behavioral Scientist* 35(4/5):517–529.

Walley, Christine J. 2004. *Rough Waters: Nature and Development in an African Marine Park.* Princeton, NJ: Princeton University Press.

Ward, B. S., and P. E. Conner. 1863. *Memoir of the Survey of the Travancore and Cochin States.* Trivandrum, India: Travancore Sircar Press.

Washbrook, David. 1997. "The Rhetoric of Democracy and Development in Late Colonial India." In S. Bose and A. Jalal, eds., *Nationalism, Democracy, and Development: State and Politics in India.* New Delhi: Oxford University Press, 36–49.

Watts, Michael, and Nancy Peluso, eds. 2001. *Violent Environments.* Ithaca, NY: Cornell University Press.

West, Harry. 2005. *Kupilikula: Governance and the Invisible Realm in Mozambique.* Chicago: University of Chicago Press.

Williams, Raymond. 1973. *The Country and the City.* London: Chatto and Windus.

Winichakul, Thongchai. 1994. *Siam Mapped: A History of the Geo-Body of a Nation.* Honolulu: University of Hawaii Press.

Wolf, Eric R. 1982. *Europe and the People Without History.* Berkeley: University of California Press.

Yang, Anand, ed. 1985. *Crime and Criminality in British India.* Tucson: University of Arizona Press.

Yesudas, R. N. 1975. *A People's Revolt in Travancore: A Backward Class Movement for Social Freedom.* Trivandrum, India: Kerala Historical Society.

———. 1980. *The History of the London Missionary Society in Travancore, 1806–1908.* Trivandrum, India: Kerala Historical Society.

Index